FREE Study Skills [

Dear Customer,

Thank you for your purchase from Mometrix! We consider it an honor and a privilege that you have purchased our product and we want to ensure your satisfaction.

As a way of showing our appreciation and to help us better serve you, we have developed a Study Skills DVD that we would like to give you for <u>FREE</u>. This DVD covers our *best practices* for getting ready for your exam, from how to use our study materials to how to best prepare for the day of the test.

All that we ask is that you email us with feedback that would describe your experience so far with our product. Good, bad, or indifferent, we want to know what you think!

To get your FREE Study Skills DVD, email <u>freedvd@mometrix.com</u> with *FREE STUDY SKILLS DVD* in the subject line and the following information in the body of the email:

- The name of the product you purchased.
- Your product rating on a scale of 1-5, with 5 being the highest rating.
- Your feedback. It can be long, short, or anything in between. We just want to know your impressions and experience so far with our product. (Good feedback might include how our study material met your needs and ways we might be able to make it even better. You could highlight features that you found helpful or features that you think we should add.)
- Your full name and shipping address where you would like us to send your free DVD.

If you have any questions or concerns, please don't hesitate to contact me directly.

Thanks again!

Sincerely,

Jay Willis
Vice President
<u>jay.willis@mometrix.com</u>
1-800-673-8175

MoGEA SECRETS

Study Guide
Your Key to Exam Success

Written and edited by the Mometrix Missouri Teacher Certification Test Team

Printed in the United States of America

This paper meets the requirements of ANSI/NISO Z39.48-1992 (Permanence of Paper).

Mometrix offers volume discount pricing to institutions. For more information or a price quote, please contact our sales department at sales@mometrix.com or 888-248-1219.

Mometrix Media LLC is not affiliated with or endorsed by any official testing organization. All organizational and test names are trademarks of their respective owners.

Paperback
ISBN 13: 978-1-63094-013-3
ISBN 10: 1-63094-013-5

Ebook
ISBN 13: 978-1-5167-0433-0
ISBN 10: 1-5167-0433-9

Hardback
ISBN 13: 978-1-5167-0558-0
ISBN 10: 1-5167-0558-0

DEAR FUTURE EXAM SUCCESS STORY

First of all, **THANK YOU** for purchasing Mometrix study materials!

Second, congratulations! You are one of the few determined test-takers who are committed to doing whatever it takes to excel on your exam. **You have come to the right place.** We developed these study materials with one goal in mind: to deliver you the information you need in a format that's concise and easy to use.

In addition to optimizing your guide for the content of the test, we've outlined our recommended steps for breaking down the preparation process into small, attainable goals so you can make sure you stay on track.

We've also analyzed the entire test-taking process, identifying the most common pitfalls and showing how you can overcome them and be ready for any curveball the test throws you.

Standardized testing is one of the biggest obstacles on your road to success, which only increases the importance of doing well in the high-pressure, high-stakes environment of test day. Your results on this test could have a significant impact on your future, and this guide provides the information and practical advice to help you achieve your full potential on test day.

Your success is our success

We would love to hear from you! If you would like to share the story of your exam success or if you have any questions or comments in regard to our products, please contact us at **800-673-8175** or **support@mometrix.com**.

Thanks again for your business and we wish you continued success!

Sincerely,
The Mometrix Test Preparation Team

Need more help? Check out our flashcards at:
http://mometrixflashcards.com/MoGEA

TABLE OF CONTENTS

INTRODUCTION _____ 1

SECRET KEY #1 – PLAN BIG, STUDY SMALL _____ 2

SECRET KEY #2 – MAKE YOUR STUDYING COUNT _____ 3

SECRET KEY #3 – PRACTICE THE RIGHT WAY _____ 4

SECRET KEY #4 – PACE YOURSELF _____ 6

SECRET KEY #5 – HAVE A PLAN FOR GUESSING _____ 7

TEST-TAKING STRATEGIES _____ 10

READING COMPREHENSION AND INTERPRETATION _____ 15

WRITING _____ 47

MATHEMATICS _____ 87

SCIENCE _____ 195

SOCIAL STUDIES _____ 218

MOGEA PRACTICE TEST _____ 234
  ENGLISH LANGUAGE ARTS _____ 234
  SCIENCE _____ 242
  MATHEMATICS _____ 252
  SOCIAL STUDIES _____ 259
  WRITING PROMPT _____ 267

ANSWER KEY AND EXPLANATIONS _____ 268
  ENGLISH LANGUAGE ARTS _____ 268
  SCIENCE _____ 272
  MATHEMATICS _____ 276
  SOCIAL STUDIES _____ 281

HOW TO OVERCOME TEST ANXIETY _____ 285
  CAUSES OF TEST ANXIETY _____ 285
  ELEMENTS OF TEST ANXIETY _____ 286
  EFFECTS OF TEST ANXIETY _____ 286
  PHYSICAL STEPS FOR BEATING TEST ANXIETY _____ 287
  MENTAL STEPS FOR BEATING TEST ANXIETY _____ 288
  STUDY STRATEGY _____ 289
  TEST TIPS _____ 291
  IMPORTANT QUALIFICATION _____ 292

HOW TO OVERCOME YOUR FEAR OF MATH _____ 293
  FALSE BELIEFS _____ 294
  MATH STRATEGIES _____ 296
  TEACHING TIPS _____ 298
  SELF-CHECK _____ 299

THANK **Y**OU _____ **300**

ADDITIONAL **B**ONUS **M**ATERIAL _____ **301**

Introduction

Thank you for purchasing this resource! You have made the choice to prepare yourself for a test that could have a huge impact on your future, and this guide is designed to help you be fully ready for test day. Obviously, it's important to have a solid understanding of the test material, but you also need to be prepared for the unique environment and stressors of the test, so that you can perform to the best of your abilities.

For this purpose, the first section that appears in this guide is the **Secret Keys**. We've devoted countless hours to meticulously researching what works and what doesn't, and we've boiled down our findings to the five most impactful steps you can take to improve your performance on the test. We start at the beginning with study planning and move through the preparation process, all the way to the testing strategies that will help you get the most out of what you know when you're finally sitting in front of the test.

We recommend that you start preparing for your test as far in advance as possible. However, if you've bought this guide as a last-minute study resource and only have a few days before your test, we recommend that you skip over the first two Secret Keys since they address a long-term study plan.

If you struggle with **test anxiety**, we strongly encourage you to check out our recommendations for how you can overcome it. Test anxiety is a formidable foe, but it can be beaten, and we want to make sure you have the tools you need to defeat it.

Secret Key #1 – Plan Big, Study Small

There's a lot riding on your performance. If you want to ace this test, you're going to need to keep your skills sharp and the material fresh in your mind. You need a plan that lets you review everything you need to know while still fitting in your schedule. We'll break this strategy down into three categories.

Information Organization

Start with the information you already have: the official test outline. From this, you can make a complete list of all the concepts you need to cover before the test. Organize these concepts into groups that can be studied together, and create a list of any related vocabulary you need to learn so you can brush up on any difficult terms. You'll want to keep this vocabulary list handy once you actually start studying since you may need to add to it along the way.

Time Management

Once you have your set of study concepts, decide how to spread them out over the time you have left before the test. Break your study plan into small, clear goals so you have a manageable task for each day and know exactly what you're doing. Then just focus on one small step at a time. When you manage your time this way, you don't need to spend hours at a time studying. Studying a small block of content for a short period each day helps you retain information better and avoid stressing over how much you have left to do. You can relax knowing that you have a plan to cover everything in time. In order for this strategy to be effective though, you have to start studying early and stick to your schedule. Avoid the exhaustion and futility that comes from last-minute cramming!

Study Environment

The environment you study in has a big impact on your learning. Studying in a coffee shop, while probably more enjoyable, is not likely to be as fruitful as studying in a quiet room. It's important to keep distractions to a minimum. You're only planning to study for a short block of time, so make the most of it. Don't pause to check your phone or get up to find a snack. It's also important to **avoid multitasking**. Research has consistently shown that multitasking will make your studying dramatically less effective. Your study area should also be comfortable and well-lit so you don't have the distraction of straining your eyes or sitting on an uncomfortable chair.

The time of day you study is also important. You want to be rested and alert. Don't wait until just before bedtime. Study when you'll be most likely to comprehend and remember. Even better, if you know what time of day your test will be, set that time aside for study. That way your brain will be used to working on that subject at that specific time and you'll have a better chance of recalling information.

Finally, it can be helpful to team up with others who are studying for the same test. Your actual studying should be done in as isolated an environment as possible, but the work of organizing the information and setting up the study plan can be divided up. In between study sessions, you can discuss with your teammates the concepts that you're all studying and quiz each other on the details. Just be sure that your teammates are as serious about the test as you are. If you find that your study time is being replaced with social time, you might need to find a new team.

2

Secret Key #2 – Make Your Studying Count

You're devoting a lot of time and effort to preparing for this test, so you want to be absolutely certain it will pay off. This means doing more than just reading the content and hoping you can remember it on test day. It's important to make every minute of study count. There are two main areas you can focus on to make your studying count:

Retention

It doesn't matter how much time you study if you can't remember the material. You need to make sure you are retaining the concepts. To check your retention of the information you're learning, try recalling it at later times with minimal prompting. Try carrying around flashcards and glance at one or two from time to time or ask a friend who's also studying for the test to quiz you.

To enhance your retention, look for ways to put the information into practice so that you can apply it rather than simply recalling it. If you're using the information in practical ways, it will be much easier to remember. Similarly, it helps to solidify a concept in your mind if you're not only reading it to yourself but also explaining it to someone else. Ask a friend to let you teach them about a concept you're a little shaky on (or speak aloud to an imaginary audience if necessary). As you try to summarize, define, give examples, and answer your friend's questions, you'll understand the concepts better and they will stay with you longer. Finally, step back for a big picture view and ask yourself how each piece of information fits with the whole subject. When you link the different concepts together and see them working together as a whole, it's easier to remember the individual components.

Finally, practice showing your work on any multi-step problems, even if you're just studying. Writing out each step you take to solve a problem will help solidify the process in your mind, and you'll be more likely to remember it during the test.

Modality

Modality simply refers to the means or method by which you study. Choosing a study modality that fits your own individual learning style is crucial. No two people learn best in exactly the same way, so it's important to know your strengths and use them to your advantage.

For example, if you learn best by visualization, focus on visualizing a concept in your mind and draw an image or a diagram. Try color-coding your notes, illustrating them, or creating symbols that will trigger your mind to recall a learned concept. If you learn best by hearing or discussing information, find a study partner who learns the same way or read aloud to yourself. Think about how to put the information in your own words. Imagine that you are giving a lecture on the topic and record yourself so you can listen to it later.

For any learning style, flashcards can be helpful. Organize the information so you can take advantage of spare moments to review. Underline key words or phrases. Use different colors for different categories. Mnemonic devices (such as creating a short list in which every item starts with the same letter) can also help with retention. Find what works best for you and use it to store the information in your mind most effectively and easily.

Secret Key #3 – Practice the Right Way

Your success on test day depends not only on how many hours you put into preparing, but also on whether you prepared the right way. It's good to check along the way to see if your studying is paying off. One of the most effective ways to do this is by taking practice tests to evaluate your progress. Practice tests are useful because they show exactly where you need to improve. Every time you take a practice test, pay special attention to these three groups of questions:

- The questions you got wrong
- The questions you had to guess on, even if you guessed right
- The questions you found difficult or slow to work through

This will show you exactly what your weak areas are, and where you need to devote more study time. Ask yourself why each of these questions gave you trouble. Was it because you didn't understand the material? Was it because you didn't remember the vocabulary? Do you need more repetitions on this type of question to build speed and confidence? Dig into those questions and figure out how you can strengthen your weak areas as you go back to review the material.

Additionally, many practice tests have a section explaining the answer choices. It can be tempting to read the explanation and think that you now have a good understanding of the concept. However, an explanation likely only covers part of the question's broader context. Even if the explanation makes sense, **go back and investigate** every concept related to the question until you're positive you have a thorough understanding.

As you go along, keep in mind that the practice test is just that: practice. Memorizing these questions and answers will not be very helpful on the actual test because it is unlikely to have any of the same exact questions. If you only know the right answers to the sample questions, you won't be prepared for the real thing. **Study the concepts** until you understand them fully, and then you'll be able to answer any question that shows up on the test.

It's important to wait on the practice tests until you're ready. If you take a test on your first day of study, you may be overwhelmed by the amount of material covered and how much you need to learn. Work up to it gradually.

On test day, you'll need to be prepared for answering questions, managing your time, and using the test-taking strategies you've learned. It's a lot to balance, like a mental marathon that will have a big impact on your future. Like training for a marathon, you'll need to start slowly and work your way up. When test day arrives, you'll be ready.

Start with the strategies you've read in the first two Secret Keys—plan your course and study in the way that works best for you. If you have time, consider using multiple study resources to get different approaches to the same concepts. It can be helpful to see difficult concepts from more than one angle. Then find a good source for practice tests. Many times, the test website will suggest potential study resources or provide sample tests.

Practice Test Strategy

If you're able to find at least three practice tests, we recommend this strategy:

UNTIMED AND OPEN-BOOK PRACTICE

Take the first test with no time constraints and with your notes and study guide handy. Take your time and focus on applying the strategies you've learned.

TIMED AND OPEN-BOOK PRACTICE

Take the second practice test open-book as well, but set a timer and practice pacing yourself to finish in time.

TIMED AND CLOSED-BOOK PRACTICE

Take any other practice tests as if it were test day. Set a timer and put away your study materials. Sit at a table or desk in a quiet room, imagine yourself at the testing center, and answer questions as quickly and accurately as possible.

Keep repeating timed and closed-book tests on a regular basis until you run out of practice tests or it's time for the actual test. Your mind will be ready for the schedule and stress of test day, and you'll be able to focus on recalling the material you've learned.

Secret Key #4 – Pace Yourself

Once you're fully prepared for the material on the test, your biggest challenge on test day will be managing your time. Just knowing that the clock is ticking can make you panic even if you have plenty of time left. Work on pacing yourself so you can build confidence against the time constraints of the exam. Pacing is a difficult skill to master, especially in a high-pressure environment, so **practice is vital**.

Set time expectations for your pace based on how much time is available. For example, if a section has 60 questions and the time limit is 30 minutes, you know you have to average 30 seconds or less per question in order to answer them all. Although 30 seconds is the hard limit, set 25 seconds per question as your goal, so you reserve extra time to spend on harder questions. When you budget extra time for the harder questions, you no longer have any reason to stress when those questions take longer to answer.

Don't let this time expectation distract you from working through the test at a calm, steady pace, but keep it in mind so you don't spend too much time on any one question. Recognize that taking extra time on one question you don't understand may keep you from answering two that you do understand later in the test. If your time limit for a question is up and you're still not sure of the answer, mark it and move on, and come back to it later if the time and the test format allow. If the testing format doesn't allow you to return to earlier questions, just make an educated guess; then put it out of your mind and move on.

On the easier questions, be careful not to rush. It may seem wise to hurry through them so you have more time for the challenging ones, but it's not worth missing one if you know the concept and just didn't take the time to read the question fully. Work efficiently but make sure you understand the question and have looked at all of the answer choices, since more than one may seem right at first.

Even if you're paying attention to the time, you may find yourself a little behind at some point. You should speed up to get back on track, but do so wisely. Don't panic; just take a few seconds less on each question until you're caught up. Don't guess without thinking, but do look through the answer choices and eliminate any you know are wrong. If you can get down to two choices, it is often worthwhile to guess from those. Once you've chosen an answer, move on and don't dwell on any that you skipped or had to hurry through. If a question was taking too long, chances are it was one of the harder ones, so you weren't as likely to get it right anyway.

On the other hand, if you find yourself getting ahead of schedule, it may be beneficial to slow down a little. The more quickly you work, the more likely you are to make a careless mistake that will affect your score. You've budgeted time for each question, so don't be afraid to spend that time. Practice an efficient but careful pace to get the most out of the time you have.

Secret Key #5 – Have a Plan for Guessing

When you're taking the test, you may find yourself stuck on a question. Some of the answer choices seem better than others, but you don't see the one answer choice that is obviously correct. What do you do?

The scenario described above is very common, yet most test takers have not effectively prepared for it. Developing and practicing a plan for guessing may be one of the single most effective uses of your time as you get ready for the exam.

In developing your plan for guessing, there are three questions to address:

- When should you start the guessing process?
- How should you narrow down the choices?
- Which answer should you choose?

When to Start the Guessing Process

Unless your plan for guessing is to select C every time (which, despite its merits, is not what we recommend), you need to leave yourself enough time to apply your answer elimination strategies. Since you have a limited amount of time for each question, that means that if you're going to give yourself the best shot at guessing correctly, you have to decide quickly whether or not you will guess.

Of course, the best-case scenario is that you don't have to guess at all, so first, see if you can answer the question based on your knowledge of the subject and basic reasoning skills. Focus on the key words in the question and try to jog your memory of related topics. Give yourself a chance to bring the knowledge to mind, but once you realize that you don't have (or you can't access) the knowledge you need to answer the question, it's time to start the guessing process.

It's almost always better to start the guessing process too early than too late. It only takes a few seconds to remember something and answer the question from knowledge. Carefully eliminating wrong answer choices takes longer. Plus, going through the process of eliminating answer choices can actually help jog your memory.

Summary: Start the guessing process as soon as you decide that you can't answer the question based on your knowledge.

How to Narrow Down the Choices

The next chapter in this book (**Test-Taking Strategies**) includes a wide range of strategies for how to approach questions and how to look for answer choices to eliminate. You will definitely want to read those carefully, practice them, and figure out which ones work best for you. Here though, we're going to address a mindset rather than a particular strategy.

Your chances of guessing an answer correctly depend on how many options you are choosing from.

How many choices you have	How likely you are to guess correctly
5	20%
4	25%
3	33%
2	50%
1	100%

You can see from this chart just how valuable it is to be able to eliminate incorrect answers and make an educated guess, but there are two things that many test takers do that cause them to miss out on the benefits of guessing:

- Accidentally eliminating the correct answer
- Selecting an answer based on an impression

We'll look at the first one here, and the second one in the next section.

To avoid accidentally eliminating the correct answer, we recommend a thought exercise called **the $5 challenge**. In this challenge, you only eliminate an answer choice from contention if you are willing to bet $5 on it being wrong. Why $5? Five dollars is a small but not insignificant amount of money. It's an amount you could afford to lose but wouldn't want to throw away. And while losing $5 once might not hurt too much, doing it twenty times will set you back $100. In the same way, each small decision you make—eliminating a choice here, guessing on a question there—won't by itself impact your score very much, but when you put them all together, they can make a big difference. By holding each answer choice elimination decision to a higher standard, you can reduce the risk of accidentally eliminating the correct answer.

The $5 challenge can also be applied in a positive sense: If you are willing to bet $5 that an answer choice *is* correct, go ahead and mark it as correct.

Summary: Only eliminate an answer choice if you are willing to bet $5 that it is wrong.

Which Answer to Choose

You're taking the test. You've run into a hard question and decided you'll have to guess. You've eliminated all the answer choices you're willing to bet $5 on. Now you have to pick an answer. Why do we even need to talk about this? Why can't you just pick whichever one you feel like when the time comes?

The answer to these questions is that if you don't come into the test with a plan, you'll rely on your impression to select an answer choice, and if you do that, you risk falling into a trap. The test writers know that everyone who takes their test will be guessing on some of the questions, so they intentionally write wrong answer choices to seem plausible. You still have to pick an answer though, and if the wrong answer choices are designed to look right, how can you ever be sure that you're not falling for their trap? The best solution we've found to this dilemma is to take the decision out of your hands entirely. Here is the process we recommend:

Once you've eliminated any choices that you are confident (willing to bet $5) are wrong, select the first remaining choice as your answer.

Whether you choose to select the first remaining choice, the second, or the last, the important thing is that you use some preselected standard. Using this approach guarantees that you will not be enticed into selecting an answer choice that looks right, because you are not basing your decision on how the answer choices look.

This is not meant to make you question your knowledge. Instead, it is to help you recognize the difference between your knowledge and your impressions. There's a huge difference between thinking an answer is right because of what you know, and thinking an answer is right because it looks or sounds like it should be right.

Summary: To ensure that your selection is appropriately random, make a predetermined selection from among all answer choices you have not eliminated.

Test-Taking Strategies

This section contains a list of test-taking strategies that you may find helpful as you work through the test. By taking what you know and applying logical thought, you can maximize your chances of answering any question correctly!

It is very important to realize that every question is different and every person is different: no single strategy will work on every question, and no single strategy will work for every person. That's why we've included all of them here, so you can try them out and determine which ones work best for different types of questions and which ones work best for you.

Question Strategies

READ CAREFULLY

Read the question and answer choices carefully. Don't miss the question because you misread the terms. You have plenty of time to read each question thoroughly and make sure you understand what is being asked. Yet a happy medium must be attained, so don't waste too much time. You must read carefully, but efficiently.

CONTEXTUAL CLUES

Look for contextual clues. If the question includes a word you are not familiar with, look at the immediate context for some indication of what the word might mean. Contextual clues can often give you all the information you need to decipher the meaning of an unfamiliar word. Even if you can't determine the meaning, you may be able to narrow down the possibilities enough to make a solid guess at the answer to the question.

PREFIXES

If you're having trouble with a word in the question or answer choices, try dissecting it. Take advantage of every clue that the word might include. Prefixes and suffixes can be a huge help. Usually they allow you to determine a basic meaning. Pre- means before, post- means after, pro - is positive, de- is negative. From prefixes and suffixes, you can get an idea of the general meaning of the word and try to put it into context.

HEDGE WORDS

Watch out for critical hedge words, such as *likely, may, can, sometimes, often, almost, mostly, usually, generally, rarely,* and *sometimes.* Question writers insert these hedge phrases to cover every possibility. Often an answer choice will be wrong simply because it leaves no room for exception. Be on guard for answer choices that have definitive words such as *exactly* and *always.*

SWITCHBACK WORDS

Stay alert for *switchbacks.* These are the words and phrases frequently used to alert you to shifts in thought. The most common switchback words are *but, although,* and *however.* Others include *nevertheless, on the other hand, even though, while, in spite of, despite, regardless of.* Switchback words are important to catch because they can change the direction of the question or an answer choice.

FACE VALUE

When in doubt, use common sense. Accept the situation in the problem at face value. Don't read too much into it. These problems will not require you to make wild assumptions. If you have to go beyond creativity and warp time or space in order to have an answer choice fit the question, then you should move on and consider the other answer choices. These are normal problems rooted in reality. The applicable relationship or explanation may not be readily apparent, but it is there for you to figure out. Use your common sense to interpret anything that isn't clear.

Answer Choice Strategies

ANSWER SELECTION

The most thorough way to pick an answer choice is to identify and eliminate wrong answers until only one is left, then confirm it is the correct answer. Sometimes an answer choice may immediately seem right, but be careful. The test writers will usually put more than one reasonable answer choice on each question, so take a second to read all of them and make sure that the other choices are not equally obvious. As long as you have time left, it is better to read every answer choice than to pick the first one that looks right without checking the others.

ANSWER CHOICE FAMILIES

An answer choice family consists of two (in rare cases, three) answer choices that are very similar in construction and cannot all be true at the same time. If you see two answer choices that are direct opposites or parallels, one of them is usually the correct answer. For instance, if one answer choice says that quantity x increases and another either says that quantity x decreases (opposite) or says that quantity y increases (parallel), then those answer choices would fall into the same family. An answer choice that doesn't match the construction of the answer choice family is more likely to be incorrect. Most questions will not have answer choice families, but when they do appear, you should be prepared to recognize them.

ELIMINATE ANSWERS

Eliminate answer choices as soon as you realize they are wrong, but make sure you consider all possibilities. If you are eliminating answer choices and realize that the last one you are left with is also wrong, don't panic. Start over and consider each choice again. There may be something you missed the first time that you will realize on the second pass.

AVOID FACT TRAPS

Don't be distracted by an answer choice that is factually true but doesn't answer the question. You are looking for the choice that answers the question. Stay focused on what the question is asking for so you don't accidentally pick an answer that is true but incorrect. Always go back to the question and make sure the answer choice you've selected actually answers the question and is not merely a true statement.

EXTREME STATEMENTS

In general, you should avoid answers that put forth extreme actions as standard practice or proclaim controversial ideas as established fact. An answer choice that states the "process should be used in certain situations, if..." is much more likely to be correct than one that states the "process should be discontinued completely." The first is a calm rational statement and doesn't even make a definitive, uncompromising stance, using a hedge word *if* to provide wiggle room, whereas the second choice is a radical idea and far more extreme.

BENCHMARK

As you read through the answer choices and you come across one that seems to answer the question well, mentally select that answer choice. This is not your final answer, but it's the one that will help you evaluate the other answer choices. The one that you selected is your benchmark or standard for judging each of the other answer choices. Every other answer choice must be compared to your benchmark. That choice is correct until proven otherwise by another answer choice beating it. If you find a better answer, then that one becomes your new benchmark. Once you've decided that no other choice answers the question as well as your benchmark, you have your final answer.

PREDICT THE ANSWER

Before you even start looking at the answer choices, it is often best to try to predict the answer. When you come up with the answer on your own, it is easier to avoid distractions and traps because you will know exactly what to look for. The right answer choice is unlikely to be word-for-word what you came up with, but it should be a close match. Even if you are confident that you have the right answer, you should still take the time to read each option before moving on.

General Strategies

TOUGH QUESTIONS

If you are stumped on a problem or it appears too hard or too difficult, don't waste time. Move on! Remember though, if you can quickly check for obviously incorrect answer choices, your chances of guessing correctly are greatly improved. Before you completely give up, at least try to knock out a couple of possible answers. Eliminate what you can and then guess at the remaining answer choices before moving on.

CHECK YOUR WORK

Since you will probably not know every term listed and the answer to every question, it is important that you get credit for the ones that you do know. Don't miss any questions through careless mistakes. If at all possible, try to take a second to look back over your answer selection and make sure you've selected the correct answer choice and haven't made a costly careless mistake (such as marking an answer choice that you didn't mean to mark). This quick double check should more than pay for itself in caught mistakes for the time it costs.

PACE YOURSELF

It's easy to be overwhelmed when you're looking at a page full of questions; your mind is confused and full of random thoughts, and the clock is ticking down faster than you would like. Calm down and maintain the pace that you have set for yourself. Especially as you get down to the last few minutes of the test, don't let the small numbers on the clock make you panic. As long as you are on track by monitoring your pace, you are guaranteed to have time for each question.

DON'T RUSH

It is very easy to make errors when you are in a hurry. Maintaining a fast pace in answering questions is pointless if it makes you miss questions that you would have gotten right otherwise. Test writers like to include distracting information and wrong answers that seem right. Taking a little extra time to avoid careless mistakes can make all the difference in your test score. Find a pace that allows you to be confident in the answers that you select.

KEEP MOVING

Panicking will not help you pass the test, so do your best to stay calm and keep moving. Taking deep breaths and going through the answer elimination steps you practiced can help to break through a stress barrier and keep your pace.

Final Notes

The combination of a solid foundation of content knowledge and the confidence that comes from practicing your plan for applying that knowledge is the key to maximizing your performance on test day. As your foundation of content knowledge is built up and strengthened, you'll find that the strategies included in this chapter become more and more effective in helping you quickly sift through the distractions and traps of the test to isolate the correct answer.

Now it's time to move on to the test content chapters of this book, but be sure to keep your goal in mind. As you read, think about how you will be able to apply this information on the test. If you've already seen sample questions for the test and you have an idea of the question format and style, try to come up with questions of your own that you can answer based on what you're reading. This will give you valuable practice applying your knowledge in the same ways you can expect to on test day.

Good luck and good studying!

Reading Comprehension and Interpretation

UNDERSTANDING LITERATURE

Reading literature is a different experience than reading non-fiction works. Our imagination is more active as we review what we have read, imagine ourselves as characters in the novel, and try to guess what will happen next. Suspense, surprise, fantasy, fear, anxiety, compassion, and a host of other emotions and feelings may be stirred by a provocative novel.

Reading longer works of fiction is a cumulative process. Some elements of a novel have a great impact, while others may go virtually unnoticed. Therefore, as novels are read with a critical eye to language, it is helpful to perceive and identify larger patterns and movements in the work as a whole. This will benefit the reader by placing characters and events in perspective, and will enrich the reading experience greatly. Novels should be savored rather than gulped. Careful reading and thoughtful analysis of the major themes of the novel are essential to a clear understanding of the work.

One of the most important skills in reading comprehension is the identification of **topics** and **main ideas.** There is a subtle difference between these two features. The topic is the subject of a text, or what the text is about. The main idea, on the other hand, is the most important point being made by the author. The topic is usually expressed in a few words at the most, while the main idea often needs a full sentence to be completely defined. As an example, a short passage might have the topic of penguins and the main idea *Penguins are different from other birds in many ways.* In most nonfiction writing, the topic and the main idea will be stated directly, often in a sentence at the very beginning or end of the text. When being tested on an understanding of the author's topic, the reader can quickly *skim* the passage for the general idea, stopping to read only the first sentence of each paragraph. A paragraph's first sentence is often (but not always) the main topic sentence, and it gives you a summary of the content of the paragraph. However, there are cases in which the reader must figure out an unstated topic or main idea. In these instances, the student must read every sentence of the text, and try to come up with an overarching idea that is supported by each of those sentences.

> **Review Video: Topics and Main Ideas**
> Visit mometrix.com/academy and enter code: 407801

While the main idea is the overall premise of a story, **supporting details** provide evidence and backing for the main point. In order to show that a main idea is correct, or valid, the author needs to add details that prove their point. All texts contain details, but they are only classified as supporting details when they serve to reinforce some larger point. Supporting details are most commonly found in informative and persuasive texts. In some cases, they will be clearly indicated with words like *for example* or *for instance,* or they will be enumerated with words like *first, second,* and *last.* However, they may not be indicated with special words. As a reader, it is important to consider whether the author's supporting details really back up his or her main point. Supporting details can be factual and correct but still not relevant to the author's point. Conversely, supporting details can

15

seem pertinent but be ineffective because they are based on opinion or assertions that cannot be proven.

Review Video: Supporting Details
Visit mometrix.com/academy and enter code: 396297

An example of a main idea is: "Giraffes live in the Serengeti of Africa." A supporting detail about giraffes could be: "A giraffe uses its long neck to reach twigs and leaves on trees." The main idea gives the general idea that the text is about giraffes. The supporting detail gives a specific fact about how the giraffes eat.

As opposed to a main idea, themes are seldom expressed directly in a text, so they can be difficult to identify. A **theme** is an issue, an idea, or a question raised by the text. For instance, a theme of William Shakespeare's *Hamlet* is indecision, as the title character explores his own psyche and the results of his failure to make bold choices. A great work of literature may have many themes, and the reader is justified in identifying any for which he or she can find support. One common characteristic of themes is that they raise more questions than they answer. In a good piece of fiction, the author is not always trying to convince the reader, but is instead trying to elevate the reader's perspective and encourage him to consider the themes more deeply. When reading, one can identify themes by constantly asking what general issues the text is addressing. A good way to evaluate an author's approach to a theme is to begin reading with a question in mind (for example, how does this text approach the theme of love?) and then look for evidence in the text that addresses that question.

Review Video: Theme
Visit mometrix.com/academy and enter code: 732074

PURPOSES FOR WRITING

In order to be an effective reader, one must pay attention to the author's **position** and purpose. Even those texts that seem objective and impartial, like textbooks, have some sort of position and bias. Readers need to take these positions into account when considering the author's message. When an author uses emotional language or clearly favors one side of an argument, his position is clear. However, the author's position may be evident not only in what he writes, but in what he doesn't write. For this reason, it is sometimes necessary to review some other texts on the same topic in order to develop a view of the author's position. If this is not possible, then it may be useful to acquire a little background personal information about the author. When the only source of information is the text, however, the reader should look for language and argumentation that seems to indicate a particular stance on the subject.

Review Video: Author's Position
Visit mometrix.com/academy and enter code: 827954

Identifying the **purpose** of an author is usually easier than identifying her position. In most cases, the author has no interest in hiding his or her purpose. A text that is meant to entertain, for instance, should be obviously written to please the reader. Most narratives, or stories, are written to entertain, though they may also inform or persuade. Informative texts are easy to identify as well. The most difficult purpose of a text to identify is persuasion, because the author has an interest in making this purpose hard to detect. When a person knows that the author is trying to convince him, he is automatically more wary and skeptical of the argument. For this reason persuasive texts often try to establish an entertaining tone, hoping to amuse the reader into agreement, or an informative tone, hoping to create an appearance of authority and objectivity.

An author's purpose is often evident in the organization of the text. For instance, if the text has headings and subheadings, if key terms are in bold, and if the author makes his main idea clear from the beginning, then the likely purpose of the text is to inform. If the author begins by making a claim and then makes various arguments to support that claim, the purpose is probably to persuade. If the author is telling a story, or is more interested in holding the attention of the reader than in making a particular point or delivering information, then his purpose is most likely to entertain. As a reader, it is best to judge an author on how well he accomplishes his purpose. In other words, it is not entirely fair to complain that a textbook is boring: if the text is clear and easy to understand, then the author has done his job. Similarly, a storyteller should not be judged too harshly for getting some facts wrong, so long as he is able to give pleasure to the reader.

> **Review Video: Purpose of an Author**
> Visit mometrix.com/academy and enter code: 497555

The author's purpose for writing will affect his writing style and the response of the reader. In a **persuasive essay**, the author is attempting to change the reader's mind or convince him of something he did not believe previously. There are several identifying characteristics of persuasive writing. One is opinion presented as fact. When an author attempts to persuade the reader, he often presents his or her opinions as if they were fact. A reader must be on guard for statements that sound factual but which cannot be subjected to research, observation, or experiment. Another characteristic of persuasive writing is emotional language. An author will often try to play on the reader's emotion by appealing to his sympathy or sense of morality. When an author uses colorful or evocative language with the intent of arousing the reader's passions, it is likely that he is attempting to persuade. Finally, in many cases a persuasive text will give an unfair explanation of opposing positions, if these positions are mentioned at all.

An **informative text** is written to educate and enlighten the reader. Informative texts are almost always nonfiction, and are rarely structured as a story. The intention of an informative text is to deliver information in the most comprehensible way possible, so the structure of the text is likely to be very clear. In an informative text, the thesis statement is often in the first sentence. The author may use some colorful language, but is likely to put more emphasis on clarity and precision. Informative essays do not typically appeal to the emotions. They often contain facts and figures, and rarely include the opinion of the author. Sometimes a persuasive essay can resemble an informative essay, especially if the author maintains an even tone and presents his or her views as if they were established fact.

The success or failure of an author's intent to **entertain** is determined by those who read the author's work. Entertaining texts may be either fiction or nonfiction, and they may describe real or imagined people, places, and events. Entertaining texts are often narratives, or stories. A text that is written to entertain is likely to contain colorful language that engages the imagination and the emotions. Such writing often features a great deal of figurative language, which typically enlivens its subject matter with images and analogies. Though an entertaining text is not usually written to persuade or inform, it may accomplish both of these tasks. An entertaining text may appeal to the reader's emotions and cause him or her to think differently about a particular subject. In any case, entertaining texts tend to showcase the personality of the author more so than do other types of writing.

When an author intends to **express feelings,** she may use colorful and evocative language. An author may write emotionally for any number of reasons. Sometimes, the author will do so because she is describing a personal situation of great pain or happiness. Sometimes an author is attempting to persuade the reader, and so will use emotion to stir up the passions. It can be easy to identify this kind of expression when the writer uses phrases like *I felt* and *I sense*. However, sometimes the author will simply describe feelings without introducing them. As a reader, it is important to recognize when an author is expressing emotion, and not to become overwhelmed by sympathy or passion. A reader should maintain some detachment so that he or she can still evaluate the strength of the author's argument or the quality of the writing.

In a sense, almost all writing is descriptive, insofar as it seeks to describe events, ideas, or people to the reader. Some texts, however, are primarily concerned with **description**. A descriptive text focuses on a particular subject, and attempts to depict it in a way that will be clear to the reader. Descriptive texts contain many adjectives and adverbs, words that give shades of meaning and create a more detailed mental picture for the reader. A descriptive text fails when it is unclear or vague to the reader. On the other hand, however, a descriptive text that compiles too much detail can be boring and overwhelming to the reader. A descriptive text will certainly be informative, and it may be persuasive and entertaining as well. Descriptive writing is a challenge for the author, but when it is done well, it can be fun to read.

WRITING DEVICES

Authors will use different stylistic and writing devices to make their meaning more clearly understood. One of those devices is comparison and contrast. When an author describes the ways in which two things are alike, he or she is **comparing** them. When the author describes the ways in which two things are different, he or she is **contrasting** them. The "compare and contrast" essay is one of the most common forms in nonfiction. It is often signaled with certain words: a comparison may be indicated with such words as *both*, *same*, *like*, *too*, and *as well*; while a contrast may be indicated by words like *but*, *however*, *on the other hand*, *instead*, and *yet*. Of course, comparisons and contrasts may be implicit without using any such signaling language. A single sentence may both compare and contrast. Consider the sentence *Brian and Sheila love ice cream, but Brian prefers vanilla and Sheila prefers strawberry*. In one sentence, the author has described both a similarity (love of ice cream) and a difference (favorite flavor).

> **Review Video: Compare and Contrast**
> Visit mometrix.com/academy and enter code: 798319

One of the most common text structures is **cause and effect**. A cause is an act or event that makes something happen, and an effect is the thing that happens as a result of that cause. A cause-and-effect relationship is not always explicit, but there are some words in English that signal causality, such as *since*, *because*, and *as a result*. As an example, consider the sentence *Because the sky was clear, Ron did not bring an umbrella*. The cause is the clear sky, and the effect is that Ron did not bring an umbrella. However, sometimes the cause-and-effect relationship will not be clearly noted. For instance, the sentence *He was late and missed the meeting* does not contain any signaling words, but it still contains a cause (he was late) and an effect (he missed the meeting). It is possible for a single cause to have multiple effects, or for a single effect to have multiple causes. Also, an effect can in turn be the cause of another effect, in what is known as a cause-and-effect chain.

Authors often use analogies to add meaning to the text. An **analogy** is a comparison of two things. The words in the analogy are connected by a certain, often undetermined relationship. Look at this analogy: moo is to cow as quack is to duck. This analogy compares the sound that a cow makes with the sound that a duck makes. Even if the word 'quack' was not given, one could figure out it is the correct word to complete the analogy based on the relationship between the words 'moo' and 'cow'. Some common relationships for analogies include synonyms, antonyms, part to whole, definition, and actor to action.

Another element that impacts a text is the author's point of view. The **point of view** of a text is the perspective from which it is told. The author will always have a point of view about a story before he draws up a plot line. The author will know what events they want to take place, how they want the characters to interact, and how the story will resolve. An author will also have an opinion on the topic, or series of events, which is presented in the story, based on their own prior experience and beliefs.

The two main points of view that authors use are first person and third person. If the narrator of the story is also the main character, or *protagonist*, the text is written in first-person point of view. In first person, the author writes with the word *I*. Third-person point of view is probably the most common point of view that authors use. Using third person, authors refer to each character using the words *he* or *she*. In third-person omniscient, the narrator is not a character in the story and tells the story of all of the characters at the same time.

Review Video: Point of View
Visit mometrix.com/academy and enter code: 383336

A good writer will use **transitional words** and phrases to guide the reader through the text. You are no doubt familiar with the common transitions, though you may never have considered how they operate. Some transitional phrases (*after, before, during, in the middle of*) give information about time. Some indicate that an example is about to be given (*for example, in fact, for instance*). Writers use them to compare (*also, likewise*) and contrast (*however, but, yet*). Transitional words and phrases can suggest addition (*and, also, furthermore, moreover*) and logical relationships (*if, then, therefore, as a result, since*). Finally, transitional words and phrases can demarcate the steps in a process (*first, second, last*). You should incorporate transitional words and phrases where they will orient your reader and illuminate the structure of your composition.

Review Video: Transitional Words and Phrases
Visit mometrix.com/academy and enter code: 197796

TYPES OF PASSAGES

A **narrative** passage is a story. Narratives can be fiction or nonfiction. However, there are a few elements that a text must have in order to be classified as a narrative. To begin with, the text must have a plot. That is, it must describe a series of events. If it is a good narrative, these events will be interesting and emotionally engaging to the reader. A narrative also has characters. These could be people, animals, or even inanimate objects, so long as they participate in the plot. A narrative passage often contains figurative language, which is meant to stimulate the imagination of the reader by making comparisons and observations. A metaphor, which is a description of one thing in terms of another, is a common piece of figurative language. *The moon was a frosty snowball* is an example of a metaphor: it is obviously untrue in the literal sense, but it suggests a certain mood for the reader. Narratives often proceed in a clear sequence, but they do not need to do so.

An **expository** passage aims to inform and enlighten the reader. It is nonfiction and usually centers around a simple, easily defined topic. Since the goal of exposition is to teach, such a passage should be as clear as possible. It is common for an expository passage to contain helpful organizing words, like *first, next, for example*, and *therefore*. These words keep the reader oriented in the text. Although expository passages do not need to feature colorful language and artful writing, they are often more effective when they do. For a reader, the challenge of expository passages is to maintain steady attention. Expository passages are not always about subjects in which a reader will naturally be interested, and the writer is often more concerned with clarity and comprehensibility than with engaging the reader. For this reason, many expository passages are dull. Making notes is a good way to maintain focus when reading an expository passage.

A **technical** passage is written to describe a complex object or process. Technical writing is common in medical and technological fields, in which complicated mathematical, scientific, and engineering ideas need to be explained simply and clearly. To ease comprehension, a technical passage usually proceeds in a very logical order. Technical passages often have clear headings and subheadings, which are used to keep the reader oriented in the text. It is also common for these passages to break sections up with numbers or letters. Many technical passages look more like an outline than a piece of prose. The amount of jargon or difficult vocabulary will vary in a technical passage depending on the intended audience. As much as possible, technical passages try to avoid language that the reader will have to research in order to understand the message. Of course, it is not always possible to avoid jargon.

A **persuasive** passage is meant to change the reader's mind or lead her into agreement with the author. The persuasive intent may be obvious, or it may be quite difficult to discern. In some cases, a persuasive passage will be indistinguishable from an informative passage: it will make an assertion and offer supporting details. However, a persuasive passage is more likely to make claims based on opinion and to appeal to the reader's emotions. Persuasive passages may not describe alternate positions and, when they do, they often display significant bias. It may be clear that a persuasive passage is giving the author's viewpoint, or the passage may adopt a seemingly objective tone. A persuasive passage is successful if it can make a convincing argument and win the trust of the reader.

A persuasive essay will likely focus on one central argument, but it may make many smaller claims along the way. These are subordinate arguments with which the reader must agree if he or she is going to agree with the central argument. The central argument will only be as strong as the subordinate claims. These claims should be rooted in fact and observation, rather than subjective judgment. The best persuasive essays provide enough supporting detail to justify claims without overwhelming the reader. Remember that a fact must be susceptible to independent verification: that is, it must be something the reader could confirm. Also, statistics are only effective when they take into account possible objections. For instance, a statistic on the number of foreclosed houses would only be useful if it was taken over a defined interval and in a defined area. Most readers are wary of statistics, because they are so often misleading. If possible, a persuasive essay should always include references so that the reader can obtain more information. Of course, this means that the writer's accuracy and fairness may be judged by the inquiring reader.

Opinions are formed by emotion as well as reason, and persuasive writers often appeal to the feelings of the reader. Although readers should always be skeptical of this technique, it is often used in a proper and ethical manner. For instance, there are many subjects that have an obvious emotional component, and therefore cannot be completely treated without an appeal to the emotions. Consider an article on drunk driving: it makes sense to include some specific examples that will alarm or sadden the reader. After all, drunk driving often has serious and tragic consequences. Emotional appeals are not appropriate, however, when they attempt to mislead the reader. For instance, in political advertisements it is common to emphasize the patriotism of the preferred candidate, because this will encourage the audience to link their own positive feelings

20

about the country with their opinion of the candidate. However, these ads often imply that the other candidate is unpatriotic, which in most cases is far from the truth. Another common and improper emotional appeal is the use of loaded language, as for instance referring to an avidly religious person as a "fanatic" or a passionate environmentalist as a "tree hugger." These terms introduce an emotional component that detracts from the argument.

HISTORY AND CULTURE

Historical context has a profound influence on literature: the events, knowledge base, and assumptions of an author's time color every aspect of his or her work. Sometimes, authors hold opinions and use language that would be considered inappropriate or immoral in a modern setting, but that was acceptable in the author's time. As a reader, one should consider how the historical context influenced a work and also how today's opinions and ideas shape the way modern readers read the works of the past. For instance, in most societies of the past, women were treated as second-class citizens. An author who wrote in 18th-century England might sound sexist to modern readers, even if that author was relatively feminist in his time. Readers should not have to excuse the faulty assumptions and prejudices of the past, but they should appreciate that a person's thoughts and words are, in part, a result of the time and culture in which they live or lived, and it is perhaps unfair to expect writers to avoid all of the errors of their times.

Even a brief study of world literature suggests that writers from vastly different cultures address similar themes. For instance, works like the *Odyssey* and *Hamlet* both tackle the individual's battle for self-control and independence. In every culture, authors address themes of personal growth and the struggle for maturity. Another universal theme is the conflict between the individual and society. In works as culturally disparate as *Native Son*, the *Aeneid*, and *1984*, authors dramatize how people struggle to maintain their personalities and dignity in large, sometimes oppressive groups. Finally, many cultures have versions of the hero's (or heroine's) journey, in which an adventurous person must overcome many obstacles in order to gain greater knowledge, power, and perspective. Some famous works that treat this theme are the *Epic of Gilgamesh*, Dante's *Divine Comedy*, and *Don Quixote*.

Authors from different genres (for instance poetry, drama, novel, short story) and cultures may address similar themes, but they often do so quite differently. For instance, poets are likely to address subject matter obliquely, through the use of images and allusions. In a play, on the other hand, the author is more likely to dramatize themes by using characters to express opposing viewpoints. This disparity is known as a dialectical approach. In a novel, the author does not need to express themes directly; rather, they can be illustrated through events and actions. In some regional literatures, like those of Greece or England, authors use more irony: their works have characters that express views and make decisions that are clearly disapproved of by the author. In Latin America, there is a great tradition of using supernatural events to illustrate themes about real life. In China and Japan, authors frequently use well-established regional forms (haiku, for instance) to organize their treatment of universal themes.

RESPONDING TO LITERATURE

When reading good literature, the reader is moved to engage actively in the text. One part of being an active reader involves making predictions. A **prediction** is a guess about what will happen next. Readers are constantly making predictions based on what they have read and what they already know. Consider the following sentence: *Staring at the computer screen in shock, Kim blindly reached over for the brimming glass of water on the shelf to her side.* The sentence suggests that Kim is agitated and that she is not looking at the glass she is going to pick up, so a reader might predict that she is going to knock the glass over. Of course, not every prediction will be accurate: perhaps

Kim will pick the glass up cleanly. Nevertheless, the author has certainly created the expectation that the water might be spilled. Predictions are always subject to revision as the reader acquires more information.

Test-taking tip: To respond to questions requiring future predictions, the student's answers should be based on evidence of past or present behavior.

Readers are often required to understand text that claims and suggests ideas without stating them directly. An **inference** is a piece of information that is implied but not written outright by the author. For instance, consider the following sentence: *Mark made more money that week than he had in the previous year.* From this sentence, the reader can infer that Mark either has not made much money in the previous year or made a great deal of money that week. Often, a reader can use information he or she already knows to make inferences. Take as an example the sentence *When his coffee arrived, he looked around the table for the silver cup.* Many people know that cream is typically served in a silver cup, so using their own base of knowledge they can infer that the subject of this sentence takes his coffee with cream. Making inferences requires concentration, attention, and practice.

Test-taking tip: While being tested on his ability to make correct inferences, the student must look for contextual clues. An answer can be *true* but not *correct*. The contextual clues will help you find the answer that is the best answer out of the given choices. Understand the context in which a phrase is stated. When asked for the implied meaning of a statement made in the passage, the student should immediately locate the statement and read the context in which it was made. Also, look for an answer choice that has a similar phrase to the statement in question.

A reader must be able to identify a text's **sequence**, or the order in which things happen. Often, and especially when the sequence is very important to the author, it is indicated with signal words like *first*, *then*, *next*, and *last*. However, sometimes a sequence is merely implied and must be noted by the reader. Consider the sentence *He walked in the front door and switched on the hall lamp.* Clearly, the man did not turn the lamp on before he walked in the door, so the implied sequence is that he first walked in the door and then turned on the lamp. Texts do not always proceed in an orderly sequence from first to last: sometimes, they begin at the end and then start over at the beginning. As a reader, it can be useful to make brief notes to clarify the sequence.

In addition to inferring and predicting things about the text, the reader must often **draw conclusions** about the information he has read. When asked for a *conclusion* that may be drawn, look for critical "hedge" phrases, such as *likely*, *may*, *can*, *will often*, among many others. When you are being tested on this knowledge, remember that question writers insert these hedge phrases to cover every possibility. Often an answer will be wrong simply because it leaves no room for exception. Extreme positive or negative answers (such as always, never, etc.) are usually not correct. The reader should not use any outside knowledge that is not gathered from the reading passage to answer the related questions. Correct answers can be derived straight from the reading passage.

LITERARY GENRES

Literary genres refer to the basic generic types of poetry, drama, fiction, and nonfiction. Literary genre is a method of classifying and analyzing literature. There are numerous subdivisions within genre, including such categories as novels, novellas, and short stories in fiction. Drama may also be subdivided into comedy, tragedy, and many other categories. Poetry and nonfiction have their own distinct divisions.

Genres often overlap, and the distinctions among them are blurred, such as that between the nonfiction novel and docudrama, as well as many others. However, the use of genres is helpful to the reader as a set of understandings that guide our responses to a work. The generic norm sets expectations and forms the framework within which we read and evaluate a work. This framework will guide both our understanding and interpretation of the work. It is a useful tool for both literary criticism and analysis.

Fiction is a general term for any form of literary narrative that is invented or imagined rather than being factual. For those individuals who equate fact with truth, the imagined or invented character of fiction tends to render it relatively unimportant or trivial among the genres. Defenders of fiction are quick to point out that the fictional mode is an essential part of being. The ability to imagine or discuss what-if plots, characters, and events is clearly part of the human experience.

Prose is derived from the Latin and means "straightforward discourse." Prose fiction, although having many categories, may be divided into three main groups:

- **Short stories**: a fictional narrative, the length of which varies, usually under 20,000 words. Short stories usually have only a few characters and generally describe one major event or insight. The short story began in magazines in the late 1800s and has flourished ever since.
- **Novels**: a longer work of fiction, often containing a large cast of characters and extensive plotting. The emphasis may be on an event, action, social problems, or any experience. There is now a genre of nonfiction novels pioneered by Truman Capote's *In Cold Blood* in the 1960s. Novels may also be written in verse.
- **Novellas**: a work of narrative fiction longer than a short story but shorter than a novel. Novellas may also be called short novels or novelettes. They originated from the German tradition and have become common forms in all of the world's literature.

Many elements influence a work of prose fiction. Some important ones are:

- **Speech and dialogue**: Characters may speak for themselves or through the narrator. Dialogue may be realistic or fantastic, depending on the author's aim.
- **Thoughts and mental processes**: There may be internal dialogue used as a device for plot development or character understanding.
- **Dramatic involvement**: Some narrators encourage readers to become involved in the events of the story, whereas others attempt to distance readers through literary devices.
- **Action**: This is any information that advances the plot or involves new interactions between the characters.
- **Duration**: The time frame of the work may be long or short, and the relationship between described time and narrative time may vary.
- **Setting and description**: Is the setting critical to the plot or characters? How are the action scenes described?
- **Themes**: This is any point of view or topic given sustained attention.
- **Symbolism**: Authors often veil meanings through imagery and other literary constructions.

Fiction is much wider than simply prose fiction. Songs, ballads, epics, and narrative poems are examples of non-prose fiction. A full definition of fiction must include not only the work itself but also the framework in which it is read. Literary fiction can also be defined as not true rather than nonexistent, as many works of historical fiction refer to real people, places, and events that are treated imaginatively as if they were true. These imaginary elements enrich and broaden literary expression.

When analyzing fiction, it is important for the reader to look carefully at the work being studied. The plot or action of a narrative can become so entertaining that the language of the work is ignored. The language of fiction should not simply be a way to relate a plot—it should also yield many insights to the judicious reader. Some prose fiction is based on the reader's engagement with the language rather than the story. A studious reader will analyze the mode of expression as well as the narrative. Part of the reward of reading in this manner is to discover how the author uses different language to describe familiar objects, events, or emotions. Some works focus the reader on an author's unorthodox use of language, whereas others may emphasize characters or storylines. What happens in a story is not always the critical element in the work. This type of reading may be difficult at first but yields great rewards.

The **narrator** is a central part of any work of fiction, and can give insight about the purpose of the work and its main themes and ideas. The following are important questions to address to better understand the voice and role of the narrator and incorporate that voice into an overall understanding of the novel:

- Who is the narrator of the novel? What is the narrator's perspective, first person or third person? What is the role of the narrator in the plot? Are there changes in narrators or the perspective of narrators?
- Does the narrator explain things in the novel, or does meaning emerge from the plot and events? The personality of the narrator is important. She may have a vested interest in a character or event described. Some narratives follow the time sequence of the plot, whereas others do not. A narrator may express approval or disapproval about a character or events in the work.
- Tone is an important aspect of the narration. Who is actually being addressed by the narrator? Is the tone familiar or formal, intimate or impersonal? Does the vocabulary suggest clues about the narrator?

A **character** is a person intimately involved with the plot and development of the novel. Development of the novel's characters not only moves the story along but will also tell the reader a lot about the novel itself. There is usually a physical description of the character, but this is often omitted in modern and postmodern novels. These works may focus on the psychological state or motivation of the character. The choice of a character's name may give valuable clues to his role in the work.

Characters are said to be flat or round. Flat characters tend to be minor figures in the story, changing little or not at all. Round characters (those understood from a well-rounded view) are more central to the story and tend to change as the plot unfolds. Stock characters are similar to flat characters, filling out the story without influencing it.

Modern literature has been greatly affected by Freudian psychology, giving rise to such devices as the interior monologue and magical realism as methods of understanding characters in a work. These give the reader a more complex understanding of the inner lives of the characters and enrich the understanding of relationships between characters.

Review Video: Characters
Visit mometrix.com/academy and enter code: 429493

Another important genre is that of **drama**: a play written to be spoken aloud. The drama is in many ways inseparable from performance. Reading drama ideally involves using imagination to visualize and re-create the play with characters and settings. The reader stages the play in his imagination, watching characters interact and developments unfold. Sometimes this involves simulating a theatrical presentation; other times it involves imagining the events. In either case, the reader is imagining the unwritten to re-create the dramatic experience. Novels present some of the same problems, but a narrator will provide much more information about the setting, characters, inner dialogues, and many other supporting details. In drama, much of this is missing, and we are required to use our powers of projection and imagination to taste the full flavor of the dramatic work. There are many empty spaces in dramatic texts that must be filled by the reader to fully appreciate the work.

Review Video: Dramas
Visit mometrix.com/academy and enter code: 216060

When reading drama in this way, there are some advantages over watching the play performed (though there is much criticism in this regard):

- Freedom of point of view and perspective: Text is free of interpretations of actors, directors, producers, and technical staging.
- Additional information: The text of a drama may be accompanied by notes or prefaces placing the work in a social or historical context. Stage directions may also provide relevant information about the author's purpose. None of this is typically available at live or filmed performances.
- Study and understanding: Difficult or obscure passages may be studied at leisure and supplemented by explanatory works. This is particularly true of older plays with unfamiliar language, which cannot be fully understood without an opportunity to study the material.

Critical elements of drama, especially when it is being read aloud or performed, include dialect, speech, and dialogue. Analysis of speech and dialogue is important in the critical study of drama. Some playwrights use speech to develop their characters. Speeches may be long or short, and written in as normal prose or blank verse. Some characters have a unique way of speaking which illuminates aspects of the drama. Emphasis and tone are both important, as well. Does the author make clear the tone in which lines are to be spoken, or is this open to interpretation? Sometimes there are various possibilities in tone with regard to delivering lines.

Dialect is any distinct variety of a language, especially one spoken in a region or part of a country. The criterion for distinguishing dialects from languages is that of mutual understanding. For example, people who speak Dutch cannot understand English unless they have learned it. But a speaker from Amsterdam can understand one from Antwerp; therefore, they speak different dialects of the same language. This is, however, a matter of degree; there are languages in which different dialects are unintelligible.

Dialect mixtures are the presence in one form of speech with elements from different neighboring dialects. The study of speech differences from one geographical area to another is called dialect geography. A dialect atlas is a map showing distribution of dialects in a given area. A dialect continuum shows a progressive shift in dialects across a territory, such that adjacent dialects are understandable, but those at the extremes are not.

Dramatic dialogue can be difficult to interpret and changes depending upon the tone used and which words are emphasized. Where the stresses, or meters, of dramatic dialogue fall can determine meaning. Variations in emphasis are only one factor in the manipulability of dramatic speech. Tone is of equal or greater importance and expresses a range of possible emotions and feelings that cannot be readily discerned from the script of a play. The reader must add tone to the words to understand the full meaning of a passage. Recognizing tone is a cumulative process as the reader begins to understand the characters and situations in the play. Other elements that influence the interpretation of dialogue include the setting, possible reactions of the characters to the speech, and possible gestures or facial expressions of the actor. There are no firm rules to guide the interpretation of dramatic speech. An open and flexible attitude is essential in interpreting dramatic dialogue.

Action is a crucial element in the production of a dramatic work. Many dramas contain little dialogue and much action. In these cases, it is essential for the reader to carefully study stage directions and visualize the action on the stage. Benefits of understanding stage directions include knowing which characters are on the stage at all times, who is speaking to whom, and following these patterns through changes of scene.

Stage directions also provide additional information, some of which is not available to a live audience. The nature of the physical space where the action occurs is vital, and stage directions help with this. The historical context of the period is important in understanding what the playwright was working with in terms of theaters and physical space. The type of staging possible for the author is a good guide to the spatial elements of a production.

Asides and soliloquies are devices that authors use in plot and character development. **Asides** indicate that not all characters are privy to the lines. This may be a method of advancing or explaining the plot in a subtle manner. **Soliloquies** are opportunities for character development, plot enhancement, and to give insight to characters' motives, feelings, and emotions. Careful study of these elements provides a reader with an abundance of clues to the major themes and plot of the work.

Art, music, and literature all interact in ways that contain many opportunities for the enrichment of all of the arts. Students could apply their knowledge of art and music by creating illustrations for a work or creating a musical score for a text. Students could discuss the meanings of texts and decide on their illustrations, or a score could amplify the meaning of the text.

Understanding the art and music of a period can make the experience of literature a richer, more rewarding experience. Students should be encouraged to use the knowledge of art and music to illuminate the text. Examining examples of dress, architecture, music, and dance of a period may be helpful in a fuller engagement of the text. Much of period literature lends itself to the analysis of the prevailing taste in art and music of an era, which helps place the literary work in a more meaningful context.

OPINIONS, FACTS, AND FALLACIES

Critical thinking skills are mastered through understanding various types of writing and the different purposes that authors have for writing the way they do. Every author writes for a purpose. Understanding that purpose, and how they accomplish their goal, will allow you to critique the writing and determine whether or not you agree with their conclusions.

Readers must always be conscious of the distinction between fact and opinion. A **fact** can be subjected to analysis and can be either proved or disproved. An **opinion**, on the other hand, is the author's personal feeling, which may not be alterable by research, evidence, or argument. If the author writes that the distance from New York to Boston is about two hundred miles, he is stating a fact. But if he writes that New York is too crowded, then he is giving an opinion, because there is no objective standard for overpopulation. An opinion may be indicated by words like *believe*, *think*, or *feel*. Also, an opinion may be supported by facts: for instance, the author might give the population density of New York as a reason for why it is overcrowded. An opinion supported by fact tends to be more convincing. When authors support their opinions with other opinions, the reader is unlikely to be moved.

Facts should be presented to the reader from reliable sources. An opinion is what the author thinks about a given topic. An opinion is not common knowledge or proven by expert sources, but it is information that the author believes and wants the reader to consider. To distinguish between fact and opinion, a reader needs to look at the type of source that is presenting information, what information backs-up a claim, and whether or not the author may be motivated to have a certain point of view on a given topic. For example, if a panel of scientists has conducted multiple studies on the effectiveness of taking a certain vitamin, the results are more likely to be factual than if a company selling a vitamin claims that taking the vitamin can produce positive effects. The company is motivated to sell its product, while the scientists are using the scientific method to prove a theory. If the author uses words such as "I think...", the statement is an opinion.

> **Review Video: Fact or Opinion**
> Visit mometrix.com/academy and enter code: 870899

In their attempt to persuade, writers often make mistakes in their thinking patterns and writing choices. It's important to understand these so you can make an informed decision. Every author has a point of view, but when an author ignores reasonable counterarguments or distorts opposing viewpoints, she is demonstrating a **bias**. A bias is evident whenever the author is unfair or inaccurate in his or her presentation. Bias may be intentional or unintentional, but it should always alert the reader to be skeptical of the argument being made. It should be noted that a biased author may still be correct. However, the author will be correct in spite of her bias, not because of it. A **stereotype** is like a bias, except that it is specifically applied to a group or place. Stereotyping is considered to be particularly abhorrent because it promotes negative generalizations about people. Many people are familiar with some of the hateful stereotypes of certain ethnic, religious, and cultural groups. Readers should be very wary of authors who stereotype. These faulty assumptions typically reveal the author's ignorance and lack of curiosity.

> **Review Video: Bias and Stereotype**
> Visit mometrix.com/academy and enter code: 644829

Sometimes, authors will **appeal to the reader's emotion** in an attempt to persuade or to distract the reader from the weakness of the argument. For instance, the author may try to inspire the pity of the reader by delivering a heart-rending story. An author also might use the bandwagon approach, in which he suggests that his opinion is correct because it is held by the majority. Some authors resort to name-calling, in which insults and harsh words are delivered to the opponent in an attempt to distract. In advertising, a common appeal is the testimonial, in which a famous person endorses a product. Of course, the fact that a celebrity likes something should not really mean anything to the reader. These and other emotional appeals are usually evidence of poor reasoning and a weak argument.

Review Video: Appeal to Emotion
Visit mometrix.com/academy and enter code: 163442

Certain *logical fallacies* are frequent in writing. A logical fallacy is a failure of reasoning. As a reader, it is important to recognize logical fallacies, because they diminish the value of the author's message. The four most common logical fallacies in writing are the false analogy, circular reasoning, false dichotomy, and overgeneralization. In a **false analogy**, the author suggests that two things are similar, when in fact they are different. This fallacy is often committed when the author is attempting to convince the reader that something unknown is like something relatively familiar. The author takes advantage of the reader's ignorance to make this false comparison. One example might be the following statement: *Failing to tip a waitress is like stealing money out of somebody's wallet.* Of course, failing to tip is very rude, especially when the service has been good, but people are not arrested for failing to tip as they would for stealing money from a wallet. To compare stingy diners with thieves is a false analogy.

Review Video: False Analogy
Visit mometrix.com/academy and enter code: 865045

Circular reasoning is one of the more difficult logical fallacies to identify, because it is typically hidden behind dense language and complicated sentences. Reasoning is described as circular when it offers no support for assertions other than restating them in different words. Put another way, a circular argument refers to itself as evidence of truth. A simple example of circular argument is when a person uses a word to define itself, such as saying *Niceness is the state of being nice*. If the reader does not know what *nice* means, then this definition will not be very useful. In a text, circular reasoning is usually more complex. For instance, an author might say *Poverty is a problem for society because it creates trouble for people throughout the community*. It is redundant to say that poverty is a problem because it creates trouble. When an author engages in circular reasoning, it is often because he or she has not fully thought out the argument, or cannot come up with any legitimate justifications.

Review Video: Circular Reasoning
Visit mometrix.com/academy and enter code: 398925

One of the most common logical fallacies is the **false dichotomy**, in which the author creates an artificial sense that there are only two possible alternatives in a situation. This fallacy is common when the author has an agenda and wants to give the impression that his view is the only sensible one. A false dichotomy has the effect of limiting the reader's options and imagination. An example of a false dichotomy is the statement *You need to go to the party with me, otherwise you'll just be bored at home*. The speaker suggests that the only other possibility besides being at the party is being bored at home. But this is not true, as it is perfectly possible to be entertained at home, or even to

go somewhere other than the party. Readers should always be wary of the false dichotomy: when an author limits alternatives, it is always wise to ask whether he is being valid.

Overgeneralization is a logical fallacy in which the author makes a claim that is so broad it cannot be proved or disproved. In most cases, overgeneralization occurs when the author wants to create an illusion of authority, or when he is using sensational language to sway the opinion of the reader. For instance, in the sentence *Everybody knows that she is a terrible teacher*, the author makes an assumption that cannot really be believed. This kind of statement is made when the author wants to create the illusion of consensus when none actually exists: it may be that most people have a negative view of the teacher, but to say that *everybody* feels that way is an exaggeration. When a reader spots overgeneralization, she should become skeptical about the argument that is being made, because an author will often try to hide a weak or unsupported assertion behind authoritative language.

Two other types of logical fallacies are **slippery slope** arguments and **hasty generalizations**. In a slippery slope argument, the author says that if something happens, it automatically means that something else will happen as a result, even though this may not be true. (i.e., just because you study hard does not mean you are going to ace the test). "Hasty generalization" is drawing a conclusion too early, without finishing analyzing the details of the argument. Writers of persuasive texts often use these techniques because they are very effective. In order to **identify logical fallacies**, readers need to read carefully and ask questions as they read. Thinking critically means not taking everything at face value. Readers need to critically evaluate an author's argument to make sure that the logic used is sound.

ORGANIZATION OF THE TEXT

The way a text is organized can help the reader to understand more clearly the author's intent and his conclusions. There are various ways to organize a text, and each one has its own purposes and uses.

Some nonfiction texts are organized to **present a problem** followed by a solution. In this type of text, it is common for the problem to be explained before the solution is offered. In some cases, as when the problem is well known, the solution may be briefly introduced at the beginning. The entire passage may focus on the solution, and the problem will be referenced only occasionally. Some texts will outline multiple solutions to a problem, leaving the reader to choose among them. If the author has an interest or an allegiance to one solution, he may fail to mention or may describe inaccurately some of the other solutions. Readers should be careful of the author's agenda when reading a problem-solution text. Only by understanding the author's point of view and interests can one develop a proper judgment of the proposed solution.

Authors need to organize information logically so the reader can follow it and locate information within the text. Two common organizational structures are cause and effect and chronological order. When using **chronological order**, the author presents information in the order that it happened. For example, biographies are written in chronological order; the subject's birth and childhood are presented first, followed by their adult life, and lastly by the events leading up to the person's death.

In **cause and effect**, an author presents one thing that makes something else happen. For example, if one were to go to bed very late, they would be tired. The cause is going to bed late, with the effect of being tired the next day.

It can be tricky to identify the cause-and-effect relationships in a text, but there are a few ways to approach this task. To begin with, these relationships are often signaled with certain terms. When an author uses words like *because*, *since*, *in order*, and *so*, she is likely describing a cause-and-effect relationship. Consider the sentence, "He called her because he needed the homework." This is a simple causal relationship, in which the cause was his need for the homework and the effect was his phone call. Not all cause-and-effect relationships are marked in this way, however. Consider the sentences, "He called her. He needed the homework." When the cause-and-effect relationship is not indicated with a keyword, it can be discovered by asking why something happened. He called her: why? The answer is in the next sentence: He needed the homework.

Persuasive essays, in which an author tries to make a convincing argument and change the reader's mind, usually include cause-and-effect relationships. However, these relationships should not always be taken at face value. An author frequently will assume a cause or take an effect for granted. To read a persuasive essay effectively, one needs to judge the cause-and-effect relationships the author is presenting. For instance, imagine an author wrote the following: "The parking deck has been unprofitable because people would prefer to ride their bikes." The relationship is clear: the cause is that people prefer to ride their bikes, and the effect is that the parking deck has been unprofitable. However, a reader should consider whether this argument is conclusive. Perhaps there are other reasons for the failure of the parking deck: a down economy, excessive fees, etc. Too often, authors present causal relationships as if they are fact rather than opinion. Readers should be on the alert for these dubious claims.

Thinking critically about ideas and conclusions can seem like a daunting task. One way to make it easier is to understand the basic elements of ideas and writing techniques. Looking at the way different ideas relate to each other can be a good way for the reader to begin his analysis. For instance, sometimes writers will write about two different ideas that are in opposition to each other. The analysis of these opposing ideas is known as **contrast**. Contrast is often marred by the author's obvious partiality to one of the ideas. A discerning reader will be put off by an author who does not engage in a fair fight. In an analysis of opposing ideas, both ideas should be presented in their clearest and most reasonable terms. If the author does prefer a side, he should avoid indicating this preference with pejorative language. An analysis of opposing ideas should proceed through the major differences point by point, with a full explanation of each side's view. For instance, in an analysis of capitalism and communism, it would be important to outline each side's view on labor, markets, prices, personal responsibility, etc. It would be less effective to describe the theory of communism and then explain how capitalism has thrived in the West. An analysis of opposing views should present each side in the same manner.

Many texts follow the **compare-and-contrast** model, in which the similarities and differences between two ideas or things are explored. Analysis of the similarities between ideas is called comparison. In order for a comparison to work, the author must place the ideas or things in an equivalent structure. That is, the author must present the ideas in the same way. Imagine an author wanted to show the similarities between cricket and baseball. The correct way to do so would be to summarize the equipment and rules for each game. It would be incorrect to summarize the equipment of cricket and then lay out the history of baseball, since this would make it impossible

30

for the reader to see the similarities. It is perhaps too obvious to say that an analysis of similar ideas should emphasize the similarities. Of course, the author should take care to include any differences that must be mentioned. Often, these small differences will only reinforce the more general similarity.

DRAWING CONCLUSIONS

Authors should have a clear purpose in mind while writing. Especially when reading informational texts, it is important to understand the logical conclusion of the author's ideas. **Identifying this logical conclusion** can help the reader understand whether he agrees with the writer or not. Identifying a logical conclusion is much like making an inference: it requires the reader to combine the information given by the text with what he already knows to make a supportable assertion. If a passage is written well, then the conclusion should be obvious even when it is unstated. If the author intends the reader to draw a certain conclusion, then all of his argumentation and detail should be leading toward it. One way to approach the task of drawing conclusions is to make brief notes of all the points made by the author. When these are arranged on paper, they may clarify the logical conclusion. Another way to approach conclusions is to consider whether the reasoning of the author raises any pertinent questions. Sometimes it will be possible to draw several conclusions from a passage, and on occasion these will be conclusions that were never imagined by the author. It is essential, however, that these conclusions be supported directly by the text.

> **Review Video: Identifying Logical Conclusions**
> Visit mometrix.com/academy and enter code: 281653

The term **text evidence** refers to information that supports a main point or points in a story, and can help lead the reader to a conclusion. Information used as *text evidence* is precise, descriptive, and factual. A main point is often followed by supporting details that provide evidence to back-up a claim. For example, a story may include the claim that winter occurs during opposite months in the Northern and Southern hemispheres. *Text evidence* based on this claim may include countries where winter occurs in opposite months, along with reasons that winter occurs at different times of the year in separate hemispheres (due to the tilt of the Earth as it rotates around the sun).

Readers interpret text and respond to it in a number of ways. Using textual support helps defend your response or interpretation because it roots your thinking in the text. You are interpreting based on information in the text and not simply your own ideas. When crafting a response, look for important quotes and details from the text to help bolster your argument. If you are writing about a character's personality trait, for example, use details from the text to show that the character acted in such a way. You can also include statistics and facts from a nonfiction text to strengthen your response. For example, instead of writing, "A lot of people use cell phones," use statistics to provide the exact number. This strengthens your argument because it is more precise.

> **Review Video: Text Evidence**
> Visit mometrix.com/academy and enter code: 486236

The text used to support an argument can be the argument's downfall if it is not credible. A text is **credible**, or believable, when the author is knowledgeable and objective, or unbiased. The author's motivations for writing the text play a critical role in determining the credibility of the text and must be evaluated when assessing that credibility. The author's motives should be for the dissemination of information. The purpose of the text should be to inform or describe, not to persuade. When an author writes a persuasive text, he has the motivation that the reader will do what they want. The extent of the author's knowledge of the topic and their motivation must be

31

evaluated when assessing the credibility of a text. Reports written about the Ozone layer by an environmental scientist and a hairdresser will have a different level of credibility.

After determining your own opinion and evaluating the credibility of your supporting text, it is sometimes necessary to communicate your ideas and findings to others. When **writing a response to a text**, it is important to use elements of the text to support your assertion or defend your position. Using supporting evidence from the text strengthens the argument because the reader can see how in depth the writer read the original piece and based their response on the details and facts within that text. Elements of text that can be used in a response include: facts, details, statistics, and direct quotations from the text. When writing a response, one must make sure they indicate which information comes from the original text and then base their discussion, argument, or defense around this information.

A reader should always be drawing conclusions from the text. Sometimes conclusions are implied from written information, and other times the information is **stated directly** within the passage. It is always more comfortable to draw conclusions from information stated within a passage, rather than to draw them from mere implications. At times an author may provide some information and then describe a counterargument. The reader should be alert for direct statements that are subsequently rejected or weakened by the author. The reader should always read the entire passage before drawing conclusions. Many readers are trained to expect the author's conclusions at either the beginning or the end of the passage, but many texts do not adhere to this format.

Drawing conclusions from information implied within a passage requires confidence on the part of the reader. **Implications** are things the author does not state directly, but which can be assumed based on what the author does say. For instance, consider the following simple passage: "I stepped outside and opened my umbrella. By the time I got to work, the cuffs of my pants were soaked." The author never states that it is raining, but this fact is clearly implied. Conclusions based on implication must be well supported by the text. In order to draw a solid conclusion, a reader should have multiple pieces of evidence, or, if he only has one, must be assured that there is no other possible explanation than his conclusion. A good reader will be able to draw many conclusions from information implied by the text, which enriches the reading experience considerably.

As an aid to drawing conclusions, the reader should be adept at **outlining** the information contained in the passage; an effective outline will reveal the structure of the passage, and will lead to solid conclusions. An effective outline will have a title that refers to the basic subject of the text, though it need not recapitulate the main idea. In most outlines, the main idea will be the first major section. It will have each major idea of the passage established as the head of a category. For instance, the most common outline format calls for the main ideas of the passage to be indicated with Roman numerals. In an effective outline of this kind, each of the main ideas will be represented by a Roman numeral and none of the Roman numerals will designate minor details or secondary ideas. Moreover, all supporting ideas and details should be placed in the appropriate place on the outline. An outline does not need to include every detail listed in the text, but it should feature all of those that are central to the argument or message. Each of these details should be listed under the appropriate main idea.

It is also helpful to **summarize** the information you have read in a paragraph or passage format. This process is similar to creating an effective outline. To begin with, a summary should accurately define the main idea of the passage, though it does not need to explain this main idea in exhaustive detail. It should continue by laying out the most important supporting details or arguments from the passage. All of the significant supporting details should be included, and none of the details included should be irrelevant or insignificant. Also, the summary should accurately report all of these details. Too often, the desire for brevity in a summary leads to the sacrifice of clarity or veracity. Summaries are often difficult to read, because they omit all of graceful language, digressions, and asides that distinguish great writing. However, if the summary is effective, it should contain much the same message as the original text.

Paraphrasing is another method the reader can use to aid in comprehension. When paraphrasing, one puts what they have read into their own words, rephrasing what the author has written to make it their own, to "translate" all of what the author says to their own words, including as many details as they can.

INFORMATIONAL SOURCES

Informational sources often come in short forms like a memo or recipe, or longer forms like books, magazines, or journals. These longer sources of information each have their own way of organizing information, but there are some similarities that the reader should be aware of.

Most books, magazines, and journals have a **table of contents** at the beginning. This helps the reader find the different parts of the book. The table of contents is usually found a page or two after the title page in a book, and on the first few pages of a magazine. However, many magazines now place the table of contents in the midst of an overabundance of advertisements, because they know readers will have to look at the ads as they search for the table. The standard orientation for a table of contents is the sections of the book listed along the left side, with the initial page number for each along the right. It is common in a book for the prefatory material (preface, introduction, etc.) to be numbered with Roman numerals. The contents are always listed in order from the beginning of the book to the end.

A nonfiction book will also typically have an **index** at the end so that the reader can easily find information about particular topics. An index lists the topics in alphabetical order. The names of people are listed with the last name first. For example, *Adams, John* would come before *Washington, George*. To the right of the entry, the relevant page numbers are listed. When a topic is mentioned over several pages, the index will often connect these pages with a dash. For instance, if the subject is mentioned from pages 35 to 42 and again on 53, then the index entry will be labeled as *35-42, 53*. Some entries will have subsets, which are listed below the main entry, indented slightly, and placed in alphabetical order. This is common for subjects that are discussed frequently in the book. For instance, in a book about Elizabethan drama, William Shakespeare will likely be an important topic. Beneath Shakespeare's name in the index, there might be listings for *death of, dramatic works of, life of*, etc. These more specific entries help the reader refine his search.

Many informative texts, especially textbooks, use **headings** and **subheadings** for organization. Headings and subheadings are typically printed in larger and bolder fonts, and are often in a different color than the main body of the text. Headings may be larger than subheadings. Also, headings and subheadings are not always complete sentences. A heading announces the topic that will be addressed in the text below. Headings are meant to alert the reader to what is about to come. Subheadings announce the topics of smaller sections within the entire section indicated by the heading. For instance, the heading of a section in a science textbook might be *AMPHIBIANS*, and within that section might be subheadings for *Frogs, Salamanders*, and *Newts*. Readers should always pay close attention to headings and subheadings, because they prime the brain for the information that is about to be delivered, and because they make it easy to go back and find particular details in a long text.

REFERENCE MATERIALS

Knowledge of reference materials such as dictionaries, encyclopedias, and manuals are vital for any reader. **Dictionaries** contain information about words. A standard dictionary entry begins with a pronunciation guide for the word. The entry will also give the word's part of speech: that is, whether it is a noun, verb, adjective, etc. A good dictionary will also include the word's origins, including the language from which it is derived and its meaning in that language. This information is known as the word's etymology.

Dictionary entries are in alphabetical order. Many words have more than one definition, in which case the definitions will be numbered. Also, if a word can be used as different parts of speech, its various definitions in those different capacities may be separated. A sample entry might look like this:

WELL: (adverb) 1. in a good way (noun) 1. a hole drilled into the earth

The correct definition of a word will vary depending on how it is used in a sentence. When looking up a word found while reading, the best way to determine the relevant definition is to substitute the dictionary's definitions for the word in the text, and select the definition that seems most appropriate.

Encyclopedias used to be the best source for general information on a range of common subjects. Many people took pride in owning a set of encyclopedias, which were often written by top researchers. Now, encyclopedias largely exist online. Although they no longer have a preeminent place in general scholarship, these digital encyclopedias now often feature audio and video clips. A good encyclopedia remains the best place to obtain basic information about a well-known topic. There are also specialty encyclopedias that cover more obscure or expert information. For instance, there are many medical encyclopedias that contain the detail and sophistication required by doctors. For a regular person researching a subject like ostriches, Pennsylvania, or the Crimean War, an encyclopedia is a good source.

A **thesaurus** is a reference book that gives synonyms of words. It is different from a dictionary because a thesaurus does not give definitions, only lists of synonyms. A thesaurus can be helpful in finding the meaning of an unfamiliar word when reading. If the meaning of a synonym is known, then the meaning of the unfamiliar word will be known. The other time a thesaurus is helpful is when writing. Using a thesaurus helps authors to vary their word choice.

A **database** is an informational source that has a different format than a publication or a memo. They are systems for storing and organizing large amounts of information. As personal computers have become more common and accessible, databases have become ever more present. The standard layout of a database is as a grid, with labels along the left side and the top. The horizontal rows and vertical columns that make up the grid are usually numbered or lettered, so that a particular square within the database might have a name like A3 or G5. Databases are good for storing information that can be expressed succinctly. They are most commonly used to store numerical data, but they also can be used to store the answers to yes-no questions and other brief data points. Information that is ambiguous (that is, has multiple possible meanings) or difficult to express in a few words is not appropriate for a database.

Often, a reader will come across a word that he does not recognize. The reader needs to know how to identify the definition of a word from its context. This means defining a word based on the words around it and the way it is used in a sentence. For instance, consider the following sentence: *The elderly scholar spent his evenings hunched over arcane texts that few other people even knew existed.*

The adjective *arcane* is uncommon, but the reader can obtain significant information about it based on its use here. Based on the fact that few other people know of their existence, the reader can assume that arcane texts must be rare and only of interest to a few people. And, because they are being read by an elderly scholar, the reader can assume that they focus on difficult academic subjects. Sometimes, words can even be defined by what they are not. For instance, consider the following sentence: *Ron's fealty to his parents was not shared by Karen, who disobeyed their every command.* Because someone who disobeys is not demonstrating *fealty*, the word can be inferred to mean something like obedience or respect.

When conducting research, it is important to depend on reputable **primary sources**. A primary source is the documentary evidence closest to the subject being studied. For instance, the primary sources for an essay about penguins would be photographs and recordings of the birds, as well as accounts of people who have studied penguins in person. A secondary source would be a review of a movie about penguins or a book outlining the observations made by others. A primary source should be credible and, if it is on a subject that is still being explored, recent. One way to assess the credibility of a work is to see how often it is mentioned in other books and articles on the same subject. Just by reading the works cited and bibliographies of other books, one can get a sense of what are the acknowledged authorities in the field.

The Internet was once considered a poor place to find sources for an essay or article, but its credibility has improved greatly over the years. Still, students need to exercise caution when performing research online. The best sources are those affiliated with established institutions, like universities, public libraries, and think tanks. Most newspapers are available online, and many of them allow the public to browse their archives. Magazines frequently offer similar services. When obtaining information from an unknown website, however, one must exercise considerably more caution. A website can be considered trustworthy if it is referenced by other sites that are known to be reputable. Also, credible sites tend to be properly maintained and frequently updated. A site is easier to trust when the author provides some information about him or herself, including some credentials that indicate expertise in the subject matter.

ORGANIZING AND UNDERSTANDING GRAPHIC INFORMATION

Two of the most common ways to organize ideas from a text, paraphrasing and summarizing, are verbal ways to organize data. Ideas from a text can also be organized using **graphic organizers**. A graphic organizer is a way to simplify information and just take key points from the text. A graphic organizer such as a timeline may have an event listed for a corresponding date on the timeline, whereas an outline may have an event listed under a key point that occurs in the text. Each reader needs to create the type of graphic organizer that works the best for him or her in terms of being able to recall information from a story. Examples include a *spider-map*, which takes a main idea from the story and places it in a bubble, with supporting points branching off the main idea, an *outline,* useful for diagramming the main and supporting points of the entire story, and a *Venn diagram,* which classifies information as separate or overlapping.

These graphic organizers can also be used by authors to enliven their presentation or text, but this may be counterproductive if the graphics are confusing or misleading. A graph should strip the author's message down to the essentials. It should have a clear title, and should be in the appropriate format. Authors may elect to use tables, line or bar graphs, or pie charts to illustrate their message. Each of these formats is correct for different types of data. The graphic should be large enough to read, and should be divided into appropriate categories. For instance, if the text is about the differences between federal spending on the military and on the space program, a pie chart or a bar graph would be the most effective choices. The pie chart could show each type of spending as a portion of total federal spending, while the bar graph would be better for directly comparing the amounts of money spent on these two programs.

In most cases, the work of interpreting information presented in graphs, tables, charts, and diagrams is done for the reader. The author will usually make explicit his or her reasons for presenting a certain set of data in such a way. However, an effective reader will avoid taking the author's claims for granted. Before considering the information presented in the graphic, the reader should consider whether the author has chosen the correct format for presentation, or whether the author has omitted variables or other information that might undermine his case. Interpreting the graphic itself is essentially an exercise in spotting trends. On a graph, for instance, the reader should be alert for how one variable responds to a change in the other. If education level increases, for example, does income increase as well? The same can be done for a table. Readers should be alert for values that break or exaggerate a trend; these may be meaningless outliers or indicators of a change in conditions.

When a reader is required to draw conclusions from the information presented in graphs, tables, charts, or diagrams, it is important to limit these conclusions to the terms of the graphic itself. In other words, the reader should avoid extrapolating from the data to make claims that are not supportable. As an example, consider a graph that compares the price of eggs to the demand. If the price and demand rise and fall together, a reader would be justified in saying that the demand for eggs and the price are tied together. However, this simple graph does not indicate which of these variables causes the other, so the reader would not be justified in concluding that the price of eggs raises or lowers the demand. In fact, demand could be tied to all sorts of other factors not included in this chart.

Review Video: Graphic Organizers
Visit mometrix.com/academy and enter code: 665513

TYPES OF TABLES AND CHARTS

Tables are presented in a standard format so that they will be easy to read and understand. At the top of the table, there will be a title. This will be a short phrase indicating the information the table or graph intends to convey. The title of a table could be something like "Average Income for Various Education Levels" or "Price of Milk Compared to Demand." A table is composed of information laid out in vertical columns and horizontal rows. Typically, each column will have a label. If "Average Income for Various Education Levels" was placed in a table format, the two columns could be labeled "Education Level" and "Average Income." Each location on the table is called a cell. Cells are defined by their column and row (e.g., second column, fifth row). The table's information is placed in these cells.

Like a table, a **graph** will typically have a title on top. This title may simply state the identities of the two axes: e.g., "Income vs. Education." However, the title may also be something more descriptive, like "A comparison of average income with level of education." In any case, bar and line graphs are laid out along two perpendicular lines, or axes. The vertical axis is called the y-axis, and the horizontal axis is called the x-axis. It is typical for the x-axis to be the independent variable and the y-axis to be the dependent variable. The independent variable is the one manipulated by the researcher or whoever put together the graph. In the above example, the independent variable would be "level of education," since the maker of the graph will define these values (high school, college, master's degree, etc.). The dependent value is not controlled by the researcher.

When selecting a graph format, it is important to consider the intention and the structure of the presentation. A bar graph, for instance, is appropriate for displaying the relations between a series of distinct quantities that are on the same scale. For instance, if one wanted to display the amount of money spent on groceries during the months of a year, a bar graph would be appropriate. The vertical axis would represent values of money, and the horizontal axis would identify the bar representing each month. A line graph also requires data expressed in common units, but it is better for demonstrating the general trend in that data. If the grocery expenses were plotted on a line graph instead of a bar graph, there would be more emphasis on whether the amount of money spent rose or fell over the course of the year. Whereas a bar graph is good for showing the relationships between the different values plotted, the line graph is good for showing whether the values tended to increase, decrease, or remain stable.

A **line graph** is a type of graph that is typically used for measuring trends over time. It is set up along a vertical and a horizontal axis. The variables being measured are listed along the left side and the bottom side of the axes. Points are then plotted along the graph, such that they correspond with their values for each variable. For instance, imagine a line graph measuring a person's income for each month of the year. If the person earned $1500 in January, there would be a point directly above January, perpendicular to the horizontal axis, and directly to the right of $1500, perpendicular to the vertical axis. Once all of the lines are plotted, they are connected with a line from left to right. This line provides a nice visual illustration of the general trends. For instance, using the earlier example, if the line sloped up, it would be clear that the person's income had increased over the course of the year.

The **bar graph** is one of the most common visual representations of information. Bar graphs are used to illustrate sets of numerical data. The graph has a vertical axis, along which numbers are listed, and a horizontal axis, along which categories, words, or some other indicators are placed. One example of a bar graph is a depiction of the respective heights of famous basketball players: the vertical axis would contain numbers ranging from five to eight feet, and the horizontal axis would contain the names of the players. The length of the bar above the player's name would illustrate his height, as the top of the bar would stop perpendicular to the height listed along the left side. In this representation, then, it would be easy to see that Yao Ming is taller than Michael Jordan, because Yao's bar would be higher.

A **pie chart**, also known as a circle graph, is useful for depicting how a single unit or category is divided. The standard pie chart is a circle within which wedges have been cut and labeled. Each of these wedges is proportional in size to its part of the whole. For instance, consider a pie chart representing a student's budget. If the student spends half her money on rent, then the pie chart will represent that amount with a line through the center of the pie. If she spends a quarter of her money on food, there will be a line extending from the edge of the circle to the center at a right angle to the line depicting rent. This illustration would make it clear that the student spends twice as much money on rent as she does on food. The pie chart is only appropriate for showing how a whole is divided.

A pie chart is effective at showing how a single entity is divided into parts. They are not effective at demonstrating the relationships between parts of different wholes. For example, it would not be as helpful to use a pie chart to compare the respective amounts of state and federal spending devoted to infrastructure, since these values are only meaningful in the context of the entire budget.

Plot lines are another way to visual represent information. Every plot line follows the same stages. One can identify each of these stages in every story they read. These stages are: the introduction, rising action, conflict, climax, falling action, and resolution. The introduction tells the reader what the story will be about and sets up the plot. The rising action is what happens that leads up to the conflict, which is some sort of problem that arises, with the climax at its peak. The falling action is what happens after the climax of the conflict. The resolution is the conclusion and often has the final solution to the problem in the conflict. A plot line looks like this:

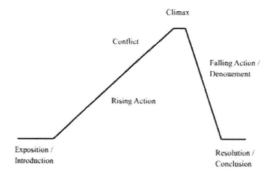

Review Video: Plot Line
Visit mometrix.com/academy and enter code: 944011

DETERMINING WORD MEANING

An understanding of the basics of language is helpful, and often vital, to understanding what you read. The term *structural analysis* refers to looking at the parts of a word and breaking it down into its different components to determine the word's meaning. Parts of a word include prefixes, suffixes, and the root word. By learning the meanings of prefixes, suffixes, and other word fundamentals, you can decipher the meaning of words which may not yet be in your vocabulary. Prefixes are common letter combinations at the beginning of words, while suffixes are common letter combinations at the end. The main part of the word is known as the root. Visually, it would look like this: prefix + root word + suffix. Look first at the individual meanings of the root word, prefix and/or suffix. Using knowledge of the meaning(s) of the prefix and/or suffix to see what information it adds to the root. Even if the meaning of the root is unknown, one can use knowledge of the prefix's and/or suffix's meaning(s) to determine an approximate meaning of the word. For example, if one sees the word *uninspired* and does not know what it means, they can use the knowledge that *un-* means 'not' to know that the full word means "not inspired." Understanding the common prefixes and suffixes can illuminate at least part of the meaning of an unfamiliar word.

Review Video: Determining Word Meanings
Visit mometrix.com/academy and enter code: 894894

Below is a list of common prefixes and their meanings:

Prefix	Definition	Examples
a	in, on, of, up, to	abed, afoot
a-	without, lacking	atheist, agnostic
ab-	from, away, off	abdicate, abjure
ad-	to, toward	advance
am-	friend, love	amicable, amatory
ante-	before, previous	antecedent, antedate
anti-	against, opposing	antipathy, antidote
auto-	self	autonomy, autobiography

38

Prefix	Definition	Examples
belli-	war, warlike	bellicose
bene-	well, good	benefit, benefactor
bi-	two	bisect, biennial
bio-	life	biology, biosphere
cata-	down, away, thoroughly	catastrophe, cataclysm
chron-	time	chronometer, synchronize
circum-	around	circumspect, circumference
com-	with, together, very	commotion, complicate
contra-	against, opposing	contradict, contravene
cred-	belief, trust	credible, credit
de-	from	depart
dem-	people	demographics, democracy
dia-	through, across, apart	diameter, diagnose
dis-	away, off, down, not	dissent, disappear
epi-	upon	epilogue
equi-	equal, equally	equivalent
ex-	out	extract
for-	away, off, from	forget, forswear
fore-	before, previous	foretell, forefathers
homo-	same, equal	homogenized
hyper-	excessive, over	hypercritical, hypertension
hypo-	under, beneath	hypodermic, hypothesis
in-	in, into	intrude, invade
in-	not, opposing	incapable, ineligible
inter-	among, between	intercede, interrupt
intra-	within	intramural, intrastate
magn-	large	magnitude, magnify
mal-	bad, poorly, not	malfunction
micr-	small	microbe, microscope
mis-	bad, poorly, not	misspell, misfire
mono-	one, single	monogamy, monologue
mor-	die, death	mortality, mortuary
neo-	new	neolithic, neoconservative
non-	not	nonentity, nonsense
ob-	against, opposing	objection
omni-	all, everywhere	omniscient
ortho-	right, straight	orthogonal, orthodox
over-	above	overbearing
pan-	all, entire	panorama, pandemonium
para-	beside, beyond	parallel, paradox
per-	through	perceive, permit
peri-	around	periscope, perimeter
phil-	love, like	philosophy, philanthropic

Prefix	Definition	Examples
poly-	many	polymorphous, polygamous
post-	after, following	postpone, postscript
pre-	before, previous	prevent, preclude
prim-	first, early	primitive, primary
pro-	forward, in place of	propel, pronoun
re-	back, backward, again	revoke, recur
retro-	back, backward	retrospect, retrograde
semi-	half, partly	semicircle, semicolon
sub-	under, beneath	subjugate, substitute
super-	above, extra	supersede, supernumerary
sym-	with, together	sympathy, symphony
trans-	across, beyond, over	transact, transport
ultra-	beyond, excessively	ultramodern, ultrasonic, ultraviolet
un-	not, reverse of	unhappy, unlock
uni-	one	uniform, unity
vis-	to see	visage, visible

Below is a list of common suffixes and their meanings:

Suffix	Definition	Examples
-able	able to, likely	capable, tolerable
-age	process, state, rank	passage, bondage
-ance	act, condition, fact	acceptance, vigilance
-arch	to rule	monarch
-ard	one that does excessively	drunkard, wizard
-ate	having, showing	separate, desolate
-ation	action, state, result	occupation, starvation
-cy	state, condition	accuracy, captaincy
-dom	state, rank, condition	serfdom, wisdom
-en	cause to be, become	deepen, strengthen
-er	one who does	teacher
-esce	become, grow, continue	convalesce, acquiesce
-esque	in the style of, like	picturesque, grotesque
-ess	feminine	waitress, lioness
-fic	making, causing	terrific, beatific
-ful	full of, marked by	thankful, zestful
-fy	make, cause, cause to have	glorify, fortify
-hood	state, condition	manhood, statehood
-ible	able, likely, fit	edible, possible, divisible
-ion	action, result, state	union, fusion
-ish	suggesting, like	churlish, childish
-ism	act, manner, doctrine	barbarism, socialism
-ist	doer, believer	monopolist, socialist
-ition	action, state, result	sedition, expedition

Suffix	Definition	Examples
-ity	state, quality, condition	acidity, civility
-ize	make, cause to be, treat with	sterilize, mechanize, criticize
-less	lacking, without	hopeless, countless
-like	like, similar	childlike, dreamlike
-logue	type of written/spoken language	prologue
-ly	like, of the nature of	friendly, positively
-ment	means, result, action	refreshment, disappointment
-ness	quality, state	greatness, tallness
-or	doer, office, action	juror, elevator, honor
-ous	marked by, given to	religious, riotous
-ship	the art or skill of	statesmanship
-some	apt to, showing	tiresome, lonesome
-th	act, state, quality	warmth, width
-tude	quality, state, result	magnitude, fortitude
-ty	quality, state	enmity, activity
-ward	in the direction of	backward, homeward

Review Video: <u>English Root Words</u>
Visit mometrix.com/academy and enter code: 896380

When defining words in a text, words often have a meaning that is more than the dictionary definition. The **denotative** meaning of a word is the literal meaning. The **connotative** meaning goes beyond the denotative meaning to include the emotional reaction a word may invoke. The connotative meaning often takes the denotative meaning a step further due to associations which the reader makes with the denotative meaning. The reader can differentiate between the denotative and connotative meanings by first recognizing when authors use each meaning. Most non-fiction, for example, is fact-based, the authors not using flowery, figurative language. The reader can assume that the writer is using the denotative, or literal, meaning of words. In fiction, on the other hand, the author may be using the connotative meaning. Connotation is one form of figurative language. The reader should use context clues to determine if the author is using the denotative or connotative meaning of a word.

Review Video: <u>Denotative and Connotative Meanings</u>
Visit mometrix.com/academy and enter code: 736707

Readers of all levels will encounter words with which they are somewhat unfamiliar. The best way to define a word in **context** is to look for nearby words that can help. For instance, unfamiliar nouns are often accompanied by examples that furnish a definition. Consider the following sentence: "Dave arrived at the party in hilarious garb: a leopard-print shirt, buckskin trousers, and high heels." If a reader was unfamiliar with the meaning of garb, he could read the examples and quickly determine that the word means "clothing." Examples will not always be this obvious. For instance, consider this sentence: "Parsley, lemon, and flowers were just a few of items he used as garnishes." Here, the possibly unfamiliar word *garnishes* is exemplified by parsley, lemon, and flowers. Readers

who have eaten in a few restaurants will probably be able to identify a garnish as something used to decorate a plate.

In addition to looking at the context of a passage, readers can often use contrasts to define an unfamiliar word in context. In many sentences, the author will not describe the unfamiliar word directly, but will instead describe the opposite of the unfamiliar word. Of course, this provides information about the word the reader needs to define. Consider the following example: "Despite his intelligence, Hector's low brow and bad posture made him look obtuse." The author suggests that Hector's appearance was opposite to his actual intelligence. Therefore, *obtuse* must mean unintelligent or stupid. Here is another example: "Despite the horrible weather, we were beatific about our trip to Alaska." The word *despite* indicates that the speaker's feelings were at odds with the weather. Since the weather is described as "horrible," *beatific* must mean something good.

In some cases, there will be very few contextual clues to help a reader define the meaning of an unfamiliar word. When this happens, one strategy the reader may employ is substitution. A good reader will brainstorm some possible synonyms for the given word, and then substitute these words into the sentence. If the sentence and the surrounding passage continue to make sense, the substitution has revealed at least some information about the unfamiliar word. Consider the sentence, "Frank's admonition rang in her ears as she climbed the mountain." A reader unfamiliar with *admonition* might come up with some substitutions like "vow," "promise," "advice," "complaint," or "compliment." All of these words make general sense of the sentence, though their meanings are diverse. The process has suggested, however, that an admonition is some sort of message. The substitution strategy is rarely able to pinpoint a precise definition, but can be effective as a last resort.

It is sometimes possible to define an unfamiliar word by looking at the descriptive words in the context. Consider the following sentence: "Fred dragged the recalcitrant boy kicking and screaming up the stairs." *Dragged*, *kicking*, and *screaming* all suggest that the boy does not want to go up the stairs. The reader may assume that *recalcitrant* means something like unwilling or protesting. In that example, an unfamiliar adjective was identified. It is perhaps more typical to use description to define an unfamiliar noun, as in this sentence: "Don's wrinkled frown and constantly shaking fist identified him as a curmudgeon of the first order." Don is described as having a "wrinkled frown and constantly shaking fist," suggesting that a *curmudgeon* must be a grumpy old man. Contrasts do not always provide detailed information about the unfamiliar word, but they at least give the reader some clues.

When a word has more than one meaning, it can be tricky to determine how it is being used in a given sentence. Consider the verb *cleave*, which bizarrely can mean either "join" or "separate." When a reader comes upon this word, she will have to select the definition that makes the most sense. So, take as an example the following sentence: "The birds cleaved together as they flew from the oak tree." Immediately, the presence of the word *together* should suggest that in this sentence *cleave* is being used to mean "*join*." A slightly more difficult example would be the sentence, "Hermione's knife cleaved the bread cleanly." It doesn't make sense for a knife to join bread together, so the word must be meant to indicate separation. Discovering the meaning of a word with multiple meanings requires the same tricks as defining an unknown word: looking for contextual clues and evaluating substituted words.

LITERARY DEVICES

Understanding how words relate to each other can often add meaning to a passage. This is explained by understanding **synonyms** (words that mean the same thing) and **antonyms** (words that mean the opposite of one another). As an example, *dry* and *arid* are synonyms, and *dry* and *wet* are antonyms. There are many pairs of words in English that can be considered synonyms, despite having slightly different definitions. For instance, the words *friendly* and *collegial* can both be used to describe a warm interpersonal relationship, so it would be correct to call them synonyms. However, *collegial* (kin to *colleague*) is more often used in reference to professional or academic relationships, while *friendly* has no such connotation. Nevertheless, it would be appropriate to call these words synonyms. If the difference between the two words is too great, however, they may not be called synonyms. *Hot* and *warm* are not synonyms, for instance, because their meanings are too distinct. A good way to determine whether two words are synonyms is to substitute one for the other and see if the sentence means the same thing. Substituting *warm* for *hot* in a sentence would convey a different meaning.

Antonyms are opposites. *Light* and *dark*, *up* and *down*, *right* and *left*, *good* and *bad*: these are all sets of antonyms. It is important to distinguish between antonyms and pairs of words that are simply different. *Black* and *gray*, for instance, are not antonyms because gray is not the opposite of black. *Black* and *white*, on the other hand, are antonyms. Not every word has an antonym. For instance, many nouns do not. What would be the antonym of *chair*, after all? On a standardized test, the questions related to antonyms are more likely to concern adjectives. Remember that adjectives are words that describe a noun. Some common adjectives include *red*, *fast*, *skinny*, and *sweet*. Of these four examples, only *red* lacks a group of obvious antonyms.

> **Review Video: Synonyms and Antonyms**
> Visit mometrix.com/academy and enter code: 105612

There are many types of language devices that authors use to convey their meaning in a more descriptive or interesting way. Understanding these concepts will help you understand what you read. These types of devices are called *figurative language* – language that goes beyond the literal meaning of the words. **Descriptive language** that evokes imagery in the reader's mind is one type of figurative language. **Exaggeration** is also one type of figurative language. Also, when you compare two things, you are using figurative language. **Similes** and **metaphors** are ways of comparing things, and both are types of figurative language commonly found in poetry. An example of figurative language (a simile in this case) is: "The child howled like a coyote when her mother told her to pick up the toys." In this example, the child's howling is compared to that of a coyote. Figurative language is descriptive in nature and helps the reader understand the sound being made in this sentence.

Alliteration is a stylistic device, or literary technique, in which successive words (more strictly, stressed syllables) begin with the same sound or letter. Alliteration is a frequent tool in poetry but it is also common in prose, particularly to highlight short phrases. An example of alliteration could be "thundering through the thickets," in which the initial th sound is used in four consecutive words. Especially in poetry, it contributes to euphony of the passage, lending it a musical air. It may act to humorous effect. Alliteration draws attention to itself, which may be a good or a bad thing. Authors should be conscious of the character of the sound to be repeated. In the above example, a *th* sound is somewhat difficult to make quickly in four consecutive words, so the phrase conveys a little of the difficulty of moving through tall grass. If the author is indeed trying to suggest this difficulty, then the alliteration is a success. Consider, however, the description of eyes as "glassy globes of glitter." This is definitely alliteration, since the initial *gl* sound is used three times.

43

However, one might question whether this awkward sound is appropriate for a description of pretty eyes. The phrase is not especially pleasant to the ear, and therefore is probably not effective as alliteration. Related to alliteration are *assonance*, the repetition of vowel sounds, and *consonance*, the repetition of consonant sounds.

> **Review Video: <u>Alliteration</u>**
> Visit mometrix.com/academy and enter code: 462837

A **figure of speech**, sometimes termed a rhetorical figure or device, or elocution, is a word or phrase that departs from straightforward, literal language. Figures of speech are often used and crafted for emphasis, freshness of expression, or clarity. However, clarity may also suffer from their use.

Note that not all theories of meaning necessarily have a concept of "literal language" (see literal and figurative language). Under theories that do not, figure of speech is not an entirely coherent concept.

As an example of the figurative use of a word, consider the sentence, "I am going to crown you." It may mean:

- I am going to place a literal crown on your head.
- I am going to symbolically exalt you to the place of kingship.
- I am going to punch you in the head with my clenched fist.
- I am going to put a second checker on top of your checker to signify that it has become a king.

> **Review Video: <u>Figure of Speech</u>**
> Visit mometrix.com/academy and enter code: 111295

A **metaphor** is a type of figurative language in which the writer equates one thing with a different thing. For instance, in the sentence "The bird was an arrow arcing through the sky," the arrow is serving as a metaphor for the bird. The point of a metaphor is to encourage the reader to think about the thing being described in a different way. Using this example, we are being asked to envision the bird's flight as being similar to the arc of an arrow, so we will imagine it to be swift, bending, etc. Metaphors are a way for the author to describe without being direct and obvious. Metaphors are a more lyrical and suggestive way of providing information. Note that the thing to which a metaphor refers will not always be mentioned explicitly by the author. For instance, consider the following description of a forest in winter: "Swaying skeletons reached for the sky and groaned as the wind blew through them." The author is clearly using *skeletons* as a metaphor for leafless trees. This metaphor creates a spooky tone while inspiring the reader's imagination.

> **Review Video: <u>Metaphor</u>**
> Visit mometrix.com/academy and enter code: 133295

Metonymy is referring to one thing in terms of another, closely related thing. This is similar to metaphor, but there is less distance between the description and the thing being described. An example of metonymy is referring to the news media as the "press," when of course the press is only the device by which newspapers are printed. Metonymy is a way of referring to something without having to repeat its name constantly. **Synecdoche**, on the other hand, is referring to a whole by one of its parts. An example of synecdoche would be calling a police officer a "badge."

Synecdoche, like metonymy, is a handy way of referring without having to overuse certain words. It also allows the writer to emphasize aspects of the thing being described. For instance, referring to businessmen as "suits" suggests professionalism, conformity, and drabness.

Hyperbole is overstatement for effect. The following sentence is an example of hyperbole: *He jumped ten feet in the air when he heard the good news*. Obviously, no person has the ability to jump ten feet in the air. The author hyperbolizes not because he believes the statement will be taken literally, but because the exaggeration conveys the extremity of emotion. Consider how much less colorful the sentence would be if the author simply said, "He jumped when he heard the good news." Hyperbole can be dangerous if the author does not exaggerate enough. For instance, if the author wrote, "He jumped two feet in the air when he heard the good news," the reader might not be sure whether this is actually true or just hyperbole. Of course, in many situations this distinction will not really matter. However, an author should avoid confusing or vague hyperbole when he needs to maintain credibility or authority with readers.

Understatement is the opposite of hyperbole: that is, it is describing something as less than it is, for effect. As an example, consider a person who climbs Mount Everest and then describes the journey as "a little stroll." This is an almost extreme example of understatement. Like other types of figurative language, understatement has a range of uses. It may convey self-deprecation or modesty, as in the above example. Of course, some people might interpret understatement as false modesty, a deliberate attempt to call attention to the magnitude of what is being discussed. For example, a woman is complimented on her enormous diamond engagement ring and says, "Oh, this little thing?" Her understatement might be viewed as snobby or insensitive. Understatement can have various effects, but it always calls attention to itself.

Review Video: Hyperbole and Understatement
Visit mometrix.com/academy and enter code: 308470

A **simile** is a figurative expression similar to a metaphor, though it requires the use of a distancing word like *like* or *as*. Some examples are "The sun was like an orange," "eager as a beaver," and "nimble as a mountain goat." Because a simile includes *like* or a*s*, it creates a little space between the description and the thing being described. If an author says that a house was "like a shoebox," the tone is slightly different than if the author said that the house *was* a shoebox. In a simile, the author indicates an awareness that the description is not the same thing as the thing being described. In a metaphor, there is no such distinction, even though one may safely assume that the author is aware of it. This is a subtle difference, but authors will alternately use metaphors and similes depending on their intended tone.

Review Video: Simile
Visit mometrix.com/academy and enter code: 642949

Another type of figurative language is **personification.** This is the description of the nonhuman as if it were human. Literally, the word means the process of making something into a person. There is a wide range of approaches to personification, from common expressions like "whispering wind" to full novels like *Animal Farm*, by George Orwell, in which the Bolshevik Revolution is reenacted by farmyard animals. The general intent of personification is to describe things in a manner that will be comprehensible to readers. When an author states that a tree "groans" in the wind, she of course does not mean that the tree is emitting a low, pained sound from its mouth. Instead, she means that the tree is making a noise similar to a human groan. Of course, this personification establishes a

45

tone of sadness or suffering. A different tone would be established if the author said the tree was "swaying" or "dancing."

Review Video: Personification
Visit mometrix.com/academy and enter code: 260066

Irony is a statement that suggests its opposite. In other words, it is when an author or character says one thing but means another. For example, imagine a man walks in his front door, covered in mud and in tattered clothes. His wife asks him, "How was your day?" and he says "Great!" The man's comment is an example of irony. As in this example, irony often depends on information the reader obtains elsewhere. There is a fine distinction between irony and sarcasm. Irony is any statement in which the literal meaning is opposite from the intended meaning, while sarcasm is a statement of this type that is also insulting to the person at whom it is directed. A sarcastic statement suggests that the other person is stupid enough to believe an obviously false statement is true. Irony is a bit more subtle than sarcasm.

Review Video: Irony
Visit mometrix.com/academy and enter code: 374204

The more words a person is exposed to, the greater their vocabulary will become. By reading on a regular basis, a person can increase the number of ways they have seen a word in context. Based on experience, a person can recall how a word was used in the past and apply that knowledge to a new context. For example, a person may have seen the word *gull* used to mean a bird that is found near the seashore. However, a *gull* can also be a person who is easily tricked. If the word is used in context in reference to a character, the reader can recognize that the character is being called a bird that is not seen as extremely intelligent. Using what the reader knows about a word can be useful when making comparisons or figuring out the meaning of a new use of a word, as in figurative language, idioms, analogies, and multiple-meaning words.

Writing

CHOOSING TOPICS

Very often the choice of a subject may be assigned or determined by someone besides the writer. When the choice is left to the writer, it is sometimes wise to allow the topic itself to "select" the writer. That is to say those topics that interest, engage, puzzle, or stimulate someone may be good choices. Engaging the writer is the most important factor in choosing a topic. Engagement notes a strong interest and spirit of inquiry about the subject. It is a signal that the subject and author are interacting in some creative sense, which usually encourages good writing. Even with an assigned topic, a particular aspect of the subject may interest the writer more than others. The key to any writer's choice of topic is the ability of a subject to inspire the author to question, speculate, inquire and interact. From this natural interest and attraction, some of the most creative writing develops.

A common problem is limiting the scope of a writing assignment. Narrowing the scope is not always enough, because the new subject may itself be too broad. Focusing on an aspect of a topic often effectively results in a topic both interesting and manageable. For example narrowing a topic like the "Civil War" to the "Battle of Antietam" may still leave an unwieldy topic. To sharpen the focus, an aspect such as "The use of artillery by Confederates at the battle of Antietam" could be selected.

UNDERSTANDING ASSIGNMENTS

Many writing assignments address specific audiences (physicians, attorneys, and teachers) and have specific goals. These writers know for whom and why they are writing. This can clarify the writing significantly. Other assignments, particularly in academic settings, may appear with no specific subject, audience, or apparent purpose. Assignments may come with some variables; a specified audience, subject, or approach and leave the rest up to the writer. Because of these variables, it is useful to consider the following questions:

- What specifically is the assignment asking the writer to do?
- What information or knowledge is necessary to fulfill the assignment?
- Can the topic be broadened or limited to more effectively complete the project?
- Are there specific parameters or other requirements for the project?
- What is the purpose of the assignment?
- Who is the intended audience for the work?
- What is the length of the assignment? Does it limit or require a certain number of pages? If so, what are the parameters?
- What is the deadline for the assignment? Sometimes preliminary materials are to be submitted before the main assignment. Considering these factors will give a writer information needed to set a schedule for the project.

LENGTH AND DOCUMENT DESIGN

Writers seldom have control over length and document design. Usually an academic assignment has a specified length, while journalists work within tight word count parameters. Document design often follows the purpose of a writing project. Specific formats are required for lab reports, research papers, and abstracts. The business world operates within fairly narrow format styles, the business letter, memo, and report allowing only a small departure from the standard format.

There are some assignments that allow the writer to choose the specific format for the work. The increased flourishes provided by computers allow a great deal of creativity in designing a visually stimulating and functional document. Improving readability is always a worthwhile goal for any project, and this is becoming much easier with available software.

DEADLINES

Deadlines are a critical element in any writing assignment. They help a writer budget their time to complete the assignment on schedule. For elaborate or complex writing projects, it is useful to create a working schedule that includes time for research, writing, revising, and editing. Breaking the process down into more workable parts with their own deadlines, helps keep a writer aware of the progress being made.

PURPOSES OF WRITING

What is the main purpose of the proposed piece? This may be very clear and focused, or ambiguous. A writer should be clear about the purpose of his writing, as this will determine the direction and elements of the work. Generally purposes may be divided into three groups:

- To entertain.
- To persuade or convince.
- To educate or inform.

Some or all of these purposes may be the goal in a given writing assignment. It is helpful to try and identify the major purpose of a writing piece, as well as any secondary purposes involved. Purpose in writing must be linked closely to the writer's goals in undertaking the assignment. In academic settings, it is usually more accurate to think in terms of several goals. A student may wish to convince the audience in an entertaining and informative fashion. However one goal should be paramount. Expectations of the instructor play an important role in an academic assignment.

> **Review Video: Purpose**
> Visit mometrix.com/academy and enter code: 511819

RECURSIVE NATURE

The process of writing is described as recursive; This means that the goals and parts of the writing process are often a seamless flow, constantly influencing each other without clear boundaries. The "steps' in the writing process occur organically, with planning, drafting and revising all taking place simultaneously, in no necessary or orderly fashion. The writer rarely pays attention to the recursive patterns. The process unfolds naturally, without attention or dependence on a predetermined sequence. The writing process is a series of recursive activities, which rarely occur in a linear fashion, rather moving back and forth between planning, drafting, revising, more planning, more drafting, polishing until the writing is complete. Forthcoming topics will cover many parts of the process individually, but they go on together as a seamless flow.

> **Review Video: Recursive Writing Process**
> Visit mometrix.com/academy and enter code: 951611

CONSIDERING AN AUDIENCE

The careful consideration of the anticipated audience is a requisite for any project. Although much of this work is intuitive, some guidelines are helpful in the analysis of an audience:

- Specifically identify your audience. Are they eclectic or share common characteristics?
- Determine qualities of the audience such as age, education, sex, culture, and special interests.

- Understand what the audience values; brevity, humor, originality, honesty are examples.
- What is the audience's attitude toward the topic; skeptical, knowledgeable, pro or con?
- Understand the writer's relationship to the audience; peer, authority, advocate, or antagonist?

Understanding the qualities of an audience allows the writer to form an organizational plan tailored to achieve the objectives of the writing with the audience in mind. It is essential to effective writing.

LEVEL OF FORMALITY

In choosing a level of formality in writing, the subject and audience should be carefully considered. The subject may require a more dignified tone, or perhaps an informal style would be best. The relationship between writer and reader is important in choosing a level of formality. Is the audience one with which you can assume a close relationship, or should a more formal tone prevail?

Most student or business writing requires some degree of formality. Informal writing is appropriate for private letters, personal e-mails, and business correspondence between close associates. Vocabulary and language should be relatively simple.

It is important to be consistent in the level of formality in a piece of writing. Shifts in levels of formality can confuse readers and detract from the message of the writing.

UNDERSTANDING THE TOPIC

Easily overlooked is the basic question of ascertaining how knowledgeable the writer is about the subject. A careful evaluation should be made to determine what is known about the topic, and what information must be acquired to undertake the writing assignment. Most people have a good sense of how to go about researching a subject, using the obvious available resources: libraries, the internet, journals, research papers and other sources. There are however some specific strategies that can help a writer learn more about a subject, and just as importantly, what is not known and must be learned. These strategies or techniques not only are useful in researching a subject, they can also be used when problems come up during the actual writing phase of the assignment. These strategies include brainstorming, free writing, looping, and questioning.

BRAINSTORMING

Brainstorming is a technique used frequently in business, industry, science, and engineering. It is accomplished by tossing out ideas, usually with several other people, in order to find a fresh approach or a creative way to approach a subject. This can be accomplished by an individual by simply free-associating about a topic. Sitting with paper and pen, every thought about the subject is written down in a word or phrase. This is done without analytical thinking, just recording what arises in the mind about the topic. The list is then read over carefully several times. The writer looks for patterns, repetitions, clusters of ideas, or a recurring theme. Although brainstorming can be done individually, it works best when several people are involved. Three to five people is ideal. This allows an exchange of ideas, points of view, and often results in fresh ideas or approaches.

FREE WRITING

Free writing is a form of brainstorming in a structured way. The method involves exploring a topic by writing about it for a certain period of time without stopping. A writer sets a time limit, and begins writing in complete sentences everything that comes to mind about the topic. Writing continues without interruption until the set period expires. When time expires, read carefully everything that has been written down. Much of it may make little or no sense, but insights and observations may emerge that the free writer did not know existed in his mind. Writing has a

49

unique quality about it of jogging loose ideas, and seeing a word or idea appear may trigger others. Freewrtiting usually results in a fuller expression of ideas than brainstorming, because thoughts and associations are written in a more comprehensive manner. Both techniques can be used to complement one another and can yield much different results.

LOOPING

Looping is a variation of freewriting that focuses a topic in short five-minute stages, or loops. Looping is done as follows:

- With a subject in mind, spend five minutes freewriting without stopping. The results are the first loop.
- Evaluate what has been written in the first loop. Locate the strongest or most recurring thought which should be summarized in a single sentence. This is the "center of gravity", and is the starting point of the next loop.
- Using the summary sentence as a starting point, another five minute cycle of freewriting takes place. Evaluate the writing and locate the "center of gravity" for the second loop, and summarize it in a single sentence. This will be the start of the third loop.
- Continue this process until a clear new direction to the subject emerges. Usually this will yield a starting point for a whole new approach to a topic.

Looping can be very helpful when a writer is blocked or unable to generate new ideas on a subject.

QUESTIONING

Asking and answering questions provides a more structured approach to investigating a subject. Several types of questions may be used to illuminate an issue.

- Questions to describe a topic. Questions such as "What is It?", "What caused it?", "What is it like or unlike?", "What is it a part of"? What do people say about it?" help explore a topic systematically.
- Questions to explain a topic. Examples include" Who, how, and what is it?", "Where does it end and begin?" What is at issue?", and "How is it done?"
- Questions to persuade include "What claims can be made about it?", "What evidence supports the claims?", "Can the claims be refuted?", and "What assumptions support the claims?"

Questioning can be a very effective device as it leads the writer through a process in a systematic manner in order to gain more information about a subject.

THESIS

A thesis states the main idea of the essay. A working or tentative thesis should be established early on in the writing process. This working thesis is subject to change and modification as writing progresses. It will serve to keep the writer focused as ideas develop.

The working thesis has two parts: a topic and a comment. The comment makes an important point about the topic. A working thesis should be interesting to an anticipated audience; it should be specific and limit the topic to a manageable scope. Theses three criteria are useful tools to measure the effectiveness of any working thesis. The writer applies these tools to ascertain:

- Is the topic of sufficient interest to hold an audience?
- Is the topic specific enough to generate interest?
- Is the topic manageable? Too broad? Too narrow? Can it be adequately researched?

50

Creating an effective thesis is an art. The thesis should be a generalization rather than a fact, and should be neither too broad or narrow in scope. A thesis prepares readers for facts and details, so it may not be a fact itself. It is a generalization that requires further proof or supporting points. Any thesis too broad may be an unwieldy topic and must be narrowed. The thesis should have a sharp focus, and avoid vague, ambivalent language. The process of bringing the thesis into sharp focus may help in outlining major sections of the work. This process is known as blueprinting, and helps the writer control the shape and sequence of the paper. Blueprinting outlines major points and supporting arguments that are used in elaborating on the thesis. A completed blueprint often leads to a development of an accurate first draft of a work. Once the thesis and opening are complete, it is time to address the body of the work.

> **Review Video: Thesis Statements**
> Visit mometrix.com/academy and enter code: 691033

FORMAL OUTLINES

A formal outline may be useful if the subject is complex, and includes many elements. here is a guide to preparing formal outlines:

- Always put the thesis at the top so it may be referred to as often as necessary during the outlining.
- Make subjects similar in generality as parallel as possible in the formal outline.
- Use complete sentences rather than phrases or sentence fragments in the outline.
- Use the conventional system of letters and numbers to designate levels of generality.
- There should be at least two subdivisions for each category in the formal outline.
- Limit the number of major sections in the outline. If there are too many major sections, combine some of them and supplement with additional sub-categories.
- Remember the formal outline is still subject to change; remain flexible throughout the process.

RESEARCH

Research is a means of critical inquiry, investigations based on sources of knowledge. Research is the basis of scientific knowledge, of inventions, scholarly inquiry, and many personal and general decisions. Much of work consists of research - finding something out and reporting on it. We can list five basic precepts about research:

- Everyone does research. To buy an car, go to a film, to investigate anything is research. We all have experience in doing research.
- Good research draws a person into a "conversation" about a topic. Results are more knowledge about a subject, understanding different sides to issues, and be able to discuss intelligently nuances of the topic.
- Research is always driven by a purpose. Reasons may vary from solving a problem to advocating a position, but research is almost always goal oriented.
- Research is shaped by purpose, and in turn the fruits of research refine the research further.
- Research is usually not a linear process; it is modified and changed by the results it yields.

Many writing assignments require research. Research is basically the process of gathering information for the writer's use. There are two broad categories of research:

1. Library research should be started after a research plan is outlined. Topics that require research should be listed, and catalogues, bibliographies, periodical indexes checked for references. Librarians are usually an excellent source of ideas and information on researching a topic.
2. Field research is based on observations, interviews, and questionnaires. This can be done by an individual or a team, depending on the scope of the field research.

The specific type and amount of research will vary widely with the topic and the writing assignment. A simple essay or story may require only a few hours of research, while a major project can consume weeks or months.

RESEARCH MATERIAL

- Primary sources are the raw material of research. This can include results of experiments, notes, and surveys or interviews done by the researcher. Other primary sources are books, letters, diaries, eyewitness accounts, and performances attended by the researcher.
- Secondary sources consist of oral and written accounts prepared by others. This includes reports, summaries, critical reviews, and other sources not developed by the researcher.

Most research writing uses both primary and secondary sources. Primary sources from first-hand accounts and secondary sources for background and supporting documentation. The research process calls for active reading and writing throughout. As research yields information, it often calls for more reading and research, and the cycle continues.

ORGANIZING INFORMATION

Organizing information effectively is an important part of research. The data must be organized in a useful manner so that it can be effectively used. Three basic ways to organize information are:

1. Spatial organization - this is useful as it lets the user "see" the information, to fix it in space. This has benefits for those individuals who are visually adept at processing information.
2. Chronological organization is the most common presentation of information. This method places information in the sequence with which it occurs. Chronological organization is very useful in explaining a process that occurs in a step-by-step pattern.
3. Logical organization includes presenting material in a logical pattern that makes intuitive sense. Some patterns that are frequently used are illustrated, definition, compare/contrast, cause/effect, problem/solution, and division/classification. Each of these methods is discussed next.

LOGICAL ORGANIZATION

There are six major types of logical organization that are frequently used:

1. Illustrations may be used to support the thesis. Examples are the most common form of this organization.
2. Definitions say what something is or is not is another way of organization. What are the characteristics of the topic?
3. Dividing or classifying information into separate items according to their similarities is a common and effective organizing method.
4. Comparing, focusing on the similarities of things, and contrasting, highlighting the differences between things is an excellent tool to use with certain kinds of information.

5. Cause and effect is a simple tool to logically understand relationships between things. A phenomenon may be traced to its causes for organizing a subject logically.
6. Problem and solution is a simple and effective manner of logically organizing material. It is very commonly used and lucidly presents information.

WRITING

AN INITIAL PLAN

After information gathering has been completed and the fruits of the research organized effectively, the writer now has a rough or initial plan for the work. A rough plan may be informal, consisting of a few elements such as "Introduction, Body, and Conclusions", or a more formal outline. The rough plan may include multiple organizational strategies within the over-all piece, or it may isolate one or two that can be used exclusively. At this stage the plan is just that, a rough plan subject to change as new ideas appear, and the organization takes a new approach. In these cases, the need for more research sometimes becomes apparent, or existing information should be considered in a new way. A more formal outline leads to an easier transition to a draft, but it can also limit the new possibilities that may arise as the plan unfolds. Until the outlines of the piece become clear, it is usually best to remain open to possible shifts in approaching the subject.

SUPPORTING THE THESIS

It is most important that the thesis of the paper be clearly expounded and adequately supported by additional points. The thesis sentence should contain a clear statement of the major theme and a comment about the thesis. The writer has an opportunity here to state what is significant or noteworthy of this particular treatment of the subject. Each sentence and paragraph in turn, should build on the thesis and support it.

Particular attention should be paid to insuring the organization properly uses the thesis and supporting points. It can be useful to outline the draft after writing, to insure that each paragraph leads smoothly to the next, and that the thesis is continually supported. The outline may highlight a weakness in flow or ideation that can be repaired. It will also spatially illustrate the flow of the argument, and provide a visual representation of the thesis and its supporting points. Often things become clearer when outlined than with a block of writing.

FIRST DRAFT

Drafting is a mysterious art, and does not easily lend itself to rules. Generally, the more detailed the formal or informal outline, the easier is the transition to a first draft. The process of drafting is a learning one, and planning, organizing, and researching may be ongoing. Drafting is an evaluative process as well, and the whole project will be under scrutiny as the draft develops. The scope may be narrowed or widened, the approach may change, and different conclusions may emerge.

The process itself is shaped by the writer's preferences for atmosphere during the writing process. Time of day or night, physical location, ambient conditions, and any useful rituals can all play into the writer's comfort and productivity. The creation of an atmosphere conducive to the writer's best work is a subtle but important aspect of writing that is often overlooked. Although excellent writing has often been done in difficult situations, it is not the best prescription for success.

EVALUATING THE DRAFT

Once a draft is finished, an evaluation is in order. This can often mean reviewing the entire process with a critical eye. There is no formal checklist that insures a complete and effective evaluation, but there are some elements that can be considered:

- It should be determined whether sufficient research was done to properly develop the assignment. Are there areas that call for additional information? If so, what type?
- What are the major strengths of the draft? Are there any obvious weaknesses? How can these be fixed?
- Who is the audience for this work and how well does the material appeal to them?
- Does the material actually accomplish the goals of the assignment? If not, what needs to be done?

This is a stage for stepping back from the project and giving it an objective evaluation. Changes made now can improve the material significantly. Take time here to formulate a final approach to the subject.

OBJECTIVE CRITICISM

Now is the time to obtain objective criticisms of the draft. It is helpful to provide readers with a list of questions to be answered about the draft. Some examples of effective questions are:

- Does the introduction catch the reader's attention? How can it be improved?
- Is the thesis clearly stated and supported by additional points?
- What type of organizational plan is used? Is it appropriate for the subject?
- Are paragraphs well developed and is there a smooth transition between them?
- Are the sentences well written and convey the appropriate meaning?
- Are words used effectively and colorfully in the text?
- What is the tone of the writing? Is it appropriate to the audience and subject?
- Is the conclusion satisfactory? Is there a sense of completion that the work is finished?
- What are main strengths and weaknesses of the writing? Are there specific suggestions for improvement?

TITLE, INTRODUCTION, AND CONCLUSION

- A good title can identify the subject, describe it in a colorful manner, and give clues to the approach and sometimes conclusion of the writing. It usually defines the work in the mind of the reader.
- A strong introduction follows the lead of the title; it draws the readers into the work, and clearly states the topic with a clarifying comment. A common style is to state the topic, and then provide additional details, finally leading to a statement of the thesis at the end. An introduction can also begin with an arresting quote, question, or strong opinion, which grabs the reader's attention.
- A good conclusion should leave readers satisfied and provide a sense of closure. Many conclusions restate the thesis and formulate general statements that grow out of it. Writers often find ways to conclude in a dramatic fashion, through a vivid image, quotation, or a warning. This in an effort to give the ending the "punch" to tie up any existing points.

An introduction announces the main point of the work. It will usually be a paragraph of 50 to 150 words, opening with a few sentences to engage the reader, and conclude with the essay's main point. The sentence stating the main point is called the thesis. If possible, the sentences leading to the thesis should attract the reader's attention with a provocative question, vivid image, description, paradoxical statement, quotation, anecdote, or a question. The thesis could also appear at the beginning of the introduction. There are some types of writing that do not lend themselves to stating a thesis in one sentence. Personal narratives and some types of business writing may be better served by conveying an overriding purpose of the text, which may or may not be stated directly. The important point is to impress the audience with the rationale for the writing.

The body of the essay should fulfill the promise of the introduction and thesis. If an informal outline has not been done, now is the time for a more formal one. Constructing the formal outline will create a "skeleton" of the paper. Using this skeleton, it is much easier to fill out the body of an essay. It is useful to block out paragraphs based on the outline, to insure they contain all the supporting points, and are in the appropriate sequence.

The conclusion of the essay should remind readers of the main point, without belaboring it. It may be relatively short, as the body of the text has already "made the case" for the thesis. A conclusion can summarize the main points, and offer advice or ask a question. Never introduce new ideas in a conclusion. Avoid vague and desultory endings, instead closing with a crisp, often positive, note. A dramatic or rhetorical flourish can end a piece colorfully.

EXAMINING PARAGRAPHS

Paragraphs are a key structural unit of prose utilized to break up long stretches of words into more manageable subsets, and to indicate a shift in topics or focus. Each paragraph may be examined by identifying the main point of the section, and insuring that every sentence supports or relates to the main theme. Paragraphs may be checked to make sure the organization used in each is appropriate, and that the number of sentences are adequate to develop the topic.

EXAMINING SENTENCES

Sentences are the building blocks of the written word, and they can be varied by paying attention to sentence length, sentence structure, and sentence openings. These elements should be varied so that writing does not seem boring, repetitive, or choppy. A careful analysis of a piece of writing will expose these stylistic problems, and they can be corrected before the final draft is written. Varying sentence structure and length can make writing more inviting and appealing to a reader.

EXAMINING WORDS

A writer's choice of words is a signature of their style. A careful analysis of the use of words can improve a piece of writing. Attention to the use of specific nouns rather than general ones can enliven language. Verbs should be active whenever possible to keep the writing stronger and energetic, and there should be an appropriate balance between numbers of nouns and verbs. Too many nouns can result in heavy, boring sentences.

EXAMINING TONE

Tone may be defined as the writer's attitude toward the topic, and to the audience. This attitude is reflected in the language used in the writing. If the language is ambiguous, tone becomes very difficult to ascertain. The tone of a work should be appropriate to the topic and to the intended audience. Some writing should avoid slang and jargon, while it may be fine in a different piece. Tone can range from humorous, to serious, and all levels in between. It may be more or less formal depending on the purpose of the writing, and its intended audience. All these nuances in tone can flavor the entire writing and should be kept in mind as the work evolves.

Tone is distinguished from mood, which is the feeling the writing evokes. Tone and mood may often be similar, but can also be significantly different. Mood often depends on the manner in which words and language are employed by the writer. In a sense tone and mood are two sides of a coin

55

which color and language enliven the total approach of a writer to his subject. Mood and tone add richness and texture to words, bringing them alive in a deliberate strategy by the writer.

EXAMINING POINT-OF-VIEW

Point-of-view is the perspective from which writing occurs. There are several possibilities:

- First Person - Is written so that the "I" of the story is a participant or observer.
- Second Person - Is a device to draw the reader in more closely. It is really a variation or refinement of the first person narrative.
- Third Person - The most traditional form of third-person point-of-view is the "omniscient narrator", in which the narrative voice, (presumed to be the writer), is presumed to know everything about the characters, plot, and action. Most novels use this point-of-view.
- A Multiple Point-Of-View - The narration is delivered from the perspective of several characters.

In modern writing, the "stream-of consciousness" technique developed fully by James Joyce where the interior monologue provides the narration through the thoughts, impressions, and fantasies of the narrator.

VOICE

Writers should find an appropriate voice that is appropriate for the subject, appeals to the intended audience, and conforms to the conventions of the genre in which the writing is done. If there is doubt about the conventions of the genre, lab reports, informal essays, research papers, business memos, and so on - a writer may examine models of these works written by experts in the field. These models can serve as examples for form and style for a particular type of writing.

Voice can also include the writer's attitude toward the subject and audience. Care should be taken that the language and tone of the writing is considered in terms of the purpose of the writing and it intended audience.

Gauging the appropriate voice for a piece is part art, and part science. It can be a crucial element in the ultimate effectiveness of the writing.

WRITING CONVENTIONS

Conventions in writing are traditional assumptions or practices used by authors of all types of text. Some basic conventions have survived through the centuries - for example the assumption that a first person narrator in a work is telling the truth - others such as having characters in melodramas speak in asides to the audience have become outmoded. Conventions are particularly important in specialized types of writing which demand specific formats and styles. This is true of scientific and research papers, as well as much of academic and business writing. This formality has relaxed somewhat in several areas but still holds true for many fields of technical writing. Conventions are particularly useful for writers working in various types of nonfiction writing, where guidelines help the writer conform to the rules expected for that field. Conventions are part of the unspoken contract between writer and audience, and should be respected.

WRITING PREPARATION

Effective writing requires preparation. The planning process includes everything done prior to drafting. Depending on the project, this could take a few minutes or several months. Elements in planning, and include considering the purpose of the writing, exploring a topic, developing a working thesis, gathering necessary materials, and developing a plan for organizing the writing.

The organizational plan may vary in length and components, from a detailed outline or a stack of research cards. The organizational plan is a guide to help draft a writing project, and may change as writing progresses, but having a guide to refer to can keep a project on track. Planning is usually an ongoing process throughout the writing, but it is essential to begin with a structure.

EDITING

Time must always be allowed for thorough and careful editing in order to insure clean and error-free work. It is helpful to create a checklist of editing to use as the manuscript is proofed. Patterns of editing problems often become apparent and understanding these patterns can eliminate them. Examples of patterns of errors include misuse of commas, difficulty in shifting tenses, and spelling problems. Once these patterns are seen, it is much easier to avoid them in the original writing. A checklist should be prepared based on every piece of writing, and should be cumulative. In this manner, progress may be checked regularly and the quantity and type of errors should be reduced over time. It is often helpful to have peer proof a manuscript, to get a fresh set of eyes on the material. Editing should be treated as an opportunity to polish and perfect a written work, rather than a chore that must be done. A good editor usually turns into a better writer over time.

PROOFREADING

As a proofreader, the goal is always to eliminate all errors. This includes typographical errors as well as any inconsistencies in spelling and punctuation. Begin by reading the prose aloud, calling out all punctuation marks and insuring that all sentences are complete and no words are left out. It is helpful to read the material again, backwards, so the focus is on each individual word, and the tendency to skip ahead is avoided.

A computer is a blessing to writers who have trouble proofreading their work. Spelling and grammar check programs may be utilized to reduce errors significantly. However it is still important for a writer to do the manual proofing necessary to insure errors of pattern are not repeated. Computers are a wonderful tool for writers but they must be employed by the writer, rather than as the writer. Skillful use of computers should result in a finely polished manuscript free of errors.

> **Review Video: <u>General Revision and Proofreading</u>**
> Visit mometrix.com/academy and enter code: 385882

REVIEWERS

Many professional and business writers work with editors who provide advice and support throughout the writing process. In academic situations, the use of reviewers is increasing, either by instructors or perhaps at an academic writing center. Peer review sessions are sometimes scheduled for class, and afford an opportunity to hear what other students feel about a piece of writing. This gives a writer a chance to serve as a reviewer.

PERSPECTIVE

TEXTUAL PERSPECTIVE

A textual knowledge of literature implies readers are taking a perspective or stance on the text. They are examining ways in which separate parts of the text relate to its overall form or structure. Textual perspectives must be used as a part of overall learning, not as an isolated feature. Textual perspective alone excludes both the author's life and the emotional experiences and attitudes of the reader. It fails to account for the readers' prior knowledge in their engagement with the work. A textual approach may include the ways in which the text shapes students' experience and emotional

engagement. Based on previous reading, social acculturation, attitudes, and a host of other factors, students bring a wealth of information into any encounter with a text. Students may compare and contrast elements of their text with other works they have read or seen to form a more rounded engagement with a work.

SOCIAL PERSPECTIVE

A rich resource for students' of literature is their own developing social knowledge. For adolescent students', social relationships are of primary importance. It is common for younger students' to impose their own social attitudes on a text, which is fertile ground for exploring how the understanding of texts is colored by social attitudes and experiences. Student's attitudes can help them reflect on the characters in a work, and can determine their relationship with the text itself.

Social perspectives can shed light on a number of important ways which can effect a reader's engagement with the text. A skillful teacher may probe these attitudes and experiences and make students' more aware of the impact of social attitudes to reading and studying a work of literature. This knowledge can become cumulative and promote more careful understanding of a literature over a period of time.

CULTURAL AND HISTORICAL CONTEXT

The cultural knowledge and background of readers effects their response to texts. They can relate the works in a context of subcultures such as peer group, mass media, school, religion, and politics, social and historical communities. Engaging with the texts, readers can better understand how characters and authors are shaped by cultural influences. Cultural elements influence reader's reactions to events, including their responses to literature.

Cultural and historical context is important in understanding the roles of women and minorities in literature. Placing works of literature in their proper cultural setting can make a work more understandable and provoke reader interest in the milieu of the day. These factors can stimulate a reader's interest in how their own cultural background impacts the engagement with the text. Thus, the cultural aspects of literature become an opportunity for the reader to gain insight into their own attitudes.

TOPICAL PERSPECTIVE

In using a topical perspective, students apply their background in a variety of different fields, for instance sports, science, politics or cooking, to the literary work they are studying. Students may then engage the text in a holistic manner, bringing all their knowledge to bear on a work. It is useful to encourage students to determine how their own information pool relates to the work. There are an infinite number of fields or topics that relate to literature.

Students are most likely to integrate topics they are currently studying into their engagement with a text. These topics would include history, science, art, and music among others. Thinking about literature from these other topical point-of-view can help students ' understand that what they are learning in other courses enhances their experience of both literature and life.

EFFECTS OF PRIOR KNOWLEDGE

HISTORY

When students employ topical knowledge of history in their study of literature, they may do much more than remember date, events, and historical figures in relation to a text. They may well apply what they know about a historical period to better understand the attitudes and relationships in a work of literature. Students learn to think historically, considering different explanations for events, or cause and effect relationships in tracing a sequence of events. For example in reading Steinbeck's novels, students may draw on what they know about the historical period of the depression. Hemingway's "Farewell To Arms" may evoke a historical picture of Europe embroiled in World War I.

Literature offers an opportunity to apply historical knowledge in the context of a work. Students understand that both literary and historical accounts of an event or character may differ significantly, and that one may illuminate the other.

SCIENTIFIC KNOWLEDGE

Students can apply their knowledge of science when reading literature. Their description of carefully observed phenomena can be used to describe a piece of writing. after reading essays by science writers, students' may be encouraged to transpose this knowledge into reading other texts. Understanding the scientific method gives readers' an opportunity to impose this process on events narrated in literature. The validity of events may be tested in the students' mind to assess the "reality" of the text.

There are many texts that take as their subject the role of the scientist in society. In reading "Frankenstein" or "Dr. Faustus", many issues can be raised about the responsibilities of scientists in conducting experiments.

The blending of science and literature is particularly compelling to some students' when they read science fiction or futuristic texts. An example would be "1984" which posits a authoritarian government controlling the lives of people.

RESEARCH PAPERS

HYPOTHESIS

The result of a focusing process is a research question, a question or problem that can be solved by through research data. A hypothesis is a tentative answer to the research question that must be supported by the research. A research question must be manageable, specific, and interesting. Additionally, it must be argumentative, capable of being proved or disproved by research.

It is helpful to explore a topic with background reading and notes before formulating a research question and a hypothesis. Create a data base where all the knowledge of a topic is written down to be utilized in approaching the task of identifying the research question. This background work will allow a narrowing to a specific question, and formulate a tentative answer, the hypothesis. The process of exploring a topic can include brainstorming, freewriting, and scanning your memory and experience for information.

OBSERVING DATA

Collecting data in the field begins with direct observation, noting phenomena in a totally objective manner, and recording it. This requires a systematic approach to observation and recording information. Prior to beginning the observation process, certain steps must be accomplished:

- Determine the purpose of the observation and review the research question and hypothesis to see that they relate to each other
- Set a limited time period for the observations
- Develop a system for recording information in a useful manner
- Obtain proper materials for taking notes

- Consider the use of cameras, video recorders, or audio tape recorders
- Use the journalistic technique of asking "who, what, where, when, and why" to garner information

RESEARCH INTERVIEWS

After determining the exact purpose of the interview, check it against the research question and hypothesis. Set up the interview in advance, specifying the amount of time needed. Prepare a written list of questions for the interview, and try out questions on peers before the interview. Prepare a copy of your questions leaving room for notes. Insure that all the necessary equipment is on hand, and record the date, time, and subject of the interview.

The interview should be businesslike, and take only the allotted time. A flexible attitude will allow for questions or comments that have not been planned for, but may prove helpful to the process. Follow-up questions should be asked whenever appropriate. A follow-up thank you note is always appreciated and may pave the way for further interviews. Be mindful at all times of the research question and hypothesis under consideration.

SURVEYS

Surveys are usually in the form of questionnaires which have the advantage of speed and rapid compilation of data. Preparation of the questionnaire is of critical importance. Tie the questionnaire to the research question as closely as possible, and include questions which will bear on the hypothesis. Questions that can be answered "yes" or "no" can be easily tabulated. The following checklist may be helpful:

- Determine the audience for the questionnaire and how best to reach them
- Draft questions that will provide short, specific answers
- Test the questions on friends or peers
- Remember to include a deadline for return of the questionnaire
- Format the questionnaire so that it is clear and easily completed
- Carefully proofread the questionnaire and insure that it is neatly reproduced

LIBRARY RESEARCH

After reviewing personal resources for information, the library is the next stop. Use index cards or notepads for documentation. Create a system for reviewing data. It is helpful to create "key words" to trigger responses from sources. Some valuable guidelines for conducting library research include:

- Consult the reference librarian for sources and ideas.
- Select appropriate general and specific reference books for examination. Encyclopedias are a good place to start. There are numerous specialized encyclopedias to assist in research.
- Survey biographical dictionaries and indexes for information.
- Review almanacs, yearbooks, and statistical data.
- Scan periodical indexes for articles on the research topic.
- Determine if there are specialized indexes and abstracts that may be helpful.
- Review the computer or card catalog for relevant references.

DRAFTING THE RESEARCH ESSAY

Before beginning the research essay, revisit the purpose, audience, and scope of the essay. An explicit thesis statement should summarize major arguments and approaches to the subject. After determining the special format of the essay, a survey of the literature on the subject is helpful. If original or first-hand research is involved, a summary of the methods and conclusions should be prepared.

A clustering strategy assembles all pertinent information on a topic in one physical place. The preparation of an outline may be based on the clusters, or a first draft may be developed without an outline. Formal outlines use a format of "Thesis statement", "Main topic", and "Supporting ideas" to shape the information. Drafting the essay can vary considerably among researchers, but it is useful to use an outline or information clusters to get started. Drafts are usually done on a point-to-point basis.

INTRODUCTION

The introduction to a research essay is particularly important as it sets the context for the essay. It needs to draw the reader into the subject, and also provide necessary background to understand the subject. It is sometimes helpful to open with the research question, and explain how the question will be answered. The major points of the essay may be forecast or previewed to prepare readers for the coming arguments.

In a research essay it is a good idea to establish the writer's credibility by reviewing credentials and experience with the subject. Another useful opening involves quoting several sources that support the points of the essay, again to establish credibility. The tone should be appropriate to the audience and subject, maintaining a sense of careful authority while building the arguments. Jargon should be kept to a minimum, and language carefully chosen to reflect the appropriate tone.

CONCLUSION

The conclusion to a research essay helps readers' summarize what they have learned. Conclusions are not meant to convince, as this has been done in the body of the essay. It can be useful to leave the reader with a memorable phrase or example that supports the argument. Conclusions should be both memorable but logical restatements of the arguments in the body of the essay.

A specific-to-general pattern can be helpful, opening with the thesis statement and expanding to more general observations. A good idea is to restate the main points in the body of the essay, leading to the conclusion. An ending that evokes a vivid image or asks a provocative question makes the essay memorable. The same effect can be achieved by a call for action, or a warning. Conclusions may be tailored to the audience's background, both in terms of language, tone, and style.

REVIEWING THE DRAFT

A quick checklist for reviewing a draft of a research essay includes:

- Introduction - Is the reader's attention gained and held by the introduction?
- Thesis - Does the essay fulfill the promise of the thesis? Is it strong enough?
- Main Points - List the main points and rank them in order of importance.
- Organization - What is the organizing principle of the essay? Does it work?
- Supporting Information - Is the thesis adequately supported? Is the thesis convincing?
- Source Material - Are there adequate sources and are they smoothly integrated into the essay?
- Conclusion - Does the conclusion have sufficient power? Does it summarize the essay well?
- Paragraphs, Sentences, and Words - Review all these for effectiveness in promoting the thesis.
- Overall Review - Evaluate the essay's strengths and weaknesses. What revisions are needed?

MODERN LANGUAGE ASSOCIATION STYLE

The Modern Language Association style is widely used in literature and languages as well as other fields. The MLA style calls for noting brief references to sources in parentheses in the text of an essay, and adding an alphabetical list of sources, called "Works Cited", at the end. Specific recommendations of the MLA include:

- Works Cited - Includes only works actually cited. List on a separate page with the author's name, title, and publication information, which must list the location of the publisher, the publishers' name, and the date of publication.
- Parenthetical Citations - MLA style uses parenthetical citations following each quotation, reference, paraphrase, or summary to a source. Each citation is made up of the author's last name and page reference, keyed to a reference in "Works Cited".
- Explanatory Notes - Explanatory notes are numbered consecutively, and identified by superscript numbers in the text. The full notes may appear as endnotes or as footnotes at the bottom of the page.

AMERICAN PSYCHOLOGICAL ASSOCIATION STYLE

The American Psychological Association style is widely followed in the social sciences. The APA parenthetical citations within the text directs readers to a list of sources. In APA style this list is called "References". References are listed on a separate page, and each line includes the author's name, publication date, title, and publication information. Publication information includes the city where the publisher is located, and the publisher's name. Underline the titles of books and periodicals , but not articles.

APA parenthetical expressions citations include the author's last name, the date of publication, and the page number. APA style allows for content footnotes for information needed to be expanded or supplemented, marked in the text by superscript numbers in consecutive order. Footnotes are listed under a separate page, headed "Footnotes" after the last page of text. All entries should be double-spaced.

REVISIONS

REVISING SENTENCES

Revising sentences is done to make writing more effective. Editing sentences is done to correct any errors. Revising sentences is usually best done on a computer, where it is possible to try several versions easily. Some writers prefer to print out a hard copy and work with this for revisions. Each works equally well and depends on the individual preference.

Spelling and grammar checks on software are a great aid to a writer but not a panacea. Many grammatical problems, such as faulty parallelism, mixed constructions, and misplaced modifiers can slip past the programs. Even if errors are caught, the writing still must be evaluated for effectiveness. A combination of software programs and writer awareness is necessary to insure an error free manuscript.

GLOBAL REVISIONS

Global revisions address the larger elements of writing. They usually affect paragraphs or sections, and may involve condensing or merging sections of text to improve meaning and flow. Sometimes material may be rearranged to better present the arguments of the essay. It is usually better for the writer to get some distance from the work before starting a global revision. Reviewers and editors can be usefully employed to make suggestions for revision. If reviewers are utilized, it is helpful to emphasize the focus on the larger themes of the work, rather than the finer points. When undertaking a global review, the writer might wish to position himself as the audience, rather than the writer. This provides some additional objectivity, and can result in a more honest appraisal of the writing and revisions that should be made. Global revisions are the last major changes a writer will make in the text. seal to persuade, inform, or entertain them. Answering these questions as objectively as possible will allow for a useful global revision.

- Purpose - Does the draft accomplish its purpose? Is the material and tone appropriate for the intended audience? Does it account for the audience's knowledge of the subject? Does it seek to persuade, inform, or entertain them?
- Focus - Does the introduction and the conclusion focus on the main point? Are all supporting arguments focused on the thesis?
- Organization and Paragraphing - Are there enough organizational cues to guide the reader? Are any paragraphs too long or too short?
- Content - Is the supporting material persuasive? Are all ideas adequately developed? Is there any material that could be deleted?
- Point -of-view - Is the draft free of distracting sifts in point-of-view? Is the point-of-view appropriate for the subject and intended audience?

PARAGRAPHS

A paragraph should be unified around a main point. A good topic sentence summarizing the paragraphs main point. A topic sentence is more general than subsequent supporting sentences. Sometime the topic sentence will be used to close the paragraph if earlier sentences give a clear indication of the direction of the paragraph. Sticking to the main point means deleting or omitting unnecessary sentences that do not advance the main point.

The main point of a paragraph deserves adequate development, which usually means a substantial paragraph. A paragraph of two or three sentences often does not develop a point well enough, particularly if the point is a strong supporting argument of the thesis. An occasional short paragraph is fine, particularly it is used as a transitional device. A choppy appearance should be avoided.

METHODS OF DEVELOPMENT:
- **Examples** are a common method of development and may be effectively used when a reader may ask "For Example?" Examples are selected instances, not an inclusive catalog. They may be used to suggest the validity of topic sentences.
- **Illustrations** are extended examples, sometimes presented in story form for interest. They usually require several sentences each, so they are used sparingly. Well selected illustrations can be a colorful and vivid way of developing a point.
- **Stories** that command reader interest, developed in a story form, can be powerful methods of emphasizing key points in a essay. Stories and illustrations should be very specific and relate directly to a point or points being made in the text. They allow more colorful language and instill a sense of human interest in a subject. Used judiciously, illustrations and stories are an excellent device.
- **Analogies** draw comparisons between items that appear to have nothing in common. Analogies are employed by writers to attempt to provoke fresh thoughts and changed feelings about a subject. They may be used to make the unfamiliar more familiar, to clarify an abstract point, or to argue a point. Although analogies are effective literary devices, they should be used thoughtfully in arguments. Two things may be alike in some respects but completely different in others.

- **Cause and effect** is a excellent device and are best used when the cause and effect are generally accepted as true. As a matter of argument, cause and effect is usually too complex and subject to other interpretations to be used effectively. A valid way of using cause and effect is to state the effect in the topic sentence of a paragraph, and add the causes in the body of the paragraph. This adds logic and form to a paragraph, and usually makes it more effective.

TYPES OF PARAGRAPHS:

- A paragraph of narration tells a story or part of a story. They are usually arranged in chronological order, but sometimes include flashbacks, taking the story back to an earlier time.
- A descriptive paragraph paints a verbal portrait of a person, place, or thing, using specific details that appeal to one or more of our senses - sight, sound, smell, taste, and touch. It conveys a real sense of being present and observing phenomena.
- A process paragraphs is related in time order, generally chronological. It usually describes a process or teaches readers how to perform the process.
- Comparing two subjects draws attention to their similarities but can also indicate a consideration of differences. To contrast is to focus only on differences. Both comparisons and contrasts may be examined point-by-point, or in succeeding paragraphs.

ORGANIZING INFORMATION:

- A grouping of items into categories based on some consistent criteria is called classification. The principle of classification a writer chooses will depend on the purpose of the classification. Most items can be classified by a number of criteria, and the selection of the specific classification will depend on the writer's aims in using this device.
- Division, on the other hand, takes one item and divides it into parts. Just as with classification, the division must be based on a valid and consistent principle. For example a body may be divided into various body systems easily, but not as easily divided into body functions, because the categories overlap.
- Definition classifies a concept or word in a general group, then distinguishes it from other members of the class. Usually simple definitions can be provided in a sentence or two, while more complex ones may need a paragraph or two to adequately define them.

COHERENCE

A smooth flow of sentences and paragraphs without gaps, shifts, or bumps leads to paragraph coherence. Ties between old information and new, can be smoothed by several strategies.

- Linking ideas clearly, from the topic sentence to the body of the paragraph is essential for a smooth transition. The topic sentence states the main point, and this should be followed by specific details, examples, and illustrations that support the topic sentence. The support may be direct or indirect. In indirect support the illustrations and examples may support a sentence that in turn supports the topic directly.
- The repetition of key words adds coherence to a paragraph. To avoid dull language, variations of the key words may be used.
- Parallel structures are often used within sentences to emphasize the similarity of ideas and connect sentences giving similar information.
- Minimize shifting sentences from one verb tense to another. These shifts affect the smooth flows of words and can disrupt the coherence of the paragraph.

TRANSITIONS

Transitions are bridges between what has been read and what is about to be read. Transitions smooth the reader's path between sentences, and inform readers of major connections to new ideas forthcoming in the text. Transitional phrases should be used with care, selecting the appropriate phrase for a transition. Tone is another important consideration in using transitional phrases, varying the tone for different audiences. For example in a scholarly essay, "in summary" would be preferable to the more informal "in short".

When working with transitional words and phrases, writers usually find a natural flow that indicates when a transition is needed. In reading a draft of the text, it should become apparent where the flow is uneven or rough. At this point, the writer can add transitional elements during the revision process. Revising can also afford an opportunity to delete transitional devices that seem heavy-handed or unnecessary.

> **Review Video: Transitions in Writing**
> Visit mometrix.com/academy and enter code: 233246

LENGTHS OF PARAGRAPHS

The comfort level for readers is paragraphs of between 100 and 200 words. Shorter paragraphs cause too much starting and stopping, and give a "choppy" effect. Paragraphs that are too long often test the attention span of the reader. Two notable exceptions to this rule exist. In scientific or scholarly papers, longer paragraphs suggest seriousness and depth. In journalistic writing, constraints are placed on paragraph size by the narrow columns in a newspaper format.

The first and last paragraphs of a text will usually be the introduction and conclusion. These special purpose paragraphs are likely to be shorter than paragraphs in the body of the work. Paragraphs in the body of the essay follow the subject's outline; one paragraph per point in short essays, and a group of paragraphs per point in longer works. Some ideas require more development than others, so it is good for a writer to remain flexible. A too long paragraph may be divided, while shorter ones may be combined.

Paragraph breaks are used for many reasons, usually as devices to improve the flow or content of the text. Some examples for beginning new paragraphs include:

- To mark off the introduction and concluding paragraphs.
- To signal a shift to a new idea or topic.
- To indicate an important shift in time or place.
- To emphasize a point by repositioning a major sentence.
- To highlight a comparison, contrast, or cause and effect relationship.
- To signal a change in speakers, voice, or tense.

ARGUMENTATIVE WRITING

Constructing a reasonable argument, the goal is not to "win" or have the last word, but rather to reveal current understanding of the question, and propose a solution to the perceived problem. The purpose of argument in a free society or a research field is to reach the best conclusion possible at the time.

Conventions of arguments vary from culture to culture. In America arguments tend to be direct rather than subtle, carefully organized rather than discursive, spoken plainly rather than poetically.

Evidence presented is usually specific and factual, while appeals to intuition or communal wisdom are rare.

Argumentative writing takes a stand on a debatable issue , and seeks to explore all sides of the issue and reach the best possible solution. Argumentative writing should not be combative, at it's strongest it is assertive.

A prelude to argumentative writing is an examination of the issue's social and intellectual contexts.

INTRODUCTION

The introduction of an essay arguing an issue should end with a thesis sentence that states a position on the issue. A good strategy is to establish credibility with readers by showing both expert knowledge and fair-mindedness. Building common ground with undecided or neutral readers is helpful.

The thesis should be supported by strong arguments that support the stated position. The main lines of argument should have a cumulative effect of convincing readers that the thesis has merit. The sum of the main lines of argument will outline the overall argumentative essay. The outline will clearly illustrate the central thesis, and subordinate claims that support it.

Evidence must be provided that support both the thesis and supporting arguments. Evidence based on reading should be documented, to show the sources. Readers must know how to check sources for accuracy and validity.

SUPPORTING EVIDENCE

Most arguments must be supported by facts and statistics. Facts are something that is known with certainty, and have been objectively verified. Statistics may be used in selective ways to for partisan purposes. It is good to check statistics by reading authors writing on both sides of an issue. This will give a more accurate idea of how valid are the statistics cited.

Examples and illustrations add an emotional component to arguments, reaching readers in ways that facts and figures cannot. They are most effective when used in combination with objective information that can be verified.

Expert opinion can contribute to a position on a question. The source should be an authority whose credentials are beyond dispute. Sometimes it is necessary to provide the credentials of the expert. Expert testimony can be quoted directly, or may be summarized by the writer. Sources must be well documented to insure their validity.

COUNTER ARGUMENTS

In addition to arguing a position, it is a good practice to review opposing arguments and attempt to counter them. This process can take place anywhere in the essay, but is perhaps best placed after the thesis is stated. Objections can be countered on a point-by-point analysis, or in a summary paragraph. Pointing out flaws in counter arguments is important, as is showing the counter arguments to have less weight than the supported thesis.

Building common ground with neutral or opposed readers can make a strong case. Sharing values with undecided readers can allow people to switch positions without giving up what they feel is important. People who may oppose a position need to feel they can change their minds without compromising their intelligence or their integrity. This appeal to open-mindedness can be a powerful tool in arguing a position without antagonizing opposing views.

FALLACIOUS ARGUMENTS

A number of unreasonable argumentative tactics are known as logical fallacies. Most fallacies are misguided uses of legitimate argumentative arguments.

Generalizing is drawing a conclusion from an array of facts using inductive reasoning. These conclusions are a probability, not a certainty. The fallacy known as a "hasty generalization" is a conclusion based on insufficient or unrepresentative evidence. Stereotyping is a hasty generalization about a group. This is common because of the human tendency to perceive selectively. Observations are made through a filter of preconceptions, prejudices, and attitudes.

Analogies point out similarities between disparate things. When an analogy is unreasonable, it is called a "false analogy". This usually consists of assuming if two things are alike in one respect, they must be alike in others. This, of course, may or may not be true. Each comparison must be independently verified to make the argument valid.

POST HOC FALLACY

Tracing cause and effect can be a complicated matter. Because of the complexity involved, writers often over-simplify it. A common error is to assume that because one event follows another, the first is the cause of the second. This common fallacy is known as "post hoc", from the Latin meaning "after this,therefore because of this".

A post hoc fallacy could run like this: "Since Abner Jones returned to the Giants lineup, the team has much better morale". The fact that Jones returned to the lineup may or may not have had an effect on team morale. The writer must show there is a cause and effect relationship between Jones' return and team morale. It is not enough to note that one event followed another. It must be proved beyond a reasonable doubt that morale was improved by the return of Jones to the lineup. The two may be true but do not necessarily follow a cause and effect pattern.

ASSUMPTIONS

When considering problems and solutions, the full range of possible options should be mentioned before recommending one solution above others. It is unfair to state there are only two alternatives, when in fact there are more options. Writers who set up a choice between their preferred option and a clearly inferior one are committing the "either...or" fallacy. All reasonable alternatives should be included in the possible solutions.

Assumptions are claims that are taken to be true without proof. If a claim is controversial, proof should be provided to verify the assumption. When a claim is made that few would agree with, the writer is guilty of a "non sequitur" (Latin for "does not follow") fallacy. Thus any assumption that is subject to debate cannot be accepted without supporting evidence is suspect.

SYLLOGISM

Deductive reasoning is constructed in a three-step method called a syllogism. The three steps are the major premise, the minor premise, and the conclusion. The major premise is a generalization, and the minor premise is a specific case. The conclusion is deduced from applying the generalization to the specific case. Deductive arguments fail if either the major or minor premise is not true, or if the conclusion does not logically follow from the premises. This means a deductive argument must stand on valid, verifiable premises, and the conclusion is a logical result of the premises.

"STRAW MAN" FALLACY

The "straw man" fallacy consists of an oversimplification or distortion of opposing views. This fallacy is one of the most obvious and easily uncovered since it relies on gross distortions. The name comes from a side setting up a position so weak (the straw man) that is easily refuted.

COMPOSITION

Composition refers to a range of activities which include the achievement of literacy, transmission of culture, preparation for writing skills in the workplace, and writing as a mode of personal expression and identity. Composition has evolved into an interdisciplinary study and an eclectic practice. Writing is always a process, performing a critical role in education.

Composition studies, like its companion, rhetoric, is a practical and theoretical study Originally it was limited to teaching and correction of student's grammar. Composition has come of age as a writing process, a complex network of interweaving social, political, and individual components.

The field now includes collaborative writing, two or more students writing together, each assuming specific responsibilities with a heavy emphasis on joint revisions. Continued innovations and experimentation are an ongoing part of composition studies.

LITERARY DEVICES

ALLUSIONS

An allusion is a reference within a text to some person, place, or event outside the text. Allusions that refer to events more or less contemporary with the text are called topical allusions. Those referring to specific persons are called personal allusions. An example of personal allusion is William Butler Yeat's reference to "golden thighed Pythagoras" in his poem " Among School Children".

Allusions may be used to summarize an important idea or point out a contrast between contemporary life and a heroic past. An example of this would be James Joyce's classical parallels in "Ulysses" in which heroic deeds in the "Odyssey" are implicitly compared to the banal aspects of everyday life in Dublin.

Allusions may also be used to summarize an important idea such as the concluding line from "King Kong", "It was beauty killed the beast".

> **Review Video: Allusion**
> Visit mometrix.com/academy and enter code: 294065

JARGON

Jargon is a specialized language used among members of a trade, profession, or group. Jargon should be avoided and used only when the audience will be familiar with the language. Jargon includes exaggerated language usually designed to impress rather than inform. Sentences filled with jargon are both wordy and difficult to understand. Jargon is commonly used in such institutions as the military, politics, sports, and art.

CLICHÉS

Clichés are sentences and phrases that have been overused to the point of triviality. They have no creativity or originality and add very little to modern writing. Writers should avoid clichés whenever possible. When editing writing, the best solution for clichés is to delete them. If this does

not seem easily accomplished, a cliché can be modified so that it is not dully predictable and trite. This often means adding phrases or sentences to change the cliché.

SLANG

Slang is an informal and sometimes private language that connotes the solidarity and exclusivity of a group such as teenagers, sports fans, ethnic groups, or rock musicians. Slang has a certain vitality, but it is not always widely understood and should be avoided in most writing. An exception could be when the audience is a specialized group who understand the jargon and slang commonly used by the members.

SEXIST LANGUAGE

Sexist language is language that stereotypes or demeans women or men, usually women. Such language is derived from stereotypical thinking, traditional pronoun use, and from words used to refer indefinitely to both sexes. Writers should avoid referring to a profession as being basically male or female, and using different conventions when referring to men and women. Pronouns "he,him,and his"should be avoided by using a pair of pronouns or revising the sentence to obviate the sexist language.

PRETENTIOUS LANGUAGE

In an attempt to sound elegant, profound, poetic, or impressive, some writers embroider their thoughts with flowery phrases, inflated language, and generally pretentious wordage. Pretentious language is often so ornate and wordy that it obscures the true meaning of the writing.

EUPHEMISMS

Euphemisms are pleasant sounding words that replace language that seems overly harsh or ugly. Euphemisms are wordy and indirect, clouding meaning through "pretty" words. However euphemisms are sometimes uses as conventions, when speaking about subjects such as death, bodily functions and sex.

DOUBLESPEAK

The term "doublespeak" was coined by George Orwell in his futuristic novel "1984". It applies to any evasive or deceptive language, particularly favored by politicians. Doublespeak is evident in advertising, journalism, and in political polemics. it should be avoided by serious writers.

FIGURES OF SPEECH

A figure of speech is an expression that uses words imaginatively rather than literally to make abstract ideas concrete. Figures of speech compare unlike things to reveal surprising similarities. The pitfalls of using figures of speech is the failure of writers to think through the images they evoke. The result can be a mixed metaphor, a combination of two or more images that do not make sense together.

In a simile the writer makes an explicit comparison, usually by introducing it with "like" or "as". An example would be " white as a sheet" or "my love is like a red, red, rose". Effective use of similes can add color and vivid imagery to language. Used carefully and sparingly, they provide a writer with an effective device to enhance meaning and style.

Figures of speech are particularly effective when used with discretion and selectively. Examples of figures of speech can be found in all genres of writing.

ALLEGORIES

Allegories are a type of narrative in which the story reflects at least one other meaning. Traditional allegory often employs personification, the use of human characters to represent abstract ideas. Early examples of the use of allegory were the medieval mystery plays in which abstractions such as Good, Evil, Penance, and Death appeared as characters.

Another type of allegory uses a surface story to refer to historical or political events. Jonathan Swift was a master at using allegory in this manner, particularly in his "Tale of a Tub" (1704), a satirical allegory of the reformation.

Allegory has been largely replaced by symbolism by modern writers. Although they are sometimes confused, symbolism bears a natural relationship to the events in a story, while in allegory the surface story is only an excuse for the secondary and more important meaning. Allegory has had a revival in postmodern writing, and is seen in much contemporary literature.

AMBIGUITY

In writing historically, ambiguity is generally viewed as an error or flaw. The word now means a literary technique in which a word or phrase conveys two or more different meanings. William Empson defines ambiguity as " any verbal nuance, however slight, which gives room for alternative reactions to the same piece of language." Empons chief purpose in defining ambiguity was to note how this device affects the interpretation of poetry. Empson identified seven types of ambiguity including the traditional meaning. These seven types of ambiguity each provided a different view of possible interpretation of text in writing. Empsons's "Seven Types of Ambiguity" was the first detailed analysis of the phenomena of multiple meanings, sometimes called plurisignation. Ambiguity can be a useful device for some types of writing but does lend itself to informative or persuasive text.

PHONETICS

Phonetics seeks to provide a descriptive terminology for the sounds of spoken language. This includes the physiology for the production of speech sounds, the classification of speech sounds including vowels and consonants, the dynamic features of speech production, and the study of instrumental phonetics, the investigation of human speech by laboratory techniques. The dynamic aspects of phonetics include voice quality, stress, rhythm, and speech melody.

Instrumental phonetics underlines both the complexity of speech production, and the subtlety of the human brain in interpreting a constantly changing flow of acoustic data as recognizable speech-sounds. The correlation between acoustic quality, auditory perception, and articulatory position is a complex and not yet fully understood process. It represents a fertile area of research for phoneticians, psychologists, and perhaps philosophers.

General phonetics classifies the speech sounds of all languages. Any one language uses only possibilities of the selections available. Sounds and how they are used in a language is the phonology of a language. Dynamic features of phonology include speech melody, stress, rhythmic organization, length and syllabicity. The central unit of phonology is the phoneme, the smallest

distinct sound in a given language. Two words are composed of different phonemes only if they differ phonetically in ways that are found to make a difference in meaning. Phonemic transcription of a word or phrase is its representation as a sequence or other combinations of phonemes.

PHONOLOGY

Phonology is a controversial and enigmatic part of linguistics. It is widely studied and defined but there is no agreement on the definition of a phoneme or phonology theory. There may be as many theories as there are phonologies in linguistics.

LINGUISTICS

Linguistics is the branch of knowledge that deals with language. Grammar, an integral part of linguistics, in its widest sense, includes the study of the structure of words and syntactic constructions, and that of sound systems. Linguistics is concerned with the lexical and grammatical categories of individual languages, and the differences between languages and the historical relations between families of languages. Each lexical entry informs us about the linguistic properties of the word. It will indicate a word's phonological, grammatical, and somatic properties.

- Grammar may be said to generate a set of phrases and sentences, so linguistics is also the study of generative grammar. Grammar must also contain a phonological component, since this determines the phonetic form of words in speech.
- Phonology, the study of sound systems and processes affecting the way words are pronounced, is another aspect of linguistics.

PSYCHOLINGUISTICS

Psycholinguistics is concerned with how linguistic competence is employed in the production and comprehension of speech.

- The first step in language comprehension is to use the phonological processor to identify sounds.
- Then the lexical processor identifies the component words.
- Finally the syntactic processor provides a syntactic representation of the sentence.
- The last step is for the semantic processor to compute a meaning representation for the sentence, on the basis of syntactical and lexical information supplied by previous steps in the process.

The relevant meaning of the words serves as the end-product of the process, and once this has been computed the sentence is understood. All stages of the psycholinguistic process take place in real time, so that measurements of each specific part of the process may be compared to the level of complexity of the grammar itself. Such is the experimental study of psycholinguistics applied.

DEVELOPMENTAL LINGUISTICS

Neurolinguistics is concerned with the physical representations of linguistic processes in the brain. The most effective way to study this is to observe the effects on language capacity in brain-injured individuals. The frontal lobe of the brain appears to be the area responsible for controlling the production of speech. As research has become more refined over the years, it is evident that language functions are located in different parts of the brain. As improved diagnostic and sophisticated imaging techniques are developed, it is anticipated that the mysteries of language capacity and competence corresponding to specific parts of the brain will become clearer. For now, our knowledge in this field is imperfect, and the process of mapping the brain for linguistic capacity and performance is limited. Neurolinguistics is closely tied to neurology and neuro-physiology.

SOCIOLINGUISTICS

Sociolinguistics is the study of the relationship between language and the structure of society. It takes into account the social backgrounds of both the speaker and the addressee, the relationship between the speaker and the addressee, and the context and manner of the interaction. Because the emphasis in sociolinguistics is on language use, the analysis of language in this field is typically based on taped recordings of everyday interactions. The sociolinguists seek to discover universal properties of languages, attempting to analyze questions such as "do all languages change in the same ways"? Answers are sought to the larger questions about universals in society in which language plays a major role. The multifaceted nature of language and its broad impact on many areas of society make this field an exciting and cutting edge part of linguistics.

MEANING

Meaning is traditionally something said to be expressed by a sentence. Modern theories in linguistics often elaborate on this. The four major theories are:

1. The meaning of a sentence is different depending on the context of the utterance.
2. Sentence meanings are part of the language system and form a level of semantic representation independent of other levels.
3. Representations are derivable from the level of syntax, given a lexicon which specifies the meaning of words and a set of semantic rules.
4. The meaning of utterances follows from separate principles that are in the domain of context or pragmatics.

Other theories assert that neither words or sentences can be assigned meanings independently of situations in which they are uttered. These theories all seek to establish a standard understanding of meaning so that linguists can refine and extend their research.

ETMOLOGY

Etymology is the study of the historical relation between a word and earlier form or forms from which it has developed. Etymology can be loosely defined as the study of the origins of words. This study may occur on different levels of linguistic approach. Word meanings and their historical antecedents are often a complicated and controversial source of study. Tracing the meaning of words often includes understanding the social, political, and cultural time that the definition existed. The evolution of words from earlier forms suggests a cross-fertilization of social contexts and common usage that is a fascinating field of study.

An etymological fallacy is that the notion that a true meaning of a word can be derived from it etymology. Modern linguistic theory provides a substantial body of knowledge that compares and evaluates etymology and provides numerous avenues for new research.

LEXICOLOGY

Lexicon is the aspect of a language that is centered on individual words or similar units. Its scope varies widely from one theory to another. In some systems, lexicon is a simple component of generative grammar. In others it is the basis for all grammatical patterns. some view a lexicon as an unstructured list, while others see it as an elaborate network of entries governed by lexical rules and shared features. Lexicon in linguistics is to be distinguished as a theory from a dictionary or part of a practical description.

Lexicology is the branch of linguistics concerned with the semantic structure of the lexicon. Lexical diffusion is the gradual spread of a phonetic or other change across the vocabulary of a language or

across a speech community? The term may also refer to the diffusion of individual lexical units within a lexicon.

Lexical decomposition is the analysis of word meanings into smaller units.

GRAMMAR

Grammar may be practically defined as the study of how words are put together or the study of sentences. There are multiple approaches to grammar in modern linguistics. Any systematic account of the structure of a language and the patterns it describes is grammar. Modern definitions of grammar state grammar is the knowledge of a language developed in the minds of the speakers.

A grammar in the broadest sense is a set of rules internalized by members of a speech community, and an account, by a linguist, of such a grammar. This internalized grammar is what is commonly called a language. Grammar is often restricted to units that have meaning. The expanded scope of grammar includes morphology and syntax, and a lexicon. Grammatical meaning is described as part of the syntax and morphology of a language as distinct from its lexicon.

The ability to learn language is determined by a biologically determined innate language facility. This widely accepted theory is known as the innateness hypothesis. The knowledge of adult grammar appears to go far beyond anything supplied by the child's linguistic experience, implying an innate ability to learn language. A language facility must incorporate a set of Universal Grammar principles which enable a child to form and interpret sentences in any natural language. Children have the ability to acquire any natural language so it follows that the contents of the innate language facility must not be specific to any one human language. Developmental linguistics is concerned with examining children's grammar and the conditions under which they emerge. The language faculty is species-specific and the ability to develop a grammar of a language is unique to human beings. The study of non-human communication forms a different field of study.

STRUCTURALIZED GRAMMAR

Structuralize grammar tends to be formal in nature as it is concerned with grammatical and phonological considerations, rather than semantics. The chief goal is to uncover the structure of a language. There are valid criticisms of the structural approach to grammar. problems exist in the available descriptive frameworks to manage, difficulties with definitions, and inconsistency and contradiction between theory and practice. These concerns have not invalidated the study of structural grammar, but have been utilized by linguists to perfect the analysis.

TRANSFORMATIONAL GRAMMAR

Transformational grammar is any grammar in which different syntactic structures are related by transformations. The main role of transformations was to relate the sentences of a language as a whole to a small set of kernel sentences. A base component of a grammar generated a deep structure for each sentence. these structures were an input to a transformational component, which was an ordered structure of transformational rules. Its output was a set of surface structures, which combined with the deep structures, formed its syntactic description. Further rules supplied its semantic representation and phonetic representation.

Transformational grammar was invented and promulgated by Noam Chomsky, a revolutionary figure in linguistics. Much of Chomsky's work has been directed to the development of a universal grammar, conceived as an account of what is inherited by the individual. Chomsky remains the dominant figure of the 20th century in linguistics.

SENTENCES

The largest structural unit normally recognized by grammar is the sentence. Any attempt to accurately define the sentence is in error. Any such definition will not bear up under Linguistic Analysis. In every language, there are a limited number of favorite sentence-types to which most others can be related. They vary from language to language. Certain utterances, while not immediately conforming to favorite sentence types, can be expanded in their context to become one sentence of a particular type. These can be called referable sentences. Other utterances that do not conform to favorite sentence types may reveal obsolete sentence types; these are proverbial sayings and are called gnomic or fossilized sentences. A very small number of utterances not conforming to the favorite sentence-types are found in prescribed social situations, such as "Hello" or "Bye".

SENTENCE PATTERNS

Sentence patterns fall into five common modes with some exceptions. They are:

1. Subject / linking verb / subject complement
2. Subject / transitive verb / direct object
3. Subject / transitive verb / indirect object / direct object
4. Subject / transitive verb / direct object / object complement
5. Subject / intransitive verb

Common exceptions to these patterns are questions and commands, sentences with delayed subjects, and passive transformations. Writers sometimes use the passive voice when the active voice would be more appropriate.

SENTENCES CLASSIFICATION

Sentences are classified in two ways:

1. according to their structure
2. according to their purpose

Writers use declarative sentences to make statements, imperative sentences to issue requests or commands, interrogative sentences to ask questions, and exclamatory sentences to make exclamations.

Depending on the number and types of clauses they contain, sentences may be classified as simple, compound, complex, or compound-complex.

Clauses come in two varieties: independent and subordinate.

1. An independent clause is a full sentence pattern that does not function within another sentence pattern; it contains a subject and modifiers plus a verb and any objects, complements, and modifiers of that verb. It either stands alone or could stand alone.
2. A subordinate clause is a full sentence pattern that functions within a sentence as an adjective, an adverb, or a noun but that cannot stand alone as a complete sentence.

SENTENCE STRUCTURES

The four major types of sentence structure are:

1. Simple sentences - Simple sentences have one independent clause with no subordinate clauses. a simple sentence may contain compound elements,- a compound subject, verb, or object for example, but does not contain more than one full sentence pattern.
2. Compound sentences - Compound sentences are composed of two or more independent clauses with no subordinate clauses. The independent clauses are usually joined with a comma and a coordinating conjunction, or with a semicolon.
3. Complex sentences - A complex sentence is composed of one independent clause with one or more dependent clauses.
4. Compound-complex sentences - A compound-complex sentence contains at least two independent clauses and at least one subordinate clause. sometimes they contain two full sentence patters that can stand alone. When each independent clause contains a subordinate clause, this makes the sentence both compound and complex.

> **Review Video: Sentence Structure**
> Visit mometrix.com/academy and enter code: 700478

CHOMSKY'S SENTENCE STRUCTURE

Deep structure is a representation of the syntax of a sentence distinguished by various criteria from its surface structure. Initially defined by Noam Chomsky as the part of the syntactic description of a of a sentence that determines its semantic interpretation by the base component of a generative grammar.

Surface sentence structure is a representation of the syntax of a sentence seen as deriving by one ore more transformations, from a an underlying deep structure. Such a sentence is in the order in which the corresponding phonetic forms are spoken. Surface structure was later broadened by Chomsky to include semantic structure. Chomsky's later minimalist program no longer takes this for granted. Minimalist theory assumes no more than a minimum of types of statements and levels of representation.

The technical analysis outlined by Chomsky over three decades forms an integral part of transformational grammar.

LANGUAGE INVESTIGATION

The investigation of a language by classification is the goal of the modern linguist. When the observer has determined the phonemic structure of a language, and has classified all its constructions, both morphological and syntactic, the resulting description will be an accurate and usable grammar of the language, accounting in the simplest way for all the utterances of the speech community.

LANGUAGE FAMILIES

A language family is a group of languages that have been developed from a single ancestor. An example would be Indo-European, of which English is one of many members. Language families are identified whenever a common origin can be accepted as certain. When a family origin in speculative or uncertain, it may be called a projected family, a proposed family, or a probable family.

Some linguists have tried to apply a biological method of classification of language families, following the genus, order, species model. They have classed languages as beginning with "superficies", "macro families", "stocks", "super stocks", or "phyla" at the top. Below those will be "subfamilies", "branches", and "groups". This attempt has proved faulty as the classifications imply more than is known about family origins. It has been difficult and largely unaccepted to class language families in these descending modes of importance.

LANGUAGE DESCRIPTIONS

The levels of language descriptions represent a distinct phase in the description of a language at which specific types of elements and the relations between them are studied or investigated.

- At the level of phonology, one studies the sound structure of a language, words or larger units that are specific to that level.
- At the level of syntax, sentences are represented as the configuration of words or morphemes standing in specific construction in relationship to one another.

Levels of language are an important part of structural linguistics, whether they focus on formal analyses or representation. Some give an order of procedures which govern the formal structural analysis of language. Others propose a hierarchy of greater or lesser degrees of abstraction, ranging from phonetics as the highest and semantics as the lowest. In many of these levels are defined by the different components of an integrated structural grammar.

MORPHOLOGY

Morphology is the grammatical structure of words and their categories. The morphological process includes any of the formal processes or operations by which the forms of words are derived from stems or roots. Types of morphological processes include affix, any element in the structure of a word other than a root; reduplication, where all or part of a form is duplicated; subtraction, where part of a form is deleted; supple ton, where one part of the morphological process replaces another; compound, where two parts of the morphological process are joined; and modification, where one part of a form is modified.

Forms of morphological classification distinguished isolating, in which each grammatical classification is represented by a single word, agglutinating, where words are easily divided into separate sections, and inflectional, concerned with inflections in languages.

FUNCTIONS OF LANGUAGE

- Language is a means of social control making human society possible. The communication of thoughts is but a small part of this.
- Language acts as an index to various things about the speaker - age, sex, physical and mental wellbeing, and personality characteristics.
- Language acts to limit classes within a society, either by accent, dialect, choice of words and grammatical features.
- Language brings human beings into relationship with the external world. It mediates between man and his environment.
- Language is the material of artistic creation, including not only literary works but poetic and oral traditions.

Any list of languages functions is arbitrary. There are dozens of other possible classifications of language functions in the literature of linguistics. The classification given above includes the basic elements of language and their societal effect.

SEMANTICS

Semantics studies the meaning of utterances and why particular utterances have the meanings they do. Semantics originally covered grammar, the account of meaningful forms, and the lexicon or body of words contained in a language. When the study of forms was separated from that of meanings, the field of generative grammar became associated with semantics. Currently, the scope of semantics will cover word meanings or lexical semantics, and the meaning of utterances studied in pragmatics, the meaning of language in everyday life.

Some narrow definitions of semantics understand the term to mean the study of problems encounted in formal semantics, excluding lexical meaning completely. This last definition is an extreme one, and is included to illustrate the broad vistas that are opened when we discuss semantics. What can be asserted is that semantics in its broadest and most common usage is the field of study in linguistics that deals with meaning in all its forms.

SPOKEN AND WRITTEN LANGUAGE

The relationship of spoken language and written form has been the subject of differences of attitudes among linguists. The spoken form is historically prior, both for the language community and the individual. It is also more complicated. For these reasons, emphasis is placed on the sound systems of languages which has led some linguists to describe the spoken form as language, and the written form as written language. Both are equal examples of language. The relationship is not a straightforward case of deriving the written from the spoken form. When a written form evolves, it tends to take on a life of its own and acquires usages different from the spoken.

Linguists are concerned with the analysis and development of language as a whole, both written and spoken. Much of the controversy in linguistic theory is concerned with both forms of languages. Linguistics is in a sense a search for the universals in language, which includes both spoken and written forms.

PARTS OF SPEECH

NOUNS

Nouns are the name of a person, place, or thing, and are usually signaled by an article (a, an, the). Nouns sometimes function as adjectives modifying other nouns. Nouns used in this manner are called noun/adjectives. Nouns are classified for a number of purposes: capitalization, word choice, count/no count nouns, and collective nouns are examples.

PRONOUNS

Pronouns is a word used in place of a noun. Usually the pronoun substitutes for the specific noun, called the antecedent. Although most pronouns function as substitutes for nouns, some can function as adjectives modifying nouns. pronouns may be classed as personal, possessive, intensive, relative, interrogative, demonstrative, indefinite, and reciprocal. pronouns can cause a number of problems for writers including pronoun-antecedent agreement, distinguishing between who and whom, and differentiating pronouns such as I and me.

77

PROBLEMS WITH PRONOUNS

Pronouns are words that substitute for nouns: he, it, them, her, me, and so on. Four frequently encountered problems with pronouns include:

1. Pronoun - antecedent agreement - The antecedent of a pronoun is the word the pronoun refers to. A pronoun and its antecedent agree when they are both singular or plural.
2. Pronoun reference - A pronoun should refer clearly to its antecedent. A pronoun's reference will be unclear if it id ambiguous, implied, vague, or indefinite.
3. Personal pronouns - Some pronouns change their case form according to their grammatical structure in a sentence. Pronouns functioning as subjects appear in the subjective case, those functioning as objects appear in the objective case, and those functioning as possessives appear in the possessive case.
4. **Who or whom** - Who, a subjective-case pronoun, can only be used subjects and subject complements. Whom, an objective case pronoun, can only be used for objects. The words who and whom appear primarily in subordinate clauses or in questions.

> **Review Video: <u>Nouns and Pronouns</u>**
> Visit mometrix.com/academy and enter code: 312073

VERBS

The verb of a sentence usually expresses action or being. It is composed of a main verb and sometimes supporting verbs. These helping verbs are forms of have, do, and be, and nine modals. The modals are "can, could, may, might, shall, should, will, would, and ought". Some verbs are followed by words that look like prepositions, but are so closely associated with the verb to be part of its meaning. These words are known as particles, and examples include "call off", "look up", and "drop off".

The main verb of a sentence is always one that would change form from base form to past tense, past participle, present participle and, -s forms. When both the past-tense and past-participle forms of a verb end in "ed", the verb is regular. In all other cases the verb is irregular. The verb "be" is highly irregular, having eight forms instead of the usual five.

- Linking verbs link the subject to a subject complement, a word or word group that completes the meaning of the subject by renaming or describing it.
- A transitive verb takes a direct object, a word or word group that names a receiver of the action. The direct object of a transitive verb is sometimes preceded by an indirect object. Transitive verbs usually appear in the active voice, with a subject doing the action and a direct object receiving the action. The direct object of a transitive verb is sometimes followed by an object complement, a word or word group that completes the direct object's meaning by renaming or describing it.
- Intransitive verbs take no objects or complements. Their pattern is subject verb.

A dictionary will disclose whether a verb is transitive or intransitive. Some verbs have both transitive and intransitive functions.

78

VERB PHRASES

A verbal phrase is a verb form that does not function as the verb of a clause. There are three major types of verbal phrases:

1. Participial phrases - These always function as adjectives. Their verbals are always present participles, always ending in "ing", or past participles frequently ending in "-d,-ed,-n.-en,or -t". Participial phrases frequently appear immediately following the noun or pronoun they modify.
2. Gerund phrases - Gerund phrases are built around present participles and they always function as nouns. : usually as subjects subject complements, direct objects, or objects of a preposition.
3. Infinitive phrases are usually structured around "to" plus the base form of the verb. They can function as nouns, as adjectives, or as adverbs. When functioning as a noun, an infinitive phrase may appear in almost any noun slot in a sentence, usually as a subject, subject complement, or direct object. Infinitive phrases functioning as adjectives usually appear immediately following the noun or pronoun they modify. adverbial phrases usually qualify the meaning of the verb.

PROBLEMS WITH VERBS

The verb is the heart of the sentence. Verbs have several potential problems including:

- Irregular verbs - Verbs that do not follow usual grammatical rules.
- Tense - Tenses indicate the time of an action in relation to the time of speaking or writing about the action.
- Mood - There are three moods in English: the indicative, used for facts, opinions, and questions; the imperative, used for orders or advice, and the subjunctive, used for wishes. The subjective mood is the most likely to cause problems. The subjective mood is used for wishes, and in "if"clauses expressing conditions contrary to facts. The subjective in such cases is the past tense form of the verb; in the case of "be", it is always "were", even if the subject is singular. The subjective mood is also used in "that' clauses following verbs such as "ask, insist, recommend, and request. The subjunctive in such cases is the base or dictionary form of the verb.

ADJECTIVES

An adjective is a word use to modify or describe a noun or pronoun. An adjective usually answers one of these question: "Which one?, What kind of?, and How many?" Adjectives usually precede the words they modify, although they sometimes follow linking verbs, in which case they describe the subject. Most adjectives have three forms: the positive, the comparative, and the superlative. The comparative should be used to compare two things, the superlative to compare three or more things.

> **Review Video: What is an Adjective?**
> Visit mometrix.com/academy and enter code: 470154

ARTICLES

Articles, sometimes classed as adjectives, are used to mark nouns. There are only three: the definite article "the" and the indefinite articles "a" and "an."

79

ADVERBS

An adverb is a word used to modify or qualify a verb, adjective, or another adverb. It usually answers one of these questions: "When?, where?, how?, and why?" Adverbs modifying adjectives or other adverbs usually intensify or limit the intensity of words they modify. The negators "not" and "never" are classified as adverbs. Writers sometimes misuse adverbs, and multilingual speakers have trouble placing them correctly. Most adverbs also have three forms: the positive, the comparative, and the superlative. The comparative should be used to compare two things, the superlative to compare three or more things.

> **Review Video: Adverbs**
> Visit mometrix.com/academy and enter code: 713951

PREPOSITIONS

A preposition is a word placed before a noun or pronoun to form a phrase modifying another word in the sentence. The prepositional phrase usually functions as an adjective or adverb. There are a limited number of prepositions in English, perhaps around 80. Some prepositions are more than one word long. "Along with", "listen to", and "next to" are some examples.

> **Review Video: What is a Preposition?**
> Visit mometrix.com/academy and enter code: 946763

CONJUNCTIONS

Conjunctions join words, phrases, or clauses, and they indicate the relationship between the elements that are joined. There are coordinating conjunctions that connect grammatically equal element, correlative conjunctions that connect pairs, subordinating conjunctions that introduces a subordinate clause, and conjunctive adverbs which may be used with a semicolon to connect independent clauses. The most common conjunctive adverbs include "then, thus, and however". Using adverbs correctly helps avoid sentence fragments and run-on sentences.

> **Review Video: Coordinating and Correlative Conjunctions**
> Visit mometrix.com/academy and enter code: 390329
>
> **Review Video: Subordinating Conjunctions**
> Visit mometrix.com/academy and enter code: 958913

SUBJECTS

The subject of a sentence names who or what the sentence is about. The complete subject is composed of the simple subject and all of its modifiers.

To find the complete subject, ask "Who" or "What", and insert the verb to complete the question. The answer is the complete subject. To find the simple subject, strip away all the modifiers in the complete subject.

In imperative sentences, the verb's subject is understood but not actually present in the sentence. Although the subject ordinarily comes before the verb, sentences that begin with "There are" or "There was", the subject follows the verb.

The ability to recognize the subject of a sentence helps in editing a variety of problems such as sentence fragments and subject-verb agreement, as well as the choice of pronouns.

> **Review Video: Subjects**
> Visit mometrix.com/academy and enter code: 444771

SUBORDINATE WORD GROUPS

Subordinate word groups cannot stand alone. They function only within sentences, as adjectives, adverbs, or nouns.

- Prepositional phrases begins with a preposition and ends with a noun or noun equivalent called its object. Prepositional phrases function as adjectives or adverbs.
- Subordinate clauses are patterned like sentences, having subject, verbs, and objects or complements. They function within sentences as adverbs, adjectives, or nouns.
- Adjective clauses modify nouns or pronouns and begin with a relative pronoun or relative adverb.
- Adverb clauses modify verbs, adjectives, and other adverbs.
- Noun clauses function as subjects, objects, or complements. In both adjective and noun clauses words may appear out of their normal order. The parts of a noun clause may also appear in their normal order.

APPOSITIVE AND ABSOLUTE PHRASES

Strictly speaking, appositive phrases are not subordinate word groups. Appositive phrases function somewhat as adjectives do, to describe nouns or pronouns. Instead of modifying nouns or pronouns however, appositive phrases rename them. In form they are nouns or nouns equivalents. Appositives are said to be in " in apposition" to the nouns or pronouns they rename. For example, in the sentence "Terriers, hunters at heart, have been dandled up to look like lap dogs", "hunters at heart" is apposition to the noun "terriers".

An absolute phrase modifies a whole clause or sentence, not just one word, and it may appear nearly anywhere in the sentence. It consists of a noun or noun equivalent usually followed by a participial phrase. Both appositive and absolute phrases can cause confusion in their usage in grammatical structures. They are particularly difficult for a person whose first language is not English.

COMMON PROBLEMS WITH SENTENCES

SUBJECT-VERB AGREEMENT

In the present tense, verbs agree with their subjects in number, (singular or plural), and in person, (first ,second, or third). The present tense ending -s is used on a verb if its subject is third person singular; otherwise the verb takes no ending. The verb "be" varies from this pattern, and alone among verbs it has special forms in both the present and past tense.

Problems with subject-verb agreement tend to arise in certain contexts:

- Words between subject and verbs.
- Subjects joined by "and".
- Subjects joined by "or" or "nor".
- Indefinite pronouns such as "someone".
- Collective nouns.

- Subject after verb.
- Who, which, and that.
- Plural form, singular meaning.
- Titles, company names, and words mentioned as words.

SENTENCE FRAGMENTS

As a rule a part of a sentence should not be treated as a complete sentence. A sentence must be composed of at least one full independent clause. An independent clause has a subject, a verb, and can stand alone as a sentence. Some fragments are clauses that contain a subject and a verb, but begin with a subordinating word. Other fragments lack a subject, verb, or both.

A sentence fragment can be repaired by combining the fragment with a nearby sentence, punctuating the new sentence correctly, or turn the fragment into a sentence by adding the missing elements. Some sentence fragments are used by writers for emphasis. Although sentence fragments are sometimes acceptable, readers and writers do not always agree on when they are appropriate. A conservative approach is to write in complete sentences only unless a special circumstance dictates otherwise.

RUN-ON SENTENCES

Run-on sentences are independent clauses that have not been joined correctly. An independent clause is a word group that does or could stand alone in a sentence. When two or more independent clauses appear in one sentence, they must be joined in one of these ways:

- Revision with a comma and a coordinating conjunction.
- Revision with a semicolon, a colon, or a dash. Used when independent clauses are closely related and their relationship is clear without a coordinating conjunction.
- Revision by separating sentences. This approach may be used when both independent clauses are long,
- or if one is a question and one is not. Separate sentences may be the best option in this case.
- Revision by restructuring the sentence. For sentence variety, consider restructuring the sentence, perhaps by turning one of the independent clauses into a subordinate phrase or clause.

Usually one of these choices will be an obvious solution to the run-on sentence. The fourth technique above is often the most effective solution, but requires the most revision.

DOUBLE NEGATIVES

Standard English allows two negatives only if a positive meaning is intended. "The team was not displeased with their performance" is an example. Double negatives used to emphasize negation are nonstandard.

Negative modifiers such as "never, no, and not" should not be paired with other negative modifiers or negative words such as " none, nobody, nothing, or neither". The modifiers "hardly, barely, and scarcely" are also considered negatives in standard English, so they should not be used with other negatives such as "not, no one, or never".

DOUBLE SUPERLATIVES

Do not use double superlatives or comparatives. When "er" or "est" has been added to an adjective or adverb, avoid using "more" or "most". Avoid expressions such as "more perfect", and "very round". Either something is or is not. It is not logical to suggest that absolute concepts come in degrees. Use the comparative to compare two things, and the superlative to compare three or more things.

PUNCTUATION

COMMAS

The comma was invented to help readers. Without it, sentence parts can run together, making meanings unclear. Various rules for comma use include:

- Use a comma before a coordinating conjunction joining independent clauses.
- Use a comma after an introductory clause or phrase.
- Use a comma between items in a series.
- Use a comma between coordinate adjectives not joined with "and". Do not use a comma between cumulative adjectives.
- Use commas to set off nonrestrictive elements. Do not use commas to set off restrictive elements.
- Use commas to set off transitional and parenthetical expressions, absolute phrases, and elements expressing contrast.
- Use commas to set off nouns of direct address, the words yes and no, interrogative tags, and interjections.
- Use commas with dates, addresses, titles, and numbers.

Some situations where commas are unnecessary include:

- Do not use a comma between compound elements that are not independent clauses.
- Do not use a comma after a phrase that begins with an inverted sentence.
- Do not use a comma between the first or after the last item in a series or before the word "although".
- Do not use a comma between cumulative adjectives, between an adjective and a noun, or between an adverb and an adjective.
- Do not use commas to set off restrictive or mildly parenthetical elements or to set off an indirect quotation.
- Do not use a comma to set off a concluding adverb clause that is essential to the meaning of the sentence or after the word "although".
- Do not use a comma to separate a verb from its subject or object. Do not use a comma after a coordinating conjunction or before a parenthesis.
- Do not use a comma with a question mark or an exclamation point.
- Use commas to prevent confusion.
- Use commas to set off direct quotations.

Review Video: Commas
Visit mometrix.com/academy and enter code: 786797

SEMICOLONS

The semicolon is used to connect major sentence elements of equal grammatical rank. Some rules regarding semicolons include:

- Use a semicolon between closely related independent clauses not joined with a coordinating conjunction.
- Use a semicolon between independent clauses linked with a transitional expression.
- Use a semicolon between items in a series containing internal punctuation.
- Avoid using a semicolon between a subordinate clause and the rest of the sentence.
- Avoid using a semicolon between an appositive word and the word it refers to.
- Avoid using a semicolon to introduce a list.
- Avoid using a semicolon between independent clauses joined by "and, but, or, nor, for, so, or yet".

> **Review Video: Semicolon Usage**
> Visit mometrix.com/academy and enter code: 370605

COLONS

The colon is used primarily to call attention to the words that follow it. In addition the colon has some other conventional uses:

- Use a colon after an independent clause to direct attention to a list, an appositive, or a quotation.
- Use a colon between independent clauses if the second summarizes or explains the first.
- Use a colon after the salutation in a formal letter, to indicate hours and minutes, to show proportions between a title and subtitle, and between city and publisher in bibliographic entries.

A colon must be preceded by a full independent clause. Avoid using colons in the following situations:

- Avoid using a colon between a verb and its object or complement.
- Avoid using a colon between a preposition and its object.
- Avoid using a colon after "such as, including, or for example."

APOSTROPHES

An apostrophe is used to indicate that a noun is possessive. Possessive nouns usually indicate ownership, as in Bill's coat or the dog's biscuit. Sometimes ownership is only loosely implied, as in the dog's coat or the forest's trees. If it is unclear whether a noun is possessive, turning into phrase may clarify it.

If the noun is plural and ends in-s, add only an apostrophe. To show joint possession, use -'s with the last noun only. To show individual possession, make all nouns possessive.

An apostrophe is often optional in plural numbers, letters, abbreviations, and words mentioned as words.

Common errors in using apostrophes include:

- Do not use an apostrophe with nouns that are not possessive.
- Do not use an apostrophe in the possessive pronouns "its, whose, his, hers, ours, yours, and theirs".

Review Video: Apostrophes
Visit mometrix.com/academy and enter code: 213068

QUOTATION MARKS

Use quotation marks to enclose direct quotations of a person's words, spoken or written. Do not use quotation marks around indirect quotations. An indirect quotation reports someone's ideas without using that person's exact words.

Set off long quotations of prose or poetry by indenting. Use single quotation marks to enclose a quotation within a quotation. Quotation marks should be used around the titles of short works: newspaper and magazine articles, poems, short stories, songs, episodes of television and radio programs, and subdivisions of books or web sites.

Quotation marks may be used to set off words used as words. Punctuation is used with quotation marks according to convention. Periods and commas are placed inside quotation marks, while colons and semicolons are placed outside quotation marks. Question marks and exclamation points are placed inside quotation marks.

Do not use quotation marks around the title of your own essay.

Review Video: Quotation Marks
Visit mometrix.com/academy and enter code: 884918

DASHES

When typing, use two hyphens to form a dash. Do not put spaces before or after the dash. Dashes are used for the following purposes:

- To set off parenthetical material that deserves emphasis.
- To set off appositives that contain commas.
- To prepare for a list, a restatement, an amplification, or a dramatic shift in tone or thought.

Unless there is a specific reason for using the dash, omit it. It can give text a choppy effect.

PARENTHESES

Parentheses are used to enclose supplemental material, minor digressions, and afterthoughts. They are also used to enclose letters or numbers labeling them items in a series. Parentheses should be used sparingly, as they break up text in a distracting manner when overused.

BRACKETS

Brackets are used to enclose any words or phrases that have been inserted into an otherwise word-for-word quotation.

ELLIPSIS MARKS

The ellipsis mark consists of three spaced periods (...), and is used to indicate when certain words have been deleted from an otherwise word-for-word quotation. If a full sentence or more is deleted

in the middle of quoted passage, a person should be inserted before the ellipsis dots. The ellipsis mark should not be used at the beginning of a quotation. It should also not be used at the end of a quotation unless some words have been deleted from the end of the final sentence.

SLASHES

The slash, (/), may be used to separate two or three lines of poetry that have been run into a text. If there are more than three lines of poetry they should be handled as an indented quotation. The slash may occasionally be used to separate paired terms such as passed/failed or either/or. In this case, apace is not placed before or after the slash. The slash should be used sparingly, only when it is clearly appropriate.

END PUNCTUATIONS

- Use a period to end all sentences except direct questions or genuine exclamations. Periods should be used in abbreviations according to convention. Problems can arise when there is a choice between a period and a question mark or exclamation point. If a sentence reports a question rather than asking it directly, it should end with a period, not a question mark.
- Question marks should be used following a direct question. If a polite request is written in the form of a question, it may be followed by a period. Questions in a series may be followed by question marks even when they are not in complete sentences.
- Exclamation marks are used after a word group or sentence that expresses exceptional feeling or deserves special emphasis. Exclamation marks should not be overused, being reserved for appropriate exclamatory interjections.

ESSAYS

Essays are generally defined to describe a prose composition, relatively brief (rarely exceeding 25 pages), dealing with a specific topic. Originally, essays tended to be informal in tone and exploratory and tentative in approach and conclusions. In more modern writing, essays have divided into the formal and informal. The formal essays have dominated the professional and scientific fields, while the informal style is written primarily to entertain or give opinions. Writers should be mindful of the style of essay their subject lends itself to, and conform to the conventions of that style.

Some types of essays, particularly scientific and academic writing, have style manuals to guide the format and conventions of the writing. The Modern Language Association and the American Psychological Association have two of the most widely followed style manuals. They are widely available for writers' reference.

Mathematics

CLASSIFICATIONS OF NUMBERS

Numbers are the basic building blocks of mathematics. Specific features of numbers are identified by the following terms:

Integer – any positive or negative whole number, including zero. Integers do not include fractions $\left(\frac{1}{3}\right)$, decimals (0.56), or mixed numbers $\left(7\frac{3}{4}\right)$.

Prime number – any whole number greater than 1 that has only two factors, itself and 1; that is, a number that can be divided evenly only by 1 and itself.

Composite number – any whole number greater than 1 that has more than two different factors; in other words, any whole number that is not a prime number. For example: The composite number 8 has the factors of 1, 2, 4, and 8.

Even number – any integer that can be divided by 2 without leaving a remainder. For example: 2, 4, 6, 8, and so on.

Odd number – any integer that cannot be divided evenly by 2. For example: 3, 5, 7, 9, and so on.

Decimal number – any number that uses a decimal point to show the part of the number that is less than one. Example: 1.234.

Decimal point – a symbol used to separate the ones place from the tenths place in decimals or dollars from cents in currency.

Decimal place – the position of a number to the right of the decimal point. In the decimal 0.123, the 1 is in the first place to the right of the decimal point, indicating tenths; the 2 is in the second place, indicating hundredths; and the 3 is in the third place, indicating thousandths.

The **decimal**, or base 10, system is a number system that uses ten different digits (0, 1, 2, 3, 4, 5, 6, 7, 8, 9). An example of a number system that uses something other than ten digits is the **binary**, or base 2, number system, used by computers, which uses only the numbers 0 and 1. It is thought that the decimal system originated because people had only their 10 fingers for counting.

Rational numbers include all integers, decimals, and fractions. Any terminating or repeating decimal number is a rational number.

Irrational numbers cannot be written as fractions or decimals because the number of decimal places is infinite and there is no recurring pattern of digits within the number. For example, pi (π) begins with 3.141592 and continues without terminating or repeating, so pi is an irrational number.

Real numbers are the set of all rational and irrational numbers.

> **Review Video: Numbers and Their Classifications**
> Visit mometrix.com/academy and enter code: 461071

87

PLACE VALUE

WRITE THE PLACE VALUE OF EACH DIGIT IN THE FOLLOWING NUMBER: 14,059.826

1: ten-thousands
4: thousands
0: hundreds
5: tens
9: ones
8: tenths
2: hundredths
6: thousandths

Review Video: Number Place Value
Visit mometrix.com/academy and enter code: 205433

WRITING NUMBERS IN WORD FORM

EXAMPLE 1

Write each number in words.

29: twenty-nine
478: four hundred seventy-eight
9,435: nine thousand four hundred thirty-five
98,542: ninety-eight thousand five hundred forty-two
302, 876: three hundred two thousand eight hundred seventy-six

EXAMPLE 2

Write each decimal in words.

0.06: six hundredths
0.6: six tenths
6.0: six
0.009: nine thousandths
0.113: one hundred thirteen thousandths
0.901: nine hundred one thousandths

ROUNDING AND ESTIMATION

Rounding is reducing the digits in a number while still trying to keep the value similar. The result will be less accurate, but will be in a simpler form, and will be easier to use. Whole numbers can be rounded to the nearest ten, hundred or thousand.

EXAMPLE 1

Round each number:

1. Round each number to the nearest ten: 11, 47, 118
2. Round each number to the nearest hundred: 78, 980, 248
3. Round each number to the nearest thousand: 302, 1274, 3756

ANSWER

1. Remember, when rounding to the nearest ten, anything ending in 5 or greater rounds up. So, 11 rounds to 10, 47 rounds to 50, and 118 rounds to 120.
2. Remember, when rounding to the nearest hundred, anything ending in 50 or greater rounds up. So, 78 rounds to 100, 980 rounds to 1000, and 248 rounds to 200.
3. Remember, when rounding to the nearest thousand, anything ending in 500 or greater rounds up. So, 302 rounds to 0, 1274 rounds to 1000, and 3756 rounds to 4000.

When you are asked to estimate the solution a problem, you will need to provide only an approximate figure or **estimation** for your answer. In this situation, you will need to round each number in the calculation to the level indicated (nearest hundred, nearest thousand, etc.) or to a level that makes sense for the numbers involved. When estimating a sum **all numbers must be rounded to the same level**. You cannot round one number to the nearest thousand while rounding another to the nearest hundred.

EXAMPLE 2

Estimate the solution to 345,932 + 96,369 by rounding each number to the nearest ten thousand.

Start by rounding each number to the nearest ten thousand: 345,932 becomes 350,000, and 96,369 becomes 100,000.

Then, add the rounded numbers: 350,000 + 100,000 = 450,000. So, the answer is approximately 450,000.

The exact answer would be 345,932 + 96,369 = 442,301. So, the estimate of 450,000 is a similar value to the exact answer.

EXAMPLE 3

A runner's heart beats 422 times over the course of six minutes. About how many times did the runner's heart beat during each minute?

"About how many" indicates that you need to estimate the solution. In this case, look at the numbers you are given. 422 can be rounded down to 420, which is easily divisible by 6. A good estimate is 420 ÷ 6 = 70 beats per minute. More accurately, the patient's heart rate was just over 70 beats per minute since his heart actually beat a little more than 420 times in six minutes.

> **Review Video: Rounding and Estimation**
> Visit mometrix.com/academy and enter code: 126243

MEASUREMENT CONVERSION

When going from a larger unit to a smaller unit, multiply the number of the known amount by the **equivalent amount**. When going from a smaller unit to a larger unit, divide the number of the known amount by the equivalent amount.

Also, you can set up conversion fractions. In these fractions, one fraction is the **conversion factor**. The other fraction has the unknown amount in the numerator. So, the known value is placed in the denominator. Sometimes the second fraction has the known value from the problem in the numerator, and the unknown in the denominator. Multiply the two fractions to get the converted measurement.

CONVERSION UNITS

METRIC CONVERSIONS

1000 mcg (microgram)	1 mg
1000 mg (milligram)	1 g
1000 g (gram)	1 kg
1000 kg (kilogram)	1 metric ton
1000 mL (milliliter)	1 L
1000 um (micrometer)	1 mm
1000 mm (millimeter)	1 m
100 cm (centimeter)	1 m
1000 m (meter)	1 km

U.S. AND METRIC EQUIVALENTS

Unit	U.S. equivalent	Metric equivalent
Inch	1 inch	2.54 centimeters
Foot	12 inches	0.305 meters
Yard	3 feet	0.914 meters
Mile	5280 feet	1.609 kilometers

CAPACITY MEASUREMENTS

Unit	U.S. equivalent	Metric equivalent
Ounce	8 drams	29.573 milliliters
Cup	8 ounces	0.237 liter
Pint	16 ounces	0.473 liter
Quart	2 pints	0.946 liter
Gallon	4 quarts	3.785 liters

WEIGHT MEASUREMENTS

Unit	U.S. equivalent	Metric equivalent
Ounce	16 drams	28.35 grams
Pound	16 ounces	453.6 grams
Ton	2,000 pounds	907.2 kilograms

FLUID MEASUREMENTS

Unit	English equivalent	Metric equivalent
1 tsp	1 fluid dram	5 milliliters
3 tsp	4 fluid drams	15 or 16 milliliters
2 tbsp	1 fluid ounce	30 milliliters
1 glass	8 fluid ounces	240 milliliters

MEASUREMENT CONVERSION PRACTICE PROBLEMS

EXAMPLE 1

a. Convert 1.4 meters to centimeters.
b. Convert 218 centimeters to meters.

90

EXAMPLE 2

a. Convert 42 inches to feet.
b. Convert 15 feet to yards.

EXAMPLE 3

a. How many pounds are in 15 kilograms?
b. How many pounds are in 80 ounces?

EXAMPLE 4

a. How many kilometers are in 2 miles?
b. How many centimeters are in 5 feet?

EXAMPLE 5

a. How many gallons are in 15.14 liters?
b. How many liters are in 8 quarts?

EXAMPLE 6

a. How many grams are in 13.2 pounds?
b. How many pints are in 9 gallons?

MEASUREMENT CONVERSION PRACTICE SOLUTIONS

EXAMPLE 1

Write ratios with the conversion factor $\frac{100 \text{ cm}}{1 \text{ m}}$. Use proportions to convert the given units.

a. $\frac{100 \text{ cm}}{1 \text{ m}} = \frac{x \text{ cm}}{1.4 \text{ m}}$. Cross multiply to get $x = 140$. So, 1.4 m is the same as 140 cm.

b. $\frac{100 \text{ cm}}{1 \text{ m}} = \frac{218 \text{ cm}}{x \text{ m}}$. Cross multiply to get $100x = 218$, or $x = 2.18$. So, 218 cm is the same as 2.18 m.

EXAMPLE 2

Write ratios with the conversion factors $\frac{12 \text{ in}}{1 \text{ ft}}$ and $\frac{3 \text{ ft}}{1 \text{ yd}}$. Use proportions to convert the given units.

a. $\frac{12 \text{ in}}{1 \text{ ft}} = \frac{42 \text{ in}}{x \text{ ft}}$. Cross multiply to get $12x = 42$, or $x = 3.5$. So, 42 inches is the same as 3.5 feet.

b. $\frac{3 \text{ ft}}{1 \text{ yd}} = \frac{15 \text{ ft}}{x \text{ yd}}$. Cross multiply to get $3x = 15$, or $x = 5$. So, 15 feet is the same as 5 yards.

EXAMPLE 3

a. 15 kilograms $\times \frac{2.2 \text{ pounds}}{1 \text{ kilogram}} = 33$ pounds

b. 80 ounces $\times \frac{1 \text{ pound}}{16 \text{ ounces}} = 5$ pounds

EXAMPLE 4

a. 2 miles $\times \frac{1.609 \text{ kilometers}}{1 \text{ mile}} = 3.218$ kilometers

b. 5 feet $\times \frac{12 \text{ inches}}{1 \text{ foot}} \times \frac{2.54 \text{ centimeters}}{1 \text{ inch}} = 152.4$ centimeters

91

EXAMPLE 5

a. $15.14 \text{ liters} \times \frac{1 \text{ gallon}}{3.785 \text{ liters}} = 4 \text{ gallons}$

b. $8 \text{ quarts} \times \frac{1 \text{ gallon}}{4 \text{ quarts}} \times \frac{3.785 \text{ liters}}{1 \text{ gallon}} = 7.57 \text{ liters}$

EXAMPLE 6

a. $13.2 \text{ pounds} \times \frac{1 \text{ kilogram}}{2.2 \text{ pounds}} \times \frac{1000 \text{ grams}}{1 \text{ kilogram}} = 6000 \text{ grams}$

b. $9 \text{ gallons} \times \frac{4 \text{ quarts}}{1 \text{ gallon}} \times \frac{2 \text{ pints}}{1 \text{ quarts}} = 72 \text{ pints}$

OPERATIONS

There are four basic mathematical operations:

ADDITION AND SUBTRACTION

Addition increases the value of one quantity by the value of another quantity. Example: $2 + 4 = 6$; $8 + 9 = 17$. The result is called the **sum**. With addition, the order does not matter. $4 + 2 = 2 + 4$.

Subtraction is the opposite operation to addition; it decreases the value of one quantity by the value of another quantity. Example: $6 - 4 = 2$; $17 - 8 = 9$. The result is called the **difference**. Note that with subtraction, the order does matter. $6 - 4 \neq 4 - 6$.

> **Review Video: <u>Addition and Subtraction</u>**
> Visit mometrix.com/academy and enter code: 521157

MULTIPLICATION AND DIVISION

Multiplication can be thought of as repeated addition. One number tells how many times to add the other number to itself. Example: 3×2 (three times two) $= 2 + 2 + 2 = 6$. With multiplication, the order does not matter. $2 \times 3 = 3 \times 2$ or $3 + 3 = 2 + 2 + 2$.

Division is the opposite operation to multiplication; one number tells us how many parts to divide the other number into. Example: $20 \div 4 = 5$; if 20 is split into 4 equal parts, each part is 5. With division, the order of the numbers does matter. $20 \div 4 \neq 4 \div 20$.

> **Review Video: <u>Multiplication and Division</u>**
> Visit mometrix.com/academy and enter code: 643326

ORDER OF OPERATIONS

Order of operations is a set of rules that dictates the order in which we must perform each operation in an expression so that we will evaluate it accurately. If we have an expression that includes multiple different operations, order of operations tells us which operations to do first. The most common mnemonic for order of operations is **PEMDAS**, or "Please Excuse My Dear Aunt Sally." PEMDAS stands for parentheses, exponents, multiplication, division, addition, and subtraction. It is important to understand that multiplication and division have equal precedence, as do addition and subtraction, so those pairs of operations are simply worked from left to right in order.

Example: Evaluate the expression $5 + 20 \div 4 \times (2 + 3) - 6$ using the correct order of operations.

- **P:** Perform the operations inside the parentheses: $(2 + 3) = 5$
- **E:** Simplify the exponents.
  - The equation now looks like this: $5 + 20 \div 4 \times 5 - 6$
- **MD:** Perform multiplication and division from left to right: $20 \div 4 = 5$; then $5 \times 5 = 25$
  - The equation now looks like this: $5 + 25 - 6$
- **AS:** Perform addition and subtraction from left to right: $5 + 25 = 30$; then $30 - 6 = 24$

> **Review Video: <u>Order of Operations</u>**
> Visit mometrix.com/academy and enter code: 259675

SUBTRACTION WITH REGROUPING

EXAMPLE 1

Demonstrate how to subtract 189 from 525 using regrouping.

First, set up the subtraction problem:

$$\begin{array}{r} 525 \\ -\ 189 \\ \hline \end{array}$$

Notice that the numbers in the ones and tens columns of 525 are smaller than the numbers in the ones and tens columns of 189. This means you will need to use regrouping to perform subtraction:

$$\begin{array}{ccc} 5 & 2 & 5 \\ - \quad 1 & 8 & 9 \\ \hline \end{array}$$

To subtract 9 from 5 in the ones column you will need to borrow from the 2 in the tens columns:

$$\begin{array}{ccc} 5 & 1 & 15 \\ - \quad 1 & 8 & 9 \\ \hline & & 6 \end{array}$$

Next, to subtract 8 from 1 in the tens column you will need to borrow from the 5 in the hundreds column:

$$\begin{array}{ccc} 4 & 11 & 15 \\ - \quad 1 & 8 & 9 \\ \hline & 3 & 6 \end{array}$$

Last, subtract the 1 from the 4 in the hundreds column:

$$\begin{array}{ccc} 4 & 11 & 15 \\ - \quad 1 & 8 & 9 \\ \hline 3 & 3 & 6 \end{array}$$

EXAMPLE 2

Demonstrate how to subtract 477 from 620 using regrouping.

First, set up the subtraction problem:

```
   620
 − 477
```

Notice that the numbers in the ones and tens columns of 620 are smaller than the numbers in the ones and tens columns of 477. This means you will need to use regrouping to perform subtraction:

```
   6   2   0
 − 4   7   7
```

To subtract 7 from 0 in the ones column you will need to borrow from the 2 in the tens column:

```
   6   1  10
 − 4   7   7
           3
```

Next, to subtract 7 from the 1 that's still in the tens column you will need to borrow from the 6 in the hundreds column:

```
   5  11  10
 − 4   7   7
       4   3
```

Lastly, subtract 4 from the 5 remaining in the hundreds column:

```
   5  11  10
 − 4   7   7
   1   4   3
```

REAL WORLD ONE OR MULTI-STEP PROBLEMS WITH RATIONAL NUMBERS

EXAMPLE 1

A woman's age is thirteen more than half of 60. How old is the woman?

"More than" indicates addition, and "of" indicates multiplication. The expression can be written as $\frac{1}{2}(60) + 13$. So, the woman's age is equal to $\frac{1}{2}(60) + 13 = 30 + 13 = 43$. The woman is 43 years old.

EXAMPLE 2

A patient was given pain medicine at a dosage of 0.22 grams. The patient's dosage was then increased to 0.80 grams. By how much was the patient's dosage increased?

The first step is to determine what operation (addition, subtraction, multiplication, or division) the problem requires. Notice the keywords and phrases "by how much" and "increased." "Increased" means that you go from a smaller amount to a larger amount. This change can be found by subtracting the smaller amount from the larger amount: 0.80 grams− 0.22 grams = 0.58 grams.

Remember to line up the decimal when subtracting:

$$\begin{array}{r} 0.80 \\ -\ 0.22 \\ \hline 0.58 \end{array}$$

EXAMPLE 3

At a hotel, $\frac{3}{4}$ of the 100 rooms are occupied today. Yesterday, $\frac{4}{5}$ of the 100 rooms were occupied. On which day were more of the rooms occupied and by how much more?

First, find the number of rooms occupied each day. To do so, multiply the fraction of rooms occupied by the number of rooms available:

$$\text{Number occupied} = \text{Fraction occupied} \times \text{Total number}$$

Today:

$$\text{Number of rooms occupied today} = \frac{3}{4} \times 100 = 75$$

Today, 75 rooms are occupied.

Yesterday:

$$\text{Number of rooms occupied} = \frac{4}{5} \times 100 = 80$$

Yesterday, 80 rooms were occupied.

The difference in the number of rooms occupied is

$$80 - 75 = 5 \text{ rooms}$$

Therefore, five more rooms were occupied yesterday than today.

> **Review Video: Rational Numbers**
> Visit mometrix.com/academy and enter code: 280645

EXAMPLE 4

At a school, 40% of the teachers teach English. If 20 teachers teach English, how many teachers work at the school?

To answer this problem, first think about the number of teachers that work at the school. Will it be more or less than the number of teachers who work in a specific department such as English? More teachers work at the school, so the number you find to answer this question will be greater than 20.

40% of the teachers are English teachers. "Of" indicates multiplication, and words like "is" and "are" indicate equivalence. Translating the problem into a mathematical sentence gives $40\% \times t = 20$, where t represents the total number of teachers. Solving for t gives $t = \frac{20}{40\%} = \frac{20}{0.40} = 50$. Fifty teachers work at the school.

EXAMPLE 5

A patient was given blood pressure medicine at a dosage of 2 grams. The patient's dosage was then decreased to 0.45 grams. By how much was the patient's dosage decreased?

The decrease is represented by the difference between the two amounts:

$$2 \text{ grams} - 0.45 \text{ grams} = 1.55 \text{ grams}.$$

Remember to line up the decimal point before subtracting.

$$
\begin{array}{r}
2.00 \\
- \quad 0.45 \\
\hline
1.55
\end{array}
$$

EXAMPLE 6

Two weeks ago, $\frac{2}{3}$ of the 60 customers at a skate shop were male. Last week, $\frac{3}{6}$ of the 80 customers were male. During which week were there more male customers?

First, you need to find the number of male customers that were in the skate shop each week. You are given this amount in terms of fractions. To find the actual number of male customers, multiply the fraction of male customers by the number of customers in the store.

Actual number of male customers = fraction of male customers × total number of customers.

Number of male customers two weeks ago $= \frac{2}{3} \times 60 = \frac{120}{3} = 40$.

Number of male customers last week $= \frac{3}{6} \times 80 = \frac{1}{2} \times 80 = \frac{80}{2} = 40$.

The number of male customers was the same both weeks.

EXAMPLE 7

Jane ate lunch at a local restaurant. She ordered a $4.99 appetizer, a $12.50 entrée, and a $1.25 soda. If she wants to tip her server 20%, how much money will she spend in all?

To find total amount, first find the sum of the items she ordered from the menu and then add 20% of this sum to the total.

$$\$4.99 + \$12.50 + \$1.25 = \$18.74$$
$$\$18.74 \times 20\% = (0.20)(\$18.74) = \$3.748 \approx \$3.75$$
$$\text{Total} = \$18.74 + \$3.75 = \$22.49.$$

Another way to find this sum is to multiply 120% by the cost of the meal.

$$\$18.74(120\%) = \$18.74(1.20) = \$22.49.$$

PARENTHESES

Parentheses are used to designate which operations should be done first when there are multiple operations. Example: $4 - (2 + 1) = 1$; the parentheses tell us that we must add 2 and 1, and then

subtract the sum from 4, rather than subtracting 2 from 4 and then adding 1 (this would give us an answer of 3).

EXPONENTS

An **exponent** is a superscript number placed next to another number at the top right. It indicates how many times the base number is to be multiplied by itself. Exponents provide a shorthand way to write what would be a longer mathematical expression. Example: $a^2 = a \times a$; $2^4 = 2 \times 2 \times 2 \times 2$. A number with an exponent of 2 is said to be "squared," while a number with an exponent of 3 is said to be "cubed." The value of a number raised to an exponent is called its power. So, 8^4 is read as "8 to the 4th power," or "8 raised to the power of 4." A negative exponent is the same as the **reciprocal** of a positive exponent. Example: $a^{-2} = \frac{1}{a^2}$.

ROOTS

A **root**, such as a square root, is another way of writing a fractional exponent. Instead of using a superscript, roots use the radical symbol ($\sqrt{}$) to indicate the operation. A radical will have a number underneath the bar, and may sometimes have a number in the upper left: $\sqrt[n]{a}$, read as "the nth root of a." The relationship between radical notation and exponent notation can be described by this equation: $\sqrt[n]{a} = a^{\frac{1}{n}}$. The two special cases of $n = 2$ and $n = 3$ are called square roots and cube roots. If there is no number to the upper left, it is understood to be a square root ($n = 2$). Nearly all of the roots you encounter will be square roots. A square root is the same as a number raised to the one-half power. When we say that a is the square root of b ($a = \sqrt{b}$), we mean that a multiplied by itself equals b: ($a \times a = b$).

A **perfect square** is a number that has an integer for its square root. There are 10 perfect squares from 1 to 100: 1, 4, 9, 16, 25, 36, 49, 64, 81, 100 (the squares of integers 1 through 10).

ABSOLUTE VALUE

A precursor to working with negative numbers is understanding what **absolute values** are. A number's absolute value is simply the distance away from zero a number is on the number line. The absolute value of a number is always positive and is written $|x|$.

EXAMPLE

Show that $|3| = |-3|$.

The absolute value of 3, written as $|3|$, is 3 because the distance between 0 and 3 on a number line is three units. Likewise, the absolute value of –3, written as $|-3|$, is 3 because the distance between 0 and -3 on a number line is three units. So, $|3| = |-3|$.

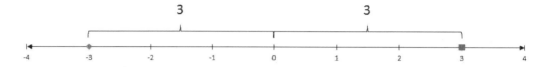

OPERATIONS WITH POSITIVE AND NEGATIVE NUMBERS

ADDITION

When adding signed numbers, if the signs are the same simply add the absolute values of the addends and apply the original sign to the sum. For example, $(+4) + (+8) = +12$ and $(-4) + (-8) = -12$. When the original signs are different, take the absolute values of the addends and subtract the smaller value from the larger value, then apply the original sign of the larger value to the difference. For instance, $(+4) + (-8) = -4$ and $(-4) + (+8) = +4$.

SUBTRACTION

For subtracting signed numbers, change the sign of the number after the minus symbol and then follow the same rules used for addition. For example, $(+4) - (+8) = (+4) + (-8) = -4$.

MULTIPLICATION

If the signs are the same the product is positive when multiplying signed numbers. For example, $(+4) \times (+8) = +32$ and $(-4) \times (-8) = +32$. If the signs are opposite, the product is negative. For example, $(+4) \times (-8) = -32$ and $(-4) \times (+8) = -32$. When more than two factors are multiplied together, the sign of the product is determined by how many negative factors are present. If there are an odd number of negative factors then the product is negative, whereas an even number of negative factors indicates a positive product. For instance, $(+4) \times (-8) \times (-2) = +64$ and $(-4) \times (-8) \times (-2) = -64$.

DIVISION

The rules for dividing signed numbers are similar to multiplying signed numbers. If the dividend and divisor have the same sign, the quotient is positive. If the dividend and divisor have opposite signs, the quotient is negative. For example, $(-4) \div (+8) = -0.5$.

THE NUMBER LINE

A number line is a graph to see the distance between numbers. Basically, this graph shows the relationship between numbers. So, a number line may have a point for zero and may show negative numbers on the left side of the line. Also, any positive numbers are placed on the right side of the line.

EXAMPLE

Name each point on the number line below:

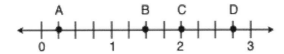

Use the dashed lines on the number line to identify each point. Each dashed line between two whole numbers is $\frac{1}{4}$. The line halfway between two numbers is $\frac{1}{2}$.

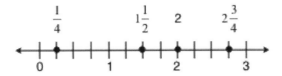

Review Video: Negative and Positive Number Line
Visit mometrix.com/academy and enter code: 816439

FRACTIONS

A **fraction** is a number that is expressed as one integer written above another integer, with a dividing line between them $\left(\frac{x}{y}\right)$. It represents the **quotient** of the two numbers "x divided by y." It can also be thought of as x out of y equal parts.

The top number of a fraction is called the **numerator**, and it represents the number of parts under consideration. The 1 in $\frac{1}{4}$ means that 1 part out of the whole is being considered in the calculation. The bottom number of a fraction is called the **denominator**, and it represents the total number of equal parts. The 4 in $\frac{1}{4}$ means that the whole consists of 4 equal parts. A fraction cannot have a denominator of zero; this is referred to as "*undefined.*"

Fractions can be manipulated, without changing the value of the fraction, by multiplying or dividing (but not adding or subtracting) both the numerator and denominator by the same number. If you divide both numbers by a common factor, you are **reducing** or simplifying the fraction. Two fractions that have the same value but are expressed differently are known as **equivalent fractions**. For example, $\frac{2}{10}, \frac{3}{15}, \frac{4}{20}$, and $\frac{5}{25}$ are all equivalent fractions. They can also all be reduced or simplified to $\frac{1}{5}$.

When two fractions are manipulated so that they have the same denominator, this is known as finding a **common denominator**. The number chosen to be that common denominator should be the least common multiple of the two original denominators. Example: $\frac{3}{4}$ and $\frac{5}{6}$; the least common multiple of 4 and 6 is 12. Manipulating to achieve the common denominator: $\frac{3}{4} = \frac{9}{12}; \frac{5}{6} = \frac{10}{12}$.

PROPER FRACTIONS AND MIXED NUMBERS

A fraction whose denominator is greater than its numerator is known as a **proper fraction**, while a fraction whose numerator is greater than its denominator is known as an **improper fraction**. Proper fractions have values *less than one* and improper fractions have values *greater than one*.

A **mixed number** is a number that contains both an integer and a fraction. Any improper fraction can be rewritten as a mixed number. Example: $\frac{8}{3} = \frac{6}{3} + \frac{2}{3} = 2 + \frac{2}{3} = 2\frac{2}{3}$. Similarly, any mixed number can be rewritten as an improper fraction. Example: $1\frac{3}{5} = 1 + \frac{3}{5} = \frac{5}{5} + \frac{3}{5} = \frac{8}{5}$.

DECIMALS

DECIMAL ILLUSTRATION

USE A MODEL TO REPRESENT THE DECIMAL: 0.24. WRITE 0.24 AS A FRACTION.

The decimal 0.24 is twenty-four hundredths. One possible model to represent this fraction is to draw 100 pennies, since each penny is worth one-hundredth of a dollar. Draw one hundred circles to represent one hundred pennies. Shade 24 of the pennies to represent the decimal twenty-four hundredths.

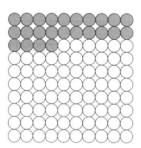

To write the decimal as a fraction, write a fraction: $\frac{\#\text{ shaded spaces}}{\#\text{ total spaces}}$. The number of shaded spaces is 24, and the total number of spaces is 100, so as a fraction 0.24 equals $\frac{24}{100}$. This fraction can then be reduced to $\frac{6}{25}$.

PERCENTAGES

Percentages can be thought of as fractions that are based on a whole of 100; that is, one whole is equal to 100%. The word **percent** means "per hundred." Fractions can be expressed as a percentage by finding equivalent fractions with a denomination of 100. Example: $\frac{7}{10} = \frac{70}{100} = 70\%$; $\frac{1}{4} = \frac{25}{100} = 25\%$.

To express a *percentage as a fraction*, divide the percentage number by 100 and reduce the fraction to its simplest possible terms. Example: $60\% = \frac{60}{100} = \frac{3}{5}$; $96\% = \frac{96}{100} = \frac{24}{25}$.

REAL WORLD PROBLEMS WITH PERCENTAGeS

A percentage problem can be presented three main ways: (1) Find what percentage of some number another number is. Example: What percentage of 40 is 8? (2) Find what number is some percentage of a given number. Example: What number is 20% of 40? (3) Find what number another number is a given percentage of. Example: What number is 8 20% of?

The three components in all of these cases are the same: a **whole** (W), a **part** (P), and a **percentage** (%). These are related by the equation: $P = W \times \%$. This is the form of the equation you would use to solve problems of type (2). To solve types (1) and (3), you would use these two forms:

$$\% = \frac{P}{W} \text{ and } W = \frac{P}{\%}$$

The thing that frequently makes percentage problems difficult is that they are most often also word problems, so a large part of solving them is figuring out which quantities are what. Example: In a school cafeteria, 7 students choose pizza, 9 choose hamburgers, and 4 choose tacos. Find the percentage that chooses tacos. To find the whole, you must first add all of the parts: $7 + 9 + 4 = 20$. The percentage can then be found by dividing the part by the whole ($\% = \frac{P}{W}$): $\frac{4}{20} = \frac{20}{100} = 20\%$.

EXAMPLE 1

What is 30% of 120?

The word *of* indicates multiplication, so 30% of 120 is found by multiplying 120 by 30%. Change 30% to a fraction or decimal, then multiply:

$$30\% = \frac{30}{100} = 0.3$$

$$120 \times 0.3 = 36$$

EXAMPLE 2

What is 150% of 20?

The word *of* indicates multiplication, so 150% of 20 is found by multiplying 20 by 150%. Change 150% to a fraction or decimal, then multiply:

$$150\% = \frac{150}{100} = 1.5$$

$$20 \times 1.5 = 30$$

Notice that 30 is greater than the original number of 20. This makes sense because you are finding a number that is more than 100% of the original number.

EXAMPLE 3

What is 14.5% of 96?

Change 14.5% to a decimal before multiplying. $0.145 \times 96 = 13.92$. Notice that 13.92 is much smaller than the original number of 96. This makes sense because you are finding a small percentage of the original number.

EXAMPLE 4

According to a survey, about 82% of engineers were highly satisfied with their job. If 145 engineers were surveyed, how many reported that they were highly satisfied?

$$82\% \text{ of } 145 = 0.82 \times 145 = 118.9$$

Because you can't have 0.9 of a person, we must round up to say that 119 engineers reported that they were highly satisfied with their jobs.

EXAMPLE 5

On Monday, Lucy spent 5 hours observing sales, 3 hours working on advertising, and 4 hours doing paperwork. On Tuesday, she spent 4 hours observing sales, 6 hours working on advertising, and 2 hours doing paperwork. What was the percent change for time spent on each task between the two days?

The three tasks are observing sales, working on advertising, and doing paperwork. To find the amount of change, compare the first amount with the second amount for each task. Then, write this difference as a percentage compared to the initial amount.

Amount of change for observing sales:

$$5 \text{ hours} - 4 \text{ hours} = 1 \text{ hour}$$

The percent of change is

$$\frac{\text{amount of change}}{\text{original amount}} \times 100\%. \frac{1 \text{ hour}}{5 \text{ hours}} \times 100\% = 20\%.$$

Lucy spent 20% less time observing sales on Tuesday than she did on Monday.

Amount of change for working on advertising:

$$6 \text{ hours} - 3 \text{ hours} = 3 \text{ hours}$$

The percent of change is

$$\frac{\text{amount of change}}{\text{original amount}} \times 100\%. \frac{3 \text{ hours}}{3 \text{ hours}} \times 100\% = 100\%.$$

Lucy spent 100% more time (or twice as much time) working on advertising on Tuesday than she did on Monday.

Amount of change for doing paperwork:

$$4 \text{ hours} - 2 \text{ hours} = 2 \text{ hours}$$

The percent of change is

$$\frac{\text{amount of change}}{\text{original amount}} \times 100\%. \frac{2 \text{ hours}}{4 \text{ hours}} \times 100\% = 50\%.$$

Lucy spent 50% less time (or half as much time) working on paperwork on Tuesday than she did on Monday.

EXAMPLE 6

A patient was given 40 mg of a certain medicine. Later, the patient's dosage was increased to 45 mg. What was the percent increase in his medication?

To find the percent increase, first compare the original and increased amounts. The original amount was 40 mg, and the increased amount is 45 mg, so the dosage of medication was increased by 5 mg ($45 - 40 = 5$). Note, however, that the question asks not by how much the dosage increased but by what percentage it increased. Percent increase $= \frac{\text{new amount} - \text{original amount}}{\text{original amount}} \times 100\%$.

$$\frac{45 \text{ mg} - 40 \text{ mg}}{40 \text{ mg}} \times 100\% = \frac{5}{40} \times 100\% = 0.125 \times 100\% = 12.5\%$$

The percent increase is 12.5%.

EXAMPLE 7

A patient was given 100 mg of a certain medicine. The patient's dosage was later decreased to 88 mg. What was the percent decrease?

The medication was decreased by 12 mg:

$$(100 \text{ mg} - 88 \text{ mg} = 12 \text{ mg})$$

To find by what percent the medication was decreased, this change must be written as a percentage when compared to the original amount.

In other words, $\frac{\text{new amount} - \text{original amount}}{\text{original amount}} \times 100\% = \text{percent change}$

So $\frac{12 \text{ mg}}{100 \text{ mg}} \times 100\% = 0.12 \times 100\% = 12\%$.

The percent decrease is 12%.

EXAMPLE 8

A barista used 125 units of coffee grounds to make a liter of coffee. The barista later reduced the amount of coffee to 100 units. By what percentage was the amount of coffee grounds reduced?

In this problem you must determine which information is necessary to answer the question. The question asks by what percentage the coffee grounds were reduced. Find the two amounts and perform subtraction to find their difference. The first pot of coffee used 125 units. The second time, the barista used 100 units. Therefore, the difference is 125 units − 100 units = 25 units. The percentage reduction can then be calculated as:

$$\frac{\text{change}}{\text{original}} = \frac{25}{125} = \frac{1}{5} = 20\%$$

EXAMPLE 9

In a performance review, an employee received a score of 70 for efficiency and 90 for meeting project deadlines. Six months later, the employee received a score of 65 for efficiency and 96 for meeting project deadlines. What was the percent change for each score on the performance review?

To find the percent change, compare the first amount with the second amount for each score; then, write this difference as a percentage of the initial amount.

Percent change for efficiency score:

$$70 - 65 = 5; \quad \frac{5}{70} \approx 7.1\%$$

The employee's efficiency decreased by about 7.1%.

Percent change for meeting project deadlines score:

$$96 - 90 = 6; \quad \frac{6}{90} \approx 6.7\%$$

The employee increased his ability to meet project deadlines by about 6.7%.

SIMPLIFY

EXAMPLE 1

Simplify the following expression:

$$\frac{\frac{2}{5}}{\frac{4}{7}}$$

Dividing a fraction by a fraction may appear tricky, but it's not if you write out your steps carefully. Follow these steps to divide a fraction by a fraction.

Step 1: Rewrite the problem as a multiplication problem. Dividing by a fraction is the same as multiplying by its **reciprocal**, also known as its **multiplicative inverse**. The product of a number and its reciprocal is 1. Because $\frac{4}{7}$ times $\frac{7}{4}$ is 1, these numbers are reciprocals. Note that reciprocals can be found by simply interchanging the numerators and denominators. So, rewriting the problem as a multiplication problem gives $\frac{2}{5} \times \frac{7}{4}$.

Step 2: Perform multiplication of the fractions by multiplying the numerators by each other and the denominators by each other. In other words, multiply across the top and then multiply across the bottom.

$$\frac{2}{5} \times \frac{7}{4} = \frac{2 \times 7}{5 \times 4} = \frac{14}{20}$$

Step 3: Make sure the fraction is reduced to lowest terms. Both 14 and 20 can be divided by 2.

$$\frac{14}{20} = \frac{14 \div 2}{20 \div 2} = \frac{7}{10}$$

The answer is $\frac{7}{10}$.

EXAMPLE 2

Simplify the following expression:

$$\frac{1}{4} + \frac{3}{6}$$

Fractions with common denominators can be easily added or subtracted. Recall that the denominator is the bottom number in the fraction and that the numerator is the top number in the fraction.

The denominators of $\frac{1}{4}$ and $\frac{3}{6}$ are 4 and 6, respectively. The lowest common denominator of 4 and 6 is 12 because 12 is the least common multiple of 4 (multiples 4, 8, 12, 16, ...) and 6 (multiples 6, 12, 18, 24, ...). Convert each fraction to its equivalent with the newly found common denominator of 12.

$$\frac{1 \times 3}{4 \times 3} = \frac{3}{12}; \frac{3 \times 2}{6 \times 2} = \frac{6}{12}$$

Now that the fractions have the same denominator, you can add them.

$$\frac{3}{12} + \frac{6}{12} = \frac{9}{12}$$

Be sure to write your answer in lowest terms. Both 9 and 12 can be divided by 3, so the answer is $\frac{3}{4}$.

EXAMPLE 3

Simplify the following expression:

$$\frac{7}{8} - \frac{8}{16}$$

The denominators of $\frac{7}{8}$ and $\frac{8}{16}$ are 8 and 16, respectively. The lowest common denominator of 8 and 16 is 16 because 16 is the least common multiple of 8 (multiples 8, 16, 24 ...) and 16 (multiples 16, 32, 48, ...). Convert each fraction to its equivalent with the newly found common denominator of 16.

$$\frac{7 \times 2}{8 \times 2} = \frac{14}{16}; \frac{8 \times 1}{16 \times 1} = \frac{8}{16}$$

Now that the fractions have the same denominator, you can subtract them.

$$\frac{14}{16} - \frac{8}{16} = \frac{6}{16}$$

Be sure to write your answer in lowest terms. Both 6 and 16 can be divided by 2, so the answer is $\frac{3}{8}$.

EXAMPLE 4

Simplify the following expression:

$$\frac{1}{2} + \left(3\left(\frac{3}{4}\right) - 2\right) + 4$$

When simplifying expressions, first perform operations within groups. Within the set of parentheses are multiplication and subtraction operations. Perform the multiplication first to get $\frac{1}{2} + \left(\frac{9}{4} - 2\right) + 4$. Then, subtract two to obtain $\frac{1}{2} + \frac{1}{4} + 4$. Finally, perform addition from left to right:

$$\frac{1}{2} + \frac{1}{4} + 4 = \frac{2}{4} + \frac{1}{4} + \frac{16}{4} = \frac{19}{4}$$

EXAMPLE 5

Simplify the following expression:

$$0.22 + 0.5 - (5.5 + 3.3 \div 3)$$

First, evaluate the terms in the parentheses $(5.5 + 3.3 \div 3)$ using order of operations. $3.3 \div 3 = 1.1$, and $5.5 + 1.1 = 6.6$.

Next, rewrite the problem: $0.22 + 0.5 - 6.6$.

Finally, add and subtract from left to right: $0.22 + 0.5 = 0.72; 0.72 - 6.6 = -5.88$. The answer is -5.88.

EXAMPLE 6

Simplify the following expression:

$$\frac{3}{2} + (4(0.5) - 0.75) + 2$$

First, simplify within the parentheses:

$$\frac{3}{2} + (2 - 0.75) + 2 =$$
$$\frac{3}{2} + 1.25 + 2$$

Finally, change the fraction to a decimal and perform addition from left to right:

$$1.5 + 1.25 + 2 = 4.75$$

EXAMPLE 7

Simplify the following expression:

$$1.45 + 1.5 + (6 - 9 \div 2) + 45$$

First, evaluate the terms in the parentheses using proper order of operations.

$$1.45 + 1.5 + (6 - 4.5) + 45$$
$$1.45 + 1.5 + 1.5 + 45$$

Finally, add from left to right.

$$1.45 + 1.5 + 1.5 + 45 = 49.45$$

CONVERTING PERCENTAGES, FRACTIONS, AND DECIMALS

Converting decimals to percentages and percentages to decimals is as simple as moving the decimal point. To *convert from a decimal to a percentage*, move the decimal point **two places to the right**. To *convert from a percentage to a decimal*, move it **two places to the left**. Example: 0.23 = 23%; 5.34 = 534%; 0.007 = 0.7%; 700% 7.00; 86% = 0.86; 0.15% = 0.0015.

It may be helpful to remember that the percentage number will always be larger than the equivalent decimal number.

> **Review Video: Converting Decimals to Fractions and Percentages**
> Visit mometrix.com/academy and enter code: 986765

EXAMPLE 1

Convert 15% to both a fraction and a decimal.

First, write the percentage over 100 because percent means "per one hundred." So, 15% can be written as $\frac{15}{100}$. Fractions should be written in the simplest form, which means that the numbers in the numerator and denominator should be reduced if possible. Both 15 and 100 can be divided by 5:

$$\frac{15 \div 5}{100 \div 5} = \frac{3}{20}$$

As before, write the percentage over 100 because percent means "per one hundred." So, 15% can be written as $\frac{15}{100}$. Dividing a number by a power of ten (10, 100, 1000, etc.) is the same as moving the decimal point to the left by the same number of spaces that there are zeros in the divisor. Since 100 has 2 zeros, move the decimal point two places to the left:

$$15\% = 0.15$$

In other words, when converting from a percentage to a decimal, drop the percent sign and move the decimal point two places to the left.

EXAMPLE 2

Write 24.36% as a fraction and then as a decimal. Explain how you made these conversions.

24.36% written as a fraction is $\frac{24.36}{100}$, or $\frac{2436}{10,000}$, which reduces to $\frac{609}{2500}$. 24.36% written as a decimal is 0.2436. Recall that dividing by 100 moves the decimal two places to the left.

> **Review Video: Converting Percentages to Decimals and Fractions**
> Visit mometrix.com/academy and enter code: 287297

EXAMPLE 3

Convert $\frac{4}{5}$ to a decimal and to a percentage.

To convert a fraction to a decimal, simply divide the numerator by the denominator in the fraction. The numerator is the top number in the fraction and the denominator is the bottom number in a fraction.

$$\frac{4}{5} = 4 \div 5 = 0.80 = 0.8$$

Percent means "per hundred."

$$\frac{4 \times 20}{5 \times 20} = \frac{80}{100} = 80\%$$

EXAMPLE 4

Convert $3\frac{2}{5}$ to a decimal and to a percentage.

The mixed number $3\frac{2}{5}$ has a whole number and a fractional part. The fractional part $\frac{2}{5}$ can be written as a decimal by dividing 5 into 2, which gives 0.4. Adding the whole to the part gives 3.4. Alternatively, note that $3\frac{2}{5} = 3\frac{4}{10} = 3.4$

To change a decimal to a percentage, multiply it by 100.

$$3.4(100) = 340\%$$

Notice that this percentage is greater than 100%. This makes sense because the original mixed number $3\frac{2}{5}$ is greater than 1.

Review Video: Converting Fractions to Percentages and Decimals
Visit mometrix.com/academy and enter code: 306233

SCIENTIFIC NOTATION

Scientific notation is a way of writing large numbers in a shorter form. The form $a \times 10^n$ is used in scientific notation, where a is greater than or equal to 1, but less than 10, and n is the number of places the decimal must move to get from the original number to a. Example: The number 230,400,000 is cumbersome to write. To write the value in scientific notation, place a decimal point between the first and second numbers, and include all digits through the last non-zero digit ($a = 2.304$). To find the appropriate power of 10, count the number of places the decimal point had to move ($n = 8$). The number is positive if the decimal moved to the left, and negative if it moved to the right. We can then write 230,400,000 as 2.304×10^8. If we look instead at the number 0.00002304, we have the same value for a, but this time the decimal moved 5 places to the right ($n = -5$). Thus, 0.00002304 can be written as 2.304×10^{-5}. Using this notation makes it simple to compare very large or very small numbers. By comparing exponents, it is easy to see that 3.28×10^4 is smaller than 1.51×10^5, because 4 is less than 5.

Review Video: Scientific Notation
Visit mometrix.com/academy and enter code: 976454

OPERATIONS WITH DECIMALS

ADDING AND SUBTRACTING DECIMALS

When adding and subtracting decimals, the decimal points must always be aligned. Adding decimals is just like adding regular whole numbers. Example: $4.5 + 2 = 6.5$.

If the problem-solver does not properly align the decimal points, an incorrect answer of 4.7 may result. An easy way to add decimals is to align all of the decimal points in a vertical column visually. This will allow one to see exactly where the decimal should be placed in the final answer. Begin adding from right to left. Add each column in turn, making sure to carry the number to the left if a column adds up to more than 9. The same rules apply to the subtraction of decimals.

> **Review Video: <u>Adding and Subtracting Decimals</u>**
> Visit mometrix.com/academy and enter code: 381101

MULTIPLYING DECIMALS

A simple multiplication problem has two components: a **multiplicand** and a **multiplier**. When multiplying decimals, work as though the numbers were whole rather than decimals. Once the final product is calculated, count the number of places to the right of the decimal in both the multiplicand and the multiplier. Then, count that number of places from the right of the product and place the decimal in that position.

For example, 12.3×2.56 has three places to the right of the respective decimals. Multiply 123×256 to get 31488. Now, beginning on the right, count three places to the left and insert the decimal. The final product will be 31.488.

> **Review Video: <u>Multiplying Decimals</u>**
> Visit mometrix.com/academy and enter code: 731574

DIVIDING DECIMALS

Every division problem has a **divisor** and a **dividend**. The dividend is the number that is being divided. In the problem $14 \div 7$, 14 is the dividend and 7 is the divisor. In a division problem with decimals, the divisor must be converted into a whole number. Begin by moving the decimal in the divisor to the right until a whole number is created. Next, move the decimal in the dividend the same number of spaces to the right. For example, 4.9 into 24.5 would become 49 into 245. The decimal was moved one space to the right to create a whole number in the divisor, and then the same was done for the dividend. Once the whole numbers are created, the problem is carried out normally: $245 \div 49 = 5$.

> **Review Video: <u>Dividing Decimals</u>**
> Visit mometrix.com/academy and enter code: 560690

OPERATIONS WITH FRACTIONS

ADDING AND SUBTRACTING FRACTIONS

If two fractions have a common denominator, they can be added or subtracted simply by adding or subtracting the two numerators and retaining the same denominator. Example: $\frac{1}{2} + \frac{1}{4} = \frac{2}{4} + \frac{1}{4} = \frac{3}{4}$. If the two fractions do not already have the same denominator, one or both of them must be manipulated to achieve a common denominator before they can be added or subtracted.

MULTIPLYING FRACTIONS

Two fractions can be multiplied by multiplying the two numerators to find the new numerator and the two denominators to find the new denominator. Example: $\frac{1}{3} \times \frac{2}{3} = \frac{1 \times 2}{3 \times 3} = \frac{2}{9}$.

DIVIDING FRACTIONS

Two fractions can be divided by flipping the numerator and denominator of the second fraction and then proceeding as though it were a multiplication. Example: $\frac{2}{3} \div \frac{3}{4} = \frac{2}{3} \times \frac{4}{3} = \frac{8}{9}$.

RATIONAL NUMBERS FROM LEAST TO GREATEST

EXAMPLE

Order the following rational numbers from least to greatest: 0.55, 17%, $\sqrt{25}$, $\frac{64}{4}$, $\frac{25}{50}$, 3.

Recall that the term **rational** simply means that the number can be expressed as a ratio or fraction. The set of rational numbers includes integers and decimals. Notice that each of the numbers in the problem can be written as a decimal or integer:

$$17\% = 0.1717$$
$$\sqrt{25} = 5$$
$$\frac{64}{4} = 16$$
$$\frac{25}{50} = \frac{1}{2} = 0.5$$

So, the answer is 17%, $\frac{25}{50}$, 0.55, 3, $\sqrt{25}$, $\frac{64}{4}$.

RATIONAL NUMBERS FROM GREATEST TO LEAST

EXAMPLE

Order the following rational numbers from greatest to least: 0.3, 27%, $\sqrt{100}$, $\frac{72}{9}$, $\frac{1}{9}$, 4.5

$$27\% = 0.27$$
$$\sqrt{100} = 10$$
$$\frac{72}{9} = 8$$
$$\frac{1}{9} \approx 0.11$$

So, the answer is $\sqrt{100}$, $\frac{72}{9}$, 4.5, 0.3, 27%, $\frac{1}{9}$.

> **Review Video: Ordering Rational Numbers**
> Visit mometrix.com/academy and enter code: 419578

FACTORS AND GREATEST COMMON FACTOR

Factors are numbers that are multiplied together to obtain a **product**. For example, in the equation $2 \times 3 = 6$, the numbers 2 and 3 are factors. A **prime number** has only two factors (1 and itself), but other numbers can have many factors.

A **common factor** is a number that divides exactly into two or more other numbers. For example, the factors of 12 are 1, 2, 3, 4, 6, and 12, while the factors of 15 are 1, 3, 5, and 15. The common factors of 12 and 15 are 1 and 3.

A **prime factor** is also a prime number. Therefore, the prime factors of 12 are 2 and 3. For 15, the prime factors are 3 and 5.

> **Review Video: Factors**
> Visit mometrix.com/academy and enter code: 920086

The **greatest common factor** (GCF) is the largest number that is a factor of two or more numbers. For example, the factors of 15 are 1, 3, 5, and 15; the factors of 35 are 1, 5, 7, and 35. Therefore, the greatest common factor of 15 and 35 is 5.

> **Review Video: Greatest Common Factor (GCF)**
> Visit mometrix.com/academy and enter code: 838699

MULTIPLES AND LEAST COMMON MULTIPLE

The least common multiple (**LCM**) is the smallest number that is a multiple of two or more numbers. For example, the multiples of 3 include 3, 6, 9, 12, 15, etc.; the multiples of 5 include 5, 10, 15, 20, etc. Therefore, the least common multiple of 3 and 5 is 15.

> **Review Video: Multiples**
> Visit mometrix.com/academy and enter code: 626738
>
> **Review Video: Multiples and Least Common Multiple (LCM)**
> Visit mometrix.com/academy and enter code: 520269

PROPORTIONS AND RATIOS

PROPORTIONS

A proportion is a relationship between two quantities that dictates how one changes when the other changes. A **direct proportion** describes a relationship in which a quantity increases by a set amount for every increase in the other quantity, or decreases by that same amount for every decrease in the other quantity. Example: Assuming a constant driving speed, the time required for a car trip increases as the distance of the trip increases. The distance to be traveled and the time required to travel are directly proportional.

Inverse proportion is a relationship in which an increase in one quantity is accompanied by a decrease in the other, or vice versa. Example: the time required for a car trip decreases as the speed increases, and increases as the speed decreases, so the time required is inversely proportional to the speed of the car.

> **Review Video: Proportions**
> Visit mometrix.com/academy and enter code: 505355

RATIOS

A **ratio** is a comparison of two quantities in a particular order. Example: If there are 14 computers in a lab, and the class has 20 students, there is a student to computer ratio of 20 to 14, commonly written as 20:14. Ratios are normally reduced to their smallest whole number representation, so 20:14 would be reduced to 10:7 by dividing both sides by 2.

> **Review Video: Ratios**
> Visit mometrix.com/academy and enter code: 996914

REAL WORLD PROBLEMS WITH PROPORTIONS AND RATIOS

EXAMPLE 1

A thermos has a leak and loses 100 mg of hot chocolate every two hours. How much hot chocolate will the thermos lose in five hours?

Using proportional reasoning, since five hours is two and a half times as long as two hours, the thermos will lose two and a half times as much hot chocolate, 2.5×100 mg $= 250$ mg, in five hours. To compute the answer, first write the amount of hot chocolate per 2 hours as a ratio: $\frac{100 \text{ mg}}{2 \text{ hours}}$. Next setup a proportion to relate the time increments of 2 hours and 5 hours: $\frac{100 \text{ mg}}{2 \text{ hours}} = \frac{x \text{ mg}}{5 \text{ hours}}$ where x is the amount of hot chocolate the thermos loses in five hours. Make sure to keep the same units in either the numerator or denominator. In this case the numerator units must be mg for both ratios and the denominator units must be hours for both ratios.

Use cross multiplication and division to solve for x:

$$\frac{100 \text{ mg}}{2 \text{ hours}} = \frac{x \text{ mg}}{5 \text{ hours}}$$

$$100(5) = 2(x)$$
$$500 = 2x$$
$$500 \div 2 = 2x \div 2$$
$$250 = x$$

Therefore, the thermos loses 250 mg every five hours.

EXAMPLE 2

At a school, for every 20 female students there are 15 male students. This same student ratio happens to exist at another school. If there are 100 female students at the second school, how many male students are there?

One way to find the number of male students is to set up and solve a proportion.

$$\frac{\text{number of female students}}{\text{number of male students}} = \frac{20}{15} = \frac{100}{\text{number of male students}}$$

Represent the unknown number of male students as the variable x.

$$\frac{20}{15} = \frac{100}{x}$$

Cross multiply and then solve for x:

$$20x = 15 \times 100 = 1500$$
$$x = \frac{1500}{20} = 75$$

Alternatively, notice that: $\frac{20 \times 5}{15 \times 5} = \frac{100}{75}$, so $x = 75$.

EXAMPLE 3

In a hospital emergency room, there are 4 nurses for every 12 patients. What is the ratio of nurses to patients? If the nurse-to-patient ratio remains constant, how many nurses must be present to care for 24 patients?

The ratio of nurses to patients can be written as 4 to 12, 4:12, or $\frac{4}{12}$. Because four and twelve have a common factor of four, the ratio should be reduced to 1:3, which means that there is one nurse present for every three patients. If this ratio remains constant, there must be eight nurses present to care for 24 patients.

EXAMPLE 4

In a bank, the banker-to-customer ratio is 1:2. If seven bankers are on duty, how many customers are currently in the bank?

Use proportional reasoning or set up a proportion to solve. Because there are twice as many customers as bankers, there must be fourteen customers when seven bankers are on duty. Setting up and solving a proportion gives the same result:

$$\frac{\text{number of bankers}}{\text{number of customers}} = \frac{1}{2} = \frac{7}{\text{number of customers}}$$

Represent the unknown number of patients as the variable x.

$$\frac{1}{2} = \frac{7}{x}$$

To solve for x, cross multiply:

$1 \times x = 7 \times 2$, so $x = 14$.

CONSTANT OF PROPORTIONALITY

When two quantities have a proportional relationship, there exists a **constant of proportionality** between the quantities; the product of this constant and one of the quantities is equal to the other quantity. For example, if one lemon costs $0.25, two lemons cost $0.50, and three lemons cost $0.75, there is a proportional relationship between the total cost of lemons and the number of lemons purchased. The constant of proportionality is the **unit price**, namely $0.25/lemon. Notice that the total price of lemons, t, can be found by multiplying the unit price of lemons, p, and the number of lemons, n: $t = pn$.

SLOPE

On a graph with two points, (x_1, y_1) and (x_2, y_2), the **slope** is found with the formula $m = \frac{y_2 - y_1}{x_2 - x_1}$; where $x_1 \neq x_2$ and m stands for slope. If the value of the slope is **positive**, the line has an *upward direction* from left to right. If the value of the slope is **negative**, the line has a *downward direction* from left to right.

UNIT RATE AS THE SLOPE

A new book goes on sale in bookstores and online stores. In the first month, 5,000 copies of the book are sold. Over time, the book continues to grow in popularity. The data for the number of copies sold is in the table below.

# of Months on Sale	1	2	3	4	5
# of Copies Sold (In Thousands)	5	10	15	20	25

So, the number of copies that are sold and the time that the book is on sale is a proportional relationship. In this example, an equation can be used to show the data: $y = 5x$, where x is the number of months that the book is on sale. Also, y is the number of copies sold. So, the slope is $\frac{\text{rise}}{\text{run}} = \frac{5}{1}$. This can be reduced to 5.

Review Video: Finding the Slope of a Line
Visit mometrix.com/academy and enter code: 766664

WORK/UNIT RATE

Unit rate expresses a quantity of one thing in terms of one unit of another. For example, if you travel 30 miles every two hours, a unit rate expresses this comparison in terms of one hour: in one hour you travel 15 miles, so your unit rate is 15 miles per hour. Other examples are how much one ounce of food costs (price per ounce) or figuring out how much one egg costs out of the dozen (price per 1 egg, instead of price per 12 eggs). The denominator of a unit rate is always 1. Unit rates are used to compare different situations to solve problems. For example, to make sure you get the best deal when deciding which kind of soda to buy, you can find the unit rate of each. If soda #1 costs $1.50 for a 1-liter bottle, and soda #2 costs $2.75 for a 2-liter bottle, it would be a better deal

to buy soda #2, because its unit rate is only $1.375 per 1-liter, which is cheaper than soda #1. Unit rates can also help determine the length of time a given event will take. For example, if you can paint 2 rooms in 4.5 hours, you can determine how long it will take you to paint 5 rooms by solving for the unit rate per room and then multiplying that by 5.

Review Video: Rates and Unit Rates
Visit mometrix.com/academy and enter code: 185363

EXAMPLE 1

Janice made $40 during the first 5 hours she spent babysitting. She will continue to earn money at this rate until she finishes babysitting in 3 more hours. Find how much money Janice earned babysitting and how much she earns per hour.

Janice will earn $64 babysitting in her 8 total hours (adding the first 5 hours to the remaining 3 gives the 8 hour total). This can be found by setting up a proportion comparing money earned to babysitting hours. Since she earns $40 for 5 hours and since the rate is constant, she will earn a proportional amount in 8 hours: $\frac{40}{5} = \frac{x}{8}$. Cross multiplying will yield $5x = 320$, and division by 5 shows that $x = 64$.

Janice earns $8 per hour. This can be found by taking her total amount earned, $64, and dividing it by the total number of hours worked, 8. Since $\frac{64}{8} = 8$, Janice makes $8 in one hour. This can also be found by finding the unit rate, money earned per hour: $\frac{64}{8} = \frac{x}{1}$. Since cross multiplying yields $8x = 64$, and division by 8 shows that $x = 8$, Janice earns $8 per hour.

EXAMPLE 2

The McDonalds are taking a family road trip, driving 300 miles to their cabin. It took them 2 hours to drive the first 120 miles. They will drive at the same speed all the way to their cabin. Find the speed at which the McDonalds are driving and how much longer it will take them to get to their cabin.

The McDonalds are driving 60 miles per hour. This can be found by setting up a proportion to find the unit rate, the number of miles they drive per one hour: $\frac{120}{2} = \frac{x}{1}$. Cross multiplying yields $2x = 120$ and division by 2 shows that $x = 60$.

Since the McDonalds will drive this same speed, it will take them another 3 hours to get to their cabin. This can be found by first finding how many miles the McDonalds have left to drive, which is $300 - 120 = 180$. The McDonalds are driving at 60 miles per hour, so a proportion can be set up to determine how many hours it will take them to drive 180 miles: $\frac{180}{x} = \frac{60}{1}$. Cross multiplying yields $60x = 180$, and division by 60 shows that $x = 3$. This can also be found by using the formula $D = r \times t$ (or distance = rate × time), where $180 = 60 \times t$, and division by 60 shows that $t = 3$.

EXAMPLE 3

It takes Andy 10 minutes to read 6 pages of his book. He has already read 150 pages in his book that is 210 pages long. Find how long it takes Andy to read 1 page and also find how long it will take him to finish his book if he continues to read at the same speed.

115

It takes Andy 1 minute and 40 seconds to read one page in his book. This can be found by finding the unit rate per one page, by dividing the total time it takes him to read 6 pages by 6. Since it takes him 10 minutes to read 6 pages, $\frac{10}{6} = 1\frac{2}{3}$ minutes, which is 1 minute and 40 seconds.

It will take Andy another 100 minutes, or 1 hour and 40 minutes to finish his book. This can be found by first figuring out how many pages Andy has left to read, which is $210-150 = 60$. Since it is now known that it takes him $1\frac{2}{3}$ minutes to read each page, then that rate must be multiplied by however many pages he has left to read (60) to find the time he'll need: $60 \times 1\frac{2}{3} = 100$, so it will take him 100 minutes, or 1 hour and 40 minutes, to read the rest of his book.

FUNCTION AND RELATION

When expressing functional relationships, the **variables** x and y are typically used. These values are often written as the **coordinates** (x, y). The x-value is the independent variable and the y-value is the dependent variable. A **relation** is a set of data in which there is not a unique y-value for each x-value in the dataset. This means that there can be two of the same x-values assigned to different y-values. A relation is simply a relationship between the x and y-values in each coordinate but does not apply to the relationship between the values of x and y in the data set. A **function** is a relation where one quantity depends on the other. For example, the amount of money that you make depends on the number of hours that you work. In a function, each x-value in the data set has one unique y-value because the y-value depends on the x-value.

> **Review Video: Definition of a Function**
> Visit mometrix.com/academy and enter code: 784611

FUNCTIONS

A **function** is an equation that has exactly one value of **output variable** (dependent variable) for each value of the **input variable** (independent variable). The set of all values for the input variable (here assumed to be x) is the domain of the function, and the set of all corresponding values of output variable (here assumed to be y) is the range of the function. When looking at a graph of an equation, the easiest way to determine if the equation is a function or not is to conduct the vertical line test. If a vertical line drawn through any value of x crosses the graph in more than one place, the equation is not a function.

DETERMINING A FUNCTION

You can determine whether an equation is a **function** by substituting different values into the equation for x. These values are called input values. All possible input values are referred to as the **domain**. The result of substituting these values into the equation is called the output, or **range**. You can display and organize these numbers in a data table. A **data table** contains the values for x and y, which you can also list as coordinates. In order for a function to exist, the table cannot contain any repeating x-values that correspond with different y-values. If each x-coordinate has a unique y-coordinate, the table contains a function. However, there can be repeating y-values that correspond with different x-values. An example of this is when the function contains an exponent. For example, if $x^2 = y$, $2^2 = 4$, and $(-2)^2 = 4$.

> **Review Video: Basics of Functions**
> Visit mometrix.com/academy and enter code: 822500

PROPERTIES OF FUNCTIONS

In functions with the notation f(x), the value substituted for x in the equation is called the argument. The domain is the set of all values for x in a function. Unless otherwise given, assume the domain is the set of real numbers that will yield real numbers for the range. This is the domain of definition.

The graph of a function is the set of all ordered pairs (x, y) that satisfy the equation of the function. The points that have zero as the value for y are called the zeros of the function. These are also the x-intercepts, because that is the point at which the graph crosses, or intercepts, the x-axis. The points that have zero as the value for x are the y-intercepts because that is where the graph crosses the y-axis.

WRITING A FUNCTION RULE USING A TABLE

If given a set of data, place the corresponding x and y-values into a table and analyze the relationship between them. Consider what you can do to each x-value to obtain the corresponding y-value. Try adding or subtracting different numbers to and from x and then try multiplying or dividing different numbers to and from x. If none of these **operations** give you the y-value, try combining the operations. Once you find a rule that works for one pair, make sure to try it with each additional set of ordered pairs in the table. If the same operation or combination of operations satisfies each set of coordinates, then the table contains a function. The rule is then used to write the equation of the function in "y =" form.

EQUATIONS AND GRAPHING

When algebraic functions and equations are shown graphically, they are usually shown on a *Cartesian coordinate plane*. The Cartesian coordinate plane consists of two number lines placed perpendicular to each other, and intersecting at the zero point, also known as the origin. The horizontal number line is known as the x-axis, with positive values to the right of the origin, and negative values to the left of the origin. The vertical number line is known as the y-axis, with positive values above the origin, and negative values below the origin. Any point on the plane can be identified by an ordered pair in the form (x,y), called coordinates. The x-value of the coordinate is called the abscissa, and the y-value of the coordinate is called the ordinate. The two number lines divide the plane into *four quadrants*: I, II, III, and IV.

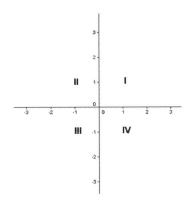

Before learning the different forms in which equations can be written, it is important to understand some terminology. A ratio of the change in the vertical distance to the change in horizontal distance is called the *slope*. On a graph with two points, (x_1, y_1) and (x_2, y_2), the slope is represented by the formula $s = \frac{y_2 - y_1}{x_2 - x_1}$; $x_1 \neq x_2$. If the value of the slope is positive, the line slopes upward from left to right. If the value of the slope is negative, the line slopes downward from left to right. If the y-coordinates are the same for both points, the slope is 0 and the line is a *horizontal line*. If the x-coordinates are the same for both points, there is no slope and the line is a *vertical line*. Two or more lines that have equal slopes are *parallel lines*. *Perpendicular lines* have slopes that are negative reciprocals of each other, such as $\frac{a}{b}$ and $\frac{-b}{a}$.

> **Review Video: Graphs of Functions**
> Visit mometrix.com/academy and enter code: 492785

Equations are made up of monomials and polynomials. A *monomial* is a single variable or product of constants and variables, such as x, $2x$, or $\frac{2}{x}$. There will never be addition or subtraction symbols in a monomial. Like monomials have like variables, but they may have different coefficients. *Polynomials* are algebraic expressions which use addition and subtraction to combine two or more monomials. Two terms make a binomial; three terms make a trinomial; etc.. The d*egree of a monomial* is the sum of the exponents of the variables. The *degree of a polynomial* is the highest degree of any individual term.

As mentioned previously, equations can be written many ways. Below is a list of the many forms equations can take.

- Standard Form: $Ax + By = C$; the slope is $\frac{-A}{B}$ and the y-intercept is $\frac{C}{B}$
- *Slope Intercept Form*: $y = mx + b$, where m is the slope and b is the y-intercept
- Point-Slope Form: $y - y_1 = m(x - x_1)$, where m is the slope and (x_1, y_1) is a point on the line
- Two-Point Form: $\frac{y - y_1}{x - x_1} = \frac{y_2 - y_1}{x_2 - x_1}$, where (x_1, y_1) and (x_2, y_2) are two points on the given line
- *Intercept Form*: $\frac{x}{x_1} + \frac{y}{y_1} = 1$, where $(x_1, 0)$ is the point at which a line intersects the x-axis, and $(0, y_1)$ is the point at which the same line intersects the y-axis

> **Review Video: Slope-Intercept and Point-Slope Forms**
> Visit mometrix.com/academy and enter code: 113216

Equations can also be written as $ax + b = 0$, where $a \neq 0$. These are referred to as **one variable linear equations**. A solution to such an equation is called a **root**. In the case where we have the equation $5x + 10 = 0$, if we solve for x we get a solution of $x = -2$. In other words, the root of the equation is -2. This is found by first subtracting 10 from both sides, which gives $5x = -10$. Next, simply divide both sides by the coefficient of the variable, in this case 5, to get $x = -2$. This can be checked by plugging -2 back into the original equation $(5)(-2) + 10 = -10 + 10 = 0$.

The **solution set** is the set of all solutions of an equation. In our example, the solution set would simply be -2. If there were more solutions (there usually are in multivariable equations) then they would also be included in the solution set. When an equation has no true solutions, this is referred to as an **empty set**. Equations with identical solution sets are *equivalent equations*. An **identity** is a term whose value or determinant is equal to 1.

SOLVING ONE-VARIABLE LINEAR EQUATIONS

Multiply all terms by the lowest common denominator to eliminate any fractions. Look for addition or subtraction to undo so you can isolate the variable on one side of the equal sign. Divide both sides by the coefficient of the variable. When you have a value for the variable, substitute this value into the original equation to make sure you have a true equation.

MANIPULATION OF FUNCTIONS

Horizontal and vertical shift occur when values are added to or subtracted from the x or y values, respectively.

If a constant is added to the y portion of each point, the graph shifts up. If a constant is subtracted from the y portion of each point, the graph shifts down. This is represented by the expression $f(x) \pm k$, where k is a constant.

If a constant is added to the x portion of each point, the graph shifts left. If a constant is subtracted from the x portion of each point, the graph shifts right. This is represented by the expression $f(x \pm k)$, where k is a constant.

Stretch, compression, and reflection occur when different parts of a function are multiplied by different groups of constants. If the function as a whole is multiplied by a real number constant greater than 1, $(k \times f(x))$, the graph is stretched vertically. If k in the previous equation is greater than zero but less than 1, the graph is compressed vertically. If k is less than zero, the graph is reflected about the x-axis, in addition to being either stretched or compressed vertically if k is less than or greater than -1, respectively. If instead, just the x-term is multiplied by a constant greater than 1 $(f(k \times x))$, the graph is compressed horizontally. If k in the previous equation is greater than zero but less than 1, the graph is stretched horizontally. If k is less than zero, the graph is reflected about the y-axis, in addition to being either stretched or compressed horizontally if k is greater than or less than -1, respectively.

CLASSIFICATION OF FUNCTIONS

There are many different ways to classify functions based on their structure or behavior. Listed here are a few common classifications.

Constant functions are given by the equation $y=b$ or $f(x) = b$, where b is a real number. There is no independent variable present in the equation, so the function has a constant value for all x. The graph of a constant function is a horizontal line of slope 0 that is positioned b units from the x-axis. If b is positive, the line is above the x-axis; if b is negative, the line is below the x-axis.

Identity functions are identified by the equation $y=x$ or $f(x) = x$, where every value of y is equal to its corresponding value of x. The only zero is the point $(0, 0)$. The graph is a diagonal line with slope 1.

In **linear functions**, the value of the function changes in direct proportion to x. The rate of change, represented by the slope on its graph, is constant throughout. The standard form of a linear equation is $ax + by = c$, where a, b, and c are real numbers. As a function, this equation is commonly written as $y = mx + b$ or $f(x) = mx + b$. This is known as the slope-intercept form, because the coefficients give the slope of the graphed function (m) and its y-intercept (b). Solve the equation $mx + b = 0$ for x to get $x = -\frac{b}{m}$, which is the only zero of the function. The domain and range are both the set of all real numbers.

A **polynomial function** is a function with multiple terms and multiple powers of x, such as:

$$f(x) = a_n x^n + a_{n-1} x^{n-1} + a_{n-2} x^{n-2} + \cdots + a_1 x + a_0$$

where n is a non-negative integer that is the highest exponent in the polynomial, and $a_n \neq 0$. The domain of a polynomial function is the set of all real numbers. If the greatest exponent in the polynomial is even, the polynomial is said to be of even degree and the range is the set of real numbers that satisfy the function. If the greatest exponent in the polynomial is odd, the polynomial is said to be odd and the range, like the domain, is the set of all real numbers.

A **quadratic function** is a polynomial function that follows the equation pattern $y = ax^2 + bx + c$, or $f(x) = ax^2 + bx + c$, where a, b, and c are real numbers and $a \neq 0$. The domain of a quadratic function is the set of all real numbers. The range is also real numbers, but only those in the subset of the domain that satisfy the equation. The root(s) of any quadratic function can be found by plugging the values of a, b, and c into the **quadratic formula**:

$$x = \frac{-b \pm \sqrt{b^2 - 4ac}}{2a}$$

If the expression $b^2 - 4ac$ is negative, you will instead find complex roots.

A quadratic function has a parabola for its graph. In the equation $f(x) = ax^2 + bx + c$, if a is positive, the parabola will open upward. If a is negative, the parabola will open downward. The axis of symmetry is a vertical line that passes through the vertex. To determine whether or not the parabola will intersect the x-axis, check the number of real roots. An equation with two real roots will cross the x-axis twice. An equation with one real root will have its vertex on the x-axis. An equation with no real roots will not contact the x-axis.

A **rational function** is a function that can be constructed as a ratio of two polynomial expressions: $f(x) = \frac{p(x)}{q(x)}$, where $p(x)$ and $q(x)$ are both polynomial expressions and $q(x) \neq 0$. The domain is the set of all real numbers, except any values for which $q(x) = 0$. The range is the set of real numbers that satisfies the function when the domain is applied. When you graph a rational function, you will have vertical asymptotes wherever $q(x) = 0$. If the polynomial in the numerator is of lesser degree than the polynomial in the denominator, the x-axis will also be a horizontal asymptote. If the numerator and denominator have equal degrees, there will be a horizontal asymptote not on the x-axis. If the degree of the numerator is exactly one greater than the degree of the denominator, the graph will have an oblique, or diagonal, asymptote. The asymptote will be along the line $y = \frac{p_n}{q_{n-1}} x + \frac{p_{n-1}}{q_{n-1}}$, where p_n and q_{n-1} are the coefficients of the highest degree terms in their respective polynomials.

A **square root function** is a function that contains a radical and is in the format $f(x) = \sqrt{ax + b}$. The domain is the set of all real numbers that yields a positive radicand or a radicand equal to zero. Because square root values are assumed to be positive unless otherwise identified, the range is all real numbers from zero to infinity. To find the zero of a square root function, set the radicand equal to zero and solve for *x*. The graph of a square root function is always to the right of the zero and always above the *x*-axis.

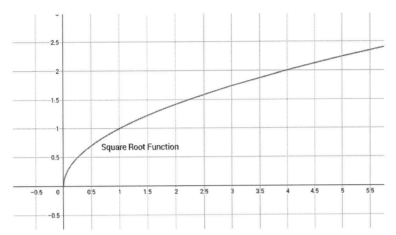

An **absolute value function** is in the format $f(x) = |ax + b|$. Like other functions, the domain is the set of all real numbers. However, because absolute value indicates positive numbers, the range is limited to positive real numbers. To find the zero of an absolute value function, set the portion inside the absolute value sign equal to zero and solve for x.

An absolute value function is also known as a piecewise function because it must be solved in pieces – one for if the value inside the absolute value sign is positive, and one for if the value is negative. The function can be expressed as

$$f(x) = \begin{cases} ax + b \text{ if } ax + b \geq 0 \\ -(ax + b) \text{ if } ax + b < 0 \end{cases}$$

This will allow for an accurate statement of the range.

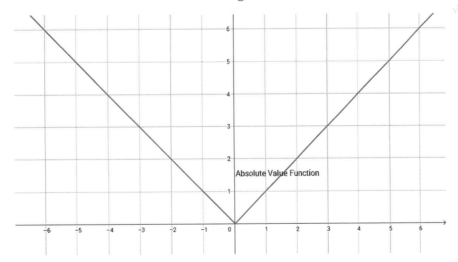

Exponential functions are equations that have the format $y = b^x$, where base $b > 0$ and $b \neq 1$. The exponential function can also be written $f(x) = b^x$.

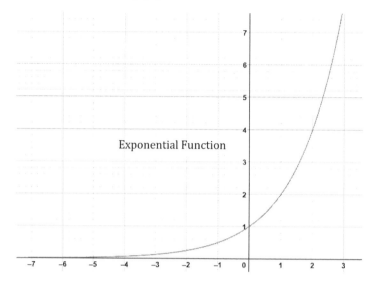

Logarithmic functions are equations that have the format $y = \log_b x$ or $f(x) = \log_b x$. The base b may be any number except one; however, the most common bases for logarithms are base 10 and base e. The log base e is known the natural logarithm, or *ln*, expressed by the function $f(x) = \ln x$.

Any logarithm that does not have an assigned value of b is assumed to be base 10: $\log x = \log_{10} x$. Exponential functions and logarithmic functions are related in that one is the inverse of the other. If $f(x) = b^x$, then $f^{-1}(x) = \log_b x$. This can perhaps be expressed more clearly by the two equations: $y = b^x$ and $x = \log_b y$.

The following properties apply to logarithmic expressions:

$$\log_b 1 = 0$$
$$\log_b b = 1$$
$$\log_b b^p = p$$
$$\log_b MN = \log_b M + \log_b N$$
$$\log_b \frac{M}{N} = \log_b M - \log_b N$$
$$\log_b M^p = p \log_b M$$

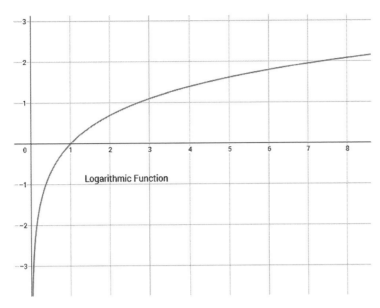

Logarithmic Function

In a **one-to-one function**, each value of x has exactly one value for y (this is the definition of a function) *and* each value of y has exactly one value for x. While the vertical line test will determine if a graph is that of a function, the horizontal line test will determine if a function is a one-to-one function. If a horizontal line drawn at any value of y intersects the graph in more than one place, the graph is not that of a one-to-one function. Do not make the mistake of using the horizontal line test exclusively in determining if a graph is that of a one-to-one function. A one-to-one function must pass both the vertical line test and the horizontal line test. One-to-one functions are also **invertible functions**.

A **monotone function** is a function whose graph either constantly increases or constantly decreases. Examples include the functions $f(x) = x$, $f(x) = -x$, or $f(x) = x^3$.

An **even function** has a graph that is symmetric with respect to the y-axis and satisfies the equation $f(x) = f(-x)$. Examples include the functions $f(x) = x^2$ and $f(x) = ax^n$, where a is any real number and n is a positive even integer.

An **odd function** has a graph that is symmetric with respect to the origin and satisfies the equation $f(x) = -f(-x)$. Examples include the functions $f(x) = x^3$ and $f(x) = ax^n$, where a is any real number and n is a positive odd integer.

Algebraic functions are those that exclusively use polynomials and roots. These would include polynomial functions, rational functions, square root functions, and all combinations of these functions, such as polynomials as the radicand. These combinations may be joined by addition, subtraction, multiplication, or division, but may not include variables as exponents.

Transcendental functions are all functions that are non-algebraic. Any function that includes logarithms, trigonometric functions, variables as exponents, or any combination that includes any of these is not algebraic in nature, even if the function includes polynomials or roots.

RELATED CONCEPTS

According to the **fundamental theorem of algebra**, every non-constant, single variable polynomial has exactly as many roots as the polynomial's highest exponent. For example, if x^4 is the largest exponent of a term, the polynomial will have exactly 4 roots. However, some of these roots may have multiplicity or be non-real numbers. For instance, in the polynomial function $f(x) = x^4 -$

$4x + 3$, the only real roots are 1 and -1. The root 1 has multiplicity of 2 and there is one non-real root $(-1 - \sqrt{2}i)$.

The **remainder theorem** is useful for determining the remainder when a polynomial is divided by a binomial. The remainder theorem states that if a polynomial function $f(x)$ is divided by a binomial $x - a$, where a is a real number, the remainder of the division will be the value of $f(a)$. If $f(a) = 0$, then a is a root of the polynomial.

The **factor theorem** is related to the remainder theorem and states that if $f(a) = 0$ then $(x - a)$ is a factor of the function.

According to the **rational root theorem,** any rational root of a polynomial function $f(x) = a_n x^n + a_{n-1}x^{n-1} + \cdots + a_1 x + a_0$ with integer coefficients will, when reduced to its lowest terms, be a positive or negative fraction such that the numerator is a factor of a_0 and the denominator is a factor of a_n. For instance, if the polynomial function $f(x) = x^3 + 3x^2 - 4$ has any rational roots, the numerators of those roots can only be factors of 4 (1, 2, 4), and the denominators can only be factors of 1 (1). The function in this example has roots of 1 $\left(\text{or } \frac{1}{1}\right)$ and -2 $\left(\text{or } -\frac{2}{1}\right)$.

Variables that vary directly are those that either both increase at the same rate or both decrease at the same rate. For example, in the functions $f(x) = kx$ or $f(x) = kx^n$, where k and n are positive, the value of $f(x)$ increases as the value of x increases and decreases as the value of x decreases.

Variables that vary inversely are those where one increases while the other decreases. For example, in the functions $f(x) = \frac{k}{x}$ or $f(x) = \frac{k}{x^n}$ where k is a positive constant, the value of y increases as the value of x decreases, and the value of y decreases as the value of x increases.

In both cases, k is the constant of variation.

APPLYING THE BASIC OPERATIONS TO FUNCTIONS

For each of the basic operations, we will use these functions as examples: $f(x) = x^2$ and $g(x) = x$.

To find the sum of two functions f and g, assuming the domains are compatible, simply add the two functions together: $(f + g)(x) = f(x) + g(x) = x^2 + x$

To find the difference of two functions f and g, assuming the domains are compatible, simply subtract the second function from the first: $(f - g)(x) = f(x) - g(x) = x^2 - x$.

To find the product of two functions f and g, assuming the domains are compatible, multiply the two functions together: $(f \cdot g)(x) = f(x) \cdot g(x) = x^2 \cdot x = x^3$.

To find the quotient of two functions f and g, assuming the domains are compatible, divide the first function by the second: $\frac{f}{g}(x) = \frac{f(x)}{g(x)} = \frac{x^2}{x} = x \; ; x \neq 0$.

The example given in each case is fairly simple, but on a given problem, if you are looking only for the value of the sum, difference, product or quotient of two functions at a particular x-value, it may be simpler to solve the functions individually and then perform the given operation using those values.

The composite of two functions f and g, written as $(f \circ g)(x)$ simply means that the output of the second function is used as the input of the first. This can also be written as $f\big(g(x)\big)$. In general, this can be solved by substituting $g(x)$ for all instances of x in $f(x)$ and simplifying. Using the example functions $f(x) = x^2 - x + 2$ and $g(x) = x + 1$, we can find that $(f \circ g)(x)$ or $f(g(x))$ is equal to $f(x+1) = (x+1)^2 - (x+1) + 2$, which simplifies to $x^2 + x + 2$.

It is important to note that $(f \circ g)(x)$ is not necessarily the same as $(g \circ f)(x)$. The process is not commutative like addition or multiplication expressions. If $(f \circ g)(x)$ does equal $(g \circ f)(x)$, the two functions are inverses of each other.

SOLVE EQUATIONS IN ONE VARIABLE

MANIPULATING EQUATIONS

Sometimes you will have variables missing in equations. So, you need to find the missing variable. To do this, you need to remember one important thing: *whatever you do to one side of an equation, you need to do to the other side*. If you subtract 100 from one side of an equation, you need to subtract 100 from the other side of the equation. This will allow you to change the form of the equation to find missing values.

EXAMPLE

Ray earns \$10 an hour at his job. Write an equation for his earnings as a function of time spent working. Determine how long Ray has to work in order to earn \$360.

The number of dollars that Ray earns is dependent on the number of hours he works, so earnings will be represented by the dependent variable y and hours worked will be represented by the independent variable x. He earns 10 dollars per hour worked, so his earning can be calculated as

$$y = 10x$$

To calculate the number of hours Ray must work in order to earn \$360, plug in 360 for y and solve for x:

$$360 = 10x$$

$$x = \frac{360}{10} = 36$$

So, Ray must work 36 hours in order to earn \$360.

Review Video: Dependent and Independent Variables and Inverting Functions
Visit mometrix.com/academy and enter code: 704764

SOLVING ONE VARIABLE LINEAR EQUATIONS

Another way to write an equation is $ax + b = 0$ where $a \neq 0$. This is known as a **one-variable linear equation**. A solution to an equation is called a **root**. Consider the following equation:

$$5x + 10 = 0$$

If we solve for x, the solution is $x = -2$. In other words, the root of the equation is –2.

The first step is to subtract 10 from both sides. This gives $5x = -10$.

Next, divide both sides by the **coefficient** of the variable. For this example, that is 5. So, you should have $x = -2$. You can make sure that you have the correct answer by substituting –2 back into the original equation. So, the equation now looks like this: $(5)(-2) + 10 = -10 + 10 = 0$.

EXAMPLE 1

Solve for x.

$$\frac{45\%}{12\%} = \frac{15\%}{x}$$

First, cross multiply; then, solve for x:

$$45x = 12 \times 15 = 180$$
$$x = \frac{180}{45} = 4\%$$

Alternatively, notice that $\frac{45\% \div 3}{12\% \div 3} = \frac{15\%}{4\%}$, so $x = 4\%$.

EXAMPLE 2

Solve for x in the following equation:

$$\frac{0.50}{2} = \frac{1.50}{x}$$

First, cross multiply; then, solve for x:

$$0.5x = 1.5 \times 2 = 3$$
$$x = \frac{3}{0.5} = 3 \times 2 = 6$$

Alternatively, notice that $\frac{0.50 \times 3}{2 \times 3} = \frac{1.50}{6}$, so $x = 6$.

EXAMPLE 3

Solve for x in the following equation:

$$\frac{40}{8} = \frac{x}{24}$$

First, cross multiply; then, solve for x:

$$8x = 40 \times 24 = 960$$
$$x = \frac{960}{8} = 120$$

Alternatively, notice that $\frac{40 \times 3}{8 \times 3} = \frac{120}{24}$, so $x = 120$.

OTHER IMPORTANT CONCEPTS

Commonly in algebra and other upper-level fields of math you find yourself working with mathematical expressions that do not equal each other. The statement comparing such expressions with symbols such as < (less than) or > (greater than) is called an *inequality*. An example of an inequality is $7x > 5$. To solve for x, simply divide both sides by 7 and the solution is shown to be $x > \frac{5}{7}$. Graphs of the solution set of inequalities are represented on a number line. Open circles are used to show that an expression approaches a number but is never quite equal to that number.

> **Review Video: Inequalities**
> Visit mometrix.com/academy and enter code: 347842

Conditional inequalities are those with certain values for the variable that will make the condition true and other values for the variable where the condition will be false. **Absolute inequalities** can have any real number as the value for the variable to make the condition true, while there is no real number value for the variable that will make the condition false. Solving inequalities is done by following the same rules as for solving equations with the exception that when multiplying or dividing by a negative number the direction of the inequality sign must be flipped or reversed. **double inequalities** are situations where two inequality statements apply to the same variable expression. An example of this is $-c < ax + b < c$.

A **weighted mean**, or weighted average, is a mean that uses "weighted" values. The formula is weighted mean $= \frac{w_1 x_1 + w_2 x_2 + w_3 x_3 \ldots + w_n x_n}{w_1 + w_2 + w_3 + \cdots + w_n}$. Weighted values, such as $w_1, w_2, w_3, \ldots w_n$ are assigned to each member of the set $x_1, x_2, x_3, \ldots x_n$. If calculating weighted mean, make sure a weight value for each member of the set is used.

GRAPHING INEQUALITIES
Graph the inequality $10 > -2x + 4$.

In order to **graph the inequality** $10 > -2x + 4$, you must first solve for x. The opposite of addition is subtraction, so subtract 4 from both sides. This results in $6 > -2x$. Next, the opposite of multiplication is division, so divide both sides by -2. Don't forget to flip the inequality symbol since you are dividing by a negative number. This results in $-3 < x$. You can rewrite this as $x > -3$. To graph an inequality, you create a number line and put a circle around the value that is being compared to x. If you are graphing a greater than or less than inequality, as the one shown, the circle remains open. This represents all of the values excluding -3. If the inequality happens to be a greater than or equal to or less than or equal to, you draw a closed circle around the value. This would represent all of the values including the number. Finally, take a look at the values that the solution represents and shade the number line in the appropriate direction. You are graphing all of the values greater than -3 and since this is all of the numbers to the right of -3, shade this region on the number line.

DETERMINING SOLUTIONS TO INEQUALITIES
Determine whether $(-2, 4)$ is a solution of the inequality $y \geq -2x + 3$.

To determine whether a coordinate is a **solution of an inequality**, you can either use the inequality or its graph. Using $(-2, 4)$ as (x, y), substitute the values into the inequality to see if it makes a true statement. This results in $4 \geq -2(-2) + 3$. Using the integer rules, simplify the right side of the inequality by multiplying and then adding. The result is $4 \geq 7$, which is a false statement. Therefore, the coordinate is not a solution of the inequality. You can also use the **graph** of an inequality to see if a coordinate is a part of the solution. The graph of an inequality is shaded over the section of the coordinate grid that is included in the solution. The graph of $y \geq -2x + 3$ includes the solid line $y = -2x + 3$ and is shaded to the right of the line, representing all of the points greater than and including the points on the line. This excludes the point $(-2, 4)$, so it is not a solution of the inequality.

CALCULATIONS USING POINTS

Sometimes you need to perform calculations using only points on a graph as input data. Using points, you can determine what the **midpoint** and **distance** are. If you know the equation for a line you can calculate the distance between the line and the point.

To find the **midpoint** of two points (x_1, y_1) and (x_2, y_2), average the x-coordinates to get the x-coordinate of the midpoint, and average the y-coordinates to get the y-coordinate of the midpoint. The formula is: midpoint $= \left(\frac{x_1+x_2}{2}, \frac{y_1+y_2}{2}\right)$.

The **distance** between two points is the same as the length of the hypotenuse of a right triangle with the two given points as endpoints, and the two sides of the right triangle parallel to the x-axis and y-axis, respectively. The length of the segment parallel to the x-axis is the difference between the x-coordinates of the two points. The length of the segment parallel to the y-axis is the difference between the y-coordinates of the two points. Use the Pythagorean theorem $a^2 + b^2 = c^2$ or $c = \sqrt{a^2 + b^2}$ to find the distance. The formula is distance $= \sqrt{(x_2 - x_1)^2 + (y_2 - y_1)^2}$.

When a line is in the format $Ax + By + C = 0$, where A, B, and C are coefficients, you can use a point (x_1, y_1) not on the line and apply the formula $d = \frac{|Ax_1 + By_1 + C|}{\sqrt{A^2+B^2}}$ to find the distance between the line and the point (x_1, y_1).

EXAMPLE

Find the distance and midpoint between points $(2, 4)$ and $(8, 6)$.

MIDPOINT

$$\text{Midpoint} = \left(\frac{x_1+x_2}{2}, \frac{y_1+y_2}{2}\right)$$
$$\text{Midpoint} = \left(\frac{2+8}{2}, \frac{4+6}{2}\right)$$
$$\text{Midpoint} = \left(\frac{10}{2}, \frac{10}{2}\right)$$
$$\text{Midpoint} = (5,5)$$

DISTANCE

$$\text{Distance} = \sqrt{(x_2 - x_1)^2 + (y_2 - y_1)^2}$$
$$\text{Distance} = \sqrt{(8 - 2)^2 + (6 - 4)^2}$$
$$\text{Distance} = \sqrt{(6)^2 + (2)^2}$$
$$\text{Distance} = \sqrt{36 + 4}$$
$$\text{Distance} = \sqrt{40} \text{ or } 2\sqrt{10}$$

SYSTEMS OF EQUATIONS

Systems of equations are a set of simultaneous equations that all use the same variables. A solution to a system of equations must be true for each equation in the system. *Consistent systems* are those with at least one solution. *Inconsistent systems* are systems of equations that have no solution.

> **Review Video: Systems of Equations**
> Visit mometrix.com/academy and enter code: 658153

SUBSTITUTION

To solve a system of linear equations by *substitution*, start with the easier equation and solve for one of the variables. Express this variable in terms of the other variable. Substitute this expression in the other equation and solve for the other variable. The solution should be expressed in the form (x, y). Substitute the values into both of the original equations to check your answer. Consider the following problem.

Solve the system using substitution:

$$x + 6y = 15$$
$$3x - 12y = 18$$

Solve the first equation for x:

$$x = 15 - 6y$$

Substitute this value in place of x in the second equation, and solve for y:

$$3(15 - 6y) - 12y = 18$$
$$45 - 18y - 12y = 18$$
$$30y = 27$$
$$y = \frac{27}{30} = \frac{9}{10} = 0.9$$

Plug this value for y back into the first equation to solve for x:

$$x = 15 - 6(0.9) = 15 - 5.4 = 9.6$$

Check both equations if you have time:

$$9.6 + 6(0.9) = 9.6 + 5.4 = 15$$
$$3(9.6) - 12(0.9) = 28.8 - 10.8 = 18$$

Therefore, the solution is $(9.6, 0.9)$.

ELIMINATION

To solve a system of equations using *elimination*, begin by rewriting both equations in standard form $Ax + By = C$. Check to see if the coefficients of one pair of like variables add to zero. If not, multiply one or both of the equations by a non-zero number to make one set of like variables add to zero. Add the two equations to solve for one of the variables. Substitute this value into one of the original equations to solve for the other variable. Check your work by substituting into the other equation. Next, we will solve the same problem as above, but using the addition method.

Solve the system using elimination:

$$x + 6y = 15$$
$$3x - 12y = 18$$

If we multiply the first equation by 2, we can eliminate the y terms:

$$2x + 12y = 30$$
$$3x - 12y = 18$$

129

Add the equations together and solve for x:

$$5x = 48$$
$$x = \frac{48}{5} = 9.6$$

Plug the value for x back into either of the original equations and solve for y:

$$9.6 + 6y = 15$$
$$y = \frac{15 - 9.6}{6} = 0.9$$

Check both equations if you have time:

$$9.6 + 6(0.9) = 9.6 + 5.4 = 15$$
$$3(9.6) - 12(0.9) = 28.8 - 10.8 = 18$$

Therefore, the solution is $(9.6, 0.9)$.

GRAPHICALLY

To solve a system of linear equations **graphically**, plot both equations on the same graph. The solution of the equations is the point where both lines cross. If the lines do not cross (are parallel), then there is **no solution**.

For example, consider the following system of equations:

$$y = 2x + 7$$
$$y = -x + 1$$

Since these equations are given in slope-intercept form, they are easy to graph; the y intercepts of the lines are $(0, 7)$ and $(0, 1)$. The respective slopes are 2 and –1, thus the graphs look like this:

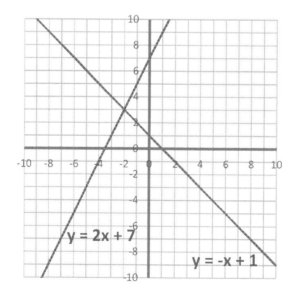

The two lines intersect at the point $(-2, 3)$, thus this is the solution to the system of equations.

Solving a system graphically is generally only practical if both coordinates of the solution are integers; otherwise the intersection will lie between gridlines on the graph and the coordinates will be difficult or impossible to determine exactly. It also helps if, as in this example, the equations are in slope-intercept form or some other form that makes them easy to graph. Otherwise, another method of solution (by substitution or elimination) is likely to be more useful.

SOLVING SYSTEMS OF EQUATIONS USING THE TRACE FEATURE

Using the **trace feature** on a calculator requires that you rewrite each equation, isolating the y-variable on one side of the equal sign. Enter both equations in the graphing calculator and plot the graphs simultaneously. Use the trace cursor to find where the two lines cross. Use the zoom feature if necessary to obtain more accurate results. Always check your answer by substituting into the original equations. The trace method is likely to be less accurate than other methods due to the resolution of graphing calculators, but is a useful tool to provide an approximate answer.

SOLVING A SYSTEM OF EQUATIONS CONSISTING OF A LINEAR EQUATION AND A QUADRATIC EQUATION

ALGEBRAICALLY

Generally, the simplest way to solve a system of equations consisting of a linear equation and a quadratic equation algebraically is through the method of **substitution**. One possible strategy is to solve the linear equation for y and then substitute that expression into the quadratic equation. After expansion and combining like terms, this will result in a new quadratic equation for x which, like all quadratic equations, may have zero, one, or two solutions. Plugging each solution for x back into one of the original equations will then produce the corresponding value of y.

For example, consider the following system of equations:

$$x + y = 1$$
$$y = (x + 3)^2 - 2$$

We can solve the linear equation for y to yield $y = -x + 1$.

Substituting this expression into the quadratic equation produces $-x + 1 = (x + 3)^2 - 2$

We can simplify this equation:

$$-x + 1 = (x + 3)^2 - 2$$
$$-x + 1 = x^2 + 6x + 9 - 2$$
$$-x + 1 = x^2 + 6x + 7$$
$$x^2 + 7x + 6 = 0$$

This quadratic equation can be factored as $(x + 1)(x + 6) = 0$. It therefore has two solutions: $x_1 = -1$ and $x_2 = -6$. Plugging each of these back into the original linear equation yields $y_1 = -x_1 + 1 = -(-1) + 1 = 2$ and $y_2 = -x_2 + 1 = -(-6) + 1 = 7$. Thus this system of equations has two solutions, $(-1, 2)$ and $(-6, 7)$.

It may help to check your work by putting each x and y value back into the original equations and verifying that they do provide a solution.

GRAPHICALLY

To solve a system of equations consisting of a linear equation and a quadratic equation **graphically**, plot both equations on the same graph. The linear equation will of course produce a straight line,

131

while the quadratic equation will produce a parabola. These two graphs will intersect at zero, one, or two points; each point of intersection is a solution of the system.

For example, consider the following system of equations:

$$y = -2x + 2$$
$$y = -2x^2 + 4x + 2$$

The linear equation describes a line with a y-intercept of $(0, 2)$ and a slope of -2.

To graph the quadratic equation, we can first find the vertex of the parabola: the x-coordinate of the vertex is $h = -\frac{b}{2a} = -\frac{4}{2(-2)} = 1$, and the y coordinate is $k = -2(1)^2 + 4(1) + 2 = 4$. Thus, the vertex lies at $(1, 4)$. To get a feel for the rest of the parabola, we can plug in a few more values of x to find more points; by putting in $x = 2$ and $x = 3$ in the quadratic equation, we find that the points $(2, 2)$ and $(3, -4)$ lie on the parabola; by symmetry thus do $(0, 2)$ and $(-1, -4)$. We can now plot both equations:

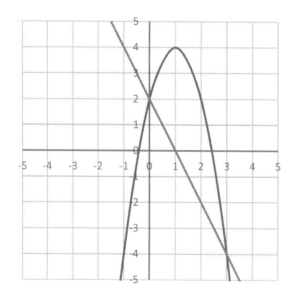

These two curves intersect at the points $(0, 2)$ and $(3, -4)$, thus these are the solutions of the equation.

POLYNOMIAL ALGEBRA

To multiply two binomials, follow the **FOIL** method. FOIL stands for:

- First: Multiply the first term of each binomial
- Outer: Multiply the outer terms of each binomial
- Inner: Multiply the inner terms of each binomial
- Last: Multiply the last term of each binomial

Using FOIL $(Ax + By)(Cx + Dy) = ACx^2 + ADxy + BCxy + BDy^2$.

EXAMPLE

Use the FOIL method on binomials $(x + 2)$ and $(x - 3)$.

First: $(x + 2)(x - 3) = (x)(x) = x^2$
Outer: $(x + 2)(x - 3) = (x)(-3) = -3x$
Inner: $(x + 2)(x - 3) = (2)(x) = 2x$
Last: $(x + 2)(x - 3) = (2)(-3) = -6$

Combine like terms:

$$(x^2) + (-3x) + (2x) + (-6) = x^2 - x - 6$$

Review Video: Multiplying Terms Using the FOIL Method
Visit mometrix.com/academy and enter code: 854792

To divide polynomials, begin by arranging the terms of each polynomial in order of one variable. You may arrange in ascending or descending order, but make sure to be consistent with both polynomials. To get the first term of the quotient, divide the first term of the dividend by the first term of the divisor. Multiply the first term of the quotient by the entire divisor and subtract that product from the dividend. Repeat for the second and successive terms until you either get a remainder of zero or a remainder whose degree is less than the degree of the divisor. If the quotient has a remainder, write the answer as a mixed expression in the form: $\text{quotient} + \frac{\text{remainder}}{\text{divisor}}$.

Rational expressions are fractions with polynomials in both the numerator and the denominator; the value of the polynomial in the denominator cannot be equal to zero. To add or subtract rational expressions, first find the common denominator, then rewrite each fraction as an equivalent fraction with the common denominator. Finally, add or subtract the numerators to get the numerator of the answer, and keep the common denominator as the denominator of the answer. When multiplying rational expressions factor each polynomial and cancel like factors (a factor which appears in both the numerator and the denominator). Then, multiply all remaining factors in the numerator to get the numerator of the product, and multiply the remaining factors in the denominator to get the denominator of the product. Remember – cancel entire factors, not individual terms. To divide rational expressions, take the reciprocal of the divisor (the rational expression you are dividing by) and multiply by the dividend.

Review Video: Simplifying Rational Polynomial Functions
Visit mometrix.com/academy and enter code: 351038

Below are patterns of some special products to remember: *perfect trinomial squares*, the *difference between two squares*, the *sum and difference of two cubes*, and *perfect cubes*.

- Perfect trinomial squares: $x^2 + 2xy + y^2 = (x + y)^2$ or $x^2 - 2xy + y^2 = (x - y)^2$
- Difference between two squares: $x^2 - y^2 = (x + y)(x - y)$
- Sum of two cubes: $x^3 + y^3 = (x + y)(x^2 - xy + y^2)$
- Note: the second factor is *not* the same as a perfect trinomial square, so do not try to factor it further.
- Difference between two cubes: $x^3 - y^3 = (x - y)(x^2 + xy + y^2)$
- Again, the second factor is *not* the same as a perfect trinomial square.
- Perfect cubes: $x^3 + 3x^2y + 3xy^2 + y^3 = (x + y)^3$ and $x^3 - 3x^2y + 3xy^2 - y^3 = (x - y)^3$

In order to **factor a polynomial**, first check for a common monomial factor. When the greatest common monomial factor has been factored out, look for patterns of special products: differences of two squares, the sum or difference of two cubes for binomial factors, or perfect trinomial squares for trinomial factors. If the factor is a trinomial but not a perfect trinomial square, look for a factorable form, such as $x^2 + (a + b)x + ab = (x + a)(x + b)$ or $(ac)x^2 + (ad + bc)x + bd = (ax + b)(cx + d)$. For factors with four terms, look for groups to factor. Once you have found the factors, write the original polynomial as the product of all the factors. Make sure all of the polynomial factors are prime. Monomial factors may be prime or composite. Check your work by multiplying the factors to make sure you get the original polynomial.

SOLVING QUADRATIC EQUATIONS

The **quadratic formula** is used to solve quadratic equations when other methods are more difficult. To use the quadratic formula to solve a quadratic equation, begin by rewriting the equation in standard form $ax^2 + bx + c = 0$, where a, b, and c are coefficients. Once you have identified the values of the coefficients, substitute those values into the quadratic formula $x = \frac{-b \pm \sqrt{b^2 - 4ac}}{2a}$. Evaluate the equation and simplify the expression. Again, check each root by substituting into the original equation. In the quadratic formula, the portion of the formula under the radical ($b^2 - 4ac$) is called the **discriminant**. If the discriminant is zero, there is only one root: $-\frac{b}{2a}$. If the discriminant is positive, there are two different real roots. If the discriminant is negative, there are no real roots.

To solve a quadratic equation by factoring, begin by rewriting the equation in standard form, if necessary. Factor the side with the variable then set each of the factors equal to zero and solve the resulting linear equations. Check your answers by substituting the roots you found into the original equation. If, when writing the equation in standard form, you have an equation in the form $x^2 + c = 0$ or $x^2 - c = 0$, set $x^2 = -c$ or $x^2 = c$ and take the square root of c. If $c = 0$, the only real root is zero. If c is positive, there are two real roots—the positive and negative square root values. If c is negative, there are no real roots because you cannot take the square root of a negative number.

> **Review Video: Factoring Quadratic Equations**
> Visit mometrix.com/academy and enter code: 336566

To solve a quadratic equation by **completing the square**, rewrite the equation so that all terms containing the variable are on the left side of the equal sign, and all the constants are on the right side of the equal sign. Make sure the coefficient of the squared term is 1. If there is a coefficient with the squared term, divide each term on both sides of the equal side by that number. Next, work with the coefficient of the single-variable term. Square half of this coefficient and add that value to both sides. Now you can factor the left side (the side containing the variable) as the square of a binomial. $x^2 + 2ax + a^2 = C \Rightarrow (x + a)^2 = C$, where x is the variable, and a and C are constants. Take the square root of both sides and solve for the variable. Substitute the value of the variable in the original problem to check your work.

QUADRATIC FUNCTION

A *quadratic function* is a function in the form $y = ax^2 + bx + c$, where a does not equal 0. While a linear function forms a line, a quadratic function forms a **parabola**, which is a u-shaped figure that either opens upward or downward. A parabola that opens upward is said to be a **positive quadratic function** and a parabola that opens downward is said to be a **negative quadratic function**. The shape of a parabola can differ, depending on the values of a, b, and c. All parabolas contain a **vertex**, which is the highest possible point, the **maximum**, or the lowest possible point, the **minimum**. This is the point where the graph begins moving in the opposite direction. A quadratic function can have zero, one, or two solutions, and therefore, zero, one, or two x-intercepts. Recall that the x-intercepts are referred to as the zeros, or roots, of a function. A quadratic function will have only one y-intercept. Understanding the basic components of a quadratic function can give you an idea of the shape of its graph.

Example graph of a positive quadratic function:

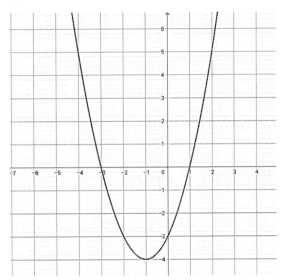

SIMPLIFYING POLYNOMIAL EXPRESSIONS

A polynomial is a group of monomials added or subtracted together. Simplifying polynomials requires combining like terms. The like terms in a polynomial expression are those that have the same variable raised to the same power. It is often helpful to connect the like terms with arrows or lines in order to separate them from the other monomials. Once you have determined the like terms, you can rearrange the polynomial by placing them together. Remember to include the sign that is in front of each term. Once the like terms are placed together, you can apply each operation and simplify. When adding and subtracting polynomials, only add and subtract the **coefficient**, or the number part; the variable and exponent stay the same.

POSITION OF PARABOLA

A **quadratic function** is written in the form $y = ax^2 + bx + c$. Changing the leading coefficient, a, in the equation changes the direction of the parabola. If the value of a is **positive**, the graph opens upward. The vertex of this parabola is the **minimum** value of the graph. If the value of a is **negative**, the graph opens downward. The vertex of this parabola is the **maximum** value of the graph. The leading coefficient, a, also affects the width of the parabola. The closer a is to 0, the wider the parabola will be. The values of b and c both affect the position of the parabola on the graph. The effect from changing b depends on the sign of a. If a is negative, increasing the value of b moves the parabola to the right and decreasing the value of b moves it to the left. If a is positive, changes to b have the opposite effect. The value of c in the quadratic equation represents the y-intercept and therefore, moves the parabola up and down the y-axis. The larger the c-value, the higher the parabola is on the graph.

FINDING ROOTS

Find the roots of $y = x^2 + 6x - 16$ and explain why these values are important.

The **roots** of a quadratic equation are the solutions when $ax^2 + bx + c = 0$. To find the roots of a quadratic equation, first replace y with 0. If $0 = x^2 + 6x - 16$, then to find the values of x, you can factor the equation if possible. When factoring a quadratic equation where $a = 1$, find the factors of

135

c that add up to b. That is the factors of -16 that add up to 6. The factors of -16 include, -4 and 4, -8 and 2 and -2 and 8. The factors that add up to equal 6 are -2 and 8. Write these factors as the product of two binomials, $0 = (x - 2)(x + 8)$. You can verify that these are the correct factors by using FOIL to multiply them together. Finally, since these binomials multiply together to equal zero, set them each equal to zero and solve for x. This results in $x - 2 = 0$, which simplifies to $x = 2$ and $x + 8 = 0$, which simplifies to $x = -8$. Therefore, the roots of the equation are 2 and -8. These values are important because they tell you where the graph of the equation crosses the x-axis. The points of intersection are $(2, 0)$ and $(-8, 0)$.

> **Review Video: <u>Finding the Missing Roots</u>**
> Visit mometrix.com/academy and enter code: 198376

SOLVING QUADRATIC EQUATIONS

METHODS

One way to find the solution or solutions of a quadratic equation is to use its **graph**. The solution(s) of a quadratic equation are the values of x when $y = 0$. On the graph, $y = 0$ is where the parabola crosses the x-axis, or the x-intercepts. This is also referred to as the **roots**, or zeros of a function. Given a graph, you can locate the x-intercepts to find the solutions. If there are no x-intercepts, the function has no solution. If the parabola crosses the x-axis at one point, there is one solution and if it crosses at two points, there are two solutions. Since the solutions exist where $y = 0$, you can also solve the equation by substituting 0 in for y. Then, try factoring the equation by finding the factors of ac that add up to equal b. You can use the guess and check method, the box method, or grouping. Once you find a pair that works, write them as the product of two binomials and set them equal to zero. Finally, solve for x to find the solutions. The last way to solve a quadratic equation is to use the **quadratic formula**. The quadratic formula is $x = \frac{-b \pm \sqrt{b^2 - 4ac}}{2a}$. Substitute the values of a, b, and c into the formula and solve for x. Remember that $\pm$ refers to two different solutions. Always check your solutions with the original equation to make sure they are valid.

EXAMPLE

List the steps used in solving $y = 2x^2 + 8x + 4$.

First, substitute 0 in for y in the quadratic equation:

$$0 = 2x^2 + 8x + 4$$

Next, try to factor the quadratic equation. If $a \neq 1$, list the factors of ac, or 8:

$$(1, 8), (-1, -8), (2, 4), (-2, -4)$$

Look for the factors of ac that add up to b, or 8. Since none do, the equation cannot be factored with whole numbers. Substitute the values of a, b, and c into the quadratic formula, $x = \frac{-b \pm \sqrt{b^2 - 4ac}}{2a}$:

$$x = \frac{-8 \pm \sqrt{8^2 - 4(2)(4)}}{2(2)}$$

Use the order of operations to simplify:

$$x = \frac{-8 \pm \sqrt{64 - 32}}{4}$$

$$x = \frac{-8 \pm \sqrt{32}}{4}$$

Reduce and simplify:

$$x = \frac{-8 \pm \sqrt{(16)(2)}}{4}$$

$$x = \frac{-8 \pm 4\sqrt{2}}{4}$$

$$x = -2 \pm \sqrt{2}$$

$$x = -2 + \sqrt{2} \text{ and}$$

$$x = -2 - \sqrt{2}$$

Check both solutions with the original equation to make sure they are valid.

Simplify the square roots and round to two decimal places.

$$x = -3.41 \text{ and } x = -0.586$$

LAWS OF EXPONENTS

Multiply $(2x^4)^2(xy)^4 \cdot 4y^3$ using the **laws of exponents**.

According the order of operations, the first step in simplifying expressions is to evaluate within the parentheses. Moving from left to right, the first set of parentheses contains a power raised to a power. The rules of exponents state that when a power is raised to a power, you *multiply* the exponents. Since $4 \times 2 = 8$, $(2x^4)^2$ can be written as $4x^8$. The second set of parentheses raises a product to a power. The **rules of exponents** state that you raise every value within the parentheses to the given power. Therefore, $(xy)^4$ can be written as x^4y^4. Combining these terms with the last term gives you, $4x^8 \cdot x^4y^4 \cdot 4y^3$. In this expression, there are powers with the same base. The rules of exponents state that you *add* powers with the same base, while multiplying the coefficients. You can group the expression as $(4x^8 \cdot x^4) \cdot (y^4 \cdot 4y^3)$ to organize the values with the same base. Then, using this rule add the exponents. The result is $4x^{12} \cdot 4y^7$, or $16x^{12}y^7$.

> **Review Video: Laws of Exponents**
> Visit mometrix.com/academy and enter code: 532558

USING GIVEN ROOTS TO FIND QUADRATIC EQUATION

EXAMPLE

Find a quadratic equation whose real roots are $x = 2$ and $x = -1$.

One way to find the roots of a quadratic equation is to factor the equation and use the **zero product property**, setting each factor of the equation equal to zero to find the corresponding root. We can use this technique in reverse to find an equation given its roots. Each root corresponds to a linear equation which in turn corresponds to a factor of the quadratic equation.

For example, the root $x=2$ corresponds to the equation $x - 2 = 0$, and the root $x = -1$ corresponds to the equation $x + 1 = 0$.

These two equations correspond to the factors $(x - 2)$ and $(x+1)$, from which we can derive the equation $(x - 2)(x + 1) = 0$, or $x^2 - x - 2 = 0$.

Any integer multiple of this entire equation will also yield the same roots, as the integer will simply cancel out when the equation is factored. For example, $2x^2 - 2x - 4 = 0$ factors as

$2(x - 2)(x + 1) = 0$.

SIMPLIFYING RATIONAL EXPRESSIONS

To *simplify a rational expression*, factor the numerator and denominator completely. Factors that are the same and appear in the numerator and denominator have a ratio of 1. The denominator, $(1 - x^2)$, is a difference of squares. It can be factored as $(1 - x)(1 + x)$. The factor $1 - x$ and the numerator $x - 1$ are opposites and have a ratio of –1. Rewrite the numerator as $-1(1 - x)$. So, the rational expression can be simplified as follows:

$$\frac{x - 1}{1 - x^2} = \frac{-1(1 - x)}{(1 - x)(1 + x)} = \frac{-1}{1 + x}$$

(Note that since the original expression is defined for $x \neq \{-1, 1\}$, the simplified expression has the same restrictions.)

> **Review Video: Reducing Rational Expressions**
> Visit mometrix.com/academy and enter code: 788868

MATRIX BASICS

A **matrix** (plural: matrices) is a rectangular array of numbers or variables, often called **elements**, which are arranged in columns and rows. A matrix is generally represented by a capital letter, with its elements represented by the corresponding lowercase letter with two subscripts indicating the row and column of the element. For example, n_{ab} represents the element in row a column b of matrix N.

$$N = \begin{bmatrix} n_{11} & n_{12} & n_{13} \\ n_{21} & n_{22} & n_{23} \end{bmatrix}$$

A matrix can be described in terms of the number of rows and columns it contains in the format $a \times b$, where a is the number of rows and b is the number of columns. The matrix shown above is a 2×3 matrix. Any $a \times b$ matrix where $a = b$ is a square matrix. A **vector** is a matrix that has exactly one column (**column vector**) or exactly one row (**row vector**).

The **main diagonal** of a matrix is the set of elements on the diagonal from the top left to the bottom right of a matrix. Because of the way it is defined, only square matrices will have a main diagonal. For the matrix shown below, the main diagonal consists of the elements $n_{11}, n_{22}, n_{33}, n_{44}$.

$$\begin{bmatrix} n_{11} & n_{12} & n_{13} & n_{14} \\ n_{21} & n_{22} & n_{23} & n_{24} \\ n_{31} & n_{32} & n_{33} & n_{34} \\ n_{41} & n_{42} & n_{43} & n_{44} \end{bmatrix}$$

A 3×4 matrix such as the one shown below would not have a main diagonal because there is no straight line of elements between the top left corner and the bottom right corner that joins the elements.

$$\begin{bmatrix} n_{11} & n_{12} & n_{13} & n_{14} \\ n_{21} & n_{22} & n_{23} & n_{24} \\ n_{31} & n_{32} & n_{33} & n_{34} \end{bmatrix}$$

A **diagonal matrix** is a square matrix that has a zero for every element in the matrix except the elements on the main diagonal. All the elements on the main diagonal must be nonzero numbers.

$$\begin{bmatrix} n_{11} & 0 & 0 & 0 \\ 0 & n_{22} & 0 & 0 \\ 0 & 0 & n_{33} & 0 \\ 0 & 0 & 0 & n_{44} \end{bmatrix}$$

If every element on the main diagonal of a diagonal matrix is equal to one, the matrix is called an **identity matrix**. The identity matrix is often represented by the letter I.

$$I = \begin{bmatrix} 1 & 0 & 0 & 0 \\ 0 & 1 & 0 & 0 \\ 0 & 0 & 1 & 0 \\ 0 & 0 & 0 & 1 \end{bmatrix}$$

A **zero matrix** is a matrix that has zero as the value for every element in the matrix.

$$\begin{bmatrix} 0 & 0 & 0 & 0 \\ 0 & 0 & 0 & 0 \\ 0 & 0 & 0 & 0 \\ 0 & 0 & 0 & 0 \end{bmatrix}$$

The zero matrix is the *identity for matrix addition*. Do not confuse the zero matrix with the identity matrix.

The **negative of a matrix** is also known as the additive inverse of a matrix. If matrix N is the given matrix, then matrix $-N$ is its negative. This means that every element n_{ab} is equal to $-n_{ab}$ in the negative. To find the negative of a given matrix, change the sign of every element in the matrix and keep all elements in their original corresponding positions in the matrix.

If two matrices have the same order and all corresponding elements in the two matrices are the same, then the two matrices are **equal matrices**.

A matrix N may be **transposed** to matrix N^T by changing all rows into columns and changing all columns into rows. The easiest way to accomplish this is to swap the positions of the row and column notations for each element. For example, suppose the element in the second row of the third column of matrix N is $n_{23} = 6$. In the transposed matrix N^T, the transposed element would be $n_{32} = 6$, and it would be placed in the third row of the second column.

$$N = \begin{bmatrix} 1 & 2 & 3 \\ 4 & 5 & 6 \end{bmatrix}; \; N^T = \begin{bmatrix} 1 & 4 \\ 2 & 5 \\ 3 & 6 \end{bmatrix}$$

To quickly transpose a matrix by hand, begin with the first column and rewrite a new matrix with those same elements in the same order in the first row. Write the elements from the second column of the original matrix in the second row of the transposed matrix. Continue this process until all columns have been completed. If the original matrix is identical to the transposed matrix, the matrices are symmetric.

The **determinant** of a matrix is a scalar value that is calculated by taking into account all the elements of a square matrix. A determinant only exists for square matrices. Finding the determinant of a 2×2 matrix is as simple as remembering a simple equation. For a 2×2 matrix $M = \begin{bmatrix} m_{11} & m_{12} \\ m_{21} & m_{22} \end{bmatrix}$, the determinant is obtained by the equation $|M| = m_{11}m_{22} - m_{12}m_{21}$. Anything larger than 2×2 requires multiple steps. Take matrix $N = \begin{bmatrix} a & b & c \\ d & e & f \\ g & h & j \end{bmatrix}$. The determinant of N is calculated as $|N| = a \begin{vmatrix} e & f \\ h & j \end{vmatrix} - b \begin{vmatrix} d & f \\ g & j \end{vmatrix} + c \begin{vmatrix} d & e \\ g & h \end{vmatrix}$ or $|N| = a(ej - fh) - b(dj - fg) + c(dh - eg)$.

There is a shortcut for 3×3 matrices: add the products of each unique set of elements diagonally left-to-right and subtract the products of each unique set of elements diagonally right-to-left. In matrix N, the left-to-right diagonal elements are (a, e, j), (b, f, g), and (c, d, h). The right-to-left diagonal elements are (a, f, h), (b, d, j), and (c, e, g). $\det(N) = aej + bfg + cdh - afh - bdj - ceg$.

Calculating the determinants of matrices larger than 3×3 is rarely, if ever, done by hand.

The **inverse** of a matrix M is the matrix that, when multiplied by matrix M, yields a product that is the identity matrix. Multiplication of matrices will be explained in greater detail shortly. Not all matrices have inverses. Only a square matrix whose determinant is not zero has an inverse. If a matrix has an inverse, that inverse is unique to that matrix. For any matrix M that has an inverse, the inverse is represented by the symbol M^{-1}. To calculate the inverse of a 2×2 square matrix, use the following pattern:

$$M = \begin{bmatrix} m_{11} & m_{12} \\ m_{21} & m_{22} \end{bmatrix}; \; M^{-1} = \begin{bmatrix} \dfrac{m_{22}}{|M|} & \dfrac{-m_{12}}{|M|} \\ \dfrac{-m_{21}}{|M|} & \dfrac{m_{11}}{|M|} \end{bmatrix}$$

Another way to find the inverse of a matrix by hand is use an augmented matrix and elementary row operations. An **augmented matrix** is formed by appending the entries from one matrix onto the end of another. For example, given a 2×2 invertible matrix $N = \begin{bmatrix} a & b \\ c & d \end{bmatrix}$, you can find the inverse N^{-1} by creating an augmented matrix by appending a 2×2 identity matrix: $\begin{bmatrix} a & b & | & 1 & 0 \\ c & d & | & 0 & 1 \end{bmatrix}$.

To find the inverse of the original 2 × 2 matrix, perform elementary row operations to convert the original matrix on the left to an identity matrix: $\begin{bmatrix} 1 & 0 & e & f \\ 0 & 1 & g & h \end{bmatrix}$.

Elementary row operations include multiplying a row by a non-zero scalar, adding scalar multiples of two rows, or some combination of these. For instance, the first step might be to multiply the second row by $\frac{b}{d}$ and then subtract it from the first row to make its second column a zero. The end result is that the 2 × 2 section on the right will become the inverse of the original matrix: $N^{-1} = \begin{bmatrix} e & f \\ g & h \end{bmatrix}$.

Calculating the inverse of any matrix larger than 2 × 2 is cumbersome and using a graphing calculator is recommended.

BASIC OPERATIONS WITH MATRICES

There are two categories of basic operations with regard to matrices: operations between a matrix and a scalar, and operations between two matrices.

SCALAR OPERATIONS

A scalar being added to a matrix is treated as though it were being added to each element of the matrix:

$$M + 4 = \begin{bmatrix} m_{11} + 4 & m_{12} + 4 \\ m_{21} + 4 & m_{22} + 4 \end{bmatrix}$$

The same is true for the other three operations.

SUBTRACTION:

$$M - 4 = \begin{bmatrix} m_{11} - 4 & m_{12} - 4 \\ m_{21} - 4 & m_{22} - 4 \end{bmatrix}$$

MULTIPLICATION:

$$M \times 4 = \begin{bmatrix} m_{11} \times 4 & m_{12} \times 4 \\ m_{21} \times 4 & m_{22} \times 4 \end{bmatrix}$$

DIVISION:

$$M \div 4 = \begin{bmatrix} m_{11} \div 4 & m_{12} \div 4 \\ m_{21} \div 4 & m_{22} \div 4 \end{bmatrix}$$

MATRIX ADDITION AND SUBTRACTION

All four of the basic operations can be used with operations between matrices (although division is usually discarded in favor of multiplication by the inverse), but there are restrictions on the situations in which they can be used. Matrices that meet all the qualifications for a given operation are called **conformable matrices**. However, conformability is specific to the operation; two matrices that are conformable for addition are not necessarily conformable for multiplication.

For two matrices to be conformable for addition or subtraction, they must be of the same dimension; otherwise the operation is not defined. If matrix M is a 3 × 2 matrix and matrix N is a

2×3 matrix, the operations $M + N$ and $M - N$ are meaningless. If matrices M and N are the same size, the operation is as simple as adding or subtracting all of the corresponding elements:

$$\begin{bmatrix} m_{11} & m_{12} \\ m_{21} & m_{22} \end{bmatrix} + \begin{bmatrix} n_{11} & n_{12} \\ n_{21} & n_{22} \end{bmatrix} = \begin{bmatrix} m_{11} + n_{11} & m_{12} + n_{12} \\ m_{21} + n_{21} & m_{22} + n_{22} \end{bmatrix}$$

$$\begin{bmatrix} m_{11} & m_{12} \\ m_{21} & m_{22} \end{bmatrix} - \begin{bmatrix} n_{11} & n_{12} \\ n_{21} & n_{22} \end{bmatrix} = \begin{bmatrix} m_{11} - n_{11} & m_{12} - n_{12} \\ m_{21} - n_{21} & m_{22} - n_{22} \end{bmatrix}$$

The result of addition or subtraction is a matrix of the same dimension as the two original matrices involved in the operation.

MATRIX MULTIPLICATION

The first thing it is necessary to understand about matrix multiplication is that it is not commutative. In scalar multiplication, the operation is commutative, meaning that $a \times b = b \times a$. For matrix multiplication, this is not the case: $A \times B \neq B \times A$. The terminology must be specific when describing matrix multiplication. The operation $A \times B$ can be described as A multiplied (or **post-multiplied**) by B, or B **pre-multiplied** by A.

For two matrices to be conformable for multiplication, they need not be of the same dimension, but specific dimensions must correspond. Taking the example of two matrices M and N to be multiplied $M \times N$, matrix M must have the same number of columns as matrix N has rows. Put another way, if matrix M has the dimensions $a \times b$ and matrix N has the dimensions $c \times d$, b must equal c if the two matrices are to be conformable for this multiplication. The matrix that results from the multiplication will have the dimensions $a \times d$. If a and d are both equal to 1, the product is simply a scalar. Square matrices of the same dimensions are always conformable for multiplication, and their product is always a matrix of the same size.

The simplest type of matrix multiplication is a 1×2 matrix (a row vector) times a 2×1 matrix (a column vector). These will multiply in the following way:

$$\begin{bmatrix} m_{11} & m_{12} \end{bmatrix} \times \begin{bmatrix} n_{11} \\ n_{21} \end{bmatrix} = m_{11}n_{11} + m_{12}n_{21}$$

The two matrices are conformable for multiplication because matrix M has the same number of columns as matrix N has rows. Because the other dimensions are both 1, the result is a scalar. Expanding our matrices to 1×3 and 3×1, the process is the same:

$$\begin{bmatrix} m_{11} & m_{12} & m_{13} \end{bmatrix} \times \begin{bmatrix} n_{11} \\ n_{21} \\ n_{31} \end{bmatrix} = m_{11}n_{11} + m_{12}n_{21} + m_{13}n_{31}$$

Once again, the result is a scalar. This type of basic matrix multiplication is the building block for the multiplication of larger matrices.

To multiply larger matrices, treat each **row from the first matrix** and each **column from the second matrix** as individual vectors and follow the pattern for multiplying vectors. The scalar value found from multiplying the first-row vector by the first column vector is placed in the first row, first column of the new matrix. The scalar value found from multiplying the second-row vector by the first column vector is placed in the second row, first column of the new matrix. Continue this pattern until each row of the first matrix has been multiplied by each column of the second vector.

Below is an example of the multiplication of a 3×2 matrix and a 2×3 matrix.

$$\begin{bmatrix} m_{11} & m_{12} \\ m_{21} & m_{22} \\ m_{31} & m_{32} \end{bmatrix} \times \begin{bmatrix} n_{11} & n_{12} & n_{13} \\ n_{21} & n_{22} & n_{23} \end{bmatrix} = \begin{bmatrix} m_{11}n_{11} + m_{12}n_{21} & m_{11}n_{12} + m_{12}n_{22} & m_{11}n_{13} + m_{12}n_{23} \\ m_{21}n_{11} + m_{22}n_{21} & m_{21}n_{12} + m_{22}n_{22} & m_{21}n_{13} + m_{22}n_{23} \\ m_{31}n_{11} + m_{32}n_{21} & m_{31}n_{12} + m_{32}n_{22} & m_{31}n_{13} + m_{32}n_{23} \end{bmatrix}$$

This process starts by taking the first column of the second matrix and running it through each row of the first matrix. Removing all but the first M row and first N column, we would see only the following:

$$[m_{11} \ \ m_{12}] \times \begin{bmatrix} n_{11} \\ n_{21} \end{bmatrix}$$

The first product would then be $m_{11}n_{11} + m_{12}n_{21}$. This process will be continued for each column of the N matrix to find the first full row of the product matrix, as shown below.

$$[m_{11} \ \ m_{12}] \times \begin{bmatrix} n_{11} \\ n_{21} \end{bmatrix} = [m_{11}n_{11} + m_{12}n_{21} \quad m_{11}n_{12} + m_{12}n_{22} \quad m_{11}n_{13} + m_{12}n_{23}]$$

After completing the first row, the next step would be to simply move to the second row of the M matrix and repeat the process until all of the rows have been finished. The result is a 3×3 matrix.

$$\begin{bmatrix} m_{11} & m_{12} \\ m_{21} & m_{22} \\ m_{31} & m_{32} \end{bmatrix} \times \begin{bmatrix} n_{11} & n_{12} & n_{13} \\ n_{21} & n_{22} & n_{23} \end{bmatrix} = \begin{bmatrix} m_{11}n_{11} + m_{12}n_{21} & m_{11}n_{12} + m_{12}n_{22} & m_{11}n_{13} + m_{12}n_{23} \\ m_{21}n_{11} + m_{22}n_{21} & m_{21}n_{12} + m_{22}n_{22} & m_{21}n_{13} + m_{22}n_{23} \\ m_{31}n_{11} + m_{32}n_{21} & m_{31}n_{12} + m_{32}n_{22} & m_{31}n_{13} + m_{32}n_{23} \end{bmatrix}$$

If the operation were done in reverse ($N \times M$), the result would be a 2×2 matrix.

$$\begin{bmatrix} n_{11} & n_{12} & n_{13} \\ n_{21} & n_{22} & n_{23} \end{bmatrix} \times \begin{bmatrix} m_{11} & m_{12} \\ m_{21} & m_{22} \\ m_{31} & m_{32} \end{bmatrix} = \begin{bmatrix} m_{11}n_{11} + m_{21}n_{12} + m_{31}n_{13} & m_{12}n_{11} + m_{22}n_{12} + m_{32}n_{13} \\ m_{11}n_{21} + m_{21}n_{22} + m_{31}n_{23} & m_{12}n_{21} + m_{22}n_{22} + m_{32}n_{23} \end{bmatrix}$$

EXAMPLE

A sporting-goods store sells baseballs, volleyballs, and basketballs.

Baseballs $3 each
Volleyballs $8 each
Basketballs $15 each

Here are the same store's sales numbers for one weekend:

	Baseballs	Volleyballs	Basketballs
Friday	5	4	4
Saturday	7	3	10
Sunday	4	3	6

Find the total sales for each day by multiplying matrices.

The first table can be represented by the following column-vector:

$$\begin{bmatrix} 3 \\ 8 \\ 15 \end{bmatrix}$$

And the second table can be represented by this matrix:

$$\begin{bmatrix} 5 & 4 & 4 \\ 7 & 3 & 10 \\ 4 & 3 & 6 \end{bmatrix}$$

Multiplying the second matrix by the first will result in a column vector showing the total sales for each day:

$$\begin{bmatrix} 5 & 4 & 4 \\ 7 & 3 & 10 \\ 4 & 3 & 6 \end{bmatrix} \times \begin{bmatrix} 3 \\ 8 \\ 15 \end{bmatrix} = \begin{bmatrix} 3 \times 5 + 8 \times 4 + 15 \times 4 \\ 3 \times 7 + 8 \times 3 + 15 \times 10 \\ 3 \times 4 + 8 \times 3 + 15 \times 6 \end{bmatrix} = \begin{bmatrix} 15 + 32 + 60 \\ 21 + 24 + 150 \\ 12 + 24 + 90 \end{bmatrix} = \begin{bmatrix} 107 \\ 195 \\ 126 \end{bmatrix}$$

From this, we can see that Friday's sales were \$107, Saturday's sales were \$195, and Sunday's sales were \$126.

SOLVING SYSTEMS OF EQUATIONS

Matrices can be used to represent the coefficients of a system of linear equations and can be very useful in solving those systems. Take for instance three equations with three variables:

$$a_1 x + b_1 y + c_1 z = d_1$$
$$a_2 x + b_2 y + c_2 z = d_2$$
$$a_3 x + b_3 y + c_3 z = d_3$$

where all a, b, c, and d are known constants.

To solve this system, define three matrices:

$$A = \begin{bmatrix} a_1 & b_1 & c_1 \\ a_2 & b_2 & c_2 \\ a_3 & b_3 & c_3 \end{bmatrix}; D = \begin{bmatrix} d_1 \\ d_2 \\ d_3 \end{bmatrix}; X = \begin{bmatrix} x \\ y \\ z \end{bmatrix}$$

The three equations in our system can be fully represented by a single matrix equation:

$$AX = D$$

We know that the identity matrix times X is equal to X, and we know that any matrix multiplied by its inverse is equal to the identity matrix.

$$A^{-1}AX = IX = X; \text{thus } X = A^{-1}D$$

Our goal then is to find the inverse of A, or A^{-1}. Once we have that, we can pre-multiply matrix D by A^{-1} (post-multiplying here is an undefined operation) to find matrix X.

Systems of equations can also be solved using the transformation of an augmented matrix in a process similar to that for finding a matrix inverse. Begin by arranging each equation of the system in the following format:

$$a_1x + b_1y + c_1z = d_1$$
$$a_2x + b_2y + c_2z = d_2$$
$$a_3x + b_3y + c_3z = d_3$$

Define matrices A and D and combine them into augmented matrix A_a:

$$A = \begin{bmatrix} a_1 & b_1 & c_1 \\ a_2 & b_2 & c_2 \\ a_3 & b_3 & c_3 \end{bmatrix}; D = \begin{bmatrix} d_1 \\ d_2 \\ d_3 \end{bmatrix}; A_a = \begin{bmatrix} a_1 & b_1 & c_1 & d_1 \\ a_2 & b_2 & c_2 & d_2 \\ a_3 & b_3 & c_3 & d_3 \end{bmatrix}$$

To solve the augmented matrix and the system of equations, use elementary row operations to form an identity matrix in the first 3×3 section. When this is complete, the values in the last column are the solutions to the system of equations:

$$\begin{bmatrix} 1 & 0 & 0 & x \\ 0 & 1 & 0 & y \\ 0 & 0 & 1 & z \end{bmatrix}$$

If an identity matrix is not possible, the system of equations has no unique solution. Sometimes only a partial solution will be possible. The following are partial solutions you may find:

$$\begin{bmatrix} 1 & 0 & k_1 & x_0 \\ 0 & 1 & k_2 & y_0 \\ 0 & 0 & 0 & 0 \end{bmatrix}$$ gives the non-unique solution $x = x_0 - k_1z; y = y_0 - k_2z$

$$\begin{bmatrix} 1 & j_1 & k_1 & x_0 \\ 0 & 0 & 0 & 0 \\ 0 & 0 & 0 & 0 \end{bmatrix}$$ gives the non-unique solution $x = x_0 - j_1y - k_1z$

This process can be used to solve systems of equations with any number of variables, but three is the upper limit for practical purposes. Anything more ought to be done with a graphing calculator.

GEOMETRIC TRANSFORMATIONS

The four *geometric transformations* are **translations, reflections, rotations**, and **dilations**. When geometric transformations are expressed as matrices, the process of performing the transformations is simplified. For calculations of the geometric transformations of a planar figure, make a $2 \times n$ matrix, where n is the number of vertices in the planar figure. Each column represents the rectangular coordinates of one vertex of the figure, with the top row containing the values of the x-coordinates and the bottom row containing the values of the y-coordinates. For example, given a planar triangular figure with coordinates (x_1, y_1), (x_2, y_2), and (x_3, y_3), the corresponding matrix is $\begin{bmatrix} x_1 & x_2 & x_3 \\ y_1 & y_2 & y_3 \end{bmatrix}$. You can then perform the necessary transformations on this matrix to determine the coordinates of the resulting figure.

TRANSLATION

A **translation** moves a figure along the x-axis, the y-axis, or both axes without changing the size or shape of the figure. To calculate the new coordinates of a planar figure following a translation, set up a matrix of the coordinates and a matrix of the translation values and add the two matrices.

$$\begin{bmatrix} h & h & h \\ v & v & v \end{bmatrix} + \begin{bmatrix} x_1 & x_2 & x_3 \\ y_1 & y_2 & y_3 \end{bmatrix} = \begin{bmatrix} h + x_1 & h + x_2 & h + x_3 \\ v + y_1 & v + y_2 & v + y_3 \end{bmatrix}$$

where h is the number of units the figure is moved along the x-axis (horizontally) and v is the number of units the figure is moved along the y-axis (vertically).

REFLECTION

To find the **reflection** of a planar figure over the x-axis, set up a matrix of the coordinates of the vertices and pre-multiply the matrix by the 2×2 matrix $\begin{bmatrix} 1 & 0 \\ 0 & -1 \end{bmatrix}$ so that $\begin{bmatrix} 1 & 0 \\ 0 & -1 \end{bmatrix} \begin{bmatrix} x_1 & x_2 & x_3 \\ y_1 & y_2 & y_3 \end{bmatrix} = \begin{bmatrix} x_1 & x_2 & x_3 \\ -y_1 & -y_2 & -y_3 \end{bmatrix}$. To find the reflection of a planar figure over the y-axis, set up a matrix of the coordinates of the vertices and pre-multiply the matrix by the 2×2 matrix $\begin{bmatrix} -1 & 0 \\ 0 & 1 \end{bmatrix}$ so that $\begin{bmatrix} -1 & 0 \\ 0 & 1 \end{bmatrix} \begin{bmatrix} x_1 & x_2 & x_3 \\ y_1 & y_2 & y_3 \end{bmatrix} = \begin{bmatrix} -x_1 & -x_2 & -x_3 \\ y_1 & y_2 & y_3 \end{bmatrix}$. To find the reflection of a planar figure over the line $y = x$, set up a matrix of the coordinates of the vertices and pre-multiply the matrix by the 2×2 matrix $\begin{bmatrix} 0 & 1 \\ 1 & 0 \end{bmatrix}$ so that $\begin{bmatrix} 0 & 1 \\ 1 & 0 \end{bmatrix} \begin{bmatrix} x_1 & x_2 & x_3 \\ y_1 & y_2 & y_3 \end{bmatrix} = \begin{bmatrix} y_1 & y_2 & y_3 \\ x_1 & x_2 & x_3 \end{bmatrix}$. Remember that the order of multiplication is important when multiplying matrices. The commutative property does not apply.

ROTATION

To find the coordinates of the figure formed by rotating a planar figure about the origin θ degrees in a counterclockwise direction, set up a matrix of the coordinates of the vertices and pre-multiply the matrix by the 2×2 matrix $\begin{bmatrix} \cos\theta & \sin\theta \\ -\sin\theta & \cos\theta \end{bmatrix}$. For example, if you want to rotate a figure 90° clockwise around the origin, you would have to convert the degree measure to 270° counterclockwise and solve the 2×2 matrix you have set as the pre-multiplier: $\begin{bmatrix} \cos 270° & \sin 270° \\ -\sin 270° & \cos 270° \end{bmatrix} = \begin{bmatrix} 0 & -1 \\ 1 & 0 \end{bmatrix}$. Use this as the pre-multiplier for the matrix $\begin{bmatrix} x_1 & x_2 & x_3 \\ y_1 & y_2 & y_3 \end{bmatrix}$ and solve to find the new coordinates.

DILATION

To find the **dilation** of a planar figure by a scale factor of k, set up a matrix of the coordinates of the vertices of the planar figure and pre-multiply the matrix by the 2×2 matrix $\begin{bmatrix} k & 0 \\ 0 & k \end{bmatrix}$ so that $\begin{bmatrix} k & 0 \\ 0 & k \end{bmatrix} \begin{bmatrix} x_1 & x_2 & x_3 \\ y_1 & y_2 & y_3 \end{bmatrix} = \begin{bmatrix} kx_1 & kx_2 & kx_3 \\ ky_1 & ky_2 & ky_3 \end{bmatrix}$. This is effectively the same as multiplying the matrix by the scalar k, but the matrix equation would still be necessary if the figure were being dilated by different factors in vertical and horizontal directions. The scale factor k will be greater than 1 if the figure is being enlarged, and between 0 and 1 if the figure is being shrunk. Again, remember that when multiplying matrices, the order of the matrices is important. The commutative property does not apply, and the matrix with the coordinates of the figure must be the second matrix.

REDUCED ROW-ECHELON FORMS

When a system of equations has a solution, finding the transformation of the augmented matrix will result in one of three reduced row-echelon forms. Only one of these forms will give a unique solution to the system of equations, however. The following examples show the solutions indicated by particular results:

$$\begin{bmatrix} 1 & 0 & 0 & x_0 \\ 0 & 1 & 0 & y_0 \\ 0 & 0 & 1 & z_0 \end{bmatrix}$$ gives the unique solution $x = x_0$; $y = y_0$; $z = z_0$

$$\begin{bmatrix} 1 & 0 & k_1 & x_0 \\ 0 & 1 & k_2 & y_0 \\ 0 & 0 & 0 & 0 \end{bmatrix}$$ gives a non-unique solution $x = x_0 - k_1 z$; $y = y_0 - k_2 z$

$$\begin{bmatrix} 1 & j_1 & k_1 & x_0 \\ 0 & 0 & 0 & 0 \\ 0 & 0 & 0 & 0 \end{bmatrix}$$ gives a non-unique solution $x = x_0 - j_1 y - k_1 z$

COMMON METRIC MEASUREMENTS

FLUIDS

1 liter = 1000 milliliters
1 liter = 1000 cubic centimeters

Note: Do not confuse *cubic centimeters* with *centiliters*. 1 liter = 1000 cubic centi*meters*, but 1 liter = 100 centi*liters*.

DISTANCE

1 meter = 1000 millimeters
1 meter = 100 centimeters

WEIGHT

1 gram = 1000 milligrams
1 kilogram = 1000 grams

MEASUREMENT PREFIXES

Kilo-: one thousand (1 *kilo*gram is one thousand grams.)
Centi-: one hundredth (1 *centi*meter is one hundredth of a meter.)
Milli-: one thousandth (1 *milli*liter is one thousandth of a liter.)

COMMON IMPERIAL MEASUREMENTS

VOLUME

1 cup = 8 fluid ounces

Note: This does NOT mean that one cup of something is the same as a half pound. Fluid ounces are measures of volume and have no correspondence with measures of weight.

1 pint = 2 cups
1 pint = 16 ounces

Again, the phrase, "A pint's a pound the world round," does not apply. A pint of something does not necessarily weigh one pound, since one fluid ounce is not the same as one ounce in weight. The expression is valid only for helping you remember the number 16, since most people can remember there are 16 ounces in a pound.

DISTANCE

1 yard = 3 feet
1 yard = 36 inches
1 mile = 5280 feet
1 mile = 1760 yards
1 acre = 43,560 square feet

VOLUME

1 quart = 2 pints
1 quart = 4 cups
1 gallon = 4 quarts
1 gallon = 8 pints
1 gallon = 16 cups

WEIGHT

1 pound = 16 ounces

Do not assume that because something weighs one pound that its volume is one pint. Ounces of weight are not equivalent to fluid ounces, which measure volume.

1 ton = 2000 pounds

In the United States, the word "ton" by itself refers to a short ton or a net ton. Do not confuse this with a long ton (also called a gross ton) or a metric ton (also spelled *tonne*), which have different measurement equivalents.

PRECISION, ACCURACY, AND ERROR

Precision: How reliable and repeatable a measurement is. The more consistent the data is with repeated testing, the more precise it is. For example, hitting a target consistently in the same spot, which may or may not be the center of the target, is precision.

Accuracy: How close the data is to the correct data. For example, hitting a target consistently in the center area of the target, whether or not the hits are all in the same spot, is accuracy.

Note: it is possible for data to be precise without being accurate. If a scale is off balance, the data will be precise, but will not be accurate. For data to have precision and accuracy, it must be repeatable and correct.

Approximate error: The amount of error in a physical measurement. Approximate error is often reported as the measurement, followed by the ± symbol and the amount of the approximate error.

Maximum possible error: Half the magnitude of the smallest unit used in the measurement. For example, if the unit of measurement is 1 centimeter, the maximum possible error is $\frac{1}{2}$ cm, written as ± 0.5 cm following the measurement. It is important to apply significant figures in reporting maximum possible error. Do not make the answer appear more accurate than the least accurate of your measurements.

LINES AND PLANES

A **point** is a fixed location in space; has no size or dimensions; commonly represented by a dot.

A **line** is a set of points that extends infinitely in two opposite directions. It has length, but no width or depth. A line can be defined by any two distinct points that it contains. A line segment is a portion of a line that has definite endpoints. A ray is a portion of a line that extends from a single point on that line in one direction along the line. It has a definite beginning, but no ending.

A **plane** is a two-dimensional flat surface defined by three non-collinear points. A plane extends an infinite distance in all directions in those two dimensions. It contains an infinite number of points, parallel lines and segments, intersecting lines and segments, as well as parallel or intersecting rays. A plane will never contain a three-dimensional figure or skew lines. Two given planes will either be parallel or they will intersect to form a line. A plane may intersect a circular conic surface, such as a cone, to form conic sections, such as the parabola, hyperbola, circle or ellipse.

Perpendicular lines are lines that intersect at right angles. They are represented by the symbol ⊥. The shortest distance from a line to a point not on the line is a perpendicular segment from the point to the line.

Parallel lines are lines in the same plane that have no points in common and never meet. It is possible for lines to be in different planes, have no points in common, and never meet, but they are not parallel because they are in different planes.

A **bisector** is a line or line segment that divides another line segment into two equal lengths. A perpendicular bisector of a line segment is composed of points that are equidistant from the endpoints of the segment it is dividing.

Intersecting lines are lines that have exactly one point in common. Concurrent lines are multiple lines that intersect at a single point.

A **transversal** is a line that intersects at least two other lines, which may or may not be parallel to one another. A transversal that intersects parallel lines is a common occurrence in geometry.

The **projection of a point on a line** is the point at which a perpendicular line drawn from the given point to the given line intersects the line. This is also the shortest distance from the given point to the line.

The **projection of a segment on a line** is a segment whose endpoints are the points formed when perpendicular lines are drawn from the endpoints of the given segment to the given line. This is similar to the length a diagonal line appears to be when viewed from above.

ANGLES

An **angle** is formed when two lines or line segments meet at a common point. It may be a common starting point for a pair of segments or rays, or it may be the intersection of lines. Angles are represented by the symbol ∠.

The **vertex** is the point at which two segments or rays meet to form an angle. If the angle is formed by intersecting rays, lines, and/or line segments, the vertex is the point at which four angles are formed. The pairs of angles opposite one another are called vertical angles, and their measures are equal.

- An *acute* angle is an angle with a degree measure less than 90°.
- A *right* angle is an angle with a degree measure of exactly 90°.
- An *obtuse* angle is an angle with a degree measure greater than 90° but less than 180°.
- A *straight angle* is an angle with a degree measure of exactly 180°. This is also a semicircle.

149

- A *reflex angle* is an angle with a degree measure greater than 180° but less than 360°.
- A *full angle* is an angle with a degree measure of exactly 360°.

Review Video: <u>Geometric Symbols: Angles</u>
Visit mometrix.com/academy and enter code: 452738

Two angles whose sum is exactly 90° are said to be **complementary**. The two angles may or may not be adjacent. In a right triangle, the two acute angles are complementary.

Two angles whose sum is exactly 180° are said to be **supplementary**. The two angles may or may not be adjacent. Two intersecting lines always form two pairs of supplementary angles. Adjacent supplementary angles will always form a straight line.

Two angles that have the same vertex and share a side are said to be **adjacent**. Vertical angles are not adjacent because they share a vertex but no common side.

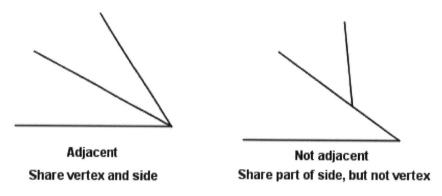

Adjacent
Share vertex and side

Not adjacent
Share part of side, but not vertex

When two parallel lines are cut by a transversal, the angles that are between the two parallel lines are **interior angles**. In the diagram below, angles 3, 4, 5, and 6 are interior angles.

When two parallel lines are cut by a transversal, the angles that are outside the parallel lines are **exterior angles**. In the diagram below, angles 1, 2, 7, and 8 are exterior angles.

When two parallel lines are cut by a transversal, the angles that are in the same position relative to the transversal and a parallel line are *corresponding angles*. The diagram below has four pairs of corresponding angles: angles 1 and 5; angles 2 and 6; angles 3 and 7; and angles 4 and 8. Corresponding angles formed by parallel lines are congruent.

When two parallel lines are cut by a transversal, the two interior angles that are on opposite sides of the transversal are called *alternate interior angles*. In the diagram below, there are two pairs of alternate interior angles: angles 3 and 6, and angles 4 and 5. Alternate interior angles formed by parallel lines are congruent.

When two parallel lines are cut by a transversal, the two exterior angles that are on opposite sides of the transversal are called *alternate exterior angles*.

In the diagram below, there are two pairs of alternate exterior angles: angles 1 and 8, and angles 2 and 7. Alternate exterior angles formed by parallel lines are congruent.

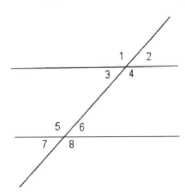

When two lines intersect, four angles are formed. The non-adjacent angles at this vertex are called vertical angles. Vertical angles are congruent. In the diagram, $\angle ABD \cong \angle CBE$ and $\angle ABC \cong \angle DBE$.

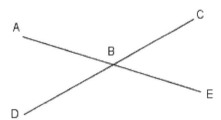

POLYGONS

Each straight line segment of a polygon is called a **side**.

The point at which two sides of a polygon intersect is called the **vertex**. In a polygon, the number of sides is always equal to the number of vertices.

A polygon with all sides congruent and all angles equal is called a **regular polygon**.

A line segment from the center of a polygon perpendicular to a side of the polygon is called the **apothem**. In a regular polygon, the apothem can be used to find the area of the polygon using the formula $A = \frac{1}{2}ap$, where a is the apothem and p is the perimeter.

A line segment from the center of a polygon to a vertex of the polygon is called a **radius**. The radius of a regular polygon is also the radius of a circle that can be circumscribed about the polygon.

- Triangle – 3 sides
- Quadrilateral – 4 sides
- Pentagon – 5 sides
- Hexagon – 6 sides
- Heptagon – 7 sides
- Octagon – 8 sides
- Nonagon – 9 sides
- Decagon – 10 sides
- Dodecagon – 12 sides

More generally, an *n*-gon is a polygon that has *n* angles and *n* sides.

The sum of the interior angles of an *n*-sided polygon is $(n-2)180°$. For example, in a triangle $n = 3$, so the sum of the interior angles is $(3-2)180° = 180°$. In a quadrilateral, $n = 4$, and the sum of the angles is $(4-2)180° = 360°$. The sum of the interior angles of a polygon is equal to the sum of the interior angles of any other polygon with the same number of sides.

A **diagonal** is a line segment that joins two non-adjacent vertices of a polygon.

A **convex polygon** is a polygon whose diagonals all lie within the interior of the polygon.

A **concave polygon** is a polygon with a least one diagonal that lies outside the polygon. In the diagram below, quadrilateral *ABCD* is concave because diagonal $\overline{AC}$ lies outside the polygon.

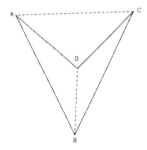

The number of diagonals a polygon has can be found by using the formula: number of diagonals $= \frac{n(n-3)}{2}$, where *n* is the number of sides in the polygon. This formula works for all polygons, not just regular polygons.

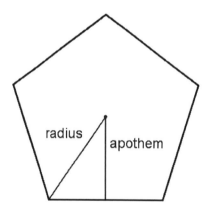

Congruent figures are geometric figures that have the same size and shape. All corresponding angles are equal, and all corresponding sides are equal. It is indicated by the symbol ≅.

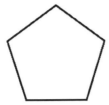 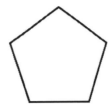

Congruent polygons

Similar figures are geometric figures that have the same shape, but do not necessarily have the same size. All corresponding angles are equal, and all corresponding sides are proportional, but they do not have to be equal. It is indicated by the symbol ∼.

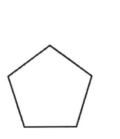 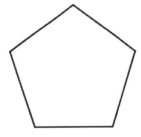

Similar polygons

Note that all congruent figures are also similar, but not all similar figures are congruent.

Review Video: Polygons, Similarity, and Congruence
Visit mometrix.com/academy and enter code: 686174

LINE OF SYMMETRY

A **line of symmetry** is a line that divides a figure or object into two symmetric parts. Each symmetric half is congruent to the other. An object may have no lines of symmetry, one line of symmetry, or more than one line of symmetry.

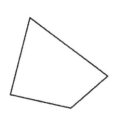 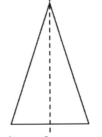 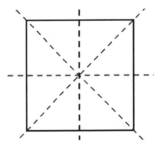

No lines of symmetry   One line of symmetry   Multiple lines of symmetry

Quadrilateral: A closed two-dimensional geometric figure composed of exactly four straight sides. The sum of the interior angles of any quadrilateral is 360°.

PARALLELOGRAM

A **parallelogram** is a quadrilateral that has exactly two pairs of opposite parallel sides. The sides that are parallel are also congruent. The opposite interior angles are always congruent, and the consecutive interior angles are supplementary. The diagonals of a parallelogram bisect each other. Each diagonal divides the parallelogram into two congruent triangles.

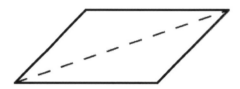

TRAPEZOID

Traditionally, a **trapezoid** is a quadrilateral that has exactly one pair of parallel sides. Some math texts define trapezoid as a quadrilateral that has at least one pair of parallel sides. Because there are no rules governing the second pair of sides, there are no rules that apply to the properties of the diagonals of a trapezoid.

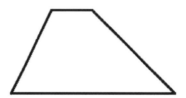

Rectangles, rhombuses, and squares are all special forms of parallelograms.

RECTANGLE

A **rectangle** is a parallelogram with four right angles. All rectangles are parallelograms, but not all parallelograms are rectangles. The diagonals of a rectangle are congruent.

RHOMBUS

A **rhombus** is a parallelogram with four congruent sides. All rhombuses are parallelograms, but not all parallelograms are rhombuses. The diagonals of a rhombus are perpendicular to each other.

SQUARE

A **square** is a parallelogram with four right angles and four congruent sides. All squares are also parallelograms, rhombuses, and rectangles. The diagonals of a square are congruent and perpendicular to each other.

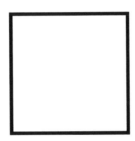

A quadrilateral whose diagonals bisect each other is a **parallelogram**. A quadrilateral whose opposite sides are parallel (2 pairs of parallel sides) is a parallelogram.

A quadrilateral whose diagonals are perpendicular bisectors of each other is a **rhombus**. A quadrilateral whose opposite sides (both pairs) are parallel and congruent is a rhombus.

A parallelogram that has a right angle is a **rectangle**. (Consecutive angles of a parallelogram are supplementary. Therefore if there is one right angle in a parallelogram, there are four right angles in that parallelogram.)

A rhombus with one right angle is a **square**. Because the rhombus is a special form of a parallelogram, the rules about the angles of a parallelogram also apply to the rhombus.

AREA AND PERIMETER FORMULAS

TRIANGLE

The *perimeter of any triangle* is found by summing the three side lengths; $P = a + b + c$. For an equilateral triangle, this is the same as $P = 3s$, where s is any side length, since all three sides are the same length.

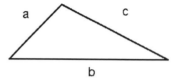

SQUARE

The *area of a square* is found by using the formula $A = s^2$, where and s is the length of one side.

The *perimeter of a square* is found by using the formula $P = 4s$, where s is the length of one side. Because all four sides are equal in a square, it is faster to multiply the length of one side by 4 than to add the same number four times. You could use the formulas for rectangles and get the same answer.

Review Video: <u>Area and Perimeter of a Square</u>
Visit mometrix.com/academy and enter code: 620902

RECTANGLE

The *area of a rectangle* is found by the formula $A = lw$, where A is the area of the rectangle, l is the length (usually considered to be the longer side) and w is the width (usually considered to be the shorter side). The numbers for l and w are interchangeable.

The *perimeter of a rectangle* is found by the formula $P = 2l + 2w$ or $P = 2(l + w)$, where l is the length, and w is the width. It may be easier to add the length and width first and then double the result, as in the second formula.

Review Video: <u>Area and Perimeter of a Rectangle</u>
Visit mometrix.com/academy and enter code: 933707

PARALLELOGRAM

The *area of a parallelogram* is found by the formula $A = bh$, where b is the length of the base, and h is the height. Note that the base and height correspond to the length and width in a rectangle, so this formula would apply to rectangles as well. Do not confuse the height of a parallelogram with the length of the second side. The two are only the same measure in the case of a rectangle.

The *perimeter of a parallelogram* is found by the formula $P = 2a + 2b$ or $P = 2(a + b)$, where a and b are the lengths of the two sides.

Review Video: <u>Area and Perimeter of a Parallelogram</u>
Visit mometrix.com/academy and enter code: 718313

Mometrix

TRAPEZOID

The *area of a trapezoid* is found by the formula $A = \frac{1}{2}h(b_1 + b_2)$, where h is the height (segment joining and perpendicular to the parallel bases), and b_1 and b_2 are the two parallel sides (bases). Do not use one of the other two sides as the height unless that side is also perpendicular to the parallel bases.

The *perimeter of a trapezoid* is found by the formula $P = a + b_1 + c + b_2$, where a, b_1, c, and b_2 are the four sides of the trapezoid.

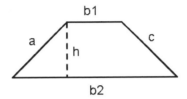

Review Video: Area and Perimeter of a Trapezoid
Visit mometrix.com/academy and enter code: 587523

TRIANGLES

An **equilateral triangle** is a triangle with three congruent sides. An equilateral triangle will also have three congruent angles, each 60°. All equilateral triangles are also acute triangles.

An **isosceles triangle** is a triangle with two congruent sides. An isosceles triangle will also have two congruent angles opposite the two congruent sides.

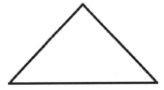

A **scalene triangle** is a triangle with no congruent sides. A scalene triangle will also have three angles of different measures. The angle with the largest measure is opposite the longest side, and the angle with the smallest measure is opposite the shortest side.

An **acute triangle** is a triangle whose three angles are all less than 90°. If two of the angles are equal, the acute triangle is also an isosceles triangle. If the three angles are all equal, the acute triangle is also an equilateral triangle.

A **right triangle** is a triangle with exactly one angle equal to 90°. All right triangles follow the Pythagorean theorem. A right triangle can never be acute or obtuse.

An **obtuse triangle** is a triangle with exactly one angle greater than 90°. The other two angles may or may not be equal. If the two remaining angles are equal, the obtuse triangle is also an isosceles triangle.

> **Review Video: Introduction to Types of Triangles**
> Visit mometrix.com/academy and enter code: 511711

TERMINOLOGY

ALTITUDE OF A TRIANGLE

A line segment drawn from one vertex perpendicular to the opposite side. In the diagram below, $\overline{BE}$, $\overline{AD}$, and $\overline{CF}$ are altitudes. The three altitudes in a triangle are always concurrent.

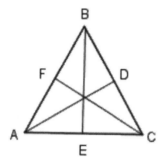

Height of a triangle

The length of the altitude, although the two terms are often used interchangeably.

Orthocenter of a triangle

The point of concurrency of the altitudes of a triangle. Note that in an obtuse triangle, the orthocenter will be outside the triangle, and in a right triangle, the orthocenter is the vertex of the right angle.

Median of a triangle

A line segment drawn from one vertex to the midpoint of the opposite side. This is not the same as the altitude, except the altitude to the base of an isosceles triangle and all three altitudes of an equilateral triangle.

Centroid of a triangle

The point of concurrency of the medians of a triangle. This is the same point as the orthocenter only in an equilateral triangle. Unlike the orthocenter, the centroid is always inside the triangle. The centroid can also be considered the exact center of the triangle. Any shape triangle can be perfectly balanced on a tip placed at the centroid. The centroid is also the point that is two-thirds the distance from the vertex to the opposite side.

PYTHAGOREAN THEOREM

The side of a triangle opposite the right angle is called the **hypotenuse**. The other two sides are called the legs. The pythagorean theorem states a relationship among the legs and hypotenuse of a right triangle: $a^2 + b^2 = c^2$, where a and b are the lengths of the legs of a right triangle, and c is the length of the hypotenuse. Note that this formula will only work with right triangles.

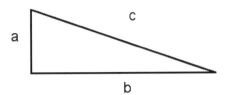

GENERAL RULES

The *triangle inequality theorem* states that the sum of the measures of any two sides of a triangle is always greater than the measure of the third side. If the sum of the measures of two sides were equal to the third side, a triangle would be impossible because the two sides would lie flat across the third side and there would be no vertex. If the sum of the measures of two of the sides was less than the third side, a closed figure would be impossible because the two shortest sides would never meet.

The sum of the measures of the interior angles of a triangle is always 180°. Therefore, a triangle can never have more than one angle greater than or equal to 90°.

In any triangle, the angles opposite congruent sides are congruent, and the sides opposite congruent angles are congruent. The largest angle is always opposite the longest side, and the smallest angle is always opposite the shortest side.

The line segment that joins the midpoints of any two sides of a triangle is always parallel to the third side and exactly half the length of the third side.

SIMILARITY AND CONGRUENCE RULES

Similar triangles are triangles whose corresponding angles are equal and whose corresponding sides are proportional. Represented by AA. Similar triangles whose corresponding sides are congruent are also congruent triangles.

Three sides of one triangle are congruent to the three corresponding sides of the second triangle. Represented as SSS.

Two sides and the included angle (the angle formed by those two sides) of one triangle are congruent to the corresponding two sides and included angle of the second triangle. Represented by SAS.

Two angles and the included side (the side that joins the two angles) of one triangle are congruent to the corresponding two angles and included side of the second triangle. Represented by ASA.

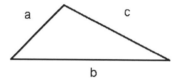

Two angles and a non-included side of one triangle are congruent to the corresponding two angles and non-included side of the second triangle. Represented by AAS.

Note that AAA is not a form for congruent triangles. This would say that the three angles are congruent, but says nothing about the sides. This meets the requirements for similar triangles, but not congruent triangles.

AREA AND PERIMETER FORMULAS

The *perimeter of any triangle* is found by summing the three side lengths; $P = a + b + c$. For an equilateral triangle, this is the same as $P = 3s$, where s is any side length, since all three sides are the same length.

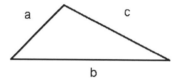

The area of any triangle can be found by taking half the product of one side length (base or b) and the perpendicular distance from that side to the opposite vertex (height or h). In equation form, $A = \frac{1}{2}bh$. For many triangles, it may be difficult to calculate h, so using one of the other formulas given here may be easier.

Another formula that works for any triangle is $A = \sqrt{s(s - a)(s - b)(s - c)}$, where A is the area, s is the semiperimeter $s = \frac{a+b+c}{2}$, and a, b, and c are the lengths of the three sides.

The area of an equilateral triangle can be found by the formula $A = \frac{\sqrt{3}}{4}s^2$, where A is the area and s is the length of a side. You could use the $30° - 60° - 90°$ ratios to find the height of the triangle and then use the standard triangle area formula, but this is faster.

The area of an isosceles triangle can be found by the formula, $A = \frac{1}{2}b\sqrt{a^2 - \frac{b^2}{4}}$, where A is the area, b is the base (the unique side), and a is the length of one of the two congruent sides. If you do not remember this formula, you can use the Pythagorean theorem to find the height so you can use the standard formula for the area of a triangle.

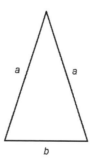

Review Video: <u>Area and Perimeter of a Triangle</u>
Visit mometrix.com/academy and enter code: 853779

160

ROTATION, CENTER OF ROTATION, AND ANGLE OF ROTATION

A *rotation* is a transformation that turns a figure around a point called the **center of rotation**, which can lie anywhere in the plane. If a line is drawn from a point on a figure to the center of rotation, and another line is drawn from the center to the rotated image of that point, the angle between the two lines is the **angle of rotation**. The vertex of the angle of rotation is the center of rotation.

> **Review Video: Rotation**
> Visit mometrix.com/academy and enter code: 602600

REFLECTION OVER A LINE AND REFLECTION IN A POINT

A reflection of a figure over a *line* (a "flip") creates a congruent image that is the same distance from the line as the original figure but on the opposite side. The **line of reflection** is the perpendicular bisector of any line segment drawn from a point on the original figure to its reflected image (unless the point and its reflected image happen to be the same point, which happens when a figure is reflected over one of its own sides).

A reflection of a figure in a *point* is the same as the rotation of the figure 180° about that point. The image of the figure is congruent to the original figure. The **point of reflection** is the midpoint of a line segment which connects a point in the figure to its image (unless the point and its reflected image happen to be the same point, which happens when a figure is reflected in one of its own points).

> **Review Video: Reflection**
> Visit mometrix.com/academy and enter code: 955068

EXAMPLE

Use the coordinate plane of the given image below to reflect the image across the *y*-axis.

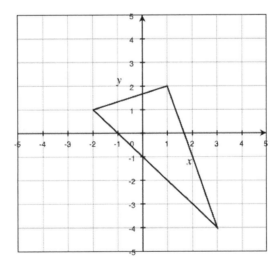

161

To reflect the image across the *y*-axis, replace each *x*-coordinate of the points that are the vertex of the triangle, *x*, with its negative, –*x*.

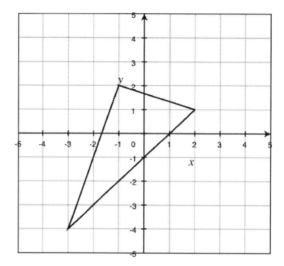

TRANSLATION

A *translation* is a transformation which slides a figure from one position in the plane to another position in the plane. The original figure and the translated figure have the same size, shape, and orientation.

Review Video: Translation
Visit mometrix.com/academy and enter code: 718628

TRANSFORMING A GIVEN FIGURE USING ROTATION, REFLECTION, AND TRANSLATION

To **rotate** a given figure: 1. Identify the point of rotation. 2. Using tracing paper, geometry software, or by approximation, recreate the figure at a new location around the point of rotation.

To **reflect** a given figure: 1. Identify the line of reflection. 2. By folding the paper, using geometry software, or by approximation, recreate the image at a new location on the other side of the line of reflection.

To **translate** a given figure: 1. Identify the new location. 2. Using graph paper, geometry software, or by approximation, recreate the figure in the new location. If using graph paper, make a chart of the x- and y-values to keep track of the coordinates of all critical points.

EVIDENCE OF TRANSFORMATION

To identify that a figure has been *rotated*, look for evidence that the figure is still face-up, but has changed its orientation.

To identify that a figure has been *reflected* across a line, look for evidence that the figure is now face-down.

To identify that a figure has been *translated*, look for evidence that a figure is still face-up and has not changed orientation; the only change is location.

To identify that a figure has been *dilated*, look for evidence that the figure has changed its size but not its orientation.

DILATION

A **dilation** is a transformation which proportionally stretches or shrinks a figure by a **scale factor**. The dilated image is the same shape and orientation as the original image but a different size. A polygon and its dilated image are similar.

EXAMPLE 1

Use the coordinate plane to create a dilation of the given image below, where the dilation is the enlargement of the original image.

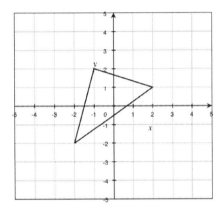

An enlargement can be found by multiplying each coordinate of the coordinate pairs located at the triangles vertices by a constant. If the figure is enlarged by a factor of 2, the new image would be:

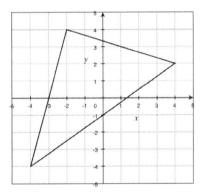

Review Video: Dilation
Visit mometrix.com/academy and enter code: 471630

TRIGONOMETRIC FORMULAS

In the diagram below, angle C is the **right angle**, and side c is the **hypotenuse**. Side a is the side adjacent to angle B and side b is the side adjacent to angle A. These formulas will work for any acute angle in a right triangle. They will *not* work for any triangle that is not a right triangle. Also, they will not work for the right angle in a right triangle, since there are not distinct adjacent and opposite sides to differentiate from the hypotenuse.

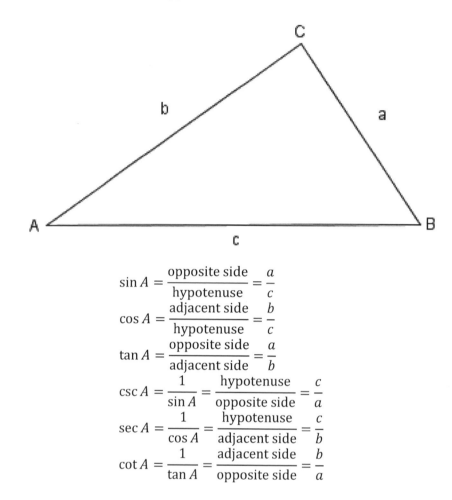

$$\sin A = \frac{\text{opposite side}}{\text{hypotenuse}} = \frac{a}{c}$$

$$\cos A = \frac{\text{adjacent side}}{\text{hypotenuse}} = \frac{b}{c}$$

$$\tan A = \frac{\text{opposite side}}{\text{adjacent side}} = \frac{a}{b}$$

$$\csc A = \frac{1}{\sin A} = \frac{\text{hypotenuse}}{\text{opposite side}} = \frac{c}{a}$$

$$\sec A = \frac{1}{\cos A} = \frac{\text{hypotenuse}}{\text{adjacent side}} = \frac{c}{b}$$

$$\cot A = \frac{1}{\tan A} = \frac{\text{adjacent side}}{\text{opposite side}} = \frac{b}{a}$$

LAWS OF SINES AND COSINES

The **law of sines** states that $\frac{\sin A}{a} = \frac{\sin B}{b} = \frac{\sin C}{c}$, where A, B, and C are the angles of a triangle, and a, b, and c are the sides opposite their respective angles. This formula will work with all triangles, not just right triangles.

The **law of cosines** is given by the formula $c^2 = a^2 + b^2 - 2ab(\cos C)$, where a, b, and c are the sides of a triangle, and C is the angle opposite side c. This formula is similar to the *pythagorean theorem*, but unlike the pythagorean theorem, it can be used on any triangle.

Review Video: <u>Cosine</u>
Visit mometrix.com/academy and enter code: 361120

CIRCLES

The **center** is the single point inside the circle that is **equidistant** from every point on the circle. (Point O in the diagram below.)

The **radius** is a line segment that joins the center of the circle and any one point on the circle. All radii of a circle are equal. (Segments OX, OY, and OZ in the diagram below.)

The **diameter** is a line segment that passes through the center of the circle and has both endpoints on the circle. The length of the diameter is exactly twice the length of the radius. (Segment XZ in the diagram below.)

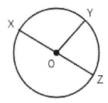

The **area of a circle** is found by the formula $A = \pi r^2$, where r is the length of the radius. If the diameter of the circle is given, remember to divide it in half to get the length of the radius before proceeding.

The **circumference** of a circle is found by the formula $C = 2\pi r$, where r is the radius. Again, remember to convert the diameter if you are given that measure rather than the radius.

Concentric circles are circles that have the same center, but not the same length of radii. A bulls-eye target is an example of concentric circles.

An **arc** is a portion of a circle. Specifically, an arc is the set of points between and including two points on a circle. An arc does not contain any points inside the circle. When a segment is drawn from the endpoints of an arc to the center of the circle, a sector is formed.

A **central angle** is an angle whose vertex is the center of a circle and whose legs intercept an arc of the circle. Angle XOY in the diagram above is a central angle. A minor arc is an arc that has a measure less than 180°. The measure of a central angle is equal to the measure of the minor arc it intercepts. A major arc is an arc having a measure of at least 180°. The measure of the major arc can be found by subtracting the measure of the central angle from 360°.

A **semicircle** is an arc whose endpoints are the endpoints of the diameter of a circle. A semicircle is exactly half of a circle.

An **inscribed angle** is an angle whose vertex lies on a circle and whose legs contain chords of that circle. The portion of the circle intercepted by the legs of the angle is called the intercepted arc. The measure of the intercepted arc is exactly twice the measure of the inscribed angle. In the following diagram, angle *ABC* is an inscribed angle. $\widehat{AC} = 2(m\angle ABC)$

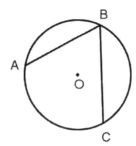

Any angle inscribed in a semicircle is a right angle. The intercepted arc is 180°, making the inscribed angle half that, or 90°. In the diagram below, angle *ABC* is inscribed in semicircle *ABC*, making angle *ABC* equal to 90°.

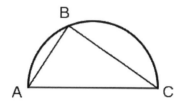

A **chord** is a line segment that has both endpoints on a circle. In the diagram below, $\overline{EB}$ is a chord.

Secant: A line that passes through a circle and contains a chord of that circle. In the diagram below, $\overleftrightarrow{EB}$ is a secant and contains chord $\overline{EB}$.

A **tangent** is a line in the same plane as a circle that touches the circle in exactly one point. While a line segment can be tangent to a circle as part of a line that is tangent, it is improper to say a tangent can be simply a line segment that touches the circle in exactly one point. In the diagram below, $\overleftrightarrow{CD}$ is tangent to circle *A*. Notice that $\overline{FB}$ is not tangent to the circle. $\overline{FB}$ is a line segment that touches the circle in exactly one point, but if the segment were extended, it would touch the circle in a second point. The point at which a tangent touches a circle is called the point of tangency. In the diagram below, point *B* is the point of tangency.

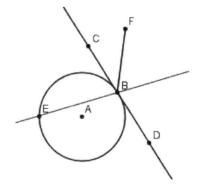

A **secant** is a line that intersects a circle in two points. Two secants may intersect inside the circle, on the circle, or outside the circle. When the two secants intersect on the circle, an inscribed angle is formed.

When two secants intersect inside a circle, the measure of each of two vertical angles is equal to half the sum of the two intercepted arcs. In the diagram below, $m\angle AEB = \frac{1}{2}(\widehat{AB} + \widehat{CD})$ and $m\angle BEC = \frac{1}{2}(\widehat{BC} + \widehat{AD})$.

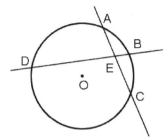

When two secants intersect outside a circle, the measure of the angle formed is equal to half the difference of the two arcs that lie between the two secants. In the diagram below, $m\angle AEB = \frac{1}{2}(\widehat{AB} - \widehat{CD})$.

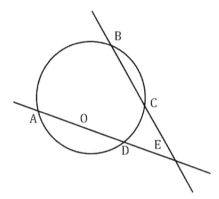

The **arc length** is the length of that portion of the circumference between two points on the circle. The formula for arc length is $s = \frac{\pi r \theta}{180°}$ where s is the arc length, r is the length of the radius, and θ is the angular measure of the arc in degrees, or $s = r\theta$, where θ is the angular measure of the arc in radians (2π radians = 360 degrees).

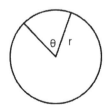

A **sector** is the portion of a circle formed by two radii and their intercepted arc. While the arc length is exclusively the points that are also on the circumference of the circle, the sector is the entire area bounded by the arc and the two radii.

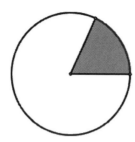

The **area of a sector** of a circle is found by the formula, $A = \frac{\theta r^2}{2}$, where A is the area, θ is the measure of the central angle in radians, and r is the radius. To find the area when the central angle is in degrees, use the formula, $A = \frac{\theta \pi r^2}{360}$, where θ is the measure of the central angle in degrees and r is the radius.

A circle is inscribed in a polygon if each of the sides of the polygon is tangent to the circle. A polygon is inscribed in a circle if each of the vertices of the polygon lies on the circle.

A circle is circumscribed about a polygon if each of the vertices of the polygon lies on the circle. A polygon is circumscribed about the circle if each of the sides of the polygon is tangent to the circle.

If one figure is inscribed in another, then the other figure is circumscribed about the first figure.

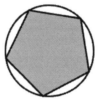

Circle circumscribed about a pentagon
Pentagon inscribed in a circle

OTHER CONIC SECTIONS

ELLIPSE

An **ellipse** is the set of all points in a plane, whose total distance from two fixed points called the foci (singular: focus) is constant, and whose center is the midpoint between the foci.

The standard equation of an ellipse that is taller than it is wide is $\frac{(y-k)^2}{a^2} + \frac{(x-h)^2}{b^2} = 1$, where a and b are coefficients. The center is the point (h, k) and the foci are the points $(h, k + c)$ and $(h, k - c)$, where $c^2 = a^2 - b^2$ and $a^2 > b^2$.

The major axis has length $2a$, and the minor axis has length $2b$.

Eccentricity (e) is a measure of how elongated an ellipse is, and is the ratio of the distance between the foci to the length of the major axis. Eccentricity will have a value between 0 and 1. The closer to 1 the eccentricity is, the closer the ellipse is to being a circle. The formula for eccentricity is $= \frac{c}{a}$.

PARABOLA

Parabola: The set of all points in a plane that are equidistant from a fixed line, called the **directrix**, and a fixed point not on the line, called the **focus**.

Axis: The line perpendicular to the directrix that passes through the focus.

For parabolas that open up or down, the standard equation is $(x - h)^2 = 4c(y - k)$, where h, c, and k are coefficients. If c is positive, the parabola opens up. If c is negative, the parabola opens down. The vertex is the point (h, k). The directrix is the line having the equation $y = -c + k$, and the focus is the point $(h, c + k)$.

For parabolas that open left or right, the standard equation is $(y - k)^2 = 4c(x - h)$, where k, c, and h are coefficients. If c is positive, the parabola opens to the right. If c is negative, the parabola opens to the left. The vertex is the point (h, k). The directrix is the line having the equation $x = -c + h$, and the focus is the point $(c + h, k)$.

HYPERBOLA

A **hyperbola** is the set of all points in a plane, whose distance from two fixed points, called foci, has a constant difference.

The standard equation of a horizontal hyperbola is $\frac{(x-h)^2}{a^2} - \frac{(y-k)^2}{b^2} = 1$, where a, b, h, and k are real numbers. The center is the point (h, k), the vertices are the points $(h + a, k)$ and $(h - a, k)$, and the foci are the points that every point on one of the parabolic curves is equidistant from and are found using the formulas $(h + c, k)$ and $(h - c, k)$, where $c^2 = a^2 + b^2$. The asymptotes are two lines the graph of the hyperbola approaches but never reaches, and are given by the equations $y = \left(\frac{b}{a}\right)(x - h) + k$ and $y = -\left(\frac{b}{a}\right)(x - h) + k$.

A **vertical hyperbola** is formed when a plane makes a vertical cut through two cones that are stacked vertex-to-vertex.

The standard equation of a vertical hyperbola is $\frac{(y-k)^2}{a^2} - \frac{(x-h)^2}{b^2} = 1$, where a, b, k, and h are real numbers. The center is the point (h, k), the vertices are the points $(h, k + a)$ and $(h, k - a)$, and the foci are the points that every point on one of the parabolic curves is equidistant from and are found using the formulas $(h, k + c)$ and $(h, k - c)$, where $c^2 = a^2 + b^2$. The asymptotes are two lines the graph of the hyperbola approaches but never reach, and are given by the equations $y = \left(\frac{a}{b}\right)(x - h) + k$ and $y = -\left(\frac{a}{b}\right)(x - h) + k$.

SOLIDS

The **surface area of a solid object** is the area of all sides or exterior surfaces. For objects such as prisms and pyramids, a further distinction is made between base surface area (B) and lateral surface area (LA). For a prism, the total surface area (SA) is $SA = LA + 2B$. For a pyramid or cone, the total surface area is $SA = LA + B$.

Review Video: How to Calculate the Volume of 3D Objects
Visit mometrix.com/academy and enter code: 163343

The **surface area of a sphere** can be found by the formula $A = 4\pi r^2$, where r is the radius. The volume is given by the formula $V = \frac{4}{3}\pi r^3$, where r is the radius. Both quantities are generally given in terms of π.

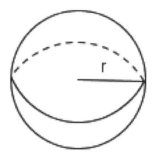

Review Video: Volume and Surface Area of a Sphere
Visit mometrix.com/academy and enter code: 786928

The **volume of any prism** is found by the formula $V = Bh$, where B is the area of the base, and h is the height (perpendicular distance between the bases). The surface area of any prism is the sum of the areas of both bases and all sides. It can be calculated as $SA = 2B + Ph$, where P is the perimeter of the base.

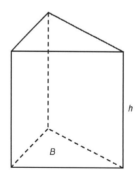

For a *rectangular prism*, the **volume** can be found by the formula $V = lwh$, where V is the volume, l is the length, w is the width, and h is the height. The surface area can be calculated as $SA = 2lw + 2hl + 2wh$ or $SA = 2(lw + hl + wh)$.

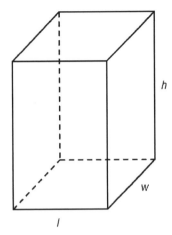

The **volume of a cube** can be found by the formula $V = s^3$, where s is the length of a side. The surface area of a cube is calculated as $SA = 6s^2$, where SA is the total surface area and s is the length of a side. These formulas are the same as the ones used for the volume and surface area of a rectangular prism, but simplified since all three quantities (length, width, and height) are the same.

Review Video: <u>Volume and Surface Area of a Cube</u>
Visit mometrix.com/academy and enter code: 664455

The **volume of a cylinder** can be calculated by the formula $V = \pi r^2 h$, where r is the radius, and h is the height. The surface area of a cylinder can be found by the formula $SA = 2\pi r^2 + 2\pi rh$. The first term is the base area multiplied by two, and the second term is the perimeter of the base multiplied by the height.

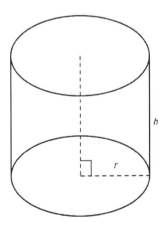

Review Video: <u>Volume and Surface Area of a Right Circular Cylinder</u>
Visit mometrix.com/academy and enter code: 226463

The **volume of a pyramid** is found by the formula $V = \frac{1}{3}Bh$, where B is the area of the base, and h is the height (perpendicular distance from the vertex to the base). Notice this formula is the same as $\frac{1}{3}$ times the volume of a prism. Like a prism, the base of a pyramid can be any shape.

> **Review Video: <u>Volume and Surface Area of a Pyramid</u>**
> Visit mometrix.com/academy and enter code: 621932

Finding the **surface area of a pyramid** is not as simple as the other shapes we've looked at thus far. If the pyramid is a right pyramid, meaning the base is a regular polygon and the vertex is directly over the center of that polygon, the surface area can be calculated as $SA = B + \frac{1}{2}Ph_s$, where P is the perimeter of the base, and h_s is the slant height (distance from the vertex to the midpoint of one side of the base). If the pyramid is irregular, the area of each triangle side must be calculated individually and then summed, along with the base.

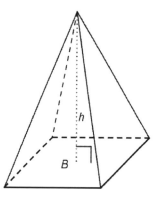

The **volume of a cone** is found by the formula $V = \frac{1}{3}\pi r^2 h$, where r is the radius, and h is the height. Notice this is the same as $\frac{1}{3}$ times the volume of a cylinder. The surface area can be calculated as $SA = \pi r^2 + \pi r s$, where s is the slant height. The slant height can be calculated using the pythagorean thereom to be $\sqrt{r^2 + h^2}$, so the surface area formula can also be written as $SA = \pi r^2 + \pi r \sqrt{r^2 + h^2}$.

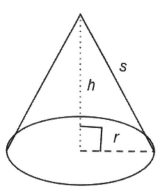

> **Review Video: <u>Volume and Surface Area of a Right Circular Cone</u>**
> Visit mometrix.com/academy and enter code: 573574

PROBABILITY TERMINOLOGY

Probability is a branch of statistics that deals with the likelihood of something taking place. One classic example is a coin toss. There are only two possible results: heads or tails. The likelihood, or probability, that the coin will land as heads is 1 out of 2 ($\frac{1}{2}$, 0.5, 50%). Tails has the same probability. Another common example is a 6-sided die roll. There are six possible results from rolling a single die, each with an equal chance of happening, so the probability of any given number coming up is 1 out of 6.

TERMS FREQUENTLY USED IN PROBABILITY

- **Event** – a situation that produces results of some sort (a coin toss)
- **Compound event** – event that involves two or more independent events (rolling a pair of dice; taking the sum)
- **Outcome** – a possible result in an experiment or event (heads, tails)
- **Desired outcome** (or success) – an outcome that meets a particular set of criteria (a roll of 1 or 2 if we are looking for numbers less than 3)
- **Independent events** – two or more events whose outcomes do not affect one another (two coins tossed at the same time)
- **Dependent events** – two or more events whose outcomes affect one another (two cards drawn consecutively from the same deck)
- **Certain outcome** – probability of outcome is 100% or 1
- **Impossible outcome** – probability of outcome is 0% or 0
- **Mutually exclusive outcomes** – two or more outcomes whose criteria cannot all be satisfied in a single event (a coin coming up heads and tails on the same toss)
- **Random variable** – refers to all possible outcomes of a single event which may be discrete or continuous.

> **Review Video: Intro to Probability**
> Visit mometrix.com/academy and enter code: 212374

CALCULATING PROBABILITY

Probability is the likelihood of a certain outcome occurring for a given event. The **theoretical probability** can usually be determined without actually performing the event. The likelihood of a outcome occurring, or the probability of an outcome occurring, is given by the formula

$$P(A) = \frac{\text{Number of acceptable outcomes}}{\text{Number of possible outcomes}}$$

where $P(A)$ is the probability of an outcome A occurring, and each outcome is just as likely to occur as any other outcome. If each outcome has the same probability of occurring as every other possible outcome, the outcomes are said to be equally likely to occur. The total number of acceptable outcomes must be less than or equal to the total number of possible outcomes. If the two are equal, then the outcome is certain to occur and the probability is 1. If the number of acceptable outcomes is zero, then the outcome is impossible and the probability is 0.

> **Review Video: Theoretical and Experimental Probability**
> Visit mometrix.com/academy and enter code: 444349

EXAMPLE:

There are 20 marbles in a bag and 5 are red. The theoretical probability of randomly selecting a red marble is 5 out of 20, ($\frac{5}{20} = \frac{1}{4}$, 0.25, or 25%).

PERMUTATIONS AND COMBINATIONS

When trying to calculate the probability of an event using the $\frac{\text{desired outcomes}}{\text{total outcomes}}$ formula, you may frequently find that there are too many outcomes to individually count them. **Permutation** and **combination formulas** offer a shortcut to counting outcomes. A permutation is an arrangement of a specific number of a set of objects in a specific order. The number of **permutations** of r items given a set of n items can be calculated as $_nP_r = \frac{n!}{(n-r)!}$. Combinations are similar to permutations, except there are no restrictions regarding the order of the elements. While ABC is considered a different permutation than BCA, ABC and BCA are considered the same combination. The number of **combinations** of r items given a set of n items can be calculated as $_nC_r = \frac{n!}{r!(n-r)!}$ or $_nC_r = \frac{_nP_r}{r!}$.

EXAMPLE:

Suppose you want to calculate how many different 5-card hands can be drawn from a deck of 52 cards. This is a combination since the order of the cards in a hand does not matter. There are 52 cards available, and 5 to be selected. Thus, the number of different hands is $_{52}C_5 = \frac{52!}{5! \times 47!} = 2{,}598{,}960$.

COMPLEMENT OF AN EVENT

Sometimes it may be easier to calculate the possibility of something not happening, or the **complement of an event**. Represented by the symbol $\bar{A}$, the complement of A is the probability that event A does not happen. When you know the probability of event A occurring, you can use the formula $P(\bar{A}) = 1 - P(A)$, where $P(\bar{A})$ is the probability of event A not occurring, and $P(A)$ is the probability of event A occurring.

ADDITION RULE

The **addition rule** for probability is used for finding the probability of a compound event. Use the formula $P(A \text{ or } B) = P(A) + P(B) - P(A \text{ and } B)$, where $P(A \text{ and } B)$ is the probability of both events occurring to find the probability of a compound event. The probability of both events occurring at the same time must be subtracted to eliminate any overlap in the first two probabilities.

CONDITIONAL PROBABILITY

Conditional probability is the probability of an event occurring once another event has already occurred. Given event A and dependent event B, the probability of event B occurring when event A has already occurred is represented by the notation $P(A|B)$. To find the probability of event B occurring, take into account the fact that event A has already occurred and adjust the total number of possible outcomes. For example, suppose you have ten balls numbered 1–10 and you want ball number 7 to be pulled in two pulls. On the first pull, the probability of getting the 7 is $\frac{1}{10}$ because there is one ball with a 7 on it and 10 balls to choose from. Assuming the first pull did not yield a 7, the probability of pulling a 7 on the second pull is now $\frac{1}{9}$ because there are only 9 balls remaining for the second pull.

MULTIPLICATION RULE

The **multiplication rule** can be used to find the probability of two independent events occurring using the formula $P(A \text{ and } B) = P(A) \times P(B)$, where $P(A \text{ and } B)$ is the probability of two independent events occurring, $P(A)$ is the probability of the first event occurring, and $P(B)$ is the probability of the second event occurring.

The multiplication rule can also be used to find the probability of two dependent events occurring using the formula $P(A \text{ and } B) = P(A) \times P(B|A)$, where $P(A \text{ and } B)$ is the probability of two dependent events occurring and $P(B|A)$ is the probability of the second event occurring after the first event has already occurred.

Before using the multiplication rule, you MUST first determine whether the two events are *dependent* or *independent*.

Use a **combination of the multiplication** rule and the rule of complements to find the probability that at least one outcome of the element will occur. This given by the general formula $P(\text{at least one event occurring}) = 1 - P(\text{no outcomes occurring})$. For example, to find the probability that at least one even number will show when a pair of dice is rolled, find the probability that two odd numbers will be rolled (no even numbers) and subtract from one. You can always use a tree diagram or make a chart to list the possible outcomes when the sample space is small, such as in the dice-rolling example, but in most cases it will be much faster to use the multiplication and complement formulas.

EXPECTED VALUE

Expected value is a method of determining expected outcome in a random situation. It is really a sum of the weighted probabilities of the possible outcomes. Multiply the probability of an event occurring by the weight assigned to that probability (such as the amount of money won or lost). A practical application of the expected value is to determine whether a game of chance is really fair. If the sum of the weighted probabilities is equal to zero, the game is generally considered fair because the player has a fair chance to at least to break even. If the expected value is less than zero, then players lose more than they win. For example, a lottery drawing might allow the player to choose any three-digit number, 000–999. The probability of choosing the winning number is 1:1000. If it costs \$1 to play, and a winning number receives \$500, the expected value is $\left(-\$1 \cdot \frac{999}{1{,}000}\right) +$ $\left(\$500 \cdot \frac{1}{1{,}000}\right) = -0.499$ or $-\$0.50$. You can expect to lose on average 50 cents for every dollar you spend.

EMPIRICAL PROBABILITY

Most of the time, when we talk about probability, we mean theoretical probability. **Empirical probability**, or experimental probability or relative frequency, is the number of times an outcome occurs in a particular experiment or a certain number of observed events. While theoretical probability is based on what *should* happen, experimental probability is based on what *has* happened. Experimental probability is calculated in the same way as theoretical, except that actual outcomes are used instead of possible outcomes.

Theoretical and experimental probability do not always line up with one another. Theoretical probability says that out of 20 coin-tosses, 10 should be heads. However, if we were actually to toss 20 coins, we might record just 5 heads. This doesn't mean that our theoretical probability is incorrect; it just means that this particular experiment had results that were different from what was predicted. A practical application of empirical probability is the insurance industry. There are no set functions that define lifespan, health, or safety. Insurance companies look at factors from hundreds of thousands of individuals to find patterns that they then use to set the formulas for insurance premiums.

OBJECTIVE PROBABILITY

Objective probability is based on mathematical formulas and documented evidence. Examples of objective probability include raffles or lottery drawings where there is a pre-determined number of possible outcomes and a predetermined number of outcomes that correspond to an event. Other cases of objective probability include probabilities of rolling dice, flipping coins, or drawing cards. Most gambling games are based on objective probability.

SUBJECTIVE PROBABILITY

Subjective probability is based on personal or professional feelings and judgments. Often, there is a lot of guesswork following extensive research. Areas where subjective probability is applicable include sales trends and business expenses. Attractions set admission prices based on subjective probabilities of attendance based on varying admission rates in an effort to maximize their profit.

SAMPLE SPACE

The total set of all possible results of a test or experiment is called a **sample space**, or sometimes a universal sample space. The sample space, represented by one of the variables S, Ω, or U (for universal sample space) has individual elements called outcomes. Other terms for outcome that may be used interchangeably include elementary outcome, simple event, or sample point. The number of outcomes in a given sample space could be infinite or finite, and some tests may yield multiple unique sample sets. For example, tests conducted by drawing playing cards from a standard deck would have one sample space of the card values, another sample space of the card suits, and a third sample space of suit-denomination combinations. For most tests, the sample spaces considered will be finite.

An **event**, represented by the variable E, is a portion of a sample space. It may be one outcome or a group of outcomes from the same sample space. If an event occurs, then the test or experiment will generate an outcome that satisfies the requirement of that event. For example, given a standard deck of 52 playing cards as the sample space, and defining the event as the collection of face cards, then the event will occur if the card drawn is a J, Q, or K. If any other card is drawn, the event is said to have not occurred.

For every sample space, each possible outcome has a specific likelihood, or probability, that it will occur. The probability measure, also called the **distribution**, is a function that assigns a real number probability, from zero to one, to each outcome. For a probability measure to be accurate, every outcome must have a real number probability measure that is greater than or equal to zero and less than or equal to one. Also, the probability measure of the sample space must equal one, and the probability measure of the union of multiple outcomes must equal the sum of the individual probability measures.

Probabilities of events are expressed as real numbers from zero to one. They give a numerical value to the chance that a particular event will occur. The probability of an event occurring is the sum of the probabilities of the individual elements of that event. For example, in a standard deck of 52 playing cards as the sample space and the collection of face cards as the event, the probability of drawing a specific face card is $\frac{1}{52} = 0.019$, but the probability of drawing any one of the twelve face cards is $12(0.019) = 0.228$. Note that rounding of numbers can generate different results. If you multiplied 12 by the fraction $\frac{1}{52}$ before converting to a decimal, you would get the answer $\frac{12}{52} =$ 0.231.

TREE DIAGRAM

For a simple sample space, possible outcomes may be determined by using a **tree diagram** or an organized chart. In either case, you can easily draw or list out the possible outcomes. For example, to determine all the possible ways three objects can be ordered, you can draw a tree diagram:

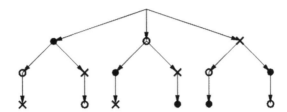

You can also make a chart to list all the possibilities:

First object	Second object	Third object
●	X	O
●	O	X
O	●	X
O	X	●
X	●	O
X	O	●

Either way, you can easily see there are six possible ways the three objects can be ordered.

If two events have no outcomes in common, they are said to be **mutually exclusive**. For example, in a standard deck of 52 playing cards, the event of all card suits is mutually exclusive to the event of all card values. If two events have no bearing on each other so that one event occurring has no influence on the probability of another event occurring, the two events are said to be independent. For example, rolling a standard six-sided die multiple times does not change that probability that a particular number will be rolled from one roll to the next. If the outcome of one event does affect the probability of the second event, the two events are said to be dependent. For example, if cards are drawn from a deck, the probability of drawing an ace after an ace has been drawn is different than the probability of drawing an ace if no ace (or no other card, for that matter) has been drawn.

In probability, the **odds in favor of an event** are the number of times the event will occur compared to the number of times the event will not occur. To calculate the odds in favor of an event, use the formula $\frac{P(A)}{1-P(A)}$, where $P(A)$ is the probability that the event will occur. Many times, odds in favor is given as a ratio in the form $\frac{a}{b}$ or $a:b$, where a is the probability of the event occurring and b is the complement of the event, the probability of the event not occurring. If the odds in favor are given as 2:5, that means that you can expect the event to occur two times for every 5 times that it does not occur. In other words, the probability that the event will occur is $\frac{2}{2+5} = \frac{2}{7}$.

In probability, the **odds against an event** are the number of times the event will not occur compared to the number of times the event will occur. To calculate the odds against an event, use the formula $\frac{1-P(A)}{P(A)}$, where $P(A)$ is the probability that the event will occur. Many times, odds against is given as a ratio in the form $\frac{b}{a}$ or $b{:}a$, where b is the probability the event will not occur (the complement of the event) and a is the probability the event will occur. If the odds against an event are given as 3:1, that means that you can expect the event to not occur 3 times for every one time it does occur. In other words, 3 out of every 4 trials will fail.

EXPERIMENTAL AND THEORETICAL PROBABILITY

Probability, P(A), is the likelihood that event A will occur. Probability is often expressed as the ratio of ways an event can occur to the total number of **outcomes**, also called the **sample space**. For example, the probability of flipping heads on a two-sided coin can be written as $\frac{1}{2}$ since there is one side with heads and a total of two sides, which means that there are two possible outcomes. Probabilities can also be expressed as decimals or percentages.

Tree diagrams are used to list all possible outcomes. Suppose you are packing for vacation and have set aside 4 shirts, 3 pairs of pants, and 2 hats. How many possible outfits are there? To construct a tree diagram, start with the first group of events, the shirts. You can use letters to label each of the articles (SA refers to the first shirt, SB refers to the second shirt, and so on). Then, from each shirt draw branches to each pair of pants that it could be paired with. Next, from each pair of pants, draw a branch to each hat that it could be paired to and finally, repeat the process with the shoes. This method allows you to list all of the possible outcomes.

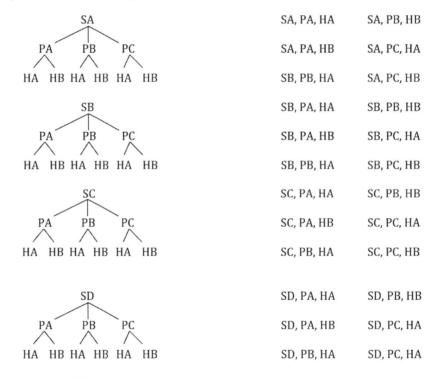

SA, PA, HA	SA, PB, HB
SA, PA, HB	SA, PC, HA
SB, PB, HA	SA, PC, HB
SB, PA, HA	SB, PB, HB
SB, PA, HB	SB, PC, HA
SB, PB, HA	SB, PC, HB
SC, PA, HA	SC, PB, HB
SC, PA, HB	SC, PC, HA
SC, PB, HA	SC, PC, HB
SD, PA, HA	SD, PB, HB
SD, PA, HB	SD, PC, HA
SD, PB, HA	SD, PC, HA

Altogether, there are 24 different combinations of shirts, pants, and hats.

ADDITION PRINCIPLE

The **addition principle** is used to determine the sample space of 2 or more events. The addition principle states that if two events, x and y, with a number of possible outcomes, n_x and n_y, have no shared outcomes, then the events are called **mutually exclusive** and the union of the events, or the total number of outcomes of the sample space, is: $x \cap y = n_x + n_y$.

For example: In a regular deck of 52 playing cards with events defined as $x =$ [drawing a jack] and $y =$ [drawing a king], there is no way for both of these to occur at the same time. Since there are 4 ways to get a jack and 4 ways to get a king the union of those events is: $x \cap y = 4 + 4 = 8$. There are 8 ways that one or the other event can occur.

If the two events share any outcomes then they are not mutually exclusive and the total number of possible outcomes for the two events is $x \cap y = n_x + n_y - (x \cup y)$. Where $(x \cup y)$ is the number of outcomes common to both events. An example of this with a regular deck of cards would be if event $x =$ [drawing a jack] and event $y =$ [drawing a spade]. Now, since there are 4 ways to draw a jack, 13 ways to draw a spade, and 1 way to draw the jack of spades, the union of the events would be $x \cap y = 4 + 13 - 1 = 16$. There are 16 ways that one or the other event can occur.

FUNDAMENTAL COUNTING PRINCIPLE

The **fundamental counting principle** deals specifically with situations in which the order that something happens affects the outcome. Specifically, the fundamental counting principle states that if one event can have x possible different outcomes, and after the first outcome has been established the event can then have y possible outcomes, then there are $x \times y$ possible different ways the outcomes can happen in that order. For example, if two dice are rolled, one at a time, there are 6 possible outcomes for the first die, and 6 possible outcomes for the second die, for a total of $6 \times 6 = 36$ total possible outcomes. Suppose you have a bag containing a penny, a nickel, a dime, a quarter, and a half dollar. There are 5 different possible outcomes the first time you pull a coin. Without replacing the first coin, there are 4 different possible outcomes for the second coin. This makes $5 \times 4 = 20$ different possible outcomes for the first two coins drawn when the order the coins are drawn makes a difference.

MULTIPLICATION COUNTING PRINCIPLE

A faster way to find the sample space without listing each individual outcome employs the **multiplication counting principle**. If one event can occur in a ways and a second event in b ways, then the two events can occur in $a \times b$ ways. In the previous example, there are 4 possible shirts, 3 possible pairs of pants, and 2 possible hats, so the possible number of combinations is $4 \times 3 \times 2$, or 24.

A similar principle is employed to determine the probability of two **independent events**. $P(A \text{ and } B) = P(A) \times P(B)$, where A is the first event and B is the second such that the outcome of B does not depend on the outcome of A. For instance, suppose you choose a marble from a bag of 2 red marbles, 7 blue marbles, and 4 green marbles. The probability that you would choose a red marble, replace it, and then choose a green marble is found by multiplying the probabilities of each independent event:

$$\frac{2}{13} \times \frac{4}{13} = \frac{8}{169}, \text{ or } 0.047, \text{ or } 4.7\%$$

This method can also be used when finding the probability of more than 2 independent events.

When two events are dependent on one another, the likelihood of the second event is affected by the outcome of the first event. This formula for finding the probability of **dependent events** is $P(A \text{ then } B) = P(A) \times P(B \text{ after } A)$. The probability that you choose a 2 and then choose a 5 from a deck of 52 cards without replacement is

$$\frac{4}{52} \times \frac{4}{51} = \frac{1}{13} \times \frac{4}{51} = \frac{4}{663} \text{ or } 0.0060, \text{ or } 0.60\%$$

Note that there are four of each number in a deck of cards, so the probability of choosing a 2 is $\frac{4}{52}$. Since you keep this card out of the deck, there are only 51 cards to choose from when selecting a 5.

Thus far, the discussion of probability has been limited to **theoretical probability, which is used to predict the likelihood of an event.** **Experimental probability** expresses the ratio of the number of times an event actually occurs to the number of **trials** performed in an experiment. Theoretically, the probability of rolling a one on an unloaded, six-sided die is $\frac{1}{6}$. Suppose you conduct an experiment to determine whether a dice is a fair one and obtain these results.

Trial #	1	2	3	4	5	6	7	8	9	10	11	12	13	14	15	16	17	18	19	20
Outcome	6	1	2	6	4	2	1	3	4	5	4	1	6	6	4	5	6	4	1	6

Out of the 20 trials, you rolled a 1 six times. $\frac{6}{20} = \frac{3}{10} = 0.30$, or 30%. This probability is different than the theoretical probability of $\frac{1}{6}$ or 16.6%. You might conclude that the die is loaded, but it would be advisable to conduct more trials to verify your conclusion: the larger the number of trials, the more accurate the experimental probability.

STATISTICS TERMINOLOGY

Statistics is the branch of mathematics that deals with collecting, recording, interpreting, illustrating, and analyzing large amounts of **data**. The following terms are often used in the discussion of data and **statistics**:

- **Data** – the collective name for pieces of *information* (singular is datum).
- **Quantitative data** – measurements (such as length, mass, and speed) that provide information about *quantities* in numbers
- **Qualitative data** – information (such as colors, scents, tastes, and shapes) that *cannot be measured* using numbers
- **Discrete data** – information that can be expressed only by a *specific value*, such as whole or half numbers. For example, since people can be counted only in whole numbers, a population count would be discrete data.
- **Continuous data** – information (such as time and temperature) that can be expressed by *any value within a given range*
- **Primary data** – information that has been *collected* directly from a survey, investigation, or experiment, such as a questionnaire or the recording of daily temperatures. Primary data that has not yet been organized or analyzed is called raw data.
- **Secondary data** – information that has been collected, sorted, and *processed* by the researcher
- **Ordinal data** – information that *can be placed in numerical order*, such as age or weight
- **Nominal data** – information that *cannot be placed in numerical order*, such as names or places.

STATISTICS

POPULATION

In statistics, the **population** is the entire collection of people, plants, etc., that data can be collected from. For example, a study to determine how well students in the area schools perform on a standardized test would have a population of all the students enrolled in those schools, although a study may include just a small sample of students from each school. A **parameter** is a numerical value that gives information about the population, such as the mean, median, mode, or standard deviation. Remember that the symbol for the mean of a population is μ and the symbol for the standard deviation of a population is σ.

SAMPLE

A **sample** is a portion of the entire population. Whereas a parameter helped describe the population, a **statistic** is a numerical value that gives information about the sample, such as mean, median, mode, or standard deviation. Keep in mind that the symbols for mean and standard deviation are different when they are referring to a sample rather than the entire population. For a sample, the symbol for mean is $\bar{x}$ and the symbol for standard deviation is s. The mean and standard deviation of a sample may or may not be identical to that of the entire population due to a sample only being a subset of the population. However, if the sample is random and large enough, statistically significant values can be attained. Samples are generally used when the population is too large to justify including every element or when acquiring data for the entire population is impossible.

INFERENTIAL STATISTICS

Inferential statistics is the branch of statistics that uses samples to make predictions about an entire population. This type of statistics is often seen in political polls, where a sample of the population is questioned about a particular topic or politician to gain an understanding about the attitudes of the entire population of the country. Often, exit polls are conducted on election days using this method. Inferential statistics can have a large margin of error if you do not have a valid sample.

SAMPLING DISTRIBUTION

Statistical values calculated from various samples of the same size make up the **sampling distribution**. For example, if several samples of identical size are randomly selected from a large population and then the mean of each sample is calculated, the distribution of values of the means would be a sampling distribution.

The **sampling distribution of the mean** is the distribution of the sample mean, $\bar{x}$, derived from random samples of a given size. It has three important characteristics. First, the mean of the sampling distribution of the mean is equal to the mean of the population that was sampled. Second, assuming the standard deviation is non-zero, the standard deviation of the sampling distribution of the mean equals the standard deviation of the sampled population divided by the square root of the sample size. This is sometimes called the standard error. Finally, as the sample size gets larger, the sampling distribution of the mean gets closer to a normal distribution via the central limit theorem.

SURVEY STUDY

A **survey study** is a method of gathering information from a small group in an attempt to gain enough information to make accurate general assumptions about the population. Once a survey study is completed, the results are then put into a summary report.

Survey studies are generally in the format of surveys, interviews, or questionnaires as part of an effort to find opinions of a particular group or to find facts about a group.

It is important to note that the findings from a survey study are only as accurate as the sample chosen from the population.

CORRELATIONAL STUDIES

Correlational studies seek to determine how much one variable is affected by changes in a second variable. For example, correlational studies may look for a relationship between the amount of time a student spends studying for a test and the grade that student earned on the test or between student scores on college admissions tests and student grades in college.

It is important to note that correlational studies cannot show a cause and effect, but rather can show only that two variables are or are not potentially correlated.

EXPERIMENTAL STUDIES

Experimental studies take correlational studies one step farther, in that they attempt to prove or disprove a cause-and-effect relationship. These studies are performed by conducting a series of experiments to test the hypothesis. For a study to be scientifically accurate, it must have both an experimental group that receives the specified treatment and a control group that does not get the treatment. This is the type of study pharmaceutical companies do as part of drug trials for new medications. Experimental studies are only valid when proper scientific method has been followed. In other words, the experiment must be well-planned and executed without bias in the testing process, all subjects must be selected at random, and the process of determining which subject is in which of the two groups must also be completely random.

OBSERVATIONAL STUDIES

Observational studies are the opposite of experimental studies. In observational studies, the tester cannot change or in any way control all of the variables in the test. For example, a study to determine which gender does better in math classes in school is strictly observational. You cannot change a person's gender, and you cannot change the subject being studied. The big downfall of observational studies is that you have no way of proving a cause-and-effect relationship because you cannot control outside influences. Events outside of school can influence a student's performance in school, and observational studies cannot take that into consideration.

RANDOM SAMPLES

For most studies, a **random sample** is necessary to produce valid results. Random samples should not have any particular influence to cause sampled subjects to behave one way or another. The goal is for the random sample to be a **representative sample**, or a sample whose characteristics give an accurate picture of the characteristics of the entire population. To accomplish this, you must make sure you have a proper **sample size**, or an appropriate number of elements in the sample.

BIASES

In statistical studies, biases must be avoided. **Bias** is an error that causes the study to favor one set of results over another. For example, if a survey to determine how the country views the president's job performance only speaks to registered voters in the president's party, the results will be skewed because a disproportionately large number of responders would tend to show approval, while a disproportionately large number of people in the opposite party would tend to express disapproval.

EXTRANEOUS VARIABLES

Extraneous variables are, as the name implies, outside influences that can affect the outcome of a study. They are not always avoidable, but could trigger bias in the result.

DATA ORGANIZATION

EXAMPLE

A nurse found the heart rates of ten different patients to be 76, 80, 90, 86, 70, 76, 72, 88, 88, and 68 beats per minute. Organize this information in a table.

There are several ways to organize data in a table. The table below is an example.

Patient Number	1	2	3	4	5	6	7	8	9	10
Heart Rate (bpm)	76	80	90	86	70	76	72	88	88	68

When making a table, be sure to label the columns and rows appropriately.

DATA ANALYSIS

MEASURES OF CENTRAL TENDENCY

The **measure of central tendency** is a statistical value that gives a general tendency for the center of a group of data. There are several different ways of describing the measure of central tendency. Each one has a unique way it is calculated, and each one gives a slightly different perspective on the data set. Whenever you give a measure of central tendency, always make sure the units are the same. If the data has different units, such as hours, minutes, and seconds, convert all the data to the same unit, and use the same unit in the measure of central tendency. If no units are given in the data, do not give units for the measure of central tendency.

MEAN

The **statistical mean** of a group of data is the same as the arithmetic average of that group. To find the mean of a set of data, first convert each value to the same units, if necessary. Then find the sum of all the values, and count the total number of data values, making sure you take into consideration each individual value. If a value appears more than once, count it more than once. Divide the sum of the values by the total number of values and apply the units, if any. Note that the mean does not have to be one of the data values in the set, and may not divide evenly.

$$\text{mean} = \frac{\text{sum of the data values}}{\text{quantity of data values}}$$

The mean of the data set {88, 72, 61, 90, 97, 68, 88, 79, 86, 93, 97, 71, 80, 84, 89, 72, 91, 95, 89, 83, 94, 90, 63, 69, 89} would be the sum of the twenty-five numbers divided by 25:

$$\frac{88 + 72 + 61 + 90 + 97 + \cdots + 94 + 90 + 63 + 69 + 89}{25}$$
$$= \frac{2078}{25}$$
$$= 83.12$$

While the mean is relatively easy to calculate and averages are understood by most people, the mean can be very misleading if used as the sole measure of central tendency. If the data set has outliers (data values that are unusually high or unusually low compared to the rest of the data values), the mean can be very distorted, especially if the data set has a small number of values. If unusually high values are countered with unusually low values, the mean is not affected as much. For example, if five of twenty students in a class get a 100 on a test, but the other 15 students have an average of 60 on the same test, the class average would appear as 70. Whenever the mean is skewed by outliers, it is always a good idea to include the median as an alternate measure of central tendency.

> **Review Video: Mean, Median, and Mode**
> Visit mometrix.com/academy and enter code: 286207

MEDIAN

The **statistical median** is the value in the middle of the set of data. To find the median, list all data values in order from smallest to largest or from largest to smallest. Any value that is repeated in the set must be listed the number of times it appears. If there are an odd number of data values, the median is the value in the middle of the list. If there is an even number of data values, the median is the arithmetic mean of the two middle values.

MODE

The **statistical mode** is the data value that occurs the most number of times in the data set. It is possible to have exactly one mode, more than one mode, or no mode. To find the mode of a set of data, arrange the data like you do to find the median (all values in order, listing all multiples of data values). Count the number of times each value appears in the data set. If all values appear an equal number of times, there is no mode. If one value appears more than any other value, that value is the mode. If two or more values appear the same number of times, but there are other values that appear fewer times and no values that appear more times, all of those values are the modes.

The big disadvantage of using the median as a measure of central tendency is that is relies solely on a value's relative size as compared to the other values in the set. When the individual values in a set of data are evenly dispersed, the median can be an accurate tool. However, if there is a group of rather large values or a group of rather small values that are not offset by a different group of values, the information that can be inferred from the median may not be accurate because the distribution of values is skewed.

The main disadvantage of the mode is that the values of the other data in the set have no bearing on the mode. The mode may be the largest value, the smallest value, or a value anywhere in between in the set. The mode only tells which value or values, if any, occurred the most number of times. It does not give any suggestions about the remaining values in the set.

DISPERSION

The **measure of dispersion** is a single value that helps to "interpret" the measure of central tendency by providing more information about how the data values in the set are distributed about the measure of central tendency. The measure of dispersion helps to eliminate or reduce the disadvantages of using the mean, median, or mode as a single measure of central tendency, and give a more accurate picture of the dataset as a whole. To have a measure of dispersion, you must know or calculate the range, standard deviation, or variance of the data set.

RANGE

The **range** of a set of data is the difference between the greatest and lowest values of the data in the set. To calculate the range, you must first make sure the units for all data values are the same, and then identify the greatest and lowest values. Use the formula $range = highest\ value - lowest\ value$. If there are multiple data values that are equal for the highest or lowest, just use one of the values in the formula. Write the answer with the same units as the data values you used to do the calculations.

STANDARD DEVIATION

Standard deviation is a measure of dispersion that compares all the data values in the set to the mean of the set to give a more accurate picture. To find the standard deviation of a population, use the formula

$$\sigma = \sqrt{\frac{\sum_{i=1}^{n}(x_i - \bar{x})^2}{n}}$$

where σ is the standard deviation of a population, x represents the individual values in the data set, $\bar{x}$ is the mean of the data values in the set, and n is the number of data values in the set. The higher the value of the standard deviation is, the greater the variance of the data values from the mean. The units associated with the standard deviation are the same as the units of the data values.

VARIANCE

The **variance** of a population, or just variance, is the square of the standard deviation of that population. While the mean of a set of data gives the average of the set and gives information about where a specific data value lies in relation to the average, the variance of the population gives information about the degree to which the data values are spread out and tell you how close an individual value is to the average compared to the other values. The units associated with variance are the same as the units of the data values squared.

PERCENTILE

Percentiles and **quartiles** are other methods of describing data within a set. *Percentiles* tell what percentage of the data in the set fall below a specific point. For example, achievement test scores are often given in percentiles. A score at the 80th percentile is one which is equal to or higher than 80 percent of the scores in the set. In other words, 80 percent of the scores were lower than that score.

QUARTILE

Quartiles are percentile groups that make up quarter sections of the data set. The first quartile is the 25th percentile. The second quartile is the 50th percentile; this is also the median of the dataset. The third quartile is the 75th percentile.

SKEWNESS

Skewness is a way to describe the symmetry or asymmetry of the distribution of values in a dataset. If the distribution of values is symmetrical, there is no skew. In general the closer the mean of a data set is to the median of the data set, the less skew there is. Generally, if the mean is to the right of the median, the data set is *positively skewed*, or right-skewed, and if the mean is to the left of the median, the data set is *negatively skewed*, or left-skewed. However, this rule of thumb is not infallible. When the data values are graphed on a curve, a set with no skew will be a perfect bell curve. To estimate skew, use the formula

$$\text{skew} = \frac{\sqrt{n(n-1)}}{n-2}\left(\frac{\frac{1}{n}\sum_{i=1}^{n}(x_i - \bar{x})^3}{\left(\frac{1}{n}\sum_{i=1}^{n}(x_i - \bar{x})^2\right)^{\frac{3}{2}}}\right)$$

where n is the number of values is the set, x_i is the i-th value in the set, and $\bar{x}$ is the mean of the set.

SIMPLE REGRESSION

In statistics, **simple regression** is using an equation to represent a relation between an independent and dependent variables. The independent variable is also referred to as the explanatory variable or the predictor, and is generally represented by the variable x in the equation. The dependent variable, usually represented by the variable y, is also referred to as the response variable. The equation may be any type of function – linear, quadratic, exponential, etc. The best way to handle this task is to use the regression feature of your graphing calculator. This will easily give you the curve of best fit and provide you with the coefficients and other information you need to derive an equation.

LINE OF BEST FIT

In a scatter plot, the **line of best fit** is the line that best shows the trends of the data. The line of best fit is given by the equation $\hat{y} = ax + b$, where a and b are the regression coefficients. The regression coefficient a is also the slope of the line of best fit, and b is also the y-coordinate of the point at which the line of best fit crosses the x-axis. Not every point on the scatter plot will be on the line of best fit. The differences between the y-values of the points in the scatter plot and the corresponding y-values according to the equation of the line of best fit are the residuals. The line of best fit is also called the least-squares regression line because it is also the line that has the lowest sum of the squares of the residuals.

CORRELATION COEFFICIENT

The **correlation coefficient** is the numerical value that indicates how strong the relationship is between the two variables of a linear regression equation. A correlation coefficient of –1 is a perfect negative correlation. A correlation coefficient of +1 is a perfect positive correlation. Correlation coefficients close to –1 or +1 are very strong correlations. A correlation coefficient equal to zero indicates there is no correlation between the two variables. This test is a good indicator of whether or not the equation for the line of best fit is accurate. The formula for the correlation coefficient is

$$r = \frac{\sum_{i=1}^{n}(x_i - \bar{x})(y_i - \bar{y})}{\sqrt{\sum_{i=1}^{n}(x_i - \bar{x})^2}\sqrt{\sum_{i=1}^{n}(y_i - \bar{y})^2}}$$

where r is the correlation coefficient, n is the number of data values in the set, (x_i, y_i) is a point in the set, and $\bar{x}$ and $\bar{y}$ are the means.

Z-SCORE

A **z-score** is an indication of how many standard deviations a given value falls from the mean. To calculate a z-score, use the formula $= \frac{x-\mu}{\sigma}$, where x is the data value, μ is the mean of the data set, and σ is the standard deviation of the population. If the z-score is positive, the data value lies above the mean. If the z-score is negative, the data value falls below the mean. These scores are useful in interpreting data such as standardized test scores, where every piece of data in the set has been counted, rather than just a small random sample. In cases where standard deviations are calculated from a random sample of the set, the z-scores will not be as accurate.

CENTRAL LIMIT THEOREM

According to the **central limit theorem**, regardless of what the original distribution of a sample is, the distribution of the means tends to get closer and closer to a normal distribution as the sample size gets larger and larger (this is necessary because the sample is becoming more all-encompassing of the elements of the population). As the sample size gets larger, the distribution of the sample mean will approach a normal distribution with a mean of the population mean and a variance of the population variance divided by the sample size.

SHAPE OF DATA DISTRIBUTION

SYMMETRY AND SKEWNESS

Symmetry is a characteristic of the shape of the plotted data. Specifically, it refers to how well the data on one side of the median *mirrors* the data on the other side.

A **skewed data** set is one that has a distinctly longer or fatter tail on one side of the peak or the other. A data set that is *skewed left* has more of its values to the left of the peak, while a set that is *skewed right* has more of its values to the right of the peak. When actually looking at the graph, these names may seem counterintuitive since, in a left-skewed data set, the bulk of the values seem to be on the right side of the graph, and vice versa. However, if the graph is viewed strictly in relation to the peak, the direction of skewness makes more sense.

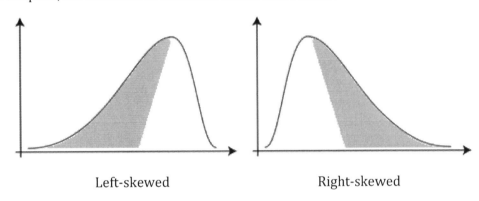

| Left-skewed | Right-skewed |

UNIMODAL VS. BIMODAL

If a distribution has a single peak, it would be considered **unimodal**. If it has two discernible peaks it would be considered **bimodal**. Bimodal distributions may be an indication that the set of data being considered is actually the combination of two sets of data with significant differences.

UNIFORMITY

A uniform distribution is a distribution in which there is *no distinct peak or variation* in the data. No values or ranges are particularly more common than any other values or ranges.

DISPLAYING INFORMATION

CHARTS AND TABLES

Charts and tables are ways of organizing information into separate rows and columns that are labeled to identify and explain the data contained in them. Some charts and tables are organized horizontally, with row lengths giving the details about the labeled information. Other charts and tables are organized vertically, with column heights giving the details about the labeled information.

FREQUENCY TABLES

Frequency tables show how frequently each unique value appears in the set. A *relative frequency table* is one that shows the proportions of each unique value compared to the entire set. Relative frequencies are given as percents; however, the total percent for a relative frequency table will not necessarily equal 100 percent due to rounding. An example of a frequency table with relative frequencies is below.

Favorite Color	Frequency	Relative Frequency
Blue	4	13%
Red	7	22%
Purple	3	9%
Green	6	19%
Cyan	12	38%

PICTOGRAPHS

A **pictograph** is a graph, generally in the horizontal orientation, that uses pictures or symbols to represent the data. Each pictograph must have a key that defines the picture or symbol and gives the quantity each picture or symbol represents. Pictures or symbols on a pictograph are not always shown as whole elements. In this case, the fraction of the picture or symbol shown represents the same fraction of the quantity a whole picture or symbol stands for. For example, a row with $3\frac{1}{2}$ ears of corn, where each ear of corn represents 100 stalks of corn in a field, would equal $3\frac{1}{2} \cdot 100 = 350$ stalks of corn in the field.

CIRCLE GRAPHS

Circle graphs, also known as *pie charts*, provide a visual depiction of the relationship of each type of data compared to the whole set of data. The circle graph is divided into sections by drawing radii to create central angles whose percentage of the circle is equal to the individual data's percentage of the whole set. Each 1% of data is equal to 3.6° in the circle graph. Therefore, data represented by a 90° section of the circle graph makes up 25% of the whole. When complete, a circle graph often looks like a pie cut into uneven wedges. The pie chart below shows the data from the frequency table referenced earlier where people were asked their favorite color.

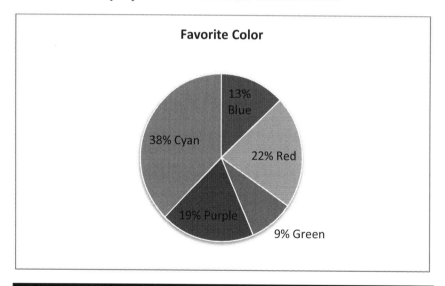

LINE GRAPHS

Line graphs have one or more lines of varying styles (solid or broken) to show the different values for a set of data. The individual data are represented as ordered pairs, much like on a Cartesian plane. In this case, the *x*- and *y*-axes are defined in terms of their units, such as dollars or time. The individual plotted points are joined by line segments to show whether the value of the data is increasing (line sloping upward), decreasing (line sloping downward) or staying the same (horizontal line). Multiple sets of data can be graphed on the same line graph to give an easy visual comparison. An example of this would be graphing achievement test scores for different groups of students over the same time period to see which group had the greatest increase or decrease in performance from year-to-year (as shown below).

Review Video: Line Graphs
Visit mometrix.com/academy and enter code: 480147

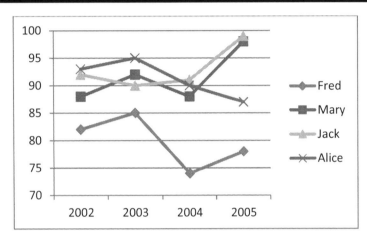

LINE PLOTS

A **line plot**, also known as a *dot plot*, has plotted points that are not connected by line segments. In this graph, the horizontal axis lists the different possible values for the data, and the vertical axis lists the number of times the individual value occurs. A single dot is graphed for each value to show the number of times it occurs. This graph is more closely related to a bar graph than a line graph. Do not connect the dots in a line plot or it will misrepresent the data.

Review Video: Line Plot
Visit mometrix.com/academy and enter code: 754610

STEM AND LEAF PLOTS

A **stem and leaf plot** is useful for depicting groups of data that fall into a range of values. Each piece of data is separated into two parts: the first, or left, part is called the stem; the second, or right, part is called the leaf. Each stem is listed in a column from smallest to largest. Each leaf that has the common stem is listed in that stem's row from smallest to largest. For example, in a set of two-digit numbers, the digit in the tens place is the stem, and the digit in the ones place is the leaf. With a stem and leaf plot, you can easily see which subset of numbers (10s, 20s, 30s, etc.) is the largest. This information is also readily available by looking at a histogram, but a stem and leaf plot also allows you to look closer and see exactly which values fall in that range. Using all of the test scores from above, we can assemble a stem and leaf plot like the one below.

Test Scores									
7	4	8							
8	2	5	7	8	8				
9	0	0	1	2	2	3	5	8	9

BAR GRAPHS

A **bar graph** is one of the few graphs that can be drawn correctly in two different configurations – both horizontally and vertically. A bar graph is similar to a line plot in the way the data is organized on the graph. Both axes must have their categories defined for the graph to be useful. Rather than placing a single dot to mark the point of the data's value, a bar, or thick line, is drawn from zero to the exact value of the data, whether it is a number, percentage, or other numerical value. Longer bar lengths correspond to greater data values. To read a bar graph, read the labels for the axes to find the units being reported. Then look where the bars end in relation to the scale given on the corresponding axis and determine the associated value.

The bar chart below represents the responses from our favorite color survey.

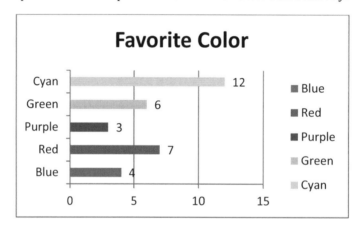

Review Video: Bar Graph
Visit mometrix.com/academy and enter code: 226729

HISTOGRAMS

At first glance, a **histogram** looks like a vertical bar graph. The difference is that a bar graph has a separate bar for each piece of data and a histogram has one continuous bar for each *range* of data. For example, a histogram may have one bar for the range 0–9, one bar for 10–19, etc. While a bar graph has numerical values on one axis, a histogram has numerical values on both axes. Each range is of equal size, and they are ordered left to right from lowest to highest. The height of each column on a histogram represents the number of data values within that range. Like a stem and leaf plot, a histogram makes it easy to glance at the graph and quickly determine which range has the greatest quantity of values. A simple example of a histogram is below.

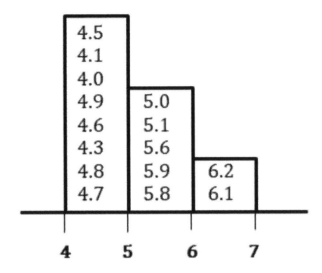

BIVARIATE DATA

Bivariate data is simply data from two different variables. (The prefix *bi-* means *two*.) In a *scatter plot*, each value in the set of data is plotted on a grid similar to a Cartesian plane, where each axis represents one of the two variables. By looking at the pattern formed by the points on the grid, you can often determine whether or not there is a relationship between the two variables, and what that relationship is, if it exists. The variables may be directly proportionate, inversely proportionate, or show no proportion at all. It may also be possible to determine if the data is linear, and if so, to find an equation to relate the two variables. The following scatter plot shows the relationship between preference for brand "A" and the age of the consumers surveyed.

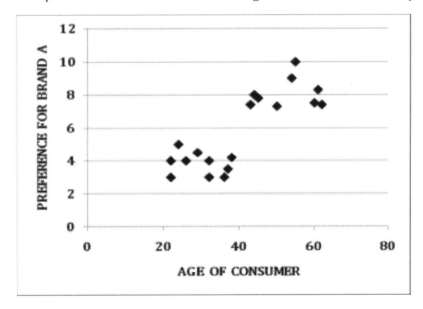

191

SCATTER PLOTS

Scatter plots are also useful in determining the type of function represented by the data and finding the simple regression. Linear scatter plots may be positive or negative. Nonlinear scatter plots are generally exponential or quadratic. Below are some common types of scatter plots:

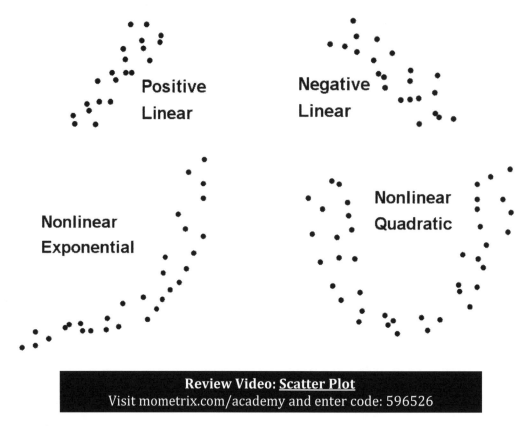

5-NUMBER SUMMARY

The **5-number summary** of a set of data gives a very informative picture of the set. The five numbers in the summary include the minimum value, maximum value, and the three quartiles. This information gives the reader the range and median of the set, as well as an indication of how the data is spread about the median.

BOX AND WHISKER PLOTS

A **box-and-whisker plot** is a graphical representation of the 5-number summary. To draw a box-and-whiskers plot, plot the points of the 5-number summary on a number line. Draw a box whose ends are through the points for the first and third quartiles. Draw a vertical line in the box through the median to divide the box in half. Draw a line segment from the first quartile point to the minimum value, and from the third quartile point to the maximum value.

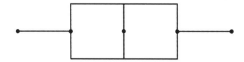

68-95-99.7 RULE

The **68–95–99.7 rule** describes how a normal distribution of data should appear when compared to the mean. This is also a description of a normal bell curve. According to this rule, 68 percent of the data values in a normally distributed set should fall within one standard deviation of the mean (34 percent above and 34 percent below the mean), 95 percent of the data values should fall within two standard deviations of the mean (47.5 percent above and 47.5 percent below the mean), and 99.7 percent of the data values should fall within three standard deviations of the mean, again, equally distributed on either side of the mean. This means that only 0.3 percent of all data values should fall more than three standard deviations from the mean. On the graph below, the normal curve is centered on the y-axis. The x-axis labels are how many standard deviations away from the center you are.

Therefore, it is easy to see how the 68-95-99.7 rule can apply.

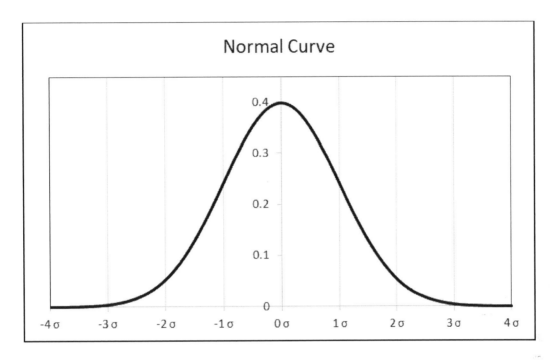

SHAPES OF FREQUENCY CURVES

The five general **shapes of frequency curves** are *symmetrical*, u-*shaped*, *skewed*, j-*shaped*, and *multimodal*. Symmetrical curves are also known as bell curves or normal curves. Values equidistant from the median have equal frequencies. U-shaped curves have two maxima – one at each end. Skewed curves have the maximum point off-center. Curves that are negative skewed, or left skewed, have the maximum on the right side of the graph so there is longer tail and lower slope on the left side. The opposite is true for curves that are positive-skewed, or right-skewed. J-shaped curves have a maximum at one end and a minimum at the other end. Multimodal curves have multiple maxima. For example, if the curve has exactly two maxima, it is called a bimodal curve.

INTERPRETATION OF GRAPHS

EXAMPLE

The following graph shows the ages of five patients being cared for in a hospital:

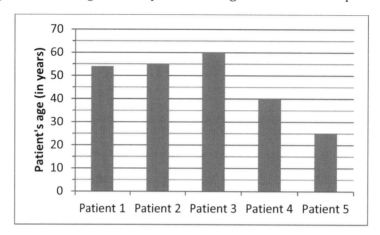

Determine the range of patient ages.

Patient 1 is 54 years old; Patient 2 is 55 years old; Patient 3 is 60 years old; Patient 4 is 40 years old; and Patient 5 is 25 years old. The range of patient ages is the age of the oldest patient minus the age of the youngest patient. In other words, $60 - 25 = 35$. The range of ages is 35 years.

CONSISTENCY BETWEEN STUDIES

EXAMPLE

In a drug study containing 100 patients, a new cholesterol drug was found to decrease low-density lipoprotein (LDL) levels in 25% of the patients. In a second study containing 50 patients, the same drug administered at the same dosage was found to decrease LDL levels in 50% of the patients. Are the results of these two studies **consistent** with one another?

Even though in both studies 25 people (25% of 100 is 25 and 50% of 50 is 25) showed improvements in their LDL levels, the results of the studies are inconsistent. The results of the second study indicate that the drug has a much higher efficacy (desired result) than the results of the first study. Because 50 out of 150 total patients showed improvement on the medication, one could argue that the drug is effective in one third (or approximately 33%) of patients. However, one should be wary of the reliability of results when they're not **reproducible** from one study to the next and when the **sample size** is fairly low.

Science

LABORATORY ACCIDENTS

Any spills or accidents should be **reported** to the teacher so that the teacher can determine the safest clean-up method. The student should start to wash off a **chemical** spilled on the skin while reporting the incident. Some spills may require removal of contaminated clothing and use of the **safety shower**. Broken glass should be disposed of in a designated container. If someone's clothing catches fire they should walk to the safety shower and use it to extinguish the flames. A fire blanket may be used to smother a **lab fire**. A fire extinguisher, phone, spill neutralizers, and a first aid box are other types of **safety equipment** found in the lab. Students should be familiar with **routes** out of the room and the building in case of fire. Students should use the **eye wash station** if a chemical gets in the eyes.

SAFETY PROCEDURES

Students should wear a **lab apron** and **safety goggles**. Loose or dangling clothing and jewelry, necklaces, and earrings should not be worn. Those with long hair should tie it back. Care should always be taken not to splash chemicals. Open-toed shoes such as sandals and flip-flops should not be worn, nor should wrist watches. Glasses are preferable to contact lenses since the latter carries a risk of chemicals getting caught between the lens and the eye. Students should always be supervised. The area where the experiment is taking place and the surrounding floor should be free of clutter. Only the lab book and the items necessary for the experiment should be present. Smoking, eating, and chewing gum are not permitted in the lab. Cords should not be allowed to dangle from work stations. There should be no rough-housing in the lab. Hands should be washed after the lab is complete.

FUME HOODS

Because of the potential safety hazards associated with chemistry lab experiments, such as fire from vapors and the inhalation of toxic fumes, a **fume hood** should be used in many instances. A fume hood carries away vapors from reagents or reactions. Equipment or reactions are placed as far back in the hood as practical to help enhance the collection of the fumes. The **glass safety shield** automatically closes to the appropriate height, and should be low enough to protect the face and body. The safety shield should only be raised to move equipment in and out of the hood. One should not climb inside a hood or stick one's head inside. All spills should be wiped up immediately and the glass should be cleaned if a splash occurs.

COMMON SAFETY HAZARDS

Some specific safety hazards possible in a chemistry lab include:

- **Fire**: Fire can be caused by volatile solvents such as ether, acetone, and benzene being kept in an open beaker or Erlenmeyer flask. Vapors can creep along the table and ignite if they reach a flame or spark. Solvents should be heated in a hood with a steam bath, not on a hot plate.
- **Explosion**: Heating or creating a reaction in a closed system can cause an explosion, resulting in flying glass and chemical splashes. The system should be vented to prevent this.
- **Chemical and thermal burns**: Many chemicals are corrosive to the skin and eyes.
- **Inhalation of toxic fumes**: Some compounds severely irritate membranes in the eyes, nose, throat, and lungs.

195

- **Absorption** of toxic chemicals such as dimethyl sulfoxide (DMSO) and nitrobenzene through the skin.
- **Ingestion** of toxic chemicals.

SAFETY GLOVES

There are many types of **gloves** available to help protect the skin from cuts, burns, and chemical splashes. There are many considerations to take into account when choosing a glove. For example, gloves that are highly protective may limit dexterity. Some gloves may not offer appropriate protection against a specific chemical. Other considerations include degradation rating, which indicates how effective a glove is when exposed to chemicals; breakthrough time, which indicates how quickly a chemical can break through the surface of the glove; and permeation rate, which indicates how quickly chemicals seep through after the initial breakthrough. Disposable latex, vinyl, or nitrile gloves are usually appropriate for most circumstances, and offer protection from incidental splashes and contact. Other types of gloves include butyl, neoprene, PVC, PVA, viton, silver shield, and natural rubber. Each offers its own type of protection, but may have drawbacks as well. **Double-gloving** can improve resistance or dexterity in some instances.

PROPER HANDLING AND STORAGE OF CHEMICALS

Students should take care when **carrying chemicals** from one place to another. Chemicals should never be taken from the room, tasted, or touched with bare hands. **Safety gloves** should be worn when appropriate and glove/chemical interactions and glove deterioration should be considered. Hands should always be **washed** thoroughly after a lab. Potentially hazardous materials intended for use in chemistry, biology, or other science labs should be secured in a safe area where relevant **Safety Data Sheets (SDS)** can be accessed. Chemicals and solutions should be used as directed and labels should be read before handling solutions and chemicals. Extra chemicals should not be returned to their original containers, but should be disposed of as directed by the school district's rules or local ordinances. Local municipalities often have hazardous waste disposal programs. Acids should be stored separately from other chemicals. Flammable liquids should be stored away from acids, bases, and oxidizers.

BUNSEN BURNERS

When using a **Bunsen burner**, loose clothing should be tucked in, long hair should be tied back, and safety goggles and aprons should be worn. Students should know what to do in case of a fire or accident. When lighting the burner, strikers should always be used instead of matches. Do not touch the hot barrel. Tongs (never fingers) should be used to hold the material in the flame. To heat liquid, a flask may be set upon wire gauze on a tripod and secured with an iron ring or clamp on a stand. The flame is extinguished by turning off the gas at the source.

SAFETY PROCEDURES RELATED TO ANIMALS

Animals to be used for **dissections** should be obtained from a company that provides animals for this purpose. Road kill or decaying animals that a student brings in should not be used. It is possible that such an animal may have a pathogen or a virus, such as rabies, which can be transmitted via the saliva of even a dead animal. Students should use gloves and should not participate if they have open sores or moral objections to dissections. It is generally accepted that biological experiments may be performed on lower-order life forms and invertebrates, but not on mammalian vertebrates and birds. No animals should be harmed physiologically. Experimental animals should be kept, cared for, and handled in a safe manner and with compassion. Pathogenic (anything able to cause a disease) substances should not be used in lab experiments.

LAB NOTEBOOKS

A **lab notebook** is a record of all pre-lab work and lab work. It differs from a lab report, which is prepared after lab work is completed. A lab notebook is a formal record of lab preparations and what was done. **Observational recordings** should not be altered, erased, or whited-out to make corrections. Drawing a single line through an entry is sufficient to make changes. Pages should be numbered and should not be torn out. Entries should be made neatly, but don't necessarily have to be complete sentences. **Entries** should provide detailed information and be recorded in such a way that another person could use them to replicate the experiment. **Quantitative data** may be recorded in tabular form, and may include calculations made during an experiment. Lab book entries can also include references and research performed before the experiment. Entries may also consist of information about a lab experiment, including the objective or purpose, the procedures, data collected, and the results.

LAB REPORTS

A **lab report** is an item developed after an experiment that is intended to present the results of a lab experiment. Generally, it should be prepared using a word processor, not hand-written or recorded in a notebook. A lab report should be formally presented. It is intended to persuade others to accept or reject a hypothesis. It should include a brief but descriptive **title** and an **abstract**. The abstract is a summary of the report. It should include a purpose that states the problem that was explored or the question that was answered. It should also include a **hypothesis** that describes the anticipated results of the experiment. The experiment should include a **control** and one **variable** to ensure that the results can be interpreted correctly. Observations and results can be presented using written narratives, tables, graphs, and illustrations. The report should also include a **summation** or **conclusion** explaining whether the results supported the hypothesis.

TYPES OF LABORATORY GLASSWARE

Two types of flasks are Erlenmeyer flasks and volumetric flasks. **Volumetric flasks** are used to accurately prepare a specific volume and concentration of solution. **Erlenmeyer flasks** can be used for mixing, transporting, and reacting, but are not appropriate for accurate measurements.

A **pipette** can be used to accurately measure small amounts of liquid. Liquid is drawn into the pipette through a bulb. The liquid measurement is read at the **meniscus**. There are also plastic disposable pipettes. A **repipette** is a hand-operated pump that dispenses solutions.

Beakers can be used to measure mass or dissolve a solvent into a solute. They do not measure volume as accurately as a volumetric flask, pipette, graduated cylinder, or burette.

Graduated cylinders are used for precise measurements and are considered more accurate than Erlenmeyer flasks or beakers. To read a graduated cylinder, it should be placed on a flat surface and read at eye level. The surface of a liquid in a graduated cylinder forms a lens-shaped curve. The measurement should be taken from the bottom of the curve. A ring may be placed at the top of tall, narrow cylinders to help avoid breakage if they are tipped over.

A **burette**, or buret, is a piece of lab glassware used to accurately dispense liquid. It looks similar to a narrow graduated cylinder, but includes a stopcock and tip. It may be filled with a funnel or pipette.

MICROSCOPES

There are different kinds of microscopes, but **optical** or **light microscopes** are the most commonly used in lab settings. Light and lenses are used to magnify and view samples. A specimen or sample is placed on a slide and the slide is placed on a stage with a hole in it. Light passes through the hole and illuminates the sample. The sample is magnified by lenses and viewed through the eyepiece. A simple microscope has one lens, while a typical compound microscope has three lenses. The light source can be room light redirected by a mirror or the microscope can have its own independent light source that passes through a condenser. In this case, there are diaphragms and filters to allow light intensity to be controlled. Optical microscopes also have coarse and fine adjustment knobs.

Other types of microscopes include **digital microscopes**, which use a camera and a monitor to allow viewing of the sample. **Scanning electron microscopes (SEMs)** provide greater detail of a sample in terms of the surface topography and can produce magnifications much greater than those possible with optical microscopes. The technology of an SEM is quite different from an optical microscope in that it does not rely on lenses to magnify objects, but uses samples placed in a chamber. In one type of SEM, a beam of electrons from an electron gun scans and actually interacts with the sample to produce an image.

Wet mount slides designed for use with a light microscope typically require a thin portion of the specimen to be placed on a standard glass slide. A drop of water is added and a cover slip or cover glass is placed on top. Air bubbles and fingerprints can make viewing difficult. Placing the cover slip at a 45-degree angle and allowing it to drop into place can help avoid the problem of air bubbles. A **cover slip** should always be used when viewing wet mount slides. The viewer should start with the objective in its lowest position and then fine focus. The microscope should be carried with two hands and stored with the low-power objective in the down position. **Lenses** should be cleaned with lens paper only. A **graticule slide** is marked with a grid line, and is useful for counting or estimating a quantity.

BALANCES

Balances such as triple-beam balances, spring balances, and electronic balances measure mass and force. An **electronic balance** is the most accurate, followed by a **triple-beam balance** and then a **spring balance**. One part of a **triple-beam balance** is the plate, which is where the item to be weighed is placed. There are also three beams that have hatch marks indicating amounts and hold the weights that rest in the notches. The front beam measures weights between 0 and 10 grams, the middle beam measures weights in 100 gram increments, and the far beam measures weights in 10 gram increments. The sum of the weight of each beam is the total weight of the object. A triple beam balance also includes a set screw to calibrate the equipment and a mark indicating the object and counterweights are in balance.

CHROMATOGRAPHY

Chromatography refers to a set of laboratory techniques used to separate or analyze **mixtures**. Mixtures are dissolved in their mobile phases. In the stationary or bonded phase, the desired component is separated from other molecules in the mixture. In chromatography, the analyte is the substance to be separated. **Preparative chromatography** refers to the type of chromatography that involves purifying a substance for further use rather than further analysis. **Analytical chromatography** involves analyzing the isolated substance. Other types of chromatography include column, planar, paper, thin layer, displacement, supercritical fluid, affinity, ion exchange, and size exclusion chromatography. Reversed phase, two-dimensional, simulated moving bed, pyrolysis, fast protein, counter current, and chiral are also types of chromatography. **Gas**

chromatography refers to the separation technique in which the mobile phase of a substance is in gas form.

REAGENTS AND REACTANTS

A **reagent** or **reactant** is a chemical agent for use in chemical reactions. When preparing for a lab, it should be confirmed that glassware and other equipment has been cleaned and/or sterilized. There should be enough materials, reagents, or other solutions needed for the lab for every group of students completing the experiment. Distilled water should be used instead of tap water when performing lab experiments because distilled water has most of its impurities removed. Other needed apparatus such as funnels, filter paper, balances, Bunsen burners, ring stands, and/or microscopes should also be set up. After the lab, it should be confirmed that sinks, workstations, and any equipment used have been cleaned. If chemicals or specimens need to be kept at a certain temperature by refrigerating them or using another storage method, the temperature should be checked periodically to ensure the sample does not spoil.

DILUTING ACIDS

When preparing a solution of **dilute acid**, always add the concentrated acid solution to water, not water to concentrated acid. Start by adding ~2/3 of the total volume of water to the graduated cylinder or volumetric flask. Next, add the concentrated acid to the water. Add additional water to the diluted acid to bring the solution to the final desired volume.

CLEANING AFTER ACID SPILLS

In the event of an **acid spill**, any clothes that have come into contact with the acid should be removed and any skin contacted with acid must be rinsed with clean water. To the extent a window can be opened or a fume hood can be turned on, do so. Do not try force circulation, such as by adding a fan, as acid fumes can be harmful if spread.

Next, pour one of the following over the spill area: sodium bicarbonate, baking soda, soda ash, or cat litter. Start from the outside of the spill and then move towards the center, in order to prevent splashing. When the clumps have thoroughly dried, sweep up the clumps and dispose of them as chemical waste.

CENTRIFUGES

A **centrifuge** is used to separate the components of a heterogeneous mixture (consisting of two or more compounds) by spinning it. The solid precipitate settles in the bottom of the container and the liquid component of the solution, called the **centrifugate**, is at the top. A well-known application of this process is using a centrifuge to separate blood cells and plasma. The heavier cells settle on the bottom of the test tube and the lighter plasma stays on top. Another example is using a salad spinner to help dry lettuce.

SPECTROPHOTOMETRY

Spectrophotometry involves measuring the amount of visible light absorbed by a colored solution. There are **analog** and **digital spectrometers** that measure percent absorbency and percent transmittance. A **single beam spectrometer** measures relative light intensity. A **double beam spectrometer** compares light intensity between a reference sample and a test sample. Spectrometers measure the wavelength of light. Spectrometry not only involves working with visible light, but also near-ultraviolet and near-infrared light. A **spectrophotometer** includes an illumination source. An output wavelength is selected and beamed at the sample, the sample absorbs light, and the detector responds to the light and outputs an analog electronic current in a usable form. A spectrophotometer may require calibration. Some types can be used to identify unknown chemicals.

ELECTROPHORESIS, CALORIMETRY, AND TITRATION

- **Electrophoresis** is the separation of molecules based on electrical charge. This is possible because particles disbursed in a fluid usually carry electric charges on their surfaces. Molecules are pulled through the fluid toward the positive end if the molecules have a negative charge and are pulled through the fluid toward the negative end if the molecules have a positive charge.
- **Calorimetry** is used to determine the heat released or absorbed in a chemical reaction.
- **Titration** helps determine the precise endpoint of a reaction. With this information, the precise quantity of reactant in the titration flask can be determined. A burette is used to deliver the second reactant to the flask and an indicator or pH meter is used to detect the endpoint of the reaction.

> **Review Video: Titration**
> Visit mometrix.com/academy and enter code: 550131

FIELD STUDIES AND RESEARCH PROJECTS

Field studies may facilitate scientific inquiry in a manner similar to indoor lab experiments. Field studies can be interdisciplinary in nature and can help students learn and apply scientific concepts and processes. **Research projects** can be conducted in any number of locations, including school campuses, local parks, national parks, beaches, or mountains. Students can practice the general techniques of observation, data collection, collaborative planning, and analysis of experiments. Field studies give students the chance to learn through hands-on applications of scientific processes, such as map making in geography, observation of stratification in geology, observation of life cycles of plants and animals, and analysis of water quality.

Students should watch out for obvious outdoor **hazards**. These include poisonous flora and fauna such as poison ivy, poison oak, and sumac. Depending on the region of the United States in which the field study is being conducted, hazards may also include rattlesnakes and black widow or brown recluse spiders. Students should also be made aware of potentially hazardous situations specific to **geographic locales** and the possibility of coming into contact with **pathogens**.

Field studies allow for great flexibility in the use of traditional and technological methods for **making observations** and **collecting data**. For example, a nature study could consist of a simple survey of bird species within a given area. Information could be recorded using still photography or a video camera. This type of activity gives students the chance to use technologies other than computers. Computers could still be used to create a slide show of transferred images or a digital lab report. If a quantitative study of birds was being performed, the simple technique of using a pencil and paper to tabulate the number of birds counted in the field could also be used. Other techniques used during field studies could include collecting specimens for lab study, observing coastal ecosystems and tides, and collecting weather data such as temperature, precipitation amounts, and air pressure in a particular locale.

METRIC AND INTERNATIONAL SYSTEM OF UNITS

The **metric system** is the accepted standard of measurement in the scientific community. The **International System of Units (SI)** is a set of measurements (including the metric system) that is almost globally accepted. The United States, Liberia, and Myanmar have not accepted this system. **Standardization** is important because it allows the results of experiments to be compared and reproduced without the need to laboriously convert measurements. The SI is based partially on the **meter-kilogram-second (MKS) system** rather than the **centimeter-gram-second (CGS) system**. The MKS system considers meters, kilograms, and seconds to be the basic units of measurement, while the CGS system considers centimeters, grams, and seconds to be the basic units of measurement. Under the MKS system, the length of an object would be expressed as 1 meter instead of 100 centimeters, which is how it would be described under the CGS system.

BASIC UNITS OF MEASUREMENT

Using the **metric system** is generally accepted as the preferred method for taking measurements. Having a **universal standard** allows individuals to interpret measurements more easily, regardless of where they are located. The basic units of measurement are: the **meter**, which measures length; the **liter**, which measures volume; and the **gram**, which measures mass. The metric system starts with a base unit and increases or decreases in units of 10. The prefix and the base unit combined are used to indicate an amount. For example, deka- is 10 times the base unit. A dekameter is 10 meters; a dekaliter is 10 liters; and a dekagram is 10 grams. The prefix hecto- refers to 100 times the base amount; kilo- is 1,000 times the base amount. The prefixes that indicate a fraction of the base unit are deci-, which is 1/10 of the base unit; centi-, which is 1/100 of the base unit; and milli-, which is 1/1000 of the base unit.

COMMON PREFIXES

The prefixes for multiples are as follows: **deka** (da), 10^1 (deka is the American spelling, but deca is also used); **hecto** (h), 10^2; **kilo** (k), 10^3; **mega** (M), 10^6; **giga** (G), 10^9; **tera** (T), 10^{12}; **peta** (P), 10^{15}; **exa** (E), 10^{18}; **zetta** (Z), 10^{21}; and **yotta** (Y), 10^{24}. The prefixes for subdivisions are as follows: **deci** (d), 10^{-1}; **centi** (c), 10^{-2}; **milli** (m), 10^{-3}; **micro** (μ), 10^{-6}; **nano** (n), 10^{-9}; **pico** (p), 10^{-12}; **femto** (f), 10^{-15}; **atto** (a), 10^{-18}; **zepto** (z), 10^{-21}; and **yocto** (y), 10^{-24}. The rule of thumb is that prefixes greater than 10^3 are capitalized. These abbreviations do not need a period after them. A decimeter is a tenth of a meter, a deciliter is a tenth of a liter, and a decigram is a tenth of a gram. Pluralization is understood. For example, when referring to 5 mL of water, no "s" needs to be added to the abbreviation.

BASIC SI UNITS OF MEASUREMENT

SI uses **second(s)** to measure time. Fractions of seconds are usually measured in metric terms using prefixes such as millisecond (1/1,000 of a second) or nanosecond (1/1,000,000,000 of a second). Increments of time larger than a second are measured in **minutes** and **hours**, which are multiples of 60 and 24. An example of this is a swimmer's time in the 800-meter freestyle being described as 7:32.67, meaning 7 minutes, 32 seconds, and 67 one-hundredths of a second. One second is equal to 1/60 of a minute, 1/3,600 of an hour, and 1/86,400 of a day. Other SI base units are the **ampere** (A) (used to measure electric current), the **kelvin** (K) (used to measure thermodynamic temperature), the **candela** (cd) (used to measure luminous intensity), and the **mole** (mol) (used to measure the amount of a substance at a molecular level). **Meter** (m) is used to measure length and **kilogram** (kg) is used to measure mass.

SIGNIFICANT FIGURES

The mathematical concept of **significant figures** or **significant digits** is often used to determine the accuracy of measurements or the level of confidence one has in a specific measurement. The significant figures of a measurement include all the digits known with certainty plus one estimated or uncertain digit. There are a number of rules for determining which digits are considered "important" or "interesting." They are: all non-zero digits are *significant*, zeros between digits are *significant*, and leading and trailing zeros are *not significant* unless they appear to the right of the non-zero digits in a decimal. For example, in 0.01230 the significant digits are 1230, and this number would be said to be accurate to the hundred-thousandths place. The zero indicates that the amount has actually been measured as 0. Other zeros are considered place holders, and are not important. A decimal point may be placed after zeros to indicate their importance (in 100. for example). **Estimating**, on the other hand, involves approximating a value rather than calculating the exact number. This may be used to quickly determine a value that is close to the actual number when complete accuracy does not matter or is not possible. In science, estimation may be used when it is impossible to measure or calculate an exact amount, or to quickly approximate an answer when true calculations would be time consuming.

GRAPHS AND CHARTS

Graphs and charts are effective ways to present scientific data such as observations, statistical analyses, and comparisons between dependent variables and independent variables. On a line chart, the **independent variable** (the one that is being manipulated for the experiment) is represented on the horizontal axis (the x-axis). Any **dependent variables** (the ones that may change as the independent variable changes) are represented on the y-axis. An **XY** or **scatter plot** is often used to plot many points. A "best fit" line is drawn, which allows outliers to be identified more easily. Charts and their axes should have titles. The x and y interval units should be evenly spaced and labeled. Other types of charts are **bar charts** and **histograms**, which can be used to compare differences between the data collected for two variables. A **pie chart** can graphically show the relation of parts to a whole.

DATA PRESENTATION

Data collected during a science lab can be organized and **presented** in any number of ways. While **straight narrative** is a suitable method for presenting some lab results, it is not a suitable way to present numbers and quantitative measurements. These types of observations can often be better presented with **tables** and **graphs**. Data that is presented in tables and organized in rows and columns may also be used to make graphs quite easily. Other methods of presenting data include illustrations, photographs, video, and even audio formats. In a **formal report**, tables and figures are labeled and referred to by their labels. For example, a picture of a bubbly solution might be labeled Figure 1, Bubbly Solution. It would be referred to in the text in the following way: "The reaction created bubbles 10 mm in size, as shown in Figure 1, Bubbly Solution." Graphs are also labeled as figures. Tables are labeled in a different way. Examples include: Table 1, Results of Statistical Analysis, or Table 2, Data from Lab 2.

STATISTICAL PRECISION AND ERRORS

Errors that occur during an experiment can be classified into two categories: random errors and systematic errors. **Random errors** can result in collected data that is wildly different from the rest of the data, or they may result in data that is indistinguishable from the rest. Random errors are not consistent across the data set. In large data sets, random errors may contribute to the variability of data, but they will not affect the average. Random errors are sometimes referred to as noise. They may be caused by a student's inability to take the same measurement in exactly the same way or by outside factors that are not considered variables, but influence the data. A **systematic error** will show up consistently across a sample or data set, and may be the result of a flaw in the experimental design. This type of error affects the average, and is also known as bias.

SCIENTIFIC NOTATION

Scientific notation is used because values in science can be very large or very small, which makes them unwieldy. A number in **decimal notation** is 93,000,000. In **scientific notation**, it is 9.3×10^7.

The first number, 9.3, is the **coefficient**. It is always greater than or equal to 1 and less than 10. This number is followed by a multiplication sign. The base is always 10 in scientific notation. If the number is greater than ten, the exponent is positive. If the number is between zero and one, the exponent is negative. The first digit of the number is followed by a decimal point and then the rest of the number. In this case, the number is 9.3. To get that number, the decimal point was moved seven places from the end of the number, 93,000,000. The number of places, seven, is the exponent.

STATISTICAL TERMINOLOGY

Mean - The average, found by taking the sum of a set of numbers and dividing by the number of numbers in the set.

Median - The middle number in a set of numbers sorted from least to greatest. If the set has an even number of entries, the median is the average of the two in the middle.

Mode - The value that appears most frequently in a data set. There may be more than one mode. If no value appears more than once, there is no mode.

Range - The difference between the highest and lowest numbers in a data set.

Standard deviation - Measures the dispersion of a data set or how far from the mean a single data point is likely to be.

Regression analysis - A method of analyzing sets of data and sets of variables that involves studying how the typical value of the dependent variable changes when any one of the independent variables is varied and the other independent variables remain fixed.

SCIENTIFIC INQUIRY

Teaching with the concept of **scientific inquiry** in mind encourages students to think like scientists rather than merely practice the rote memorization of facts and history. This belief in scientific inquiry puts the burden of learning on students, which is a much different approach than expecting them to simply accept and memorize what they are taught. The standards for science as inquiry are intended to be comprehensive, encompassing a student's K-12 education. More are addressed as students gain knowledge. The **National Science Education Standards** state that engaging students in inquiry helps them develop the following five skills:

- Understand scientific concepts.
- Appreciate "how we know" what we know in science.
- Understand the nature of science.
- Develop the skills necessary to become independent inquirers about the natural world.
- Develop the skills necessary to use the skills, abilities, and attitudes associated with science.

SCIENTIFIC KNOWLEDGE

The National Science Education Standards suggest that **science** as a whole and its unifying concepts and processes are a way of thought that is taught throughout a student's K-12 education. There are eight areas of content, and all the concepts, procedures, and underlying principles contained within make up the body of **scientific knowledge**. The areas of content are: unifying concepts and processes in science, science as inquiry, physical science, life science, earth and space science, science and technology, science in personal and social perspectives, and history and nature of science. Specific unifying concepts and processes included in the standards and repeated throughout the content areas are: systems, order, and organization; evidence, models, and explanation; change, constancy, and measurement; evolution and equilibrium; and form and function.

HISTORY OF SCIENTIFIC KNOWLEDGE

When one examines the history of **scientific knowledge**, it is clear that it is constantly **evolving**. The body of facts, models, theories, and laws grows and changes over time. In other words, one scientific discovery leads to the next. Some advances in science and technology have important and long-lasting effects on science and society. Some discoveries were so alien to the accepted beliefs of the time that not only were they rejected as wrong, but were also considered outright blasphemy. Today, however, many beliefs once considered incorrect have become an ingrained part of scientific knowledge, and have also been the basis of new advances. Examples of advances include: Copernicus's heliocentric view of the universe, Newton's laws of motion and planetary orbits, relativity, geologic time scale, plate tectonics, atomic theory, nuclear physics, biological evolution, germ theory, industrial revolution, molecular biology, information and communication, quantum theory, galactic universe, and medical and health technology.

IMPORTANT TERMINOLOGY

- A **scientific fact** is considered an objective and verifiable observation.
- A **scientific theory** is a greater body of accepted knowledge, principles, or relationships that might explain why something happens.
- A **hypothesis** is an educated guess that is not yet proven. It is used to predict the outcome of an experiment in an attempt to solve a problem or answer a question.
- A **law** is an explanation of events that always leads to the same outcome. It is a fact that an object falls. The law of gravity explains why an object falls. The theory of relativity, although generally accepted, has been neither proven nor disproved.
- A **model** is used to explain something on a smaller scale or in simpler terms to provide an example. It is a representation of an idea that can be used to explain events or applied to new situations to predict outcomes or determine results.

SCIENTIFIC INQUIRY AND SCIENTIFIC METHOD

Scientists use a number of generally accepted techniques collectively known as the **scientific method**. The scientific method generally involves carrying out the following steps:

- Identifying a problem or posing a question
- Formulating a hypothesis or an educated guess
- Conducting experiments or tests that will provide a basis to solve the problem or answer the question
- Observing the results of the test
- Drawing conclusions

An important part of the scientific method is using acceptable experimental techniques. Objectivity is also important if valid results are to be obtained. Another important part of the scientific method is peer review. It is essential that experiments be performed and data be recorded in such a way that experiments can be reproduced to verify results.

SCIENTIFIC INQUIRY SKILLS FOR ELEMENTARY STUDENTS

The six abilities that **grades K-4 students** should acquire are as follows:

- They should be able to ask questions about objects, organisms, and events in the environment.
- They should be able to devise a simple investigation to answer a question.
- They should be able to use tools such as magnifying glasses, rulers, and balances to gather data and make observations.
- They should be able to use the gathered data and observations to provide an explanation.
- They should be able to talk about, draw pictures, or use another method to communicate the results of an investigation and what they learned.
- With respect to the nature of scientific inquiry and scientists, students should understand that investigations involve formulating questions and answers, using different methods of discovering and disclosing answers, using basic tools, observing, sharing answers, and looking at and understanding others' work.

SCIENTIFIC INQUIRY SKILLS FOR MIDDLE GRADE STUDENTS

The five abilities that **grades 5-8 students** should acquire are as follows:

- They should be able to reformulate and clarify questions until they can be answered through scientific investigation.
- They should be able to create and carry out a scientific investigation, interpret the data to provide explanations, and use further data to revise explanations.
- They should be able to identify the tools necessary to gather and analyze data. They should be able to use computer hardware and software to store, organize, and gather data.
- They should be able to provide descriptions and explanations, create models, and make predictions based on the body of knowledge they possess.
- They should be able to explain cause and effect relationships using explanations and data from experiments.

SCIENTIFIC INQUIRY SKILLS FOR OLDER STUDENTS

The six abilities that **grades 9-12 students** should acquire are as follows:

- They should be able to identify questions and concepts that guide scientific investigation. In other words, they should be able to create a hypothesis and an appropriate experiment to test that hypothesis.
- They should be able to design and conduct a scientific investigation from start to finish. This includes being able to guide the inquiry by choosing the proper technologies and methods, determining variables, selecting an appropriate method for presenting data, and conducting peer review.
- They should be able to use technology and mathematics in investigations.
- They should be able to formulate and revise scientific explanations and models.
- They should be able to recognize and analyze alternative explanations. In other words, they should be able to devise other possibilities based on the current body of knowledge.
- They should be able to communicate and defend a scientific argument in both written and oral form.

GREENHOUSE EFFECT

The **greenhouse effect** refers to a naturally occurring and necessary process. **Greenhouse gases**, which are ozone, carbon dioxide, water vapor, and methane, trap infrared radiation that is reflected toward the atmosphere. Without the greenhouse effect, it is estimated that the temperature on Earth would be 30 degrees less on average. The problem occurs because human activity generates more greenhouse gases than necessary. Practices that increase the amount of greenhouse gases include the burning of natural gas and oil, farming practices that result in the release of methane and nitrous oxide, factory operations that produce gases, and deforestation practices that decrease the amount of oxygen available to offset greenhouse gases. Population growth also increases the volume of gases released. Excess greenhouse gases cause more infrared radiation to become trapped, which increases the temperature at the Earth's surface.

OZONE DEPLETION

Ultraviolet light breaks O2 into two very reactive oxygen atoms with unpaired electrons, which are known as **free radicals**. A free radical of oxygen pairs with another oxygen molecule to form **ozone** (O3). Ultraviolet light also breaks ozone (O3) into O2 and a free radical of oxygen. This process usually acts as an ultraviolet light filter for the planet. Other free radical catalysts are produced by natural phenomena such as volcanic eruptions and by human activities. When these enter the atmosphere, they disrupt the normal cycle by breaking down ozone so it cannot absorb more ultraviolet radiation. One such catalyst is the chlorine in chlorofluorocarbons (CFCs). CFCs were used as aerosols and refrigerants. When a CFC like CF2Cl2 is broken down in the atmosphere, chlorine free radicals are produced. These act as catalysts to break down ozone. Whether a chlorine free radical reacts with an ozone or oxygen molecule, it is able to react again.

HUMAN IMPACTS ON ECOSYSTEMS

Human impacts on **ecosystems** take many forms and have many causes. They include widespread disruptions and specific niche disturbances. Humans practice many forms of **environmental manipulation** that affect plants and animals in many biomes and ecosystems. Many human practices involve the consumption of natural resources for food and energy production, the changing of the environment to produce food and energy, and the intrusion on ecosystems to provide shelter. These general behaviors include a multitude of specific behaviors, including the use and overuse of pesticides, the encroachment upon habitat, over hunting and over fishing, the introduction of plant and animal species into non-native ecosystems, and the introduction of hazardous wastes and chemical byproducts into the environment. These behaviors have led to a number of consequences, such as acid rain, ozone depletion, deforestation, urbanization, accelerated species loss, genetic abnormalities, endocrine disruption in populations, and harm to individual animals.

GLOBAL WARMING

Global warming may cause the permanent loss of glaciers and permafrost. There might also be increases in air pollution and acid rain. Rising temperatures may lead to an increase in sea levels as polar ice melts, lower amounts of available fresh water as coastal areas flood, species extinction because of changes in habitat, increases in certain diseases, and a decreased standard of living for humans. Less fresh water and losses of habitat for humans and other species can also lead to decreased agricultural production and food supply shortages. Increased desertification leads to habitat loss for humans and other species. There may be more moisture in the atmosphere due to evaporation.

ACID RAIN AND EUTROPHICATION

Acid rain is made up water droplets for which the pH has been lowered due atmospheric pollution. The common sources of this pollution are **sulfur** and **nitrogen** that have been released through the burning of fossil fuels. This can lead to a lowering of the pH of lakes and ponds, thereby destroying aquatic life, or damaging the leaves and bark of trees. It can also destroy buildings, monuments, and statues made of rock.

Eutrophication is the depletion of oxygen in a body of water. It may be caused by an increase in the amount of nutrients, particularly **phosphates**, which leads to an increase in plant and algae life that use up the oxygen. The result is a decrease in water quality and death of aquatic life. Sources of excess phosphates may be detergents, industrial run-off, or fertilizers that are washed into lakes or streams.

WASTE DISPOSAL METHODS

- <u>Landfills</u> – **Methane** (CH_4) is a greenhouse gas emitted from landfills. Some is used to generate electricity and some gets into the atmosphere. CO_2 is also emitted, and landfill gas can contain nitrogen, oxygen, water vapor, sulfur, mercury, and radioactive contaminants such as tritium. **Landfill leachate** contains acids from car batteries, solvents, heavy metals, pesticides, motor oil, paint, household cleaning supplies, plastics, and many other potentially harmful substances. Some of these are dangerous when they get into the ecosystem.
- <u>Incinerators</u> – These contribute to air pollution in that they can release nitric and sulfuric oxides, which cause **acid rain**.
- <u>Sewage</u> – When dumped in raw form into oceans, sewage can introduce **fecal contaminants** and **pathogenic organisms**, which can harm ocean life and cause disease in humans.

EFFECTS OF CONSUMERISM

Economic growth and quality of living are associated with a wasteful cycle of production. Goods are produced as cheaply as possible with little or no regard for the **ecological effects**. The ultimate goal is profitability. The production process is wasteful, and often introduces **hazardous byproducts** into the environment. Furthermore, byproducts may be dumped into a landfill instead of recycled. When consumer products get dumped in landfills, they can leach **contamination** into groundwater. Landfills can also leach gases. These are or have been dumping grounds for illegal substances, business and government waste, construction industry waste, and medical waste. These items also get dumped at illegal dump sites in urban and remote areas.

ETHICAL AND MORAL CONCERNS

Ethical and moral concerns related to genetic engineering arise in the scientific community and in smaller communities within society. Religious and moral beliefs can conflict with the economic interests of businesses, and with research methods used by the scientific community. For example, the United States government allows genes to be patented. A company has patented the gene for breast and ovarian cancer and will only make it available to researchers for a fee. This leads to a decrease in research, a decrease in medical solutions, and possibly an increase in the occurrence of breast and ovarian cancers. The possibility of lateral or incidental discoveries as a result of research is also limited. For example, a researcher working on a genetic solution to treat breast cancer might accidentally discover a cure for prostate cancer. This, however, would not occur if the researcher could not use the patented gene in the first place.

ENERGY PRODUCTION

- Coal-fired power plants: These generate electricity fairly cheaply, but are the largest source of **greenhouse gases**.
- Gasoline: Gasoline is cheap, generates less CO_2 than coal, and requires less water than coal. But it nevertheless releases a substantial amount of CO_2 in the aggregate and is a limited resource. The burning of gas and other fossil fuels releases carbon dioxide (a greenhouse gas) into the atmosphere.
- Nuclear power plants: A small nuclear power plant can cheaply produce a large amount of electricity. But the waste is potentially harmful and a substantial amount of **water** is required to generate electricity. The cost of storing and transporting the **radioactive waste** is also very large.
- Hydropower: Hydropower is sustainable and environmentally benign once established. A disadvantage is that the building of a dam and the re-routing of a river can be very **environmentally disruptive**.
- Wind power: Wind power is sustainable, non-polluting, and requires little to no cooling water. But it will not produce power in the absence of **wind** and requires a large area over which the turbines can be laid out.
- Solar power: Solar power is sustainable, can be used for a single house or building, and generates peak energy during times of peak usage. But production is limited to when the sun is shining, the panels themselves are expensive to make, and making the panels generates harmful **toxins**.
- Geothermal power: Geothermal power is sustainable, relatively cheap, and non-polluting. Disadvantages are that it can only be utilized in areas with specific **volcanic activity**.

REMOTE SENSING

Remote sensing refers to the gathering of data about an object or phenomenon without physical or intimate contact with the object being studied. The data can be viewed or recorded and stored in many forms (visually with a camera, audibly, or in the form of data). Gathering weather data from a ship, satellite, or buoy might be thought of as remote sensing. The monitoring of a fetus through the use of ultrasound technology provides a remote image. Listening to the heartbeat of a fetus is another example of remote sensing. Methods for remote sensing can be grouped as radiometric, geodetic, or acoustic. Examples of **radiometric remote sensing** include radar, laser altimeters, light detection and ranging (LIDAR) used to determine the concentration of chemicals in the air, and radiometers used to detect various frequencies of radiation. **Geodetic remote sensing** involves measuring the small fluctuations in Earth's gravitational field. Examples of **acoustic remote sensing** include underwater sonar and seismographs.

CELL PHONES AND GPS

A **cell phone** uses **radio waves** to communicate information. When speaking into a cell phone, the user's voice is converted into an electrical signal which is transmitted via radio waves to a cell tower, then to a satellite, then to a cell tower near the recipient, and then to the recipient's cell phone. The recipient's cell phone converts the digital signal back into an electrical signal.

A similar process occurs when data is transmitted over the **Internet** via a wireless network. The cell phone will convert any outgoing communication into a radio wave that will be sent to a wireless router. The router is "wireless" in the sense that the router is not wired to the phone. But the router is connected to the Internet via a cable. The router converts the radio signal into digital form and sends the communication through the Internet. The same basic process also occurs when a cell phone receives information from the Internet.

Wireless networks use radio frequencies of 2.4 GHz or 5 GHz.

Global Positioning System (GPS) is a system of **satellites** that orbit the Earth and communicate with mobile devices to pinpoint the mobile device's **position**. This is accomplished by determining the distance between the mobile device and at least three satellites. A mobile device might calculate a distance of 400 miles between it and the first satellite. The possible locations that are 400 miles from the first satellite and the mobile device will fall along a circle. The possible locations on Earth relative to the other two satellites will fall somewhere along different circles. The point on Earth at which these three circles intersect is the location of the mobile device. The process of determining position based on distance measurements from three satellites is called **trilateration**.

DEVELOPING SCIENTIFIC UNDERSTANDING

Scientific understanding involves not merely the knowledge of scientific theories and equations, but a comprehension of how science is done, how we come to know these theories (and how confident we are in them), and how the different domains of science fit together. Students are unlikely to develop a good scientific understanding merely by being presented with isolated facts. Rather, research suggests that a scientific understanding is best fostered by **inquiry** and by **problem-based learning** approaches, which help students develop their own critical thinking and reasoning skills. In these methods, students are not just provided with facts and theories to memorize but are led to "discover" principles on their own, through experimentation and analogy. The instructor must still provide guidance in the process; if students are completely left to their own devices they may be confused or arrive at incorrect conclusions that may do more harm than good. Furthermore, assessments used in the classroom should promote **higher-order learning**, focusing not just on repetition of facts but on reasoning and evaluation of claims. It is critical that students understand that science is a process and a way of knowing, not a collection of facts.

PRIOR KNOWLEDGE

Students vary in their prior knowledge and capabilities, and science instruction is not a one-size-fits-all process. Sometimes prior knowledge helps student, in that they already have some knowledge about the subject in question, but sometimes prior knowledge may seem to conflict with the new information being taught—a dilemma sometimes called the "**paradox of continuity**". Learning therefore can require a **conceptual change**, in a way that allows the students to reformulate their understanding to fit new information.

Students' experience and developmental characteristics can also affect their science learning. Some students learn more effectively through different **learning styles**, or modalities: some learn best from what they see (**visual learners**), others from what they hear (**auditory learners**), still others from handling objects (**tactile learners**), and others from active participation (**kinesthetic learners**). **Abstract thinking** develops during adolescence and may develop more rapidly in some students than others; students who have not fully developed this capability may benefit from more structured teaching methods. Adolescents tend to be at a stage in their social development in which they learn well in cooperative group activities.

PLANNING ACTIVITIES

Instructors should be aware of and sensitive to students' different preferred styles of learning and prepare lessons that engage all these styles. The instructor should also try to tie lessons to students' individual interests in order to promote active engagement. A **positive learning environment** is one that adapts to students' individual needs and that often involves students working cooperatively.

In science in particular it's important for instructors not to exclude women and minorities, since they *have* been excluded so much in the past that it's easy to do so unconsciously. The instructor should make an effort to mention scientists of different ethnicities and genders and make it clear that women and minorities can be capable scientists.

English learners, too, have their own needs that must be addressed. The instructor can help English learners, for instance, by speaking slowly and clearly, by writing down and providing definitions of key terms, by using visual aids and graphic organizers (which also may help visual learners who are not English language learners), and by giving access to translating devices if necessary. English learners can also benefit from working in groups with capable English speakers who can help explain instructions and procedures they don't understand.

MOTIVATION AND ENGAGEMENT

Regardless of how clearly and accurately an instructor explains the topic, the students may not learn if they're unengaged and not paying attention. Therefore, it's important for the teacher to engage the students' interest and keep their attention. One of the advantages of inquiry-based learning is that it actively involves the students and keeps them more engaged than direct students by relating the topic to their interests and goals and finding ways to tie the topics in to the students' own experiences, prior knowledge, and daily lives. This requires the teacher to get to know the students and their interests, but this has other benefits as well: the students are also more engaged when there is a good relationship between the teachers and students.

Students also tend to be more engaged by collaborative group activities than by working on their own. Adolescents are at a stage in their social development in which they are increasingly driven to form social attachments with their peers. They are comfortable working in groups and benefit from collaborative learning environments.

TEXTS USED IN THE CLASSROOM

Science instruction often involves the students acquiring information from textbooks and handouts, but not all students may be able to effectively use these texts without guidance. Most textbooks have various features designed to make it easier to locate information: an **index**, a **table of contents**, often a **glossary** and/or a list of important variables and formulas. An instructor can explain how to use these features at the beginning of the year, and perhaps even assign an activity that involves making use of them.

It may also be helpful to teach **active reading** techniques. One such technique is **pre-reading**—skimming and reading the headings before reading the text in depth, making predictions and building background knowledge. The instructor can also encourage active reading techniques through providing graphic organizers or techniques like **SQ3R**—a method that involves the student first surveying the chapter, then formulating questions about each section, then reading the section, reciting the main ideas (putting them in their own words), and reviewing the material.

In the modern classroom, textbooks aren't the only kind of text that students can take advantage of. An effective teacher can also show students how to find information online, through web searches and reference sites.

TOTAL SCHOOL PROGRAM

While the science teachers plan the curriculum for their classes, they must also be aware of the **total school program**—the overall objectives for the students' learning in all subjects. The science teacher must be aware of school-wide objectives, and make sure that they are being adequately met in his or her class. The science instructor may also have a role in *setting* those objectives, in conjunction with other teachers and administrators; the science instructor in this case should work cooperatively with the rest of the team and ensure that any issues unique or important to the science classroom are properly addressed and incorporated into the objectives.

The science teacher must also be mindful of the statewide objectives. Standards lay out the curriculum requirements for the course and specifies topics that must be covered. Students must master these topics to be ready not only for standardized exams, but to ensure that no gaps in understanding exist prior to advancing to the next grade-level.

SUPPORTIVE LEARNING ENVIRONMENT

Creating a learning environment that supports student inquiries involves both setting certain procedures and expectations in the class and providing resources that lend themselves to inquiry-based learning. To encourage inquiry-based learning, the instructor should encourage students to ask questions, but try to guide them toward finding answers for themselves rather than giving direct answers to their questions. The instructor should pose questions that require higher-order thinking rather than rote recall or yes or no answers and include a time for reflection in each lesson. Lessons in inquiry-based classrooms are centered around projects and experiments rather than lectures—in fact, one increasingly popular technique is to **"flip the classroom"**, having the students read the lesson or watch video lectures you provide as their homework and freeing up class time for discussion and analysis.

An inquiry-centered classroom environment should put a priority on student collaboration. The instructor should give the students assignments that involve their working together as much as practical. It is helpful to have some online resources that facilitate collaboration and sharing of information, such as a class website, and perhaps a class blog and wiki. Many online resources allow students to share documents and work on them together.

PARTICIPATION IN SCIENTIFIC INVESTIGATION

Scientific investigations are an important part of science teaching, and it is vital that all students are given the opportunity to participate. Ideally, there will be enough space and equipment for the students to work in small groups on an experiment, but in practice this may not be possible. In this case, one solution is to have rotating stations in the classroom, where for one day or for part of the period one group works on one experiment, while another group works on a different activity that uses different equipment; as they rotate through the different stations, all the students will have the opportunity to do every activity, but not in the same order.

Another important part of making it possible for all students to participate in scientific investigations is to ensure that they all have the means to understand and carry out the instructions. Going over the procedure in a lecture may not be enough; it may be better to have a written handout and/or a screencast that the students can watch and refer back to as needed. Students with special needs must also be accommodated; for instance, English language learners can be given definitions of key terms.

ACTIVE LEARNING, INQUIRY, AND REFLECTION

Active learning and inquiry-based learning are two related pedagogical techniques that have been shown by research to be effective in teaching science. **Active learning** refers to teaching by making the student an active participant in the learning process. A class in which the instructor lectures, the students take notes, and the students later demonstrate their learning of the topic by taking a written exam is *not* engaged in active learning, and is not likely to be as effective. Active learning can include experiments that the students perform, interactive online simulations of processes that they can't physically experience in the classroom, having the students create presentations and projects rather than have exams and worksheets as the main assessments.

Inquiry-based learning is a form of teaching by asking questions, having discussions, and helping students do their own research rather than just presenting them with lists of facts and formulas to be learned. Inquiry-based learning is effective not only because it involves the students directly, but because allowing them to formulate their own questions engages their curiosity and critical thinking. **Reflection** is also an important part of inquiry-based learning, having students think back on what they learned and how they learned it.

MODELING SCIENTIFIC THOUGHT

Modeling, in a pedagogical context, refers to *showing* the students what they should do, rather than telling them. This doesn't mean just demonstrating an activity at the front of the classroom while the students watch passively; effective modeling also involves the students as active participants. The important thing is that the teacher sets an example of the principles he or she wants to convey.

To model scientific attitudes, therefore, means to demonstrate and embody those attitudes. To instill curiosity and skepticism in students, the teacher should display those attributes. If the teacher doesn't know the answer to a question, the teacher should not be afraid to say "I don't know"—but should follow that by trying to find the answer, by looking it up online or by performing an experiment. When discussing a topic and coming up with questions about it, the instructor should come up with questions as well—ideally questions the instructor honestly doesn't know the answer to. On the other hand, the instructor should not be too quick to accept answers—not, for instance, immediately latching onto the first answer the instructor finds online, but looking for multiple sources of information, and analyzing their credibility.

INQUIRY-BASED SCIENTIFIC INVESTIGATION

An **inquiry-based scientific investigation** is one that follows the **scientific method**. While the scientific method is often formalized in different ways, there are some essential aspects. The investigator formulates a specific **question** that the investigation will answer. Usually this question is based on an **observation** that the investigation is intended to explain. The investigator then does some background **research**, reviewing previously published information on the subject in question. For a professional scientist, this will usually involve reading articles in scientific journals; in a classroom setting a web search may suffice. The investigator may formulate a **hypothesis**—a proposed possible answer to the question.

The investigator decides how to **gather evidence** to find an answer to the question and prove or disprove the hypothesis, designing an **experiment** that will test the hypothesis, and selecting the proper tools to carry it out. The investigator makes **predictions** as to what will happen in the experiment if the hypothesis is true, and if it is not. The investigator then carries out the experiment, gathers data, and analyzes the results, drawing **conclusions** based on the data.

There remain other important steps: **communication** of the results to others, defending the results, and possibly formulating further questions.

FORMULATING SCIENTIFIC QUESTIONS

Formulating scientific questions is an important part of an inquiry-based investigation; an investigation starts with a specific question, and then an experiment is designed to answer that question. The question usually is based on an observation: the student observes a phenomenon and then formulates a question about what the student observed. The question should be as concrete, objective, quantitative, and measurable as possible. "Why did this object move?" is a vague and abstract question that cannot be easily answered. "Did this object move because of this force?" is more concrete. "What is the relationship between this force and the motion of this object?" is a good quantitative question that can potentially be answered by experiment.

To help the student to formulate a question, the instructor can first guide students through an observation, encouraging the students to think of anything about the observation they're curious about or that they don't understand. The instructor can then help the students come up with questions addressing the subject of their curiosity, and then gradually guide the students into making the questions more specific and measurable.

HYPOTHESES

The **hypothesis** is an educated guess as to the answer to the central question of a scientific investigation. It is an important part of the investigation because it helps guide the inquiry and suggest specific lines of investigation that can prove or disprove the hypothesis: the experiment at the heart of the investigation should be designed such that it will have different results depending on whether or not the hypothesis is correct.

It is important that the hypothesis is an *educated* guess; the student may not know the answer to the question, but there should be some basis for choosing the hypothesis—by extrapolation from known cases, or by analogy with similar scenarios. If the student has trouble coming up with a hypothesis, the instructor might prompt the student to think of similar situations the student understands better, or to research such situations that have been investigated before, and then to consider what those situations imply about the present question. Even a very loose analogy can be enough to make a hypothesis—for the purposes of the investigation, it doesn't matter that the student chooses a hypothesis that turns out to be *right*, only that it relates to the question.

SCIENTIFIC RESULTS

There are many methods that can be used to analyze and evaluate scientific results. Often **graphs** help investigators and readers visualize data better. If one variable is plotted against another and the points seem to form a straight line, that is evidence that a linear relationship may exist between these variables; if they form a parabola, they may have a quadratic relationship; and so on. In more advanced classes, **statistical methods** may be useful, from methods as simple as taking the **mean** of multiple measurements and comparing the means of sets of data rather than the individual points, to methods as complex as calculating **standard deviations** and **correlation coefficients**. All of these methods help show the relationships between quantities and can help to evaluate possible explanations of a result.

Error analysis is another important part of evaluating results. Students should have an idea of what possible sources of error exist in the experiment, and whether they are **random** or **systematic**. Random error can be identified by taking repeated measurements and seeing how close they are; identifying systematic error involves a more thoughtful consideration of what could lead results to be off in one direction or the other.

HIGHER-LEVEL THINKING SKILLS

Students should be encouraged to engage in not just rote memorization and learning of procedures, but in higher-order thinking as well that involves putting together what they've learned in constructive ways. The most commonly used model of different levels of thinking in education is **Bloom's taxonomy**, which divides cognitive processes into six categories or levels. The lowest level, **Remember**, involves simple recall of data. The next, **Understand**, requires students to be able to explain or discuss concepts in their own words. Then comes **Apply**, using the concepts in practice; **Analyze**, drawing connections and comparisons between ideas; **Evaluate**, judging and justifying ideas; and **Create**, synthesizing something new from the concepts.

It's easy to design activities that utilize the lower levels of Bloom's Taxonomy, but engaging the higher orders of thinking is more difficult—but is important for developing a more thorough understanding of a topic. Some verbs commonly associated with each level of Bloom's Taxonomy give clues as to how to promote them. "Create", for example, is associated with the verbs "construct", "plan", and "design" (among others)—certainly designing an experiment to answer a specific question fits here. "Evaluate" is associated with "appraise", "argue", and "justify"—students could be asked to assess a scientific claim and argue for or against it.

SYSTEMATIC OBSERVATIONS AND MEASUREMENTS

In a scientific investigation, observations are not haphazard; there are certain systematic principles that must be followed for useful observations. As far as possible, the observations should be **quantitative**; there should be some measured value recorded, and not simply a qualitative observation such as "it is longer". Measurements should be taken by a consistent method and recorded with proper units—and with an estimate of their **uncertainty**. A measurement taken with a meter stick with markings every millimeter, for instance, has an uncertainty of ±0.5 mm.

It is also important when making observations to vary only one quantity at a time. If you want to measure how a plant's growth is affected by temperature and by amount of light, it isn't useful to change both factors for each measurement—that would make it impossible to see how much of the effect was produced by each change. Rather, it is better to do (at least) one set of measurements in which the temperature is held constant and the amount of light is changed, and another where the reverse is true, so that the effects of each factor can be isolated. In many cases, an **experimental control** is also desirable.

STUDENTS' PRIOR KNOWLEDGE

Prior knowledge refers to the knowledge the student has about the subject matter before it's covered in class. This may come from previous classes, from books and television, from peers or parents, from experience, or from other sources. It's useful to know what prior knowledge students possess before the lesson begins, and there are a number of ways of finding out. One way is through **formative assessments**, assessments that are designed not to test what the student has learned but to test what the students know in order to guide lesson planning. Another popular way of testing prior knowledge is a **K-W-L chart**, in which students write down what they *know* about the topic, what they *want* to know, and, after the lesson, what they *learned*.

The instructor can use the students' prior knowledge as a starting point for the lesson; having the students share what they already know can help introduce the topic. Prior knowledge may also guide the instructor's approach to the topic, since it may carry some assumptions or preconceptions that will affect the way the student might react to different presentations. In some cases, prior knowledge may even lead to misconceptions that must be overcome.

PERFORMANCE IN INQUIRY-BASED INVESTIGATIONS

The stereotypical classroom assessment may be a multiple-choice quiz, but this is not generally the most effective way of assessing student learning in an inquiry-based classroom. There may be a place for written exams as summative assessments, but more effective assessment methods will engage students' higher-order thinking processes and may involve collaboration and active participation.

214

For example, in a science class, a lab report can be a useful assessment; after performing an experiment, students may be asked to turn in a written account of the procedure and results. Along similar lines, a laboratory journal that students keep during an experiment can also be used for assessment, or a field journal for longer-term projects. The instructor may require students to compile all their work in a portfolio, to be turned in at the end of the semester or at shorter intervals; this can serve as a summative assessment in lieu of or in addition to a traditional exam. To assess the student's participation in a classroom activity as objectively as possible, rather than make a subjective judgment call the instructor can use checklists or a detailed rubric prepared ahead of time.

ASSESSMENT AND INSTRUCTION

An **assessment** is an activity designed to measure students' knowledge, learning, or abilities, such as an exam. Assessments are not limited to testing how much the student has learned after a lesson; there are also formative assessments used before or during a lesson to test the student's prior knowledge and how well they are learning the topic.

There are important relationships between assessment and instruction, and the two must be designed together. Formative assessments guide instruction, since the instructor should take into account students' prior knowledge in planning a lesson, and if a formative assessment shows that students are not learning what the instructor expects, the instructor should use that information to try a different pedagogical approach. As for summative assessments, they should be designed to match the learning objectives; the instructor should make sure that the summative assessment is designed to test that the students have met the specific instructional goals of the lessons.

ONGOING ASSESSMENT

Ongoing assessment is vital in science instruction for several reasons. For one thing, formative assessments are important so that the instructor can be informed of the students' prior knowledge and plan the lesson accordingly. If the instructor learns from a formative assessment that the students lack some prior knowledge necessary to the lesson, then the instructor will have to be sure to cover that first; if the instructor learns that the students have a significant misconception about the topic, then the instructor may have to plan for a conceptual change. During the lesson, further formative assessments can monitor students' learning and inform the instructor whether the students are absorbing the information and methodologies that the instructor intends them to absorb, or whether the pace of the lesson should be changed or different pedagogical methods adopted.

Ongoing assessments can also benefit the students by reinforcing the subject matter. The assessments give the students another opportunity to put what they have learned to use, and may help them better retain it. They also give the students an idea of how well they are learning, and what topics they might need to review or about which they should ask more questions.

TYPES OF ASSESSMENTS

Assessments are divided into two main categories: **formative assessments** that measure how well students have learned the subject matter, and **summative assessments** that are used before or during a lesson to test the student's prior knowledge and how well they are learning the topic. Both these types of assessment are important, and both can be carried out in a number of ways. Assessments can also be **formal**—data-driven, standardized assessments the results of which can be compared against preset benchmarks—or **informal**—less structured assessments based around performance and content. An effective science classroom utilizes a variety of different assessment methods.

For example, a **performance assessment** is an assessment that requires the student to demonstrate skills by completing a task, rather than by selecting a pre-set answer or filling in a blank. A **self-assessment** is an activity in which the student assesses his or her own work, perhaps using a rubric provided by the instructor; these are often not graded and serve to inform the student of his or her own learning. A **peer assessment** is an activity in which the student's work is assessed not by the instructor, but by a fellow student.

COMBATTING MISCONCEPTIONS

One of the reasons it's important to gauge students' prior knowledge of a topic is because some of that prior knowledge may be incorrect or misleading, and the student may have misconceptions about the topic that must be overcome. Simply telling the students that their prior beliefs were incorrect is unlikely to be effective, and may in fact be counterproductive, leading to their misconceptions being reinforced instead of removed. Rather, a better goal is to bring about a **conceptual change**, a gradual revision and rearrangement of prior knowledge to accommodate new ideas, in which the student is an active participant.

There are several research-based methods of bringing about conceptual change. One method is to promote **cognitive conflict**: presenting data or demonstrations that contradict the students' prior conceptions, and guiding the students into finding a resolution to the conflict. Another is the use of **refutational texts** that discuss and refute various views on the topic. Other methods include **collaborative argumentation**, in which students are encouraged to discuss, defend, and evaluate their positions; and **persuasive pedagogy**, applying methods of persuasion such as response shaping and reinforcing.

RELIABILITY AND VALIDITY

Two measurements of the soundness of an assessment are reliability and validity. An assessment is **reliable** if it yields consistent results; students' scores on the assessment should not depend on external circumstances and should be similar for different questions that test the same skill. An assessment is **valid** if it measures what it is meant to measure. These two qualities can vary independently; it is possible for an exam to have a high reliability but a low validity, or vice versa.

The reliability of an assessment can be affected by many factors. Longer tests tend to be more reliable; tests with a short time limit so that many students cannot complete all the questions, or must rush to do so, tend to be less reliable. Reliability is also affected by difficulty; a test is most reliable when the questions are not so easy that almost every student answers the questions correctly, but not so hard that almost none do. An assessment will tend to be more valid if it is designed to cover all the material, and only the material, that it is supposed to cover. It will be less valid if it has hidden biases against certain categories of student.

ASSESSMENT AS A LEARNING EXPERIENCE

Though an obvious purpose of assessments is to allow the instructor to assign students a grade in the class, the assessments themselves can provide learning experiences. For one thing, as the students see what questions on the assessment they are unable to answer, or do not answer correctly, this helps them see what topics they have not fully learned and may need to further review. On the other hand, the questions that the students got right will help build their confidence and perhaps help them better remember in the future what they learned about those topics. Assessments also give students further practice with the methods and concepts they are testing, which may further work to reinforce them. They may also help students to learn new problem-solving strategies; as students go over the assessment after the fact and discuss how they were

supposed to solve a particular problem, the answer might give them information about a strategy they were previously unaware of or underutilizing.

EQUITABLE USE OF ASSESSMENTS

One important consideration that must be kept in mind in designing assessments is that they must be **equitable**—they must not be biased toward or against any part of the student population. Every student must have an adequate opportunity to demonstrate his or her skills and knowledge. There are many biases that may carelessly enter into assessments: cultural biases, language biases, biases against students with special needs.

There are a number of steps that instructors can take to ensure that assessments are equitable. Questions should not rely on "common knowledge" that may not be common to students of different cultures. Students with special needs must be provided with adequate accommodations. English language learners should be given definitions or paraphrases of difficult words and sentences. Other steps that can be taken toward making assessments more equitable include clearly laying out learning outcomes and grading rubrics; using many different methods of assessment that allow students to show their accomplishments in different ways; and ensuring that the subject matter covered in assessments is closely matched to what the instructor teaches in class.

SHARING CRITERIA AND RESULTS

It's important to share the evaluation criteria of assessments with students so that the students will know what to expect from the assessments and prepare accordingly, and so that during the assessment they will know where to best focus their time and attention. If the students have no idea how an assessment will be graded, then the assessment is not fair or equitable; students will not know what aspects of the assessment they should focus on the most and doing well on the assessment may be largely a matter of luck. Sharing the rubric for the assessment ahead of time makes the instructor's expectations clear and ensures that the students know what specifically they will be tested on and can prepare accordingly.

It is also important to share the results of assessments with the students. If the students know the results of their assessments, they can gauge their own progress and learning, and decide where they need to focus in the future and what topics they may need to revisit. Knowing their assessment results may also help students evaluate their study strategies and judge whether or not they are working and how or if they might need to be revised.

Social Studies

INTERPRETING MAPS

The **map legend** is an area that provides interpretation information such as the key, the scale, and how to interpret the map. The **key** is the area that defines symbols, abbreviations, and color schemes used on the map. Any feature identified on the map should be defined in the key. The **scale** is a feature of the map legend that tells how distance on the map relates to distance on the ground. It can either be presented mathematically in a ratio or visually with a line segment. For example, it could say that one inch on the map equals one foot on the ground, or it could show a line segment and tell how much distance on the map the line symbolizes. **Latitude** and **longitude** are often shown on maps to relate their area to the world. Latitude shows how far a location is north or south from the earth's equator, and longitude shows how far a location is east or west from the earth's prime meridian. Latitude runs from 90 N (North Pole) – 0 (equator) – 90 S (South Pole), and longitude runs 180 E (international date line) – 0 (prime meridian) – 180 W (international date line).

Review Video: 5 Elements of any Map
Visit mometrix.com/academy and enter code: 437727

POPULAR MAP PROJECTIONS

- **Globe**: Earth's features are shown on a sphere. No distortion of distances, directions, or areas occurs.
- **Mercator**: projects Earth's features onto a cylinder wrapped around a globe. Generates a rectangular map that is not distorted at the equator but is greatly distorted near the poles. Lines of latitude and longitude form a square grid.
- **Robinson**: projects Earth's features onto an oval-looking map. Areas near the poles are truer to size than in the Mercator. Some distortion affects every point.
- **Orthographic**: Earth's features are shown on a circle, which is tangent to the globe at any point chosen by the mapmaker. Generates a circular, 3D-appearing map similar to how Earth is seen from space.
- **Conic maps**: A family of maps drawn by projecting the globe's features onto a cone set onto the globe. Some distortion affects most points.
- **Polar maps**: A circle onto which the land around the poles has been projected. Provides much less distortion of Antarctica and the land around the North Pole than other map types.

CARTOGRAPHIC DISTORTION AND ITS INFLUENCE ON MAP PROJECTIONS

Cartographic distortion is the distortion caused by projecting a three-dimensional structure, in this case the surface of the earth, onto the two-dimensional surface of a map. Numerous map projections have been developed to minimize distortion, but the only way to eliminate distortion completely is to render the earth in three dimensions. Most map projections have minimal distortion in some location, usually the center, and the distortion becomes greater close to the edges of the map. Some map projections try to compromise and distribute the distortion more evenly across the map. Different categories of maps preserve, or do not distort, different features. Maps that preserve directions accurately are **azimuthal**, and maps that preserve shapes properly are **conformal**. Area-preserving maps are called **equal-area maps**, and maps that preserve distance are called **distance-preserving**. Maps that preserve the shortest routes are **gnomonic projections**.

COMPARING MAPS OF THE SAME PLACE FROM DIFFERENT TIME PERIODS

Maps of the same place from different time periods can often be initially aligned by **geographic features**. Political and land-use boundaries are most likely to change between time periods, whereas locations of waterways and geologic features such as mountains are relatively constant. Once geographic features have been used to align maps, they can be compared side-by-side to examine the changing locations of human settlement, smaller waterways, etc. This kind of map interpretation, at the smallest scale, provides information about how small groups of humans **interact with their environment**. For example, such analysis might show that major cities began around ports, and then moved inland as modes of transportation, like railroads and cars, became more common. Lands that were initially used for agriculture might become incorporated into a nearby city as the population grows. This kind of map analysis can also show the evolution of the **socio-economics** of an area, providing information about the relative importance of economic activities (manufacturing, agriculture or trade) and even the commuting behavior of workers.

NATURAL, POLITICAL, AND CULTURAL FEATURES ON MAPS

Map legends will provide information about the types of natural, political, or cultural features on a map. Some maps show only one of these three features. **Natural features** such as waterways, wetlands, beaches, deserts, mountains, highlands and plains can be compared between regions by type, number, distribution, or any other physical characteristic. **Political features** such as state and county divisions or roads and railroads can be compared numerically, but examining their geographic distribution may be more informative. This provides information on settlement density and population. In addition, road and railroad density may show regions of intense urbanization, agricultural regions, or industrial centers. **Cultural features** may include roads and railroads, but might also include historic areas, museums, archaeological digs, early settlements and even campgrounds. Comparing and contrasting the number, distribution, and types of these features may provide information on the history of an area, the duration of settlement of an area, or the current use of the area (for example, many museums are found in current-day cultural centers).

COMPARING MAPS WITH DATASETS OR TEXTS

Maps can provide a great deal of information about an area by showing specific locations where certain types of settlement, land use, or population growth occurred. **Datasets** and **texts** can provide more specific information about events that can be hypothesized from maps. This specific information may provide dates of significant events (for example, the date of a fire that gutted a downtown region, forcing suburban development) or important numerical data (e.g., population growth by year). Written datasets and texts enable map interpretation to become concrete and allow observed trends to be linked with specific causes ("Real estate prices rose in 2004, causing middle-class citizens to move northwest of the city"). Without specific information from additional sources, inferences drawn from maps cannot be put in **context** and interpreted in more than a vague way.

EVALUATING GRAPHIC FORMATS

The type of information being conveyed guides the choice of **format**. Textual information and numeric information must be displayed with different techniques. Text-only information may be most easily summarized in a diagram or a timeline. If text includes numeric information, it may be converted into a chart that shows the size of groups, connects ideas in a table or graphic, or shows information in a hybridized format. Ideas or opinions can be effectively conveyed in political cartoons. Numeric information is often most helpfully presented in tables or graphs. When information will be referred to and looked up again and again, tables are often most helpful for the reader. When the trends in the numeric information are more important than the numbers themselves, graphs are often the best choice. Information that is linked to the land and has a spatial component is best conveyed using maps.

USING ELECTRONIC RESOURCES AND PERIODICALS FOR REFERENCE

Electronic resources are often the quickest, most convenient way to get background information on a topic. One of the particular strengths of **electronic resources** is that they can also provide primary-source multimedia video, audio, or other visual information on a topic that would not be accessible in print. Information available on the Internet is not often carefully screened for accuracy or for bias, so choosing the **source** of electronic information is often very important. Electronic encyclopedias can provide excellent overview information, but publicly edited resources like Wikipedia are open to error, rapid change, incompleteness, or bias. Students should be made aware of the different types and reliabilities of electronic resources, and they should be taught how to distinguish between them. Electronic resources can often be too detailed and overwhelm students with irrelevant information. **Periodicals** provide current information on social science events, but they too must be screened for bias. Some amount of identifiable bias can actually be an important source of information, because it indicates prevailing culture and standards. Periodicals generally have tighter editorial standards than electronic resources, so completeness and overt errors are not usually as problematic. Periodicals can also provide primary-source information with interviews and photographs.

USING ENCYCLOPEDIAS, BIBLIOGRAPHIES, OR ALMANACS FOR SOCIAL SCIENCE RESEARCH

Encyclopedias are ideal for getting background information on a topic. They provide an overview of the topic, and link it to other concepts that can provide additional keywords, information, or subjects. They can help students narrow their topic by showing the sub-topics within the overall topic, and by relating it to other topics. **Encyclopedias** are often more useful than the Internet because they provide a clearly organized, concise overview of material. **Bibliographies** are bound collections of references to periodicals and books, organized by topic. Students can begin researching more efficiently after they identify a topic, look it up in a bibliography, and look up the references listed there. This provides a branching network of information a student can follow. A pitfall of bibliographies is that when in textbooks or other journal articles, the references in them are chosen to support the author's point of view, and so may be limited in scope. **Almanacs** are volumes of facts published annually. They provide numerical information on just about every topic, and are organized by subject or geographic region. They are often helpful for supporting arguments made using other resources, and do not provide any interpretation of their own.

PRIMARY AND SECONDARY RESOURCES

Primary resources provide information about an event from the perspective of people who were present at the event. They might be letters, autobiographies, interviews, speeches, artworks, or anything created by people with first-hand experience. **Primary resources** are valuable because they provide not only facts about the event, but also information about the surrounding circumstances; for example, a letter might provide commentary about how a political speech was received. The Internet is a source of primary information, but care must be taken to evaluate the perspective of the website providing that information. Websites hosted by individuals or special-interest organizations are more likely to be biased than those hosted by public organizations, governments, educational institutions, or news associations.

Secondary resources provide information about an event, but were not written at the time the event occurred. They draw information from primary sources. Because secondary sources were written later, they have the added advantage of historical perspective, multiple points of view, or resultant outcomes. Newsmagazines that write about an event even a week after it occurred count as secondary sources. Secondary sources tend to analyze events more effectively or thoroughly than primary sources.

FORMULATING RESEARCH QUESTIONS OR HYPOTHESES

Formulating research questions or hypotheses is the process of finding questions to answer that have not yet been asked. The first step in the process is reading **background information**. Knowing about a general topic and reading about how other people have addressed it helps identify areas that are well understood. Areas that are not as well understood may either be lightly addressed in the available literature, or distinctly identified as a topic that is not well understood and deserves further study. Research questions or hypotheses may address such an unknown aspect, or they may focus on drawing parallels between similar, well-researched topics that have not been connected before. Students usually need practice in developing research questions that are of the appropriate scope so that they will find enough information to answer the question, yet not so much that they become overwhelmed. Hypotheses tend to be more specific than research questions.

COLLECTING INFORMATION, ORGANIZING AND REPORTING RESULTS

The first step of writing a research paper involves narrowing down on a **topic**. The student should first read background information to identify areas that are interesting or need further study and that the student does not have a strong opinion about. The research question should be identified, and the student should refer to general sources that can point to more specific information. When he begins to take notes, his information must be **organized** with a clear system to identify the source. Any information from outside sources must be acknowledged with **footnotes** or a **bibliography**. To gain more specific information about his topic, the student can then research bibliographies of the general sources to narrow down on information pertinent to his topic. He should draft a thesis statement that summarizes the main point of the research. This should lead to a working **outline** that incorporates all the ideas needed to support the main point in a logical order. A rough draft should incorporate the results of the research in the outlined order, with all citations clearly inserted. The paper should then be edited for clarity, style, flow, and content.

ANALYZING ARTIFACTS

Artifacts, or everyday objects used by previous cultures, are useful for understanding life in those cultures. Students should first discover, or be provided with, a **description** of the item. This description should tell during what period the **artifact** was used and what culture used it. From that description and/or from examination of the artifact, students should be able to discuss what the artifact is, what it is made of, its potential uses, and the people who likely used it. They should then be able to draw **conclusions** from all these pieces of evidence about life in that culture. For example, analysis of coins from an early American archaeological site might show that settlers brought coins with them, or that some classes of residents were wealthy, or that trade occurred with many different nations. The interpretation will vary depending on the circumstances surrounding the artifact. Students should consider these circumstances when drawing conclusions.

IDENTIFYING MAIN IDEAS IN A DOCUMENT

Main ideas in a paragraph are often found in the **topic sentence**, which is usually the first or second sentence in the paragraph. Every following sentence in the paragraph should relate to that initial information. Sometimes, the first or second sentence doesn't obviously set up the main idea. When that happens, each sentence in the paragraph should be read carefully to find the **common theme** between them all. This common theme is the main idea of the paragraph. Main ideas in an entire document can be found by analyzing the structure of the document. Frequently, the document begins with an introductory paragraph or abstract that will summarize the main ideas. Each paragraph often discusses one of the main ideas and contributes to the overall goal of the document. Some documents are divided up into chapters or sections, each of which discusses a main idea. The way that main ideas are described in a document (either in sentences, paragraphs, or chapters) depends on the length of the document.

ORGANIZING INFORMATION CHRONOLOGICALLY AND ANALYZING THE SEQUENCE OF EVENTS

To organize information chronologically, each piece of information must be associated with a time or a date. Events are ordered according to the time or date at which they happened. In social sciences, chronological organization is the most straightforward way to arrange information, because it relies on a uniform, fixed scale – the passage of time. Information can also be organized based on any of the "who, what, when, where, why?" principles.

Analyzing the sequence of chronological events involves not only examining the event itself, but the preceding and following events. This can put the event in question into perspective, showing how a certain thing might have happened based on preceding history. One large disadvantage of chronological organization is that it may not highlight important events clearly relative to less important events. Determining the relative importance of events depends more strongly on interpreting their relationships to neighboring events.

RECOGNIZING CAUSE-AND-EFFECT RELATIONSHIPS, AND COMPARING SIMILARITIES AND DIFFERENCES

Cause-and-effect relationships are simply linkages between an event that happened (the **effect**) because of some other event (the **cause**). Effects are always chronologically ordered after causes. Effects can be found by asking why something happened, or looking for information following words like so, consequently, since, because, therefore, this led to, as a result, and thus. Causes can be found by asking what happened. **Comparing similarities and differences** involves mentally setting two concepts next to each other and then listing the ways they are the same and the ways they are different. The level of comparison varies by student level; for example, younger students may compare the physical characteristics of two animals while older students compare the themes of a book. Similarity/difference comparisons can be done by listing written descriptions in a point-by-point approach, or they can be done in several graphic ways. Venn diagrams are commonly used to organize information, showing non-overlapping clouds filled with information about the different characteristics of A and B, and the overlapping area shows ways in which A and B are the same. Idea maps using arrows and bubbles can also be developed to show these differences.

DISTINGUISHING BETWEEN FACT AND OPINION

Students easily recognize that **facts** are true statements that everyone agrees on, such as an object's name or a statement about a historical event. Students also recognize that **opinions** vary about matters of taste, such as preferences in food or music, that rely on people's interpretation of facts. Simple examples are easy to spot. **Fact-based passages** include certainty-grounded words like is, did, or saw. On the other hand, **passages containing opinions** often include words that indicate possibility rather than certainty, such as would, should or believe. First-person verbs also indicate

222

opinions, showing that one person is talking about his experience. Less clear are examples found in higher-level texts. For example, primary-source accounts of a Civil War battle might include facts ("X battle was fought today") and also opinions ("Union soldiers are not as brave as Confederate soldiers") that are not clearly written as such ("I believe Union soldiers..."). At the same time as students learn to interpret sources critically (Was the battle account written by a Southerner?), they should practice sifting fact from these types of opinion. Other examples where fact and opinion blend together are self-authored internet websites.

> **Review Video: Fact or Opinion**
> Visit mometrix.com/academy and enter code: 870899

DETERMINING THE ADEQUACY, RELEVANCE, AND CONSISTENCY OF INFORMATION

Before information is sought, a list of **guiding questions** should be developed to help determine whether information found is adequate, relevant, and consistent. These questions should be based on the **research goals**, which should be laid out in an outline or concept map. For example, a student writing a report on Navajo social structure might begin with questions concerning the general lifestyle and location of Navajos, and follow with questions about how Navajo society was organized. While researching his questions, he will come up with pieces of information. This information can be compared to his research questions to determine whether it is **relevant** to his report. Information from several sources should be compared to determine whether information is **consistent**. Information that is **adequate** helps answer specific questions that are part of the research goals. Inadequate information for this particular student might be a statement such as "Navajos had a strong societal structure," because the student is probably seeking more specific information.

DRAWING CONCLUSIONS AND MAKING GENERALIZATIONS ABOUT A TOPIC

Students reading about a topic will encounter different facts and opinions that contribute to their overall impression of the material. The student can critically examine the material by thinking about what facts have been included, how they have been presented, what they show, what they relate to outside the written material, and what the author's conclusion is. Students may agree or disagree with the author's conclusion, based on the student's interpretation of the facts the author presented. When working on a research project, a student's research questions will help him gather details that will enable him to **draw a conclusion** about the research material.

Generalizations are blanket statements that apply to a wide number of examples. They are similar to conclusions, but do not have to summarize the information as completely as conclusions. Generalizations in reading material may be flagged by words such as all, most, none, many, several, sometimes, often, never, overall, or in general. Generalizations are often followed by supporting information consisting of a list of facts. Generalizations can refer to facts or the author's opinions, and they provide a valuable summary of the text overall.

INTERPRETING CHARTS AND TABLES

Charts used in social science are a visual representation of data. They combine graphic and textual elements to convey information in a concise format. Often, **charts** divide the space up in blocks, which are filled with text and/or pictures to convey a point. Charts are often organized in tabular form, where blocks below a heading all have information in common. Charts also divide information into conceptual, non-numeric groups (for example, "favorite color"), which are then plotted against a numerical axis (e.g., "number of students"). Charts should be labeled in such a way that a reader can locate a point on the chart and then consult the surrounding axes or table headings to understand how it compares to other points. **Tables** are a type of chart that divides textual information into rows and columns. Each row and column represents a characteristic of the information. For example, a table might be used to convey demographic information. The first column would provide "year," and the second would provide "population." Reading across the rows, one could see that in the year 1966, the population of Middletown was 53,847. Tracking the columns would show how frequently the population was counted.

INTERPRET GRAPHS AND DIAGRAMS

Graphs are similar to charts, except that they graphically show numeric information on both axes. For example, a **graph** might show population through the years, with years on the X-axis and population on the Y-axis. One advantage of graphs is that population during the time in between censuses can be estimated by locating that point on the graph. Each axis should be labeled to allow the information to be interpreted correctly, and the graph should have an informative title.

Diagrams are usually drawings that show the progression of events. The drawings can be fairly schematic, as in a flow chart, or they can be quite detailed, as in a depiction of scenes from a battle. Diagrams usually have arrows connecting the events or boxes shown. Each event or box should be labeled to show what it represents. Diagrams are interpreted by following the progression along the arrows through all events.

> **Review Video: Terminology for Tables and Graphs**
> Visit mometrix.com/academy and enter code: 355505
>
> **Review Video: Understanding Charts and Tables**
> Visit mometrix.com/academy and enter code: 882112

USING TIMELINES IN SOCIAL SCIENCE

Timelines are used to show the relationships between people, places, and events. They are ordered chronologically, and usually are shown left-to-right or top-to-bottom. Each event on the **timeline** is associated with a date, which determines its location on the timeline. On electronic resources, timelines often contain hyperlinks associated with each event. Clicking on the event's hyperlink will open a page with more information about the event. **Cause-and-effect relationships** can be observed on timelines, which often show a key event and then resulting events following in close succession. These can be helpful for showing the order of events in time or the relationships between similar events. They help make the passage of time a concrete concept, and show that large periods pass between some events, and other events cluster very closely.

USING POLITICAL CARTOONS IN SOCIAL SCIENCE STUDIES

Political cartoons are drawings that memorably convey an opinion. These opinions may be supportive or critical, and may summarize a series of events or pose a fictional situation that summarizes an attitude. **Political cartoons** are therefore secondary sources of information that provide social and cultural context about events. Political cartoons may have captions that help describe the action or put it in context. They may also have dialogue, labels, or other recognizable cultural symbols. For example, Uncle Sam frequently appears in political cartoons to represent the United States Government. Political cartoons frequently employ caricature to call attention to a situation or a person. The nature of the caricature helps show the cartoonist's attitude toward the issue being portrayed. Every element of the cartoon is included to support the artist's point, and should be considered in the cartoon's interpretation. When interpreting political cartoons, students should examine what issue is being discussed, what elements the artist chose to support his or her point, and what the message is. Considering who might agree or disagree with the cartoon is also helpful in determining the message of the cartoon.

QUESTIONING STRATEGY IN RECIPROCAL TEACHING

Good readers will, throughout the process of reading, ask questions. Students first identify the kind of information significant enough for the substance of a question when those questions are first generated. They then ask this information in the form of a question and test themselves to find out if they might answer their own questions. The generation of questions is a flexible strategy insofar as students can be taught and encouraged to ask questions on a number of different levels. When students know before reading that they need to think of questions about the text, they then read while aware of the important ideas in that text. This helps increase comprehension, process the meaning and make inferences and connections to prior information before forming a question.

USING COMPUTERS TO BETTER MANAGE THE CLASSROOM

Since businesses use computers to their advantage in making their companies more efficient, teachers also can use computers in managing their classrooms. Teachers can use the computer to do traditional paperwork and help free them from a number of tasks that are classified as noninstructional. A computer will not make a business a success by itself. And a teacher must know, like the business manager, what programs will do and how they are used. Teachers can use computers to:

- Keep student progress records, test, cumulative and average scores.
- Prepare notes to individual students.
- Keep records of attendance.
- Keep an inventory of supplies that include what quantities are available and where they are located.
- Generate tests and worksheets. They sometimes can help score tests. Students may also be able to take the test on the computer.
- Produce posters and calendars.
- Send parents notes.

HURDLES STUDENTS FACE STUDYING AT HOME

Students may have difficulties with homework because parents come home tired after a hectic day and are unable to properly monitor the students' assignments. The personal difficulties students have and priorities that compete with classwork also are some of the obstacles for studying work at home. Often times the parents do not realize that there is a problem. Some parents are too tired and busy with homemaking chores that finding time to check their children's assignments carefully becomes difficult. Students also have many more extracurricular activities in which to participate and other options such as jobs, sports, activities, television and the Internet. Students also have personal difficulties such as an unstable home life, a lack of adult role models or drug problems.

STRATEGIES TO HAVE STUDENTS COMPLETE HOMEWORK ASSIGNMENTS

Teachers should make known their expectations early in the school year before the first homework is assigned. The teacher should go over the ground rules with the students. An explanation of expectations that is written down helps to increase the chances for students successfully completing homework. Students should know:

- Homework is important and has meaning.
- Doing assignments or not doing them has consequences such as lower grades if the assignments are not done.

225

- Students need to be held to a high standard. Research has shown that students make better gains academically when teachers set high expectations and tell the students of their expectations. Students also should know how much and when homework will be assigned.

CREATING ASSIGNMENTS WITH PURPOSE HELPS IN COMPLETING HOMEWORK AND STUDY SKILLS

Assignments that are made for work to be done outside of class should be done so with a purpose rather than to provide busy work. Good from the homework helps contribute to the class and is much like finishing a project. Among the major purposes of homework are:

- Review and practice of what the students have learned.
- To get ready for the next day's class.
- Improving overall study skills by learning to use resources such as the library, reference material, encyclopedias, or the Internet.
- Exploring subjects more deeply than time allows while in class. In elementary school, as well as to a certain extent in junior high and high school, homework can:
- Teach the children the fundamentals of working independently.
- Encourage self-discipline through time management and meeting deadlines.

TEST-TAKING TIPS BENEFITING INTERMEDIATE STUDENTS

When it is time to take a test, the student should:

- Think positively about doing the best that he or she can do.
- Take some deep breaths and relax. Breathe slowly. Clear the mind of worries and anxious thoughts.
- Push the feet down on the floor to the count of five. Push them harder and hard. Relax and then repeat.
- Visualize by closing the eyes and picturing oneself in a happy and peaceful place.
- Bring all materials needed for the test.
- Listen carefully to the directions and ask if they are not understood.
- Reread the directions carefully
- Look over the entire test to see what must be done before beginning.
- Determine how much time there is to spend on each question, allowing more time for essay questions.
- Skip difficult questions and go back later to answer those skipped.

IMPORTANCE OF CHECKING WORK WHEN TAKING TESTS IN ELEMENTARY CLASSES

Some students finish the test early and do not check their answers. This should be a habit that they develop. When they check their work, they need to ensure that the answers are correctly marked on the answer sheet. They should make sure the answers match the number of questions on the answer sheet. Students should have time to check and reconsider their work if time has been efficiently managed. Students should be encouraged to change answers when they think a better answer is appropriate. Students need reinforcement that their word should be checked daily. Teachers can do this by refusing to accept work until it is confirmed the work has been checked.

IMPORTANCE OF CAREFULLY READING ENTIRE TEST ITEMS AND ALL POSSIBLE ANSWERS FOR ELEMENTARY STUDENTS

Students should not stop reading an item when they believe they have a right answer or that a better answer might be available to them. They should consider each possible option or alternative and then select the best answer. Students should be encouraged to very carefully go over each question and pay particular attention to key terms. This information may be translated by the student into different forms, such as changing the question into their own words or substituting common words. They can use their knowledge to anticipate what an answer might be and to select an answer that appears similar to the one they predicted. These skills may be practiced in regular classroom activity.

TEACHER PLANNING AND PREPARATION

Despite the status of the teacher's knowledge on instructional matters, he or she does select certain curricular content, makes decisions about groupings and allocates specific time periods for activities. These are at the crux of teacher preparation and planning. Teachers must turn curricular goals and related content into a plan that works. This includes textbook and material selection, content strategies, learning assessments for particular pupils, scheduling lessons and detailing instruction for particular days. The planning may be informal or it may be formal and explicit. A skillful teacher plans his or her school day. Teachers have perceptions of the students' needs in different subject areas. Teachers have a central portion of what defines education taken away if they become hindered in actualizing their plans.

MEAN, MEDIAN, AND MODE

- Mean – A number that typifies a set of numbers, such as a geometric mean or an arithmetic mean. The average value of a set of numbers.
- Mode - The number or range of numbers in a set that occurs the most frequently.
- Median - The middle value in a distribution, above and below which lie an equal number of values.

TRADITIONAL AND STANDARDIZED FORMS OF ASSESSMENTS, WHEN TO USE, AND USING STUDENTS' WORK TO GUIDE INSTRUCTION

- Identify what students are doing correctly
- Identify the concepts that your class is developing
- Point our your students misconceptions and errors
- Identify appropriate measures of scoring aptitude.
- Figure out appropriate methods of remediation and acceleration
- Know the appropriate uses of rubrics

INSTRUCTIONAL APPROACHES TO CLASSROOM MANAGEMENT AND STUDENT MOTIVATION

- Model-based classroom management
- Concise and efficient instructions
- Developmentally and age appropriate instruction
- Large (whole) group instruction
- Small group instruction

Be able to create and maintain an atmosphere that encourages questions, conjectures, problem solving, and experimentation

RETEACHING, ENRICHMENT, AND EXTENSIONS

- Reteaching - The act of teaching over again
- Enrichment – Above and beyond the given
- Extensions - small add-ons that help in teaching

OVERVIEW OF CLASSROOM MANAGEMENT

- Organization - The state or manner of being organized
- Discipline - Training expected to produce a specific character or pattern of behavior, especially training that produces moral or mental improvement.
- Procedures - A set of established forms or methods for conducting the affairs of an organized body
- Learner responsibility – the student must have responsibility for their actions or non-action
- Interventions – Interference so as to modify a process or situation.

HELPING ACHIEVE POSITIVE LEARNING OUTCOMES FROM HIGH TEACHER EXPECTATIONS

Most teachers have high hopes for their students. Some may be better than others at communicating those expectations. Others might unconsciously expect less of students who show little interest in learning or who have significant barriers to hurdle. But by holding all students to high standards most teacher believe they can help students achieve their full potential. Studies do show that students tend to internalize beliefs teachers have about their ability. When students are not expected to make a lot of progress, they may tend to take on a defeatist outlook. Some student may think their teachers believe they are not capable of handling demanding assignments. Teachers must see themselves as responsible for finding ways to raise performance despite whatever circumstances the students face.

HOME, CULTURAL AND PARENTAL INVOLVEMENT

Most of the differences in academic achievement can be explained by the quantity and quality of reading materials in the home, the number of pages read for homework, the number of days absent from schools, the number of hours in which TV is watched and the presence of two parents in the home. There are other factors within these factors as well. One factor is the activities in which children engage at home such as reading storybooks, visiting libraries or playing word games. Another factor is the potential difference between the home and school cultures. Culture is used in this sense as a broad sense to include the behavior and attitudes of parents. If there is a wide gap between the home culture and school culture, children may perceive tasks such as reading as devaluing their identity.

EFFECT OF PEER INFLUENCE ON LEARNING

Peer influence on children's behavior as well as on learning is well recognized in psychological literature. Peer influence can operate both ways, positive and negative. Teachers will try normally exploit the positive influence on peers and promote many of the learning experiences the children may have by organizing them into small groups in which they can become involved in learning. The negative aspects of peer influence are obvious when parents of children expect him and her to show interest in school work and spend time on homework but many of the children's peers do not have the same goals on their agendas. It is under such circumstances that it might become necessary to have the child discontinue his or her association with those peers who are negative influences.

LITERACY PROBLEMS WITHIN THE SCHOOL SYSTEM

A big problem behind high rates of illiteracy in America is that students are not always taught properly in their educational environments. Within school systems, education is not giving the youth what it needs to achieve later goals in life. Goals are also not set high because the goals they are trying to reach reflect what the students have learned up to that point in life and not what they should have learned. In order for these students to achieve higher education levels, they will need to be encouraged to want to learn and set higher goals that they one day reach. Some say that to

accomplish this, the teaching methods and disciplines in schools will have to be altered to suit all students and their needs, despite their backgrounds.

Ensuring Literacy for Students of Lower Socioeconomic Classes

There are disagreements among scholars as to the direct correlation between a child's socioeconomic level and comprehension levels in school. Some see a direct correlation others say the correlation is more in degrees. Despite the socioeconomic status, the students still need to learn and that the most important time for students to learn language, according to some academics, is before they enter the education system. Children from a low socioeconomic black or Hispanic family may have worse phonemic awareness that Anglo children and experts have suggested that teachers adjust their styles of teaching to meet the children with those needs. Certain reasons exist for certain social groups having a difficult time reaching the top. In order to reach the top one needs to have a good foundation and that foundation is being able to read and to communicate.

Improving School Literacy Levels

Schools found to be low-performing from assessments sometimes have to adjust their entire curriculum. When such changes take place, there are many aims that are incorporated, much more than just a single program or a single type of instruction. These aims may include helping students' lifelong skills, improving the quality of teaching, learning to make sure all teachers recognize the role that language plays in learning. Among possible strands in a strategy for an entire school, that students in years 7 and 8 read in their form period time or that all year 7 pupils have a literacy hour each week. The focus might include having staff mark all children's books for spelling and grammar as well as content, that all departments provide a glossary of subject-specific words for pupils and that all departments would use a writing frame to provide writing structure for children in each subject.

Curriculum Components

Scope and sequence - effective instruction focusing on the essential skills and concepts commonly found on standardized tests.

Curricular materials - Equipment and materials needed to teach a subject

Learner objectives - The establishing of objectives, types and levels of objectives, of what will be taught.

Nature of Parental Education and Socioeconomic Status

The exact nature of the impact parental education and social economic status has on student achievement although it does have an impact. Studies have found that parental education and family socioeconomic status alone are not necessarily predictors of how students will achieve academically. Studies have found that parental education accounts for about a quarter of the variance in student test scores while socioeconomic status accounts for slightly more than a quarter. Other research indicates that dysfunctional home environments, low expectations from parents, parenting that is ineffective, differences in language and high mobility levels may account for the low achievement levels among those students that come from lower socioeconomic levels.

Negative Peer Influences of Learning

Students, teenagers specifically, look to each other to learn and this sometimes brings about problems. Teenagers are growing and learning and through this development the students look toward each other to acquire what their peers deem to be acceptable. In many instances this may lead to inaccurate understandings. Teenagers purposely acquire knowledge sometimes that is

unmistakably wrong and continue to use it in everyday situations. Some students are so influenced by their culture that, even though they are capable of speaking properly, they will not do so for fear they will not fit in with their peers. These students who are properly taught will acknowledge to adults they are speaking in slang yet still do so because their culture has shaped them to do so.

INCORPORATING THE HISPANIC CULTURE IN READING LESSONS FOR ELEMENTARY STUDENTS

Children can be find places on the map of the United States with names that come from the Spanish language such as San Francisco, Los Angeles, Pueblo. An activity can be done that invites students to use the library, class or Internet to find Hispanic Americans in history. Students can be invited to design a postage stamp of the Hispanic Heritage stamp series that might show a famous Hispanic American or some aspect of the Hispanic-American culture or history. Students can be given a list of Spanish words and be invited to find the English equivalent such as "ensalada" -- "salad." Invite students to create books to help them learn the Spanish words for the numbers one to 10 and for the common colors. For example, 1 -- uno, yellow -- amarillo.

IEP

Special education teachers help to develop an Individualized Education Program (IEP) for each special education student. The IEP sets personalized goals for each student and is tailored to the student's individual needs and ability. When appropriate, the program includes a transition plan outlining specific steps to prepare students with disabilities for middle school or high school or, in the case of older students, a job or postsecondary study. Teachers review the IEP with the student's parents, school administrators, and the student's general education teacher. Teachers work closely with parents to inform them of their child's progress and suggest techniques to promote learning at home.

OBSERVATIONS ASSESSING PREDICTION SKILLS

Teachers observing students will hear the language of prediction. Students might say "I think ... " or "I wonder if ... " By observing, the teachers can view certain reading behaviors that students show. When observing students making predictions about fiction text, the teacher should look out for these reading behaviors:

- Do students look at the text cover and make predictions that are based on the title or illustration?
- Do students stop prediction-making while he or she is reading?
- When reading the text, do the students make predictions based on clues from the illustration or text?

These behaviors should be observed for nonfiction text reading:

- Do students use headings or subheadings in order to make predictions?
- Do students use charts, graphs, illustrations or maps to make predictions?
- Doe students predict what is likely to be learned based on clues from the illustration or text?

EFFECTIVELY USING PARAPROFESSIONAL SKILLS AND TIME

Especially with special education, teachers cannot get to each classroom and paraprofessionals are often sent into classrooms to help students with special needs. Regardless of the use, the roles and routines in which the paraprofessional is used needs to be carefully and clearly laid out. An educator might want to keep notes after discussing the use of a paraprofessional with colleagues.

Say the paraprofessional is in the classroom for reading a half-hour each day. No guidance has been given the teacher. One might consider the routines that could be put into place for that time period. Ensure that it would not take up too much time for the teacher and be within what is expected in the skills of a paraprofessional. One might discuss the benefits of the paraprofessional helping with readers who struggle. Also one might plot the progress of students that are being helped by the paraprofessional.

ESTABLISHING A SUCCESSFUL LEARNING CENTER

Learning centers should be established one at a time. Clear rules and routines for using each center should be understood. A chart should be posted at each center that indicates the rules such as how many children should be in the center or what materials and equipment may be used. The center should be closely supervised at first. Teachers can determine when children are able to work both independently or cooperatively. Possible centers include a writing center, an alphabet center, a science center, a writing center or other centers. These can be changed throughout the year. Learning centers help play an important part in classroom management. Effective classrooms have a combination of direct instruction, cooperative learning, independent practice and learning center activities.

UNDERSTANDING REASON FOR ASSIGNMENTS HELPS STUDENTS STUDY

While students may appreciate understanding an assignment's purpose, the purpose might now become clear until students are mid-way through the assignment or have completed it. Students need to know what it is that is expected of them. There should be clear communication or scant confusion over what is the value of the assignment. The teacher should not just tell a student to read something or answer questions without knowing why they are doing it. Students should be given the bigger picture of just how their assignments fit in the realm of what they study. This is even though the student may not entirely appreciate the project's significance until it is finished or partially finished.

HELPING STUDENTS BETTER UNDERSTAND AND STUDY WITH FOCUSING ASSIGNMENTS

Assignments that are focused are less difficult for students to complete and to understand. Assignments that try to reinforce an overabundant number of ideas is not likely to help a student learn. This is especially the case for students who have not yet developed abstract thinking to the point where they can successfully integrate many of the concepts. Assignments need not be a large, overwhelming dissertation about what it is the teacher expects. The assignment should stick to one issue or concept. and it should ask for maybe four or five examples. A teacher can easily determine if the students are getting what is being sought and if not, help can be given in studying for the objective. Focus and the appropriate background information is also important in class discussions of assigned readings. Some children can be frustrated trying to get at the reading all at once.

HELPING STUDENTS THINK THROUGH WHILE STUDYING WITH CHALLENGING ASSIGNMENTS

Homework can give a student the ability to apply concepts that are beyond the controlled environment of a classroom. It can also help students collect and connect information from a variety of sources, subjects and places. The best assignments challenge students to expand or break away from how they normally think. Such an assignment might combine two unassociated ideas. Assignments can range from listing what one finds in a desk drawer to writing paragraphs about family members. In those assignments, students can break the punctuation or capitalization rules in order to better learn the rules. Integrating topics also helps the thinking process, such as putting together an art, writing and science class.

HELPING STUDENTS STUDY AND COMPLETE THEIR WORK BY VARYING ASSIGNMENTS

If all assignments are alike, students will get bored. Mixing approaches and styles should be tried. All students will not be interested in a given assignment, but mixing it up creates better chances that some of the homework will be enjoyed by the students. Short-term assignments can help students better practice and review material already covered in class. Long-term projects allow students to vary the pace of their work, get into subjects of interest to them and to manage time and deadlines. Variety may also help stimulate the teachers. Students are given more opportunities to better learn when the teacher is enthusiastic. The teachers might try not teaching the same topics or points year in and year out.

ENHANCING STUDYING BY TYING ASSIGNMENTS TO THE PRESENT

Students may often feel that they can relate to assignments about events from long ago in the past. It is hard to teach most types of history unless they are related somehow to the present. But assignments can draw comparisons between what is happening today and events years or centuries ago. For instance, students might approach an assignment on a Civil War battle by contrasting it with more modern battles. They might see the battle through the eyes of a television war correspondent who interviews the principal leaders and ask what they might do differently if they were to "do over" the battle. Students learn the specifics of such battles through these interviews and can appreciate the significance of the events that took place. This is a way of piquing interest in study.

HELPING STUDENTS STUDY A SUBJECT BY MATCHING SKILLS, INTERESTS AND NEEDS

The chances are greater that a student will complete his or her homework assignments if they:

- Are not too hard or too easy.
- Match children's preferred learning styles.
- Let students work on material that they really like. Assignments cannot be customized for every student. But teachers can give assignments to a heterogeneous class that varies in content, format and style. This will better the chance that all students will have some elements of the assignments that are of interest.

Teachers can give the students choices. The student may be expected to master all the same material but it can be done in different ways. This helps student feel they control parts of their learning which encourages studying and helps them to enjoy an assignment that they otherwise would not.

CURRICULUM STANDARDS

Standards focus on developing coherency across grade levels, teaching for understanding, and relevancy of subject matter, helping courses to build upon each other in age appropriate ways. This farsighted statement sets an excellent vision for what students should be learning. The standards are broken into ten areas within two broader categories. Process Standards, the first category, define how students should "do" the content and how they should be able to use their knowledge. The second category, the Content Standards, deal with the content that students should learn.

CONTROVERSY OVER TEACHER EXPECTATIONS ON LEARNING OUTCOMES

The original Pygmalion study gave teachers false information about the learning potential of certain students in the 1-6 grades in a San Francisco elementary school. Teachers were told student had been tested and found to be on the edge of a period of rapid intellectual growth but the student had actually been selected at random. At the end of the experimental period, some of the targeted student exhibited superior scores on IQ tests compared to those of similar abilities. The results led researchers to claim that inflated expectations of teachers for target students actually caused accelerated intellectual growth in the students. A numbers of studies have since taken place and some found technical defects serious enough to cast doubt on the original findings. Whether one accepts or doubts the Pygmalion study, clearly educators and public are very interested in the power of expectations affecting the outcomes of students.

POSITIVE EFFECT ON STUDENT OUTCOMES WITH HIGHER TEACHER EXPECTATIONS SUPPLEMENTED WITH OTHER MEASURES

Self-fulfilling prophecies such as those argued as the outcome of the Pygmalion study on teacher expectations are the most dramatic form of teacher expectation effects because they involve changes in the behavior of children. Sustaining expectations are situations in which teachers fail to see student potential and do not respond by encouraging the student to fulfill their potential. But both actually involve change. High expectations may not be the magic trick needed to close achievement gaps. But raising expectations can make a difference when the effort is accompanied by a relevant and rigorous curriculum, adequate materials and current textbooks. This, along with effective teaching strategies, good classroom management, tutoring programs, uncrowded classrooms and involved parents just to name a few.

PRIOR KNOWLEDGE

Prior knowledge is a combination of one's attitudes, experiences and knowledge which already exist. Attitudes can range from beliefs about ourselves as learners or being aware of our own strengths and weaknesses. It can also be our level of motivation and responsibility for our own learning. The experiences from our daily activities, especially ones with our friends and families, give us a background from which we derive most of our understanding. Individual events in our lives provide us experiences from which to draw from; both bad and good and influence how we deal with future situations. This knowledge is drawn from a wide variety of things, from knowledge of specific content areas and the concepts within, to the goals that we have for ourselves academically.

ORAL QUESTIONING IN CLASS

One easy way for teachers to conduct a formative assessment in class is to briefly quiz students on the material covered. Indeed, whether it is to be done for a grade or not, it is generally useful to recapitulate the previous day's lesson at the beginning of class. Oftentimes, this can be best accomplished by allowing students to articulate the material, and to critique one another's understanding. Some probing questions from the teacher can ensure that the recent material is understood in the context of the material that has already been learned. It is not always necessary to formally grade students on their participation or performance in an informal question-and-answer session; the main thing is to develop an idea of the students' progress.

MoGEA Practice Test

English Language Arts

Questions 1 through 3 are based on the following text:

Jo's face was a study next day, for the secret rather weighed upon her, and she found it hard not to look mysterious and important. Meg observed it, but did not trouble herself to make inquiries, for she had learned that the best way to manage Jo was by the law of contraries, so she felt sure of being told everything if she did not ask. She was rather surprised, therefore, when the silence remained unbroken, and Jo assumed a patronizing air, which decidedly aggravated Meg, who in turn assumed an air of dignified reserve and devoted herself to her mother. This left Jo to her own devices, for Mrs. March had taken her place as nurse, and bade her rest, exercise, and amuse herself after her long confinement. Amy being gone, Laurie was her only refuge, and much as she enjoyed his society, she rather dreaded him just then, for he was an incorrigible tease, and she feared he would coax the secret from her.

(*Little Women* by Louisa May Alcott)

1. From what point of view is this passage written?

    a. First person
    b. Second person
    c. Third person
    d. Fourth person

2. The phrase "was a study" implies that

    a. Jo looked jubilant.
    b. Jo looked secretive.
    c. Jo looked disheveled.
    d. Jo looked angry.

3. What can you infer about Laurie?

    a. He was stoic.
    b. He was taciturn.
    c. He was unruly.
    d. He was uncanny.

Questions 4 through 7 are based on the following text:

There Will Come Soft Rains

By Sara Teasdale

(1)   There will come soft rains and the smell of the ground,
        And swallows circling with their shimmering sound;
        And frogs in the pools singing at night,
        And wild plum trees in tremulous white;
(5)   Robins will wear their feathery fire
        Whistling their whims on a low fence-wire;
        And not one will know of the war, not one
        Will care at last when it is done.
        Not one would mind, neither bird nor tree
(10) If mankind perished utterly;
        And Spring herself, when she woke at dawn,
        Would scarcely know that we were gone

4. Which line uses personification?

    a. Line 2
    b. Line 4
    c. Line 7
    d. Line 11 ✓

5. The "we" used in line 12 refers to

    ✓ a. all of mankind.
    b. the victors of the war.
    c. Americans.
    d. the poet and the reader.

6. This poem is an example of a(n)

    a. sonnet.
    ✓ b. rhymed verse.
    c. free verse.
    d. lyric.

7. Which of these statements offers the best summary of the poem?

    ✓ a. Nature does not care about the affairs of mankind.
    b. It is the government's responsibility to fight a war.
    c. War has a devastating impact on nature.
    d. Wars should not be fought in the spring.

Questions 8 through 10 are based on the following text:

    Archaeological Sites are concentrations of artifacts, rock art or features that reflect activities conducted by past human cultures. Archaeological sites are also areas or buildings where historic human events occurred, such as mining camps or railroad construction sites. These areas are usually, but not always, accompanied by artifacts.

Cultural Resources are usually archaeological sites. They are also *areas* or *localities* that are considered by Native Americans to have been or are presently significant in the exercise of their respective Native American religions or traditional lifeway customs.

Artifacts are objects that show evidence of use or alteration by humans. There are three kinds of artifacts:

- Prehistoric artifacts were used prior to written history, which is considered in North America to have been before the arrival of Europeans. Examples of prehistoric artifacts are arrowheads, manos and metates, and ceramic materials.
- Historic artifacts were used during written history, but more than 50 years ago. Historic artifacts include purple glass bottles, tin cans sealed with solder, and parts of wagons.
- Recent artifacts were used within the last 50 years and are generally not considered of archaeological significance. (U.S. Department of the Interior)

8. What is a prehistoric artifact?
    a. An artifact found on an archaeological site
    b. A purple glass bottle
    c. An item used within the last 50 years
  ✓ d. An item used prior to written history

9. What is the main idea of the first paragraph?
  ✓ a. Archaeological sites are areas of artifacts, rock art or features that reflect activities of past human cultures.
    b. Artifacts are objects that show evidence of use by humans.
    c. Artifacts include purple glass bottles, tin cans sealed with solder, and parts of wagons.
    d. Archaeological sites can include mining camps and railroad construction sites.

10. What would be a logical implication based on this passage?
  ✓ a. Cultural Resources always contain recent artifacts.
    b. A site that contains recent artifacts would not be of interest to an archaeologist.
    c. Arrowheads can be found in mining camps and railroad construction sites.
    d. Prehistoric artifacts are the most important of the three types of artifacts.

Questions 11 through 14 are based on the following text:

Mary Ainsworth described three major categories of infant attachment: secure, anxious/avoidant, and anxious/ambivalent. After years of additional research by many investigators, Mary Main and Judith Solomon in 1986 identified a fourth pattern: anxious/disorganized/disoriented.

These four major patterns of attachment describe unique sets of behavior:

Secure: Securely attached babies are able to use the attachment figure as an effective secure base from which to explore the world. When such moderately stressful events as brief (3-minute) separations in an unfamiliar environment occur, these securely attached babies approach or signal to the attachment figure at reunion and achieve a degree of proximity or contact which suffices to terminate attachment behavior. They accomplish this with little or no open or masked anger, and soon return to exploration or play.

Avoidant: Babies with avoidant attachments are covertly anxious about the attachment figure's responsiveness and have developed a defensive strategy for managing their anxiety. Upon the attachment figure's return after the same moderately stressful events, these avoidant babies show mild version of the "detachment" behavior which characterizes many infants after separations of two or three weeks; that is, they fail to greet the mother, ignore her overtures and act as if she is of little importance.

Ambivalent: In babies with anxious/ambivalent attachments, both anxiety and mixed feelings about the attachment figure are readily observable. At reunion after brief separations in an unfamiliar environment, they mingle openly angry behavior with their attachment behavior.

Disorganized/Disoriented: Babies classified in this group appear to have no consistent strategy for managing separation from and reunion with the attachment figure. Some appear to be clinically depressed; some demonstrate mixtures of avoidant behavior, openly angry behavior and attachment behavior. Others show odd, often uncomfortable and disturbing behaviors. These infant are often seen in studies of high-risk samples of severely maltreated, very disturbed or depressed babies, but also appear in normal middle-class samples. (U.S. Department of Health and Human Services)

11. It can be inferred from this passage that Mary Ainsworth is a

    a. Botanist
    b. Biologist
√ c. Psychologist
    d. Entomologist

12. This passage is mainly about

    a. three categories of infant attachment.
√ b. four major patterns of infant attachment.
    c. secure infant attachment.
    d. high risk babies.

13. This passage would most likely be found in a

    a. human resources handbook.
√ b. human development textbook.
    c. philosophy textbook.
    d. physiology textbook.

14. Babies with avoidant attachments

    a. show odd, uncomfortable behaviors.
    b. are openly angry.
    c. show masked anger.
√ d. act as if the mother is of no importance.

15. What literary movement is a type of realistic fiction that developed in France, America and England in late the 19th century?

    a. Romanticism

    b. Realism

    c. Naturalism

    d. Classicism

16. Who wrote the 1891 novel *Tess of the D'urbervilles*?

    a. Emily Bronte

    b. Charles Dickens

    c. Thomas Hardy

    d. Edgar Allan Poe

17. Which author was among the founders of the Modernist movement and authored *A Room of One's Own* in 1929?

    a. Fyodor Dostoevsky

    b. Francis Bacon

    c. Charles Dickens

    d. Virginia Woolf

18. Which author's works have explored the experience and roles of black women in American society?

    a. Toni Morrison

    b. Washington Irving

    c. Richard Wright

    d. Flannery O'Conner

19. Which author is associated with the Contemporary movement?

    a. Homer

    b. Henry David Thoreau

    c. George Orwell

    d. William Shakespeare

20. Catherine and Heathcliff are main characters from which novel?

    a. Jane Eyre

    b. Wuthering Heights

    c. The Awakening

    d. The Scarlett Letter

21. What is one strategy for prewriting?

    a. Clustering

    b. Reconsidering arguments

    c. Retell, Recite, Relate

    d. Getting the reader's attention

22. The main difference between a topic outline and a sentence outline is

a. a topic outline helps arrange ideas.
b. ideas are numbered or lettered in a sentence outline.
c. ideas are fully stated in a sentence outline.
d. a sentence outline only uses brief phrases or single words.

23. If a student is writing a thesis on brain disorders, the best source of information would be a(n):

a. medical journals.
b. encyclopedia.
c. webpage.
d. newspaper.

24. Which is the best revision of this sentence?

I will start the music after the guests have arrived.

a. After the guests have arrived, I will start the music.
b. I will start the music after the guests arrive.
c. I start the music when the guests have arrived.
d. I will have started the music when the guests have arrived.

25. Which sentence is incorrect?

a. Shawna graduated from college.
b. Shawna graduated college.
c. The college graduated Shawna.
d. Shawna was graduated from college.

26. Which is not a main step in the writing process?

a. Revising
b. Editing
c. Publishing
d. Brainstorming

27. What is the goal of the drafting stage of the writing process?

a. Correcting work before publication
b. Making content clear, interesting and complete
c. Getting ideas down on paper without undue concern for mechanics
d. Brainstorming ideas

28. When creating an outline, it is important to use

a. prepositions.
b. progressivism.
c. abbreviation.
d. subordination.

29. What takes place in the revision stage of the writing process?

a. Correcting errors in grammar, spelling and punctuation
b. Making major changes in content and structure
c. Brainstorming ideas
d. Getting ideas down on paper

30. Which sentence is an example of passive voice?

a. Debbie Knuteson won the award.
b. The doctor admitted Joan to the hospital yesterday.
c. James was released from prison in 1951.
d. The veterinarian injected the puppy with three vaccines.

31. Which of the following is a compound-complex sentence?

a. The dog lived in the backyard, but the cat, who knew he was superior, lived inside the house.
b. She ate her breakfast, and then brushed her teeth.
c. When she arrived, the train had already left.
d. Facts can be proven.

32. Which of the following is the best example of parallel sentence structure?

a. She enjoys dessert, walking on the beach, and songs from the 1980s.
b. I like to eat pies, playing soccer games, and mysteries.
c. The sheriff tried to make the law explicit, accurate, and fair.
d. He is adorable, wears a feather in his hat, and has a cunning way about him.

33. Which correction, if any, should be made in this sentence?

Servicing the air conditioner every summer, the appliance seemed to run better.

a. Servicing the air conditioner every summer, there is an easy way to keep your appliance cooling your home.
b. Servicing the air conditioner every summer, Joan found she could have a much lower electric bill.
c. Servicing the air conditioner every summer, the appliance was kept in excellent condition.
d. No correction is required.

34. Identify the error in this sentence:

The baking <u>of</u> homemade meals <u>have</u> increased <u>during</u> the <u>current</u> economy.

a. of
b. have
c. during
d. current

35. Identify the error in this sentence.

No matter how diligent Jonas tries, he still fails to complete his homework.

a. Adjective and adverb error
b. Antecedent agreement error
c. Dangling modifier
d. Verb tense error

36. Which correction should be made in this sentence?

After the new neighbors moved in, <u>Russell found there excessively loud music very aggravating.</u>

a. Russell found their excessively loud music very aggravating.
b. Russell was aggravated by their excessively loud music.
c. Russell found their excessively loud music very annoying.
d. Russell found them aggravating.

37. What correction, if any, should be made in this sentence?

> Major remodeling is necessary, in instances where mold and dry rot, have destroyed infrastructure.

a. Major remodeling is necessary in instances where mold and dry rot have destroyed infrastructure.
b. Major remodeling is necessary, in instances where mold and dry rot have destroyed infrastructure.
c. Major remodeling is necessary in instances where mold, and dry rot, have destroyed infrastructure.
d. No correction is required.

38. Which sentence is incorrectly punctuated?

a. My son's smile reminds me of his father.
b. I drove to the grocery store, the Laundromat, and the library that is just down the street.
c. "I am going to lunch," she said. "I haven't finished my work, but I need to eat now."
d. They drove all day to see the snow, however, it had all melted by the time they got there.

39. Identify the error in this sentence.

> The teacher gave stickers to whomever had stood in line quietly.

a. Punctuation error
b. Verb tense error
c. Subject and object form error
d. Dangling modifier

40. Which title is not punctuated correctly?

a. A Christmas Carol, by Charles Dickens
b. "The Road Not Taken," by Robert Frost
c. "The Raven," by Edgar Allan Poe
d. "The Heart of Darkness," by Joseph Conrad

Science

1. If you were testing the effectiveness of a cream that reduced the signs of wrinkles around women's eyes, which of the following would be a good control group?

a. Rats with no wrinkles

b. A group of women with no wrinkles around their eyes who are given the cream

c. A group of women with wrinkles who are given a harmless cream that has no effect

d. A group of women with wrinkles around their eyes

2. Which step of the scientific method involves independent variables?

a. Make an observation

b. Ask a question

c. Formulate a hypothesis

d. Conduct an experiment

3. Which of these units of measurement is used to measure bicyclist's energy expenditure?

a. ergs

b. nanometers

c. milligrams

d. cubic centimeters

4. Convert 0.0000000736 to scientific notation.

a. 7.36×108

b. $736 \times 10 - 8$

c. 7.36×10^{-8}

d. $736 \times 10 - 8$

5. The true diameter of electrical wire 3.67 cm. Three measurements of the wire produce the following values: 3.9 cm, 3.9 cm, and 3.9 cm. Which of the following statements is true concerning the measurements?

a. They are neither precise nor accurate.

b. They are precise and accurate.

c. They are precise but not accurate.

d. They are accurate but not precise.

6. Science can be differentiated from non-science because scientific results

a. are repeatable.

b. always take place in a laboratory.

c. are based on single events.

d. are formed from opinions.

7. Which of the following is formed by meiosis?

a. spores

b. embryos

c. DNA

d. chromosomes

8. Most of the energy in a food chain is concentrated in the level of the

    a. primary producers.
    b. primary consumers.
    c. secondary consumers.
    d. tertiary consumers.

9. In a mixture of NaCl and H_2O, what piece of equipment should be used to separate the mixture?

    a. magnet
    b. hotplate
    c. funnel
    d. drill

10. A scientist wants to measure the direction and duration of the movement of the ground. Which of the following instruments will the scientist most likely use?

    a. a laser light with holograph
    b. a seismograph
    c. an electron microscope
    d. a stereoscope

Questions 11 and 12 are based on the following figures and text:

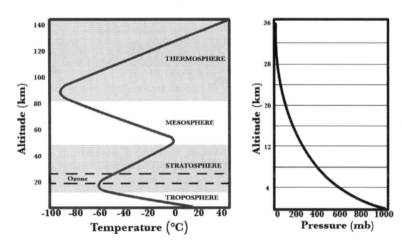

The Earth's atmosphere is comprised of multiple layers with very different temperature characteristics. Closest to the surface, the *troposphere* contains approximately 75 percent of the atmosphere's mass and 99 percent of its water vapor and aerosols. Temperature fluctuations cause constant mixing of air in the troposphere through convection, but it generally becomes cooler as altitude increases.

The *stratosphere* is heated by the absorption of ultraviolet radiation from the sun. Since its lower layers are composed of cooler, heavier air, there is no convective mixing in the stratosphere, and it is quite stable.

The *mesosphere* is the atmospheric layer directly above the stratosphere. Here, temperature decreases as altitude increases due to decreased solar heating and, to a degree, CO_2. In the lower atmosphere, CO_2 acts as a greenhouse gas by absorbing infrared radiation from the earth's surface. In the mesosphere, CO_2 cools the atmosphere by radiating heat into space.

Above this layer lies the *thermosphere*. At these altitudes, atmospheric gases form layers according to their molecular masses. Temperatures increase with altitude due to absorption of solar radiation by the small amount of residual oxygen. Temperatures are highly dependent on solar activity, and can rise to 1,500°C.

11. Commercial jetliners typically cruise at altitudes of 9-12 km, in the lower reaches of the stratosphere. Which of the following might be the reason for this choice of cruising altitude?
a. Jet engines run more efficiently at colder temperatures.
b. There is less air resistance than at lower altitudes.
c. There is less turbulence than at lower altitudes.
d. All of the above are possible reasons.

12. The lowest temperatures in the Earth's atmosphere are recorded within the
a. Troposphere
b. Stratosphere
c. Mesosphere
d. Thermosphere

13. The major advantage of sexual reproduction over asexual forms is that
a. it requires two individuals.
b. it promotes diversity.
c. it produces more offspring.
d. it involves chromosomes.

Questions 14 and 15 are based on the following text:

Isotopes

The nucleus of an atom contains both protons and neutrons. Protons have a single positive electric charge, while neutrons have a charge of zero. The number of protons that a nucleus contains, called the atomic number and abbreviated as Z, determines the identity of an atom of matter. For example, hydrogen contains a single proton (Z =1), whereas helium contains two (Z = 2). Atoms of a single element may differ in terms of the number of neutrons in their atomic nuclei, however. The total number of protons and neutrons in an atom is referred to as the atomic mass, or M. Helium typically has an atomic mass equal to 4, but there is another helium isotope for which M = 3. This form of helium has the same number of protons, but only one neutron.

In an atomic fusion reaction, nuclei collide with one another with enough force to break them apart. The resulting nuclei may have a lower atomic mass than the reactants, with the difference being released as energy. Electric charge, however, is always conserved.

14. Two atoms of helium-3 (atomic mass = 3) collide in a fusion reaction to produce a single atom of helium-4 (atomic mass = 4). What might be another product of this reaction?

    a. A neutron
    b. A proton
    c. Two electrons
    d. Two protons

15. Hydrogen atoms usually contain a single nucleon (nucleon refers to either a neutron or a proton). Deuteriumand tritium are isotopes of hydrogen containing two and three nucleons, respectively. How many electrons orbit the tritium nucleus if the atom is electrically neutral?

    a. 0
    b. 1
    c. 2
    d. 3

Questions 16 and 17 are based on the following figures and text:

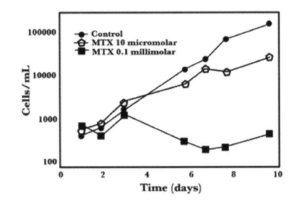

Cancer cells of the murine erythroleukemia (MEL) cell line were cultured in normal grob. wth medium (control) and in two different concentrations of the anti-cancer drug c. methotrexate (MTX) for a period of ten days. Samples were removed periodically, and td. he number of cells per milliliter of culture was determined. Each point in the figure represents the mean of five determinations.

16. The growth of cells in the absence of drugs in this experiment can best be described as:

    a. linear
    b. exponential
    c. derivative
    d. inhibited

17. Which of the following statements is supported by the data?

    a. Methotrexate does not inhibit cell growth.
    b. millimolar methotrexate inhibits the growth of bacteria.
    c. 10 micromolar methotrexate effectively suppresses cell growth.
    d. 100 micromolar methotrexate effectively suppresses cell growth.

18. A person heterozygous for the recessive gene for blue eyes marries a person who is homozygous for the trait. What is the probability that the couple's third child will have blue eyes?

    a. 0.0
    b. 0.25
    c. 0.50
    d. 1.0

19. A solar eclipse is

    a. when the moon comes between the sun and the earth
    b. the path of the sun across the celestial sphere
    c. a geometrical curve
    d. when the earth comes between the moon and the sun

20. Pollination involves which plant parts?

    a. xylem and petiole
    b. apical meristem and floral meristem
    c. anther and stigma
    d. root hairs and stroma

21. Which agricultural product takes the most energy to produce?

    a. rice
    b. potatoes
    c. beef
    d. wheat

Questions 22 and 23 are based on the following figure and text:

Rock Cycle

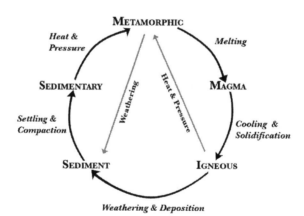

Rocks are created and destroyed in a recurrent process known as the rock cycle. Rocks are made from minerals, which are naturally occurring, crystalline solids of characteristic chemical composition. The actions of heat, pressure, and erosion can change the form of these minerals drastically. *Igneous* rocks form when molten magma is exuded from the Earth's molten core, and then cools and solidifies near the surface. *Sedimentary* rocks are made of fragments of other rocks worn by weathering or erosion. Sand particles form sediments as they settle to the bottom, and are eventually compacted into stone by the weight above them, a process called *lithification*. Heat and pressure can change the crystal structure of these minerals, altering them into denser *metamorphic* rocks, and as these sink deeper into the hot core, they melt again into magma.

22. A process that can lead to igneous rock formation is

a. weathering.
b. sedimentation.
c. erosion.
d. volcanic activity.

23. Which of the following rock types is formed at the greatest distances below the Earth's surface?

a. Igneous
b. Metamorphic
c. Sedimentary
d. Slate

24. Read the following paragraph:

An experiment was conducted to determine whether taking an aspirin every day could reduce the chance of a heart attack. Scientists gave a group of 600 heart attack survivors who were in a health and fitness program one aspirin per day for three years. The study found that the people in the study had a much smaller chance of having another heart attack than the national average for heart attack survivors. The scientists concluded that taking aspirin lowers your risk of a heart attack.

What is the main flaw of this study?

a. The number of people examined in the study was too small.
b. The results of the study may be due to the health regimen the participants were on, not the aspirin.
c. The study did not have a long enough duration to have accurate results.
d. There was no control group.

25. The pilot of an eastbound plane determines wind speed relative to his aircraft. He measures a wind velocity of 320 km/h, with the wind coming from the east. An observer on the ground sees the plane pass overhead, and measures its velocity as 290 km/h. What is the wind velocity relative to the observer?

a. 30 km/h east-to-west
b. 30 km/h west-to-east
c. 320 km/h east-to-west
d. 290 km/h east-to-west

26. During periods that are unfavorable for growth, some plants become dormant. Which season would these plants most likely lie dormant in North America?

a. Summer
b. Fall
c. Winter
d. Spring

27. Which is the smallest unit of measure, out of the following choices?

a. microliter
b. megaliter
c. deciliter
d. milliliter

28. Put 9×10^6 in standard notation.

a. 9,000,000
b. 90,000,000
c. 0.000009
d. 0.0000009

29. What is oxidation?

a. The exchange of carbon dioxide for oxygen
b. The reduction of the number of chromosomes per cell
c. Cave formations resulting from the dripping of mineralized water
d. A change in the chemical composition of iron

30. A recycling company collects sorted materials from its clients. The materials are weighed and then processed for re-use. The chart shows the weights of various classes of materials that were collected by the company during a representative month.

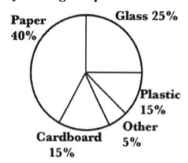

Which of the following statements is NOT supported by the data in the chart?

a. Paper products, including cardboard, make up a majority of the collected materials.
b. One quarter of the materials collected are made of glass.
c. More plastic is collected than cardboard.
d. Plastic and cardboard together represent a larger portion of the collected materials than glass bottles.

Questions 31 and 32 are based on the following passage:

> The fossilized remains of a bat have been found in volcanic rock dated to A.D. 79. Scientists studying the bat believe it to be an extinct species.

31. Which of the following statements is the best conclusion based on the data provided?

a. The volcanic eruption caused the extinction of this species of bat.
b. The only casualties from the eruption were bats.
c. The bat was probably from the same period as the volcanic eruption.
d. Bats never survive volcanic eruptions.

32. What would be the best way for scientists to confirm that the bat is an extinct species?

a. Compare the fossilized remains of this bat with the fossilized remains of other species b. killed in the eruption.

c. Search for live specimens of the fossilized species.

d. Compare the fossilized remains of this bat with bats known to be from that species. Test the genetic make-up of the fossilized bat.

33. A Tsunami may be caused by

a. earthquakes

b. volcanoes

c. landslides

d. A, B and C

Questions 34–37 are based upon the following figure and text:

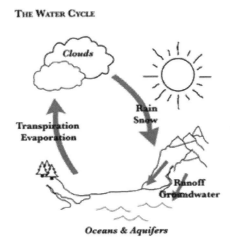

THE WATER CYCLE

Energy from the sun heats the water in the oceans and causes it to evaporate, forming water vapor that rises through the atmosphere. Cooler temperatures at high altitudes cause this vapor to condense and form clouds. Water droplets in the clouds condense and grow, eventually falling to the ground as precipitation. This continuous movement of water above and below ground is called the hydrologic cycle, or water cycle, and it is essential for life on our planet. All the Earth's stores of water, including that found in clouds, oceans, underground, etc., are known as the *hydrosphere*.

Water can be stored in several locations as part of the water cycle. The largest reservoirs are the oceans, which hold about 95% of the world's water, more than 300,000,000 cubic miles. Water is also stored in polar ice caps, mountain snowcaps, lakes and streams, plants, and below ground in aquifers. Each of these reservoirs has a characteristic *residence time*, which is the average amount of time a water molecule will spend there before moving on. Some typical residence times are shown in the table.

Average reservoir residence times of water.

Reservoir	Residence Time
Atmosphere	9 days
Oceans	3,000 years
Glaciers and Ice Caps	100 years
Soil Moisture	2 months
Underground Aquifers	10,000 years

The water cycle can change over time. During cold climatic periods, more water is stored as ice and snow, and the rate of evaporation is lower. This affects the level of the Earth's oceans. During the last ice age, for instance, oceans were 400 feet lower than today. Human activities that affect the water cycle include agriculture, dam construction, deforestation, and industrial activities.

34. Another name for the water cycle is

a. the hydrosphere.
b. the atmosphere.
c. the residence cycle.
d. the hydrologic cycle.

35. Water is stored underground, as well as in oceans and ice caps. Such underground storage reservoirs are called

a. storage tanks.
b. aquifers.
c. evaporators.
d. runoff.

36. Other than atmospheric water, water molecules spend the least time in

a. aquifers.
b. oceans.
c. glaciers.
d. soil.

37. Which of the following statements is NOT true?

a. Cutting down trees affects the water cycle.
b. Ocean levels rise during an ice age.
c. Oceans hold most of the world's water.
d. Clouds are formed because of cold temperatures.

38. What is the best use for a barometer?

a. measuring temperature
b. measuring atmospheric pressure
c. observing remote objects
d. viewing objects too small for the naked eye to see

39. Sn is the symbol for which element?

    a. Sulfur
    b. Selenium
    c. Scandium
    d. Tin

40. What is often used to transport a measured volume of liquid?

    a. a pipette
    b. a graduated cylinder
    c. a beaker
    d. a slide

Mathematics

1. A blouse normally sells for $138, but is on sale for 25% off. What is the cost of the blouse?

    a. $67
    b. $103.50
    c. $34.50
    d. $113

2. The following table shows the distance from a point to a moving car at various times.

d	Distance	50	70	110
t	Time	2	3	5

If the speed of the car is constant, which of the following equations describes the distance from the point to the car?

    a. $d = 25\,t$
    b. $d = 35\,t$
    c. $d = 55\,t$
    d. $d = 20\,t + 10$

3. There are n musicians in a marching band. All play either a drum or a brass instrument. If p represents the fraction of musicians playing drums, how many play a brass instrument?

    a. $pn - 1$
    b. $p(n - 1)$
    c. $(p - 1)n$
    d. $(1 - p)n$

4. Set A = {(-6,-3), (-4,2), (9,0)}

   Set B = {(-4,2), (-6,-1), (-6,-3), (7,1)}

What is the intersection of sets A and B?

    a. {(9,0)}
    b. {(-6,-3)}
    c. {(-6,-3), (-4,2)}
    d. {(-6,-4), (-4,2), (-6,-1), (9,0), (7,1)}

5. Which of the following is an example of an irrational number?

    a. -8
    b. 1/4
    c. $\sqrt{2}$
    d. 28

6. Which of the following is an example of the commutative property?

    a. 8 + 12 = 12 + 8
    b. 20 + 0 = 20
    c. 9(3 + 6) = 9 • 3 + 9 • 6
    d. 2 + -2 = 0

7. An MP3 player is set to play songs at random from the fifteen songs it contains in memory. Any song can be played at any time, even if it is repeated. There are 5 songs by Band A, 3 songs by Band B, 2 by Band C, and 5 by Band D. If the player has just played two songs in a row by Band D, what is the probability that the next song will also be by Band D?

    a. 1 in 5
    b. 1 in 3
    c. 1 in 9
    d. 1 in 27

8. Referring again to the MP3 player described in Question 7, what is the probability that the next two songs will both be by Band B?

    a. 1 in 25
    b. 1 in 3
    c. 1 in 5
    d. 1 in 9

9. To determine a student's grade, a teacher throws out the lowest grade obtained on 5 tests, averages the remaining grades, and rounds up to the nearest integer. If Betty scored 72, 75, 88, 86, and 90 on her tests, what grade will she receive?

    a. 68
    b. 85
    c. 88
    d. 84.8

10. Simplify the following expression: 6x + 2y - 3 + 4x + 5y + 6

    a. 10x + 7y + 3
    b. 24x + 7y + 9
    c. 17xy + 3
    d. 2x + 7y + 3

11. What is the value of the expression $-3 \times 5^2 + 2(4-18) + 33$?

    a. -130
    b. -70
    c. -20
    d. 74

12. A box of laundry detergent contains 16.5 oz of product. What is the maximum number of loads that can be washed if each load requires a minimum of ¾ oz of detergent?

    a. 10
    b. 50
    c. 22
    d. 18

13. A crane raises one end of a 3300 lb steel beam. The other end rests upon the ground. If the crane supports 30% of the beam's weight, how many pounds does it support?

    a. 330 lbs
    b. 990 lbs
    c. 700 lbs
    d. 1100 lbs

14. A taxi service charges $5.50 for the first 1/5th of a mile, $1.50 for each additional 1/5th of a mile, and 20¢ per minute of waiting time. Joan took a cab from her place to a flower shop 8 miles away, where she bought a bouquet, then another 3.6 miles to her mother's place. The driver had to wait 9 minutes while she bought the bouquet. What was the fare?

    a. $20
    b. $120.20
    c. $92.80
    d. $91

15. Prizes are to be awarded to the best pupils in each class of an elementary school. The number of students in each grade is shown in the table, and the school principal wants the number of prizes awarded in each grade to be proportional to the number of students. If there are twenty prizes, how many should go to fifth grade students?

Grade	1	2	3	4	5
Students	35	38	38	33	36

    a. 5
    b. 4
    c. 7
    d. 3

16. Solve the following equation: $x + 16 = 3x + 32$

    a. $-16 = 2x$
    b. $x = -8$
    c. $x = -16$
    d. $x = -32$

17. Translate the following into mathematical symbols:

    46 is less than the difference of 17 and a number

    a. $46 < x - 17$
    b. $46 > 17 - x$
    c. $46 < 17 - x$
    d. $17 - x < 46$

18. Solve the inequality: |x + 6| < 9

    a. (-15, 3)
    b. (3, 3)
    c. (-15, -3)
    d. (6, -9)

19. Solve the quadratic equation: $x^2 + 3x = -2$

    a. x = 1, 2
    b. x = -2, -3
    c. x = 2, 1
    d. x = -2, -1

20. What is a reflex angle?

    a. an angle that measures less than 90°
    b. an angle that measures more than 90°, but less than 180°
    c. an angle that measures 180° exactly
    d. an angel that measures more than 180°

21. What geometric figure is this?

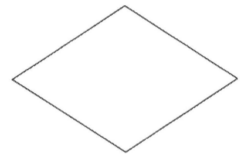

    a. rhombus
    b. trapezoid
    c. pentagon
    d. square

22. How are the following polygons related?

 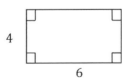

    a. They are congruent.
    b. They are acute.
    c. They are similar.
    d. They are adjacent.

23. Find the perimeter of a triangle with sides measuring 6 centimeters, 12 centimeters and 14 centimeters.

    a. 18 cm
    b. 24 cm
    c. 28 cm
    d. 32 cm

24. The radius of a circle is 6 inches. What is the area?

    a. 18.84 in²
    b. 37.68 in²
    c. 87.98 in²
    d. 113.04 in²

25. Find the volume of a cube with the length of each side as 12 cm.

    1.   36 cm³
    2.   650 cm³
    3.   1,728 cm³
    4.   2,421 cm³

26. Find the surface area of a sphere with the radius of 1.5 cm.

    a. 28.26 cm²
    b. 7.065 cm²
    c. 18.84 cm²
    d. 14.13 cm²

27. Find the length of c based on the right triangle below.

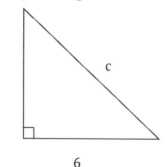

    a. 7 cm
    b. 10 cm
    c. 14 cm
    d. 20 cm

28. What is the surface area, in square inches, of a cube if the length of one side is 3 inches?

    a. 9
    b. 27
    c. 54
    d. 18

29. Which of the following values is closest to the diameter of a circle with an area of 314 square inches?

a. 20 inches
b. 10 inches
c. 100 inches
d. 31.4 inches

30. A circle has a perimeter of 35 feet. What is its diameter?

a. 11.14 feet
b. 6.28 feet
c. 5.57 feet
d. 3.5 feet

31. Two angles of a triangle measure 15 and 70 degrees, respectively. What is the size of the third angle?

a. 90 degrees
b. 80 degrees
c. 75 degrees
d. 95 degrees

32. A metal rod used in manufacturing must be as close as possible to 15 inches in length. The tolerance of the length, L, in inches, is specified by the inequality $| L - 15 | \leq 0.01$. What is the minimum length permissible for the rod?

a. 14.9 inches
b. 14.99 inches
c. 15.01 inches
d. 15.1 inches

33. The town of Fram will build a water storage tank on a hill overlooking the town. The tank will be a right circular cylinder of radius R and height H. The plot of ground selected for the installation is large enough to accommodate a circular tank 60 feet in diameter. The planning commission wants the tank to hold 1,000,000 cubic feet of water, and they intend to use the full area available. Which of the following is the minimum acceptable height?

a. 655 ft
b. 455 ft
c. 355 ft
d. 255 ft

34. A teacher can grade 20 math tests per hour. If she starts grading test at 10:30 a.m., which of the following is the best estimate as to when she will be done grading 134 tests?

a. 3:00 p.m.
b. 4:00 p.m.
c. 4:30 p.m.
d. 5:00 p.m.

35. Define this symbol: $A \cap B$

a. A is a subset of B.
b. The set of all elements that are in A or B, or both.
c. The set of all elements that are in both A and B.
d. A set with no elements.

36. Translate the following into mathematical symbols:

The quotient of 56 and a number is 8

a. $56/x = 8$
b. $56x = 8$
c. $x/56 = 8$
d. $8 \cdot 56 = x$

37. What is the next number in the series?

132, 123, 115, 108, 102

a. 82
b. 87
c. 92
d. 97

38. What is the mode of the following numbers?

37, 46, 52, 52, 61, 63

a. 37
b. 52
c. 55
d. 311

39. If a = 3 and b = 4, simplify the following expression: 6a + b -7

a. 12
b. 15
c. 20
d. 22

40. $10x - 36 + 4x - 6 + x = 3$. What is the value of x?

a. 3
b. 4
c. 6
d. 10

Social Studies

1. Peter the Great's reign was dominated by his efforts to

    a. keep Portugal out of the War of Spanish Succession.
    b. create a reform program called the Peronísmo.
    c. modernize and Westernize Russia.
    d. prevent the union of England and Normandy.

2. Which list is in the correct chronological order?

    a. Great Schism, Norman Conquest, French Revolution
    b. Great Schism, French Revolution, Norman Conquest
    c. Norman Conquest, Great Schism, French Revolution
    d. French Revolution, Norman Conquest, Great Schism

3. Marxism had a profound influence on the development of

    a. the Bolshevik political movement.
    b. Autumn Harvest Uprising.
    c. the National Socialist German Workers' Party
    d. the Greek Civil war

4. The Lincoln-Douglas debates resulted in

    a. the declaration of Illinois as a slave state.
    b. the split of the Democratic Party.
    c. the election of Douglas as president in 1860.
    d. the election of Lincoln to the senate in 1858.

5. What major U.S. event took place around the same time that the Judiciary Act set up the federal judiciary system?

    a. The Neutrality Act was passed.
    b. The United States entered WWII.
    c. The Korean War ended.
    d. George Washington was inaugurated president.

6. What invention increased the value and demand for slaves in the South?

    a. the combine
    b. the steam engine
    c. the cotton gin
    d. the automobile

7. What significance did *Brown* v. *Board of Education of Topeka* have on the system if education in the United States?

    a. Students were educated separately but equally.
    b. Students were taught creationism.
    c. Students were taught evolution.
    d. The "separate but equal" ruling was reversed.

8. What was generally the sentiment towards Chinese laborers in the United States in 1882?

a. Chinese laborers were viewed as cheap laborers and were generally discriminated against.
b. Chinese laborers were highly valued members of the United States society.
c. Chinese laborers were forced out of the country.
d. Chinese laborers were welcomed through several immigration laws.

9. Iran, Iraq, and Kuwait all border what body of water?

a. Indian Ocean
b. Red Sea
c. Persian Gulf
d. Caspian Sea

10. The majority of residents of Brazil identify themselves as

a. Roman Catholic
b. Buddhist
c. Muslim
d. Jewish

11. Which economic/political system has the following characteristics:

- private ownership of property
- property and capital provides income for the owner
- freedom to compete for economic gain
- profit motive driving the economy.

a. fascism
b. capitalism
c. communism
d. Marxism

12. Which of these would not be found in a democracy?

a. a congress
b. a parliament
c. a prime minister
d. a dictator

13. A researcher is collecting data for her study on parenting. She hypothesized that countries where mothers carry their infants on their person have children who have more secure attachments as toddlers. Which method would be the most helpful in collecting data for this study?

a. Interviewing parents in the United States about their methods of carrying babies.
b. Determining methods of carrying babies and studying the toddlers in several countries.
c. Researching popular methods of carrying infants on the internet.
d. Collecting data on the number of strollers sold in several countries.

Question 14 refers to the following chart:

Jail Inmates by Sex and Race				
Year	1990	1995	2000	2005
Male	365,821	448,000	543,120	646,807
Female	37,198	51,300	70,414	93,963
Juveniles	2,301	7,800	7,613	6,759
White	169,600	203,300	260,500	331,000
Black	172,300	220,600	256,300	290,500
Hispanic	58,100	74,400	94,100	111,900
[Source: U.S. Dept. of Justice; does not include federal or state prisons.]				

14. Based on the chart, which of the following statements is NOT accurate?

a. Fewer women than men are incarcerated in each year sampled.

b. The rate of jail incarceration rose for every subgroup of prisoner.

c. In 2000 and in 2005, more whites were incarcerated in jails than any other race.

d. Rate of Hispanic jailing has steadily increased over the fifteen years represented.

15. Which institution is responsible for promoting international peace and maintaining observance of international law?

a. United Nations

b. British Parliament

c. European Economic Community

d. Southeast Asia Treaty Organization

16. What events took place while Joseph Stalin was in power?

a. Russian Revolution of 1905

b. World War II

c. Russo-Japanese War

d. Punic Wars

17. What contributed to the weakening and collapse of the League of Nations?

a. The failure of the United States to join

b. The beginning of World War I

c. The signing of the Treaty of Versailles

d. The beginning of the Persian Wars

18. Who became the commander of the Confederate army of northern Virginia at the beginning of the Civil War?

a. Abraham Lincoln

b. Thomas "Stonewall" Jackson

c. Robert E. Lee

d. Jefferson Davis

19. Which list is in the correct chronological order?

a. Great Depression, Revolutionary War, first moon landing

b. Revolutionary War, first moon landing, Great Depression

c. First moon landing, Great Depression, Revolutionary War

d. Revolutionary War, Great Depression, first moon landing

20. Which invention had a major role in communication during the Civil War?

a. Morse Code
b. Telephone
c. Radio
d. Computer

21. The Dred Scott case involved the Supreme Court ruling on

a. Women's voting rights
b. Civil rights
c. Miranda Rights
d. Right to an attorney

22. The Andes Mountain Range is located on which continent?

a. North America
b. South America
c. Australia
d. Asia

23. What ornamental figures are found in Gothic architecture?

a. dragons
b. phoenixes
c. gargoyles
d. Tuscan columns

24. What effect does the Sahara Desert have on trade?

a. Caravans have to skirt the desert.
b. Oases make trade possible.
c. Due to massive amounts of rain, trade routes are unpredictable.
d. Trade across the Sahara Desert has never existed due to the inhospitable conditions.

25. India's economy can be best described as

a. a third-world country.
b. one of the lowest producing economies in the world.
c. a market-based system.
d. an agricultural stronghold.

26. Which of the following countries can be described as a constitutional democratic monarchy?

a. Thailand
b. Mexico
c. Australia
d. South Africa

27. Read the following passage:

Islam spread to Europe during the medieval period, bringing scientific and technological insights. The Muslim emphasis on knowledge and learning can be traced to an emphasis on both in the Qur'an [Koran], the holy book of Islam. Because of this emphasis, scholars preserved some of the Greek and Roman texts that were lost to the rest of Europe. The writings of Aristotle, among others, were saved by Muslim translators. Islamic scholars modified a Hindu number system, which became the more commonly used Arabic system, which replaced Roman numerals. They also developed algebra and invented the astrolabe, a device for telling time that also helped sailors to navigate. In medicine, Muslim doctors cleaned wounds with antiseptics, closed the wounds with gut and silk sutures, and were among the first to use sedatives.

Based on the information above, which of the following conclusions is likely true?

a. People of Muslim faith were braver than others when facing surgery.
b. Fewer Muslim patients died of wound infections than did their European counterparts.
c. The silk market expanded because of the Muslim use of silk sutures.
d. No one would read Aristotle today had the Muslims not saved the translations.

Questions 28 and 29 refer to the following chart:

United States Foreign Trade 1960–1970

(by Category Percentages)

Category	1960		1970	
	Exports	**Imports**	**Exports**	**Imports**
Chemicals	8.7	5.3	9.0	3.6
Crude materials (except fuel)	13.7	18.3	10.8	8.3
Food and beverages, including tobacco	15.6	22.5	11.8	15.6
Machinery and transport	34.3	9.7	42.0	28.0
Mineral fuels and related materials	4.1	10.5	3.7	7.7

28. In 1960, which of the following categories had the greatest disparity between percentage of both exports and imports?

a. chemicals
b. crude materials
c. food and beverages
d. machinery and transport

29. Which category saw the greatest percentage decrease in imports between 1960 and 1970?

    a. chemicals

    b. crude materials

    c. food and beverages

    d. machinery and transport

Questions 30 and 31 refer to the following chart:

Women in the Labor Force, Selected Years

Year	Women in Labor Force (thousands)	Percentage of Total Labor Force
1900	5,114	18.1
1920	8,430	20.4
1940	12,845	24.3
1950	18,412	28.8
1970	31,560	36.7

30. In what year on the chart did women first make up more than 25 percent of the total labor force?

    a. 1900

    b. 1920

    c. 1940

    d. 1950

31. How could you express the change in percentage of women as part of the total labor force from 1900 to 1970?

    a. The percentage rate declined by half.

    b. The percentage rate remained steady.

    c. The percentage rate doubled.

    d. The percentage rate fluctuated up and down over the years.

32. When the euro was introduced in January 2002, a single euro was valued at 88 cents in United States currency. In the summer of 2008, at one point it required $1.60 U.S. to buy 1 euro. In late October 2008, the euro fell to its lowest level against the dollar in two years. Which of the following statements represents an accurate conclusion?

    a. The world in 2008 was headed for another Great Depression.

    b. The dollar regained strength after significant devaluing against the euro.

    c. The euro remains the world's strongest currency.

    d. Investors need to keep buying stocks.

33. In 1957, President Dwight Eisenhower sent federal troops to Little Rock, Arkansas. They were to enforce integration at Little Rock Central High School, although the governor of the state had tried to prevent integration. Eisenhower's action is an example that illustrates

    a. showing a governor that he had no real power in state government.

    b. trying to keep federal troops out of Vietnam.

    c. states' rights being more important than federal law.

    d. upholding federal law if state or local officials will not.

Questions 34 – 36 refer to the following chart

Ethnic Groups in Selected Central American Countries

Country	Honduras	Nicaragua	El Salvador	Costa Rica	Belize
Mestizo [European and Native American]	90%	69%	90%		49%
Amerindian	7%	5%	1%	1%	
Black	2%	9%		3%	
White	1%	17%	9%	94%	
Chinese				1%	
Creole [African and European]					25%
Maya					11%

34. To which nation would you go to study the living traditions of the Mayans?

a. Honduras

b. Costa Rica

c. Belize

d. Nicaragua

35. Which of the following conclusions is valid?

a. The Creole population is the largest ethnic group in Latin America.

b. The Maya have completely died out.

c. Few people in Nicaragua are of mixed heritage.

d. The Amerindian population of many Central American countries was destroyed by war and disease.

36. Based on your general knowledge, how do you explain the large Creole population of Belize?

a. Belize is near the Caribbean, where many Africans were once enslaved.

b. Belize has long been a trading partner with West African nations.

c. Many Creole who once lived in New Orleans left after Hurricane Katrina.

d. The Creole came to Belize to start new restaurants.

37. Which of the following countries is NOT located along the Indian Ocean?

a. Cameroon

b. Somalia

c. Mozambique

d. Kenya

38. ARTICLE XXVII (Ratified July 1, 1971) of the United States Constitution states:

Section 1. The right of citizens of the United States, who are eighteen years of age or older, to vote shall not be denied or abridged by the United States or by any State on account of age.

This amendment to the Constitution was ratified in part because of what historical reality?

a. Women gained the right to vote.
b. Suffrage was extended to all African Americans.
c. Young men were being drafted to serve in the Vietnam War.
d. The number of people under 21 years of age increased.

Questions 39 and 40 refer to the following passage:

In 1969, 13 African American members of the House of Representatives gathered to form the Congressional Black Caucus (CBC). They felt that a unified voice for minorities was needed. President Richard Nixon met with the group two years later; his weak response to their list of 60 recommendations increased their efforts. These efforts included ending apartheid in South Africa, reforming welfare, expanding educational opportunities and development of businesses by minorities. For nearly 20 years, the CBC has proposed an alternative annual budget; it generally varies widely from the budget that the president submits. In 2008, the organization has 43 members from both urban and rural areas. The CBC is sometimes called the conscience of Congress.

39. Which of the following statements is true?

a. The Congressional Black Caucus was founded immediately following the Civil War.
b. The major goal of the CBC is to elect an African American president.
c. Since its founding, the organization has grown by about 30 members.
d. The first president to recognize the CBC was Jimmy Carter.

40. Which of the following statements is an opinion?

a. The Congressional Black Caucus began in 1969.
b. The CBC is often referred to as Congress's conscience.
c. Every year for two decades, the CBC has proposed a national budget.
d. Apartheid was the worst political system of the twentieth century.

Writing Prompt

Imagine you are attending a college that is contemplating a change to electronic textbooks. All students who attend the school will be offered the opportunity to access their textbooks through an electronic textbook search engine. Supporters argue that switching to the e-textbooks will save students money and will be a more environmentally friendly choice over traditional printed textbooks.

The Student Council has asked students to submit statements expressing their opinions on the issue, and you have decided to submit a statement.

In an organized, coherent, and supported essay directed to the Student Council, explain what you think the college should do and why it should do so. Address the pros and cons of switching to an electronic textbook system.

Answer Key and Explanations

English Language Arts

1. C: Point of view refers to the vantage point from which a story is written. First person uses the pronoun *I*. Second person uses the pronoun *you*. Third person uses the pronouns *he/she/they*. There is no fourth person point of view. This passage was written in the third person.

2. B: The words "mysterious" and "important" used in the sentence help the reader deduce that Jo looked secretive. Jo neither looked jubilant, or joyful; disheveled, or disarrayed; or angry.

3. C: The last sentence states that Laurie was "an incorrigible tease." From this statement you can infer that Laurie was unruly or unmanageable. Stoic means not showing passion or emotion. Taciturn means silent. Uncanny means supernatural. There is nothing in the passage to imply he had any of these characteristics.

4. D: Personification is a metaphor in which a thing or abstraction is represented   as a person. Personification is used throughout this poem. However, of the answer choices given, line 11 is the best choice. The author personifies spring as a female.

5. A: The fifth stanza gives clues to whom "we" refers.

"Not one would mind, neither bird nor tree

If mankind perished utterly"

"We" is referencing mankind.

6. B: This is an example of a rhymed verse poem. The last two words of each line rhymes in every stanza. A sonnet is a poem of fourteen lines following a set rhyme scheme and logical structure. Often, poets use iambic pentameter when writing sonnets. A free verse poem is written without using strict meter or rhyme. A lyric poem is a short poem that expresses personal feelings, which may or may not be set to music.

7. A: Answer choice A gives the best summary of the poem. The poem imagines nature reclaiming the earth after humanity has been wiped out by a war. The poet imagines how little the human race will be missed.

8. D: According to the passage, a prehistoric artifact is an item used by humans prior to written history. The other answer choices are details included in the passage, but not the definition of prehistoric artifacts.

9. A: The first paragraph gives the definition of an archaeological site, choice A. The other answer choices are details covered in the passage, but not the main idea of the first paragraph.

10. B: Since the passage states that recent artifacts are not of archaeological significance, a logical implication is that a site containing recent artifacts would not be of interest to an archaeologist. Answer choices A, C, and D are not true based on the information given in the passage.

11. C: Since this passage is about the characteristics of human behavior, it can be inferred that Mary Ainsworth is a psychologist. A botanist studies plants. A biologist studies plant and animal life. An entomologist studies insects.

12. B: This passage describes four major patterns of infant attachment.

13. B: This passage addresses infant behavior and would most likely be found in a human development textbook.

14. D: The paragraph that describes the avoidant attachment pattern states that the infant acts as if the mother is of no importance.

15. C: Naturalism is a type of realistic fiction. The Naturalist movement took place in France, America, and England in the late 19th and early 20th centuries. Naturalists believed that people were controlled by both outer and inner forces.

16. C: Thomas Hardy wrote *Tess of the D'urbervilles* in 1891. This novel is about a young girl who is seduced and ends up pregnant. Hardy also wrote *Far from the Madding Crowd* and *Return of the Native*. All of his novels were criticized because the plots and characters were seen as indecent and immoral.

17. D: Virginia Woolf had a powerful effect on the modern novel. Other authors that influenced the Modernist movement include T. S. Eliot, Ezra Pound, James Joyce, and Gertrude Stein. The Modernist movement took place in the late 19th and early 20th centuries. The authors questioned traditional forms of literature and in doing so, wrote novels and poems that were full of modern thought.

18. A: Toni Morrison's novels focus on black women and their search for a place within American culture and society. She often uses fantasy to explore the themes of racism, gender bias, and class conflict. She is both a Nobel Prize and Pulitzer Prize winner. Her novels include *The Bluest Eye*, *Sula*, *Song of Solomon*, and *Beloved*.

19. C: Authors of the Contemporary movement wrote from 1945 to the present. George Orwell wrote *Animal Farm* in 1945 and *1984* in 1949.

20. B: Heathcliff and Catherine are main characters in *Wuthering Heights*, written by Emily Bronte in 1847.

21. A: Clustering is a prewriting strategy. The writer starts with a circle in the middle that contains a main idea and then draws lines to other, smaller circles that contain sub-ideas or issues related to the main idea. Other prewriting strategies include free-writing, brainstorming, tagmemics, and journalistic techniques.

22. C: The headings and subheadings of a topic outline are words or phrases, and it is brief. The headings and subheadings of a sentence outline are full sentences, and it is longer and more detailed.

23. A: The best source for information would be a medical journal. While the other sources may have information on the topic, the medical journal would have the most reliable information.

24. B: No matter what the tense of the main part of a sentence, the verb that follows *after* should be in the simple present (*arrive*) or the simple past (*arrived*). In this case, it should be the simple present.

25. B: Use *graduate* with the preposition *from*, unless the noun comes first in the sentence.

26. D: Although brainstorming can be used as part of the prewriting step, it is not main step in the writing process. The five steps of the writing process are Prewriting, Drafting, Revising, Editing, and Publishing.

27. C: The goal of the drafting stage is to get ideas down on paper without undue concern for mechanics. Errors will be corrected in the editing stage.

28. D: There are four main components to an effective outline. Subordination means that the information in the heading is more general, while the subheadings are more specific. For example:

I. Visit and Evaluate College Websites

    A. Note important statistic

    B. Look for interesting classes

The other three components of an effective outline include parallelism, coordination, and division.

29. B: Revising is the time to reconsider the topic, the audience, and the purpose of writing. Rethinking the approach may lead to major changes in content and structure.

30. C: The passive voice is used to eliminate the necessity of naming the agent of the action when the agent is unknown or unimportant. Here is an example of this sentence using the active voice:

    Prison authorities released James from prison in 1951.

31. A: A compound-complex sentence has two or more independent clauses and one or more dependent clauses.

32. C: Parallel sentence structure uses parallel grammatical form between coordinated elements. Option C uses the following grammatical structure after the word law: adjective--adjective--adjective.

33. B: When a sentence begins with a modifying word, phrase, or clause, the subject must be modified by that modifier. When a modifier improperly modifies something, it is called a "dangling modifier." Option B introduces a person into the subject position and corrects the dangling modifier.

34. B: The subject of this sentence is *the baking* and the verb is *have increased*. However, *baking* is a singular subject, so the correct verb form is *has* increased. This is an example of incorrect subject-verb agreement.

35. A: This is an adjective and adverb error. Adjectives modify nouns and pronouns; adverbs modify verbs, adjectives, and other adverbs. *Attentive* is modifying Jonas' diligence. *Tries* is a verb, so *diligent* needs to be an adverb to make this sentence grammatically correct.

No matter how diligently Jonas tries, he still fails to complete his homework.

36. C: This sentence contains both a homonym error (their/there) and a confused pair (annoy/aggravate). The use of *aggravate* to mean *annoy* is sometimes objected to because it departs from the etymological meaning "to make heavier."

37. A: This is an example of superfluous commas.

38. D: When conjunctive adverbs (*however, furthermore,* and *therefore*) are used in place of coordinating conjunctions to combine two sentences into one a semicolon is needed before the conjunctive adverb.

39. C: "Who" is the subject form of the pronoun and "whom" is the object form. This sentence should read:

> "The teacher gave stickers to whoever had stood in line quietly."

40. D: The titles of books, movies, plays, magazines and newspapers are written in italics. The titles of poems, stories, and paintings are written with quotation marks.

Science

1. C: The best control group would be women with wrinkles around their eyes using a harmless cream that has no effect. A scientific control group is used to minimize the unintended influence of other variables on a scientific study. Such extraneous variables include researcher bias, environmental changes, and biological variation. Scientific controls ensure that data are valid, and are a vital part of the scientific method.

2. D: The Scientific method is set of steps used to solve scientific problems. The steps are making an observation, asking a question, formulating a hypothesis, conducting an experiment, analyzing data, and drawing a conclusion. Independent variables are used in experiments to ensure that only a single variable is tested.

3. A: An erg is a centimeter-gram-second unit of energy. An ergometer is used to measure ergs. They are often used on exercise equipment. Portable ergometers can be mounted on bicycles to measure the rider's energy expenditure. A nanometer is a measurement of length. A milligram is a unit of mass or weight. A cubic centimeter is measurement of volume.

4. C: In scientific notation, the numerical portion will be "7.36". Count how many places the decimal point has to move to get from where it is now to where it needs to be. The power on 10 has to be –8 because that's how many places the decimal point needs to be moved.

5. C: All three measurements differ in value from the true length. This means they are not accurate. However, all three the measurements are equal in, so they are precise.

6. A: In order for something to be considered scientific fact, the results must be repeatable. Scientific study does not always take place in a laboratory. Scientific fact is never based on a single event. Only after the same experiments are conducted numerous times with the same results is the hypothesis accepted as fact. Science is not based on opinions.

7. A: Meiosis is a process that cuts the number of chromosomes per cell is cut in half. In animals, meiosis results in the formation of gametes, while in other organisms it results in spores.

8. A: A food chain shows how energy is transferred from one organism to another. A producer uses the energy from the sun to make its own food. Most of the energy in a food chain is in the level of the producer.

9. B: A mixture of NaCl and H_2O is salt and water. The only way to separate salt from water is to boil the mixture which evaporates the water, leaving the salt behind.

10. B: Movement of the ground, or an earthquake, generates seismic waves. These movements can be detected with a sensitive instrument called a seismograph.

11. D: The graph shows that temperatures in the lower stratosphere are -50°C or lower, permitting more efficient engine operation. The text indicates that 75% of the Earth's atmosphere is in the troposphere, which is below the stratosphere. It also states that convective mixing of air, and therefore the effects of weather, are characteristic of the troposphere. In the stratosphere, temperature-based layering of air leads to a stable environment. All of these effects combine to allow jets to operate with the best fuel efficiency possible in the lower reaches of the atmosphere.

12. D: This can be read from the graph. The thermosphere contains both the coldest and the highest temperatures in the atmospheric regions beneath outer space. In the thermosphere, atmospheric gases form layers of relatively pure molecular species. In its lower reaches, CO2 contributes to cooling through radiative emission, as in the mesosphere. In its upper reaches, molecular oxygen absorbs solar radiation and causes significant warming.

13. B: Sexual reproduction allows the genetic information from two parents to mix. Recombination events between the two parental copies of individual genes may occur, creating new genes. The production of new genes and of new gene combinations leads to an increase in diversity within the population, which is a great advantage in terms of adapting to changes in the environment.

14. D: The charge must be conserved in the reaction. Since the reactants, two helium atoms, each have two protons, they will have a total electric charge of +4. The reaction product, helium-4, also has two protons, and therefore has a total charge of +2. Two positive charges are lacking to balance the reaction. Of the choices given, only D, with two protons, has a charge of +2.

15. B: Since tritium is an isotope of hydrogen, the nucleus contains a single proton, giving it a charge of +1. The extra neutrons do not contribute to the charge. Electrons have a charge of -1. In order to neutralize the single positive charge of the nuclear proton, a single orbiting electron is required.

16. B: The vertical axis of this graph is an exponential scale, with each regularly-spaced tick mark corresponding to a ten-fold increase in the quantity being measured. The curve corresponding to the control cells, those grown in the absence of the drug, shows a cell concentration of approximately 500 cells/mL at the start, 5000 cells/mL after 4 days, and 50,000 cells per mL after 8 days, indicating an exponential growth pattern in which the number of cells increases by a factor of ten every four days.

17. D: The effects of two concentrations of methotrexate (MTX) on the growth of cancer cells are shown by the open pentagons and solid squares in the figure. These growth curves may be compared to the growth of untreated cells (the control) shown by the solid circles. It can be seen that, at a concentration of 10 micromoles per liter (10 micromolar), cell growth is slightly inhibited when compared to the control. At the greater concentration of 100 micromoles per liter (equivalent to 0.1 millimolar), the cells do not grow at all. The experiment is concerned with cancer cells, not bacteria, so choice B is incorrect.

18. C: The heterozygous parent will have the genotype Bb and the homozygous parent will have the genotype bb. The possible genotypes of the offspring are Bb, Bb, bb, and bb. Thus, 50 percent of the offspring will be homozygous and 50 percent will be heterozygous. Birth order is not important as each child has the same probability of having blue eyes.

19. A: A solar eclipse is when the moon moves between the Sun and the Earth. When viewed from the Earth, the moon and the Sun are about the same size, and thus the moon can completely block the sun.

20. C: Pollination is the fertilization of plants. It involves the transfer of pollen from the anther to the stigma, either by wind or by insects.

21. C: Energy is lost when matter is transferred from one trophic level to another. It requires energy to produce the food for the cattle, and therefore it takes more energy to produce beef than any of the plant crops.

22. D: Volcanic activity allows molten magma to reach the surface of the Earth, where it cools and solidifies into rock—a process akin to freezing. As the diagram and text both indicate, these types of rocks are known as igneous rocks. Examples of igneous rocks are obsidian and basalt. The type of igneous rock formed depends upon the chemical composition of the magma.

23. B: Metamorphic rocks ("metamorphic" means "changed form") are formed at great depths, usually from sedimentary precursors. As more and more sediment accumulates above them, the increased pressure and heat forces the relatively open crystal structure of the sedimentary rocks to collapse and adopt a denser structure. Examples of metamorphic rocks are quartz and gneiss.

24. B: The flaw in this study is that it does not observe a single variable, but several variables at the same time. The participants were taking aspirin and participating in a health regime.

25. A: The velocities of both the wind and the aircraft can be represented by vectors, with the length of the vector representing the speed, and the direction of the vector representing the direction of either the wind or the airplane. Since the wind speed opposes that of the plane, the pilot will measure the sum of the actual wind speed plus that of his aircraft:

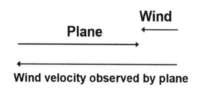

26. C: Since the winter is most unfavorable for plant growth in North America, some plants go dormant during this season.

27. A: A microliter is a millionth of a liter.

28. A: Move the decimal point six positions to the right.

29. D: Oxidation, also known as rusting, is the result of a change in the chemical composition of the iron.

30. C: The chart shows that plastic and cardboard materials both comprise 15% of the collected materials, and therefore it is incorrect to say that there is more plastic than cardboard. They are present in equal quantities.

31. C: If the bat was found in the lava from a volcanic eruption dated in 79 A.D., it is a reasonable conclusion that the bat came from that period.

32. C: To determine if this bat is from a particular species, the remains must be compared with the remains of the other members of the species.

33. D: A tsunami, sometimes referred to as a tidal wave, is a large wave or series of waves caused by the displacement of a large volume of water. While the most common cause is an earthquake, large landslides (either falling into the sea or taking place under water) or explosive volcanic action may also result in a tsunami.

34. D: The term *hydrologic cycle* is defined in the first paragraph, where it is described as being equivalent to the *water cycle*. It is derived from the Greek root *hydros*, which means "water."

35. B: The second paragraph gives examples of different storage reservoirs for water in the water cycle. Underground aquifers are one of the examples given. An *aquifer* (a word derived from the Latin roots *aqua*—meaning water, and *ferre*—meaning "to bear") is any geologic formation containing ground water.

36. D: According to the table, the average residence time of water in soil is only two months. Only its residence time in the atmosphere, 9 days, is shorter. Residence time is defined in the text as the average amount of time that a water molecule spends in each of the reservoirs shown in the table before it moves on to the next reservoir of the water cycle.

37. B: According to the final paragraph of the text, ocean levels actually fall during an ice age. This is because more water is stored in ice caps and glaciers when the prevailing temperatures are very cold, and therefore less water remains in the oceans.

38. B: A barometer is an instrument for measuring atmospheric pressure, used especially in weather forecasting.

39. D: Sn is the symbol for tin.

40. C: A pipette is used to transport a measured volume of liquid. Graduated cylinders are used to measure liquids. A beaker is used for stirring, mixing, or heating liquids. They can be used to measure liquids, but are less accurate than a graduated cylinder. A slide holds objects for examination under a microscope.

Mathematics

1. B: 25% off is equivalent to, $25 * \frac{\$138}{100} = \$34.50$, and therefore the sale price becomes: $138 -\$34.50 = \$103.50$.

2. D: Inspection of the data shows that the distance traveled by the car during any 1-unit interval (velocity) is 20 units. However, the first data point shows that the car is 50 units from the point of origin at time 2, so it had a 10-unit head start before time measurement began. Answers A-C only fit the data at single points. They do not fit the whole set.

3. D: The fraction of those playing drums plus the fraction of those playing a brass instrument must total 1. The number that play drums is therefore *pn*, and the number playing brass must be (1-*p*)*n*.

4. C: The intersection of two sets, *A* and *B*, is the set that contains all elements of *A* that also belong to *B* (or equivalently, all elements of *B* that also belong to *A*), but no other elements.

5. C: An irrational number is a real number that cannot be expressed as a ratio of two integers.

6. A: The commutative property states that changing the order of something does not change the end result.

7. B: The probability of playing a song by any band is proportional to the number of songs by that band over the total number of songs, or $\frac{5}{15} = \frac{1}{3}$ for Band D. The probability of playing any particular song is not affected by what has been played previously, because the choice is random.

8. A: Since 3 of the 15 songs are by Band B, the probability that any one song will be by that band is $\frac{3}{15} = \frac{1}{5}$. The probability that two successive events will occur is the product of the probabilities for any one event or, in this case, $\frac{1}{5} \times \frac{1}{5} = \frac{1}{25}$.

9. B: The lowest score, 68, is eliminated. The average of the remaining four grades   is:

$$Avg = \frac{75 + 88 + 86 + 90}{4} = 84.75$$

Rounding up to the nearest integer gives a final grade of 85.

10. A: This expression can be simplified by identifying like terms and then grouping and combining like terms:

6*x* and +4*x* are like terms, and can be combined to give +10*x*,

+2*y* and +5*y* combine to give +7*y*, and

-3 and +6 combine to give +3.

Therefore after simplifying, this expression becomes:

$$10x + 7y + 3$$

11. B: Use the order of operations to find the value for this expression: parentheses, exponents, multiplication and division, addition and subtraction:

$$-3 \times 5^2 + 2(4-18) + 33$$
$$= -3 \times 5^2 + 2(-14) + 33$$
$$= -3 \times 25 + 2(-14) + 33$$
$$= -75 + (-28) + 33$$
$$= -70$$

12. C: 16.5 x 4/3 = 22

13. B: 30% of 3300 = 0.3 x 3300 = 990

14. C: The total distance traveled was 8 + 3.6 = 11.6 miles. The first 1/5th of a mile is charged at the higher rate. Since 1/5th = 0.2, the remainder of the trip is 11.4 miles. Thus, the fare for the distance traveled is computed as $5.50 + 5 × 11.4 × $1.50 = $91. To this the charge for waiting time must be added, which is simply 9 x 20¢ = 180¢ = $1.80. Finally, add the two charges, $91 + $1.80 = $92.80.

15. B: First determine the proportion of students in Grade 5. Since the total number of students is 180, this proportion is $\frac{36}{180} = 0.2$, or 20%. Then determine the same proportion of the total prizes, which is 20% of twenty, or $0.2 \times 20 = 4$.

16. B: Given the equation $x + 16 = 3x + 32$,

Subtract x from each side:

$$16 = 2x + 32$$

Subtract 32 from each side.

$$-16 = -2x$$

Divide both sides by 2:

$$x = -8$$

17. C: First write "46 is less than" using 46 and the less than symbol:

$$46 <$$

Difference means subtract. When "difference of" is used, write the numbers in the same order as they appear in the sentence:

$$17 - x$$

The sentence should read:

$$46 < 17 - x$$

18. A: The inequality is solved by writing a double inequality equivalent to the given inequality but without absolute value:

$$-9 < x + 6 < 9$$

Solve the double inequality by subtracting 6:

$$-15 < x < 3$$

The above solution set is written in interval form as follows:

$$(-15, 3)$$

19. D: Write the quadratic equation with right side equal to 0.

$$x^2 + 3x + 2 = 0$$

Factor the equation.

$$(x + 2)(x+1) = 0$$

Set each equation to equal zero.

$$x + 2 = 0 \text{ or } x +1 = 0$$

Solve each equation:

$$x = -2 \text{ and } x = -1 \text{ or } x = -2, -1$$

20. D: A reflex angle measures more than 180°. An angle that measures less than 90° is an acute angle. An angle that measures more than 90°, but less than 180° is an obtuse angle. An angle that measures 180° exactly is a straight angle.

21. A: A rhombus is four-sided polygon having all four sides of equal length. The sum of the angles of a rhombus is 360 degrees.

22. C: Similar polygons are polygons for which all corresponding angles are congruent and all corresponding sides are proportional.

23. D: To find the perimeter of a triangle, take the sum of the length of each side.

24. D: The formula for the area of a circle is $A = \pi r^2$.

$$A = \pi \bullet r \bullet r$$
$$A = 3.14 \bullet (6 \text{ in}) \bullet (6\text{in})$$
$$A = 3.14 \bullet (36 \text{ in}^2)$$
$$A = 113.04 \text{ in}^2$$

25. C: The formula for the volume of a cube is $V = L^3$.

$$12^3 = 1{,}728 \text{ cm}^3$$

26. A: The formula for the surface area of a sphere is A = 4πr².

$$A = 4 \bullet \Pi \bullet r \bullet r$$
$$A = 4 \bullet 3.14 \bullet (1.5 \text{ cm}) \bullet (1.5 \text{ cm})$$
$$A = 12.56 \bullet (2.25 \text{ cm}^2)$$
$$A = 28.26 \text{ cm}^2$$

27. B: Use the Pythagorean Theorem to solve this problem: a² + b² = c²

$$8^2 + 6^2 = c^2$$
$$64 + 36 = c^2$$
$$100 = c^2$$
$$\sqrt{100} = 10$$

28. C: The surface of a cube is obtained by multiplying the area of each face by 6, as there are 6 faces. The area of each face is the square of the length of one edge. Therefore, $A = 6 \times 3^2 = 6 \times 9 = 54$.

29. A: The area A of a circle is given by $A = \pi \times r^2$, where r is the radius. Because π is approximately 3.14, we can solve for $r = \sqrt{\frac{A}{\pi}} = \sqrt{\frac{314}{3.14}} = \sqrt{100} = 10$. Now, the diameter d is twice the radius, or $d = 2 \times 10 = 20$.

30. A: The perimeter of a circle is given by $2\pi r$, where r is the radius. We solve for $r = \frac{35}{2\pi} = 5.57$, and double this value to obtain the diameter $d = 11.14$ feet.

31. D: The sum of angles in a triangle equals 180 degrees. Therefore, solve for the remaining angle as 180 – (15 + 70) = 95 degrees.

32. B: The inequality specifies that the difference between L and 15 inches must be less or equal to 0.01. For choice B, | 14.99 – 15 | = | -0.01 | = 0.01, which is equal to the specified tolerance and therefore meets the condition.

33. C: The volume of a right circular cylinder is equal to its height multiplied by the area of its base, A. Since the base is circular, $A = \pi R^2$, where R, the radius, is half the diameter, or 30 feet. Therefore: $V = H \times \pi R^2$.

Solving for H,

$$H = \frac{V}{\pi R^2} = \frac{1,000,000}{\pi \times 30^2} = \frac{1,000,000}{\pi \times 900} = 353.7 ft$$

34. D: The teacher is grading 134 tests, which can be estimated at 130 tests. Divide the total number of tests by the number of tests she can grade in an hour to determine how many hours it will take to grade the tests:

$$130 \div 20 = 6.5 \text{ hours}$$

She started grading at 10:30 a.m., so 6.5 hours later will be 5:00 p.m.

35. C: This is the symbol for set intersection. "A intersect B" is the set of all elements that are in both A and B.

36. A: The quotient means divide. 56 is the numerator and x is the denominator. "Is 8" means "equals 8." The problem should read: $56/x = 8$

37. D: The pattern is subtracting one less number each time:

$$132 - 9 = 123$$
$$123 - 8 = 115$$
$$115 - 7 = 108$$
$$108 - 6 = 102$$

The next number to be subtracted is 5, so $102 - 5 = 97$

38. B: The mode is the number that appears the most. 52 appears the most in this series of numbers.

39. B: $6 \cdot 3 + 4 - 7$

$$= 18 + 4 - 7$$
$$= 15$$

40. A: Simplify the equation:

$$10x - 36 + 4x - 6 + x = 3$$
$$15x - 42 = 3$$
$$15x = 45$$
$$x = 3$$

Social Studies

1. C: Peter the Great (Peter I) was the Russian czar from 1682–1725. His reign was dominated by his efforts to modernize and Westernize Russia. He was responsible for bringing Russia into the European sphere, creating the first Russian navy, and controlling nobility, among other things.

2. C: The Norman Conquest was the English historical period beginning in 1066. It   began with the defeat of Anglo-Saxon King Harold II. With this defeat, the customs, laws, and language of the Normans was introduced in England. The Great Schism was the division in the Roman Catholic Church from 1378–1417 when two rival popes emerged.

The French Revolution was the prolonged political and social struggle between 1789 and 1799 in France. It encompassed the regicide of the king, Louis XVI, and the queen, Marie-Antoinette, included the Reign of Terror, the establishment of the First Republic, and led to the rise of Napoleon Bonaparte as Emperor of France, leading Europe to war.

3. A: Marxism is a term applied to the political, economic, and social theories advanced by Marx and Engels. Marx's theories had a profound influence on the development of Socialist movements and were the basis for the Bolshevik political movement lead by Lenin.

4. B: The debates between Lincoln, a Republican, and Douglas, a Democrat, resulted in Douglas making statements about slavery that the South would not accept. This resulted in the split of the Democratic Party and the defeat of Douglas in the presidential election in 1860.

5. D: The Judiciary Act established the Supreme Court, district courts, circuit courts, and the office of attorney general in 1789. George Washington was inaugurated president in 1789.

6. C: Eli Whitney invented the cotton gin in 1794. The gin enabled one worker to produce 50 pounds of cleaned cotton in one day. This made cotton a profitable crop and increased the demand for and value of slaves in the South.

7. D: In 1954 the Warren Court unanimously reversed the separate but equal ruling of *Plessy* v. *Ferguson* in 1896.

8. A: In 1880, ill sentiment was high against Chinese laborers. This sentiment lead   to the reversal of the Burlingame Treaty of 1868, and thus legal immigration was stopped for a period of 10 years.

9. C: Iran, Iraq, and Kuwait all border the Persian Gulf.

10. A: The national religion of Brazil is Roman Catholicism.

11. B: These characteristics describe capitalism.

12. D: A dictator is a leader with absolute power without respect to constitutional limitations. This would not be found in a democracy. Democracy is rule by the people; government by the consent of the governed.

13. B: Determining methods of carrying babies and studying the toddlers in several countries would be the best method for gathering data for this study.

14. B: The rate of incarceration for juveniles did decrease after 1995. Answer A is a correct statement. Fewer women than men are incarcerated in each year sampled, even though the number of females incarcerated is growing. Response C is also accurate; in the years specified, more whites were incarcerated in jails than any other race. The chart clearly shows an increase in the number of Hispanics being jailed, making response D an accurate statement. Sadly, the fifth response, likewise, is true; the number of black inmates jumps by nearly half a million every five years.

15. A: The United Nations is an international organization of nations formed in 1945. Its main purpose is to promote international peace and security, maintain observance of international law, and promote economic and social progress.

16. B: Stalin became dictator of the Soviet Union in 1924. He died in 1953. World War II was a worldwide conflict fought from 1939–1945.

17. A: The League of Nations was an international organization formed to maintain peace and security in the post-World War I world. The fact that the United States did not join seriously weakened the League.

18. C: Robert E. Lee declined Lincoln's offer to command the U.S. Army at the outbreak of the Civil War. He instead chose to become the commander of the Confederate army of northern Virginia. In the final phases of the war, he was the commander of all Confederate forces.

19. D: The correct order is Revolutionary War (1776–1783), Great Depression (1929), first moon landing (1969).

20. A: Samuel Morse invented a code of dots and dashes that became known as Morse Code and in 1844 the first message was transmitted over a telegraph line. Morse code played an important role in communications during the Civil War.

21. B: In the Dred Scot case of 1857, the Supreme Court ruled that Dred Scott was not a citizen and had no right to bring his case to court.

22. B: The Andes mountain range is the world's longest continental mountain range. It lies as a continuous chain of mountains along the western coast of South America.

23. C: Gothic architecture often uses gargoyles, grotesque creatures with open mouths. They served as gutters, directing water away from walls.

24. B: Trade has been a part of the Sahara desert for centuries. Without the oases, this would have been impossible. An oasis is an area fed by an underground spring. Where oases were found in the Sahara, communities were established. This allowed traders to cross the desert by traveling from one oasis to another.

25. C: In recent years, India's economy has been shaping into a market-based economy. This is an economic system that relies on supply and demand to set prices, rather than having prices set by the government.

26. A: A constitutional democratic monarchy is a country where the head of state is a monarch. The monarch shares power with a government that is organized by a constitution. Thailand's government meets this definition.

27. B: By using antiseptics, Muslim doctors prevented the infection that often led to loss of limbs or life among Europeans. The other responses are opinion or not supported by the paragraph. We have no way of comparing the bravery of Muslim people with those of other faiths when facing surgery, so Choice A can be eliminated. Likewise, Choice C is incorrect; there would not be sufficient rise in silk use for sutures to account for an expanded silk market. It is not clear that the Muslims were the only people to have translations of the works of Aristotle, nor does the passage suggest such.

28. D: Machinery and transport jumped from 34.3 to 42.0 percent in exports and from 9.7 to 28.0 percent in imports. Chemicals increased exports slightly, from 8.7 to 9.0. Imports declined slightly, from 5.3 to 3.6; thus Choice A is incorrect. Crude material exports declined from 13.7 to 10.8 while imports declined from 18.3 to 8.3, making Choice B incorrect. The decline in exports of food and beverages was just under 4 percent, while imports declined 7 percent; therefore, Choice C is not an accurate choice.

29. B: Crude material imports declined by 10 percentage points. All other categories saw imports that declined less than 10 points over the decade. Chemicals decreased in that time by only 1.7 percent, making Choice A inaccurate. Choice C is also incorrect; food and beverages decreased during those ten years by just over 7 percent. Imports of machinery and transport nearly tripled, rather than decreased, which means Choice D is incorrect.

30. D: By 1950, the number of women in the workforce had climbed to 28.8 percent—the first time the percentage was above 25 percent. Choice A is incorrect because women in 1900 made up only 18 percent of the workforce. By 1920, women still comprised only 20.4 of the workforce, making Choice B inaccurate. In 1940, 24.3 percent of women were in the labor force, but the question asks for a percentage higher than 25.

31. C: The percentage of women in the workforce steadily increased through seven decades (and beyond). By 1970, when it reached 36.7 percent, it was double the 18.1 percent of 1900. Choice A is wrong because the rate did not decline. The second response is also incorrect; the rate did not remain steady, but climbed. The fourth answer is not accurate; the rate did not vary up and down, but rather increased steadily.

32. B: Although the nation faced recession, the U.S. Dollar made a comeback in world currency during the fall of 2008. Choice A cannot be concluded from the information given, which focuses solely on the dollar and euro rather than on the entire world. Choice C is incorrect as well; the euro fell in 2008 against the dollar. The wisdom of buying stocks cannot be concluded from the information given; therefore, Choice D is not viable.

33. D: It is the duty of the President to see that federal laws are enforced. National laws are not subject to state laws or interpretations in matters constitutionally delegated to the federal government. Choice A is not correct, as the governor of a state does have power; he cannot act, however, in defiance of constitutional federal law. Choice B is incorrect as well, as the conflict in Vietnam had nothing to do with the situation in Arkansas. Choice C, finally, is incorrect, as the constitution outlines powers delegated to both levels of government, with regard to different spheres of influence.

34. C: The Mayan population of Belize stands at about 10 percent. The first option, Honduras, does not have a Mayan presence. Thus it is incorrect. Choice B, Costa Rica, does not have a statistically significant Mayan population either, making this a false choice. Choice D suggests Nicaragua, but it does not have enough Maya to show up on the chart at all.

35. D: Only in Belize does the Amerindian population exceed 10 percent, and that by a slim margin. Choice A is incorrect because the Creole population is not the largest ethnic group in the entire region but makes up about a fourth of Belize's population. The second response is also false; the Maya make up about 10 percent of the Belize population. Choice C is not correct; more than two-thirds of Nicaragua's people are of mixed descent.

36. A: Choice A is most accurate. Belize is close to Haiti and Jamaica, both of which have a high concentration of people of African descent. There is no evidence of trade between Belize and the nations of West Africa, making Choice B wrong. It is possible that many Creole in New Orleans did leave after Hurricane Katrina; however, there is no indication that they went to Belize, making the third response wrong. Choice D cannot be supported.

37. A: Cameroon is on the Atlantic coast, south of Nigeria and north of Gabon. Choice B is not accurate. Somalia is bordered by both the Indian Ocean and the Gulf of Aden; its capital, Mogadishu, is on the Indian Ocean. Choice C is incorrect; Mozambique, near the southern part of the continent, is bordered by the Indian Ocean. Choice D, Kenya, near the middle of the African continent, likewise, is an inaccurate choice. Kenya is also bordered by the Indian Ocean.

38. C: Young people protested being old enough to fight and die for their country while being denied voting rights. Choice A is incorrect because women had gained the right to vote with passage of the Nineteenth Amendment in 1920. Choice B is also wrong. African American males were guaranteed suffrage following the Civil War; African American females gained the right in 1920. The baby boom ended in 1964, so Choice D is not correct.

39. C: In 1969, there were 13 members; in 2008, there were 43, an increase of 30. The first response is not correct. The Civil War ended in 1865; it was more than 100 years later that the CBC was formed. The second option is also incorrect; nothing in the passage suggests a goal of a black president. Choice D is wrong; the passage specifically states that the alternative budget varies widely from the one that the president submits.

40. D: One key to an opinion statement is the use of superlatives. This sentence states apartheid was the worst political system, an opinion that could be challenged, given Nazism and fascism during World War II. All other statements can be verified as fact.

How to Overcome Test Anxiety

Just the thought of taking a test is enough to make most people a little nervous. A test is an important event that can have a long-term impact on your future, so it's important to take it seriously and it's natural to feel anxious about performing well. But just because anxiety is normal, that doesn't mean that it's helpful in test taking, or that you should simply accept it as part of your life. Anxiety can have a variety of effects. These effects can be mild, like making you feel slightly nervous, or severe, like blocking your ability to focus or remember even a simple detail.

If you experience test anxiety—whether severe or mild—it's important to know how to beat it. To discover this, first you need to understand what causes test anxiety.

Causes of Test Anxiety

While we often think of anxiety as an uncontrollable emotional state, it can actually be caused by simple, practical things. One of the most common causes of test anxiety is that a person does not feel adequately prepared for their test. This feeling can be the result of many different issues such as poor study habits or lack of organization, but the most common culprit is time management. Starting to study too late, failing to organize your study time to cover all of the material, or being distracted while you study will mean that you're not well prepared for the test. This may lead to cramming the night before, which will cause you to be physically and mentally exhausted for the test. Poor time management also contributes to feelings of stress, fear, and hopelessness as you realize you are not well prepared but don't know what to do about it.

Other times, test anxiety is not related to your preparation for the test but comes from unresolved fear. This may be a past failure on a test, or poor performance on tests in general. It may come from comparing yourself to others who seem to be performing better or from the stress of living up to expectations. Anxiety may be driven by fears of the future—how failure on this test would affect your educational and career goals. These fears are often completely irrational, but they can still negatively impact your test performance.

Review Video: <u>3 Reasons You Have Test Anxiety</u>
Visit mometrix.com/academy and enter code: 428468

285

Mometrix

Elements of Test Anxiety

As mentioned earlier, test anxiety is considered to be an emotional state, but it has physical and mental components as well. Sometimes you may not even realize that you are suffering from test anxiety until you notice the physical symptoms. These can include trembling hands, rapid heartbeat, sweating, nausea, and tense muscles. Extreme anxiety may lead to fainting or vomiting. Obviously, any of these symptoms can have a negative impact on testing. It is important to recognize them as soon as they begin to occur so that you can address the problem before it damages your performance.

> **Review Video: 3 Ways to Tell You Have Test Anxiety**
> Visit mometrix.com/academy and enter code: 927847

The mental components of test anxiety include trouble focusing and inability to remember learned information. During a test, your mind is on high alert, which can help you recall information and stay focused for an extended period of time. However, anxiety interferes with your mind's natural processes, causing you to blank out, even on the questions you know well. The strain of testing during anxiety makes it difficult to stay focused, especially on a test that may take several hours. Extreme anxiety can take a huge mental toll, making it difficult not only to recall test information but even to understand the test questions or pull your thoughts together.

> **Review Video: How Test Anxiety Affects Memory**
> Visit mometrix.com/academy and enter code: 609003

Effects of Test Anxiety

Test anxiety is like a disease—if left untreated, it will get progressively worse. Anxiety leads to poor performance, and this reinforces the feelings of fear and failure, which in turn lead to poor performances on subsequent tests. It can grow from a mild nervousness to a crippling condition. If allowed to progress, test anxiety can have a big impact on your schooling, and consequently on your future.

Test anxiety can spread to other parts of your life. Anxiety on tests can become anxiety in any stressful situation, and blanking on a test can turn into panicking in a job situation. But fortunately, you don't have to let anxiety rule your testing and determine your grades. There are a number of relatively simple steps you can take to move past anxiety and function normally on a test and in the rest of life.

> **Review Video: How Test Anxiety Impacts Your Grades**
> Visit mometrix.com/academy and enter code: 939819

Physical Steps for Beating Test Anxiety

While test anxiety is a serious problem, the good news is that it can be overcome. It doesn't have to control your ability to think and remember information. While it may take time, you can begin taking steps today to beat anxiety.

Just as your first hint that you may be struggling with anxiety comes from the physical symptoms, the first step to treating it is also physical. Rest is crucial for having a clear, strong mind. If you are tired, it is much easier to give in to anxiety. But if you establish good sleep habits, your body and mind will be ready to perform optimally, without the strain of exhaustion. Additionally, sleeping well helps you to retain information better, so you're more likely to recall the answers when you see the test questions.

Getting good sleep means more than going to bed on time. It's important to allow your brain time to relax. Take study breaks from time to time so it doesn't get overworked, and don't study right before bed. Take time to rest your mind before trying to rest your body, or you may find it difficult to fall asleep.

Review Video: The Importance of Sleep for Your Brain
Visit mometrix.com/academy and enter code: 319338

Along with sleep, other aspects of physical health are important in preparing for a test. Good nutrition is vital for good brain function. Sugary foods and drinks may give a burst of energy but this burst is followed by a crash, both physically and emotionally. Instead, fuel your body with protein and vitamin-rich foods.

Also, drink plenty of water. Dehydration can lead to headaches and exhaustion, especially if your brain is already under stress from the rigors of the test. Particularly if your test is a long one, drink water during the breaks. And if possible, take an energy-boosting snack to eat between sections.

Review Video: How Diet Can Affect your Mood
Visit mometrix.com/academy and enter code: 624317

Along with sleep and diet, a third important part of physical health is exercise. Maintaining a steady workout schedule is helpful, but even taking 5-minute study breaks to walk can help get your blood pumping faster and clear your head. Exercise also releases endorphins, which contribute to a positive feeling and can help combat test anxiety.

When you nurture your physical health, you are also contributing to your mental health. If your body is healthy, your mind is much more likely to be healthy as well. So take time to rest, nourish your body with healthy food and water, and get moving as much as possible. Taking these physical steps will make you stronger and more able to take the mental steps necessary to overcome test anxiety.

Review Video: How to Stay Healthy and Prevent Test Anxiety
Visit mometrix.com/academy and enter code: 877894

Mental Steps for Beating Test Anxiety

Working on the mental side of test anxiety can be more challenging, but as with the physical side, there are clear steps you can take to overcome it. As mentioned earlier, test anxiety often stems from lack of preparation, so the obvious solution is to prepare for the test. Effective studying may be the most important weapon you have for beating test anxiety, but you can and should employ several other mental tools to combat fear.

First, boost your confidence by reminding yourself of past success—tests or projects that you aced. If you're putting as much effort into preparing for this test as you did for those, there's no reason you should expect to fail here. Work hard to prepare; then trust your preparation.

Second, surround yourself with encouraging people. It can be helpful to find a study group, but be sure that the people you're around will encourage a positive attitude. If you spend time with others who are anxious or cynical, this will only contribute to your own anxiety. Look for others who are motivated to study hard from a desire to succeed, not from a fear of failure.

Third, reward yourself. A test is physically and mentally tiring, even without anxiety, and it can be helpful to have something to look forward to. Plan an activity following the test, regardless of the outcome, such as going to a movie or getting ice cream.

When you are taking the test, if you find yourself beginning to feel anxious, remind yourself that you know the material. Visualize successfully completing the test. Then take a few deep, relaxing breaths and return to it. Work through the questions carefully but with confidence, knowing that you are capable of succeeding.

Developing a healthy mental approach to test taking will also aid in other areas of life. Test anxiety affects more than just the actual test—it can be damaging to your mental health and even contribute to depression. It's important to beat test anxiety before it becomes a problem for more than testing.

Review Video: <u>Test Anxiety and Depression</u>
Visit mometrix.com/academy and enter code: 904704

Study Strategy

Being prepared for the test is necessary to combat anxiety, but what does being prepared look like? You may study for hours on end and still not feel prepared. What you need is a strategy for test prep. The next few pages outline our recommended steps to help you plan out and conquer the challenge of preparation.

STEP 1: SCOPE OUT THE TEST

Learn everything you can about the format (multiple choice, essay, etc.) and what will be on the test. Gather any study materials, course outlines, or sample exams that may be available. Not only will this help you to prepare, but knowing what to expect can help to alleviate test anxiety.

STEP 2: MAP OUT THE MATERIAL

Look through the textbook or study guide and make note of how many chapters or sections it has. Then divide these over the time you have. For example, if a book has 15 chapters and you have five days to study, you need to cover three chapters each day. Even better, if you have the time, leave an extra day at the end for overall review after you have gone through the material in depth.

If time is limited, you may need to prioritize the material. Look through it and make note of which sections you think you already have a good grasp on, and which need review. While you are studying, skim quickly through the familiar sections and take more time on the challenging parts. Write out your plan so you don't get lost as you go. Having a written plan also helps you feel more in control of the study, so anxiety is less likely to arise from feeling overwhelmed at the amount to cover.

STEP 3: GATHER YOUR TOOLS

Decide what study method works best for you. Do you prefer to highlight in the book as you study and then go back over the highlighted portions? Or do you type out notes of the important information? Or is it helpful to make flashcards that you can carry with you? Assemble the pens, index cards, highlighters, post-it notes, and any other materials you may need so you won't be distracted by getting up to find things while you study.

If you're having a hard time retaining the information or organizing your notes, experiment with different methods. For example, try color-coding by subject with colored pens, highlighters, or post-it notes. If you learn better by hearing, try recording yourself reading your notes so you can listen while in the car, working out, or simply sitting at your desk. Ask a friend to quiz you from your flashcards, or try teaching someone the material to solidify it in your mind.

STEP 4: CREATE YOUR ENVIRONMENT

It's important to avoid distractions while you study. This includes both the obvious distractions like visitors and the subtle distractions like an uncomfortable chair (or a too-comfortable couch that makes you want to fall asleep). Set up the best study environment possible: good lighting and a comfortable work area. If background music helps you focus, you may want to turn it on, but otherwise keep the room quiet. If you are using a computer to take notes, be sure you don't have any other windows open, especially applications like social media, games, or anything else that could distract you. Silence your phone and turn off notifications. Be sure to keep water close by so you stay hydrated while you study (but avoid unhealthy drinks and snacks).

Also, take into account the best time of day to study. Are you freshest first thing in the morning? Try to set aside some time then to work through the material. Is your mind clearer in the afternoon or evening? Schedule your study session then. Another method is to study at the same time of day that you will take the test, so that your brain gets used to working on the material at that time and will be ready to focus at test time.

STEP 5: STUDY!

Once you have done all the study preparation, it's time to settle into the actual studying. Sit down, take a few moments to settle your mind so you can focus, and begin to follow your study plan. Don't give in to distractions or let yourself procrastinate. This is your time to prepare so you'll be ready to fearlessly approach the test. Make the most of the time and stay focused.

Of course, you don't want to burn out. If you study too long you may find that you're not retaining the information very well. Take regular study breaks. For example, taking five minutes out of every hour to walk briskly, breathing deeply and swinging your arms, can help your mind stay fresh.

As you get to the end of each chapter or section, it's a good idea to do a quick review. Remind yourself of what you learned and work on any difficult parts. When you feel that you've mastered the material, move on to the next part. At the end of your study session, briefly skim through your notes again.

But while review is helpful, cramming last minute is NOT. If at all possible, work ahead so that you won't need to fit all your study into the last day. Cramming overloads your brain with more information than it can process and retain, and your tired mind may struggle to recall even previously learned information when it is overwhelmed with last-minute study. Also, the urgent nature of cramming and the stress placed on your brain contribute to anxiety. You'll be more likely to go to the test feeling unprepared and having trouble thinking clearly.

So don't cram, and don't stay up late before the test, even just to review your notes at a leisurely pace. Your brain needs rest more than it needs to go over the information again. In fact, plan to finish your studies by noon or early afternoon the day before the test. Give your brain the rest of the day to relax or focus on other things, and get a good night's sleep. Then you will be fresh for the test and better able to recall what you've studied.

STEP 6: TAKE A PRACTICE TEST

Many courses offer sample tests, either online or in the study materials. This is an excellent resource to check whether you have mastered the material, as well as to prepare for the test format and environment.

Check the test format ahead of time: the number of questions, the type (multiple choice, free response, etc.), and the time limit. Then create a plan for working through them. For example, if you have 30 minutes to take a 60-question test, your limit is 30 seconds per question. Spend less time on the questions you know well so that you can take more time on the difficult ones.

If you have time to take several practice tests, take the first one open book, with no time limit. Work through the questions at your own pace and make sure you fully understand them. Gradually work up to taking a test under test conditions: sit at a desk with all study materials put away and set a timer. Pace yourself to make sure you finish the test with time to spare and go back to check your answers if you have time.

After each test, check your answers. On the questions you missed, be sure you understand why you missed them. Did you misread the question (tests can use tricky wording)? Did you forget the information? Or was it something you hadn't learned? Go back and study any shaky areas that the practice tests reveal.

Taking these tests not only helps with your grade, but also aids in combating test anxiety. If you're already used to the test conditions, you're less likely to worry about it, and working through tests until you're scoring well gives you a confidence boost. Go through the practice tests until you feel comfortable, and then you can go into the test knowing that you're ready for it.

Test Tips

On test day, you should be confident, knowing that you've prepared well and are ready to answer the questions. But aside from preparation, there are several test day strategies you can employ to maximize your performance.

First, as stated before, get a good night's sleep the night before the test (and for several nights before that, if possible). Go into the test with a fresh, alert mind rather than staying up late to study.

Try not to change too much about your normal routine on the day of the test. It's important to eat a nutritious breakfast, but if you normally don't eat breakfast at all, consider eating just a protein bar. If you're a coffee drinker, go ahead and have your normal coffee. Just make sure you time it so that the caffeine doesn't wear off right in the middle of your test. Avoid sugary beverages, and drink enough water to stay hydrated but not so much that you need a restroom break 10 minutes into the test. If your test isn't first thing in the morning, consider going for a walk or doing a light workout before the test to get your blood flowing.

Allow yourself enough time to get ready, and leave for the test with plenty of time to spare so you won't have the anxiety of scrambling to arrive in time. Another reason to be early is to select a good seat. It's helpful to sit away from doors and windows, which can be distracting. Find a good seat, get out your supplies, and settle your mind before the test begins.

When the test begins, start by going over the instructions carefully, even if you already know what to expect. Make sure you avoid any careless mistakes by following the directions.

Then begin working through the questions, pacing yourself as you've practiced. If you're not sure on an answer, don't spend too much time on it, and don't let it shake your confidence. Either skip it and come back later, or eliminate as many wrong answers as possible and guess among the remaining ones. Don't dwell on these questions as you continue—put them out of your mind and focus on what lies ahead.

Be sure to read all of the answer choices, even if you're sure the first one is the right answer. Sometimes you'll find a better one if you keep reading. But don't second-guess yourself if you do immediately know the answer. Your gut instinct is usually right. Don't let test anxiety rob you of the information you know.

If you have time at the end of the test (and if the test format allows), go back and review your answers. Be cautious about changing any, since your first instinct tends to be correct, but make sure you didn't misread any of the questions or accidentally mark the wrong answer choice. Look over any you skipped and make an educated guess.

At the end, leave the test feeling confident. You've done your best, so don't waste time worrying about your performance or wishing you could change anything. Instead, celebrate the successful

completion of this test. And finally, use this test to learn how to deal with anxiety even better next time.

Important Qualification

Not all anxiety is created equal. If your test anxiety is causing major issues in your life beyond the classroom or testing center, or if you are experiencing troubling physical symptoms related to your anxiety, it may be a sign of a serious physiological or psychological condition. If this sounds like your situation, we strongly encourage you to seek professional help.

How to Overcome Your Fear of Math

The word *math* is enough to strike fear into most hearts. How many of us have memories of sitting through confusing lectures, wrestling over mind-numbing homework, or taking tests that still seem incomprehensible even after hours of study? Years after graduation, many still shudder at these memories.

The fact is, math is not just a classroom subject. It has real-world implications that you face every day, whether you realize it or not. This may be balancing your monthly budget, deciding how many supplies to buy for a project, or simply splitting a meal check with friends. The idea of daily confrontations with math can be so paralyzing that some develop a condition known as *math anxiety*.

But you do NOT need to be paralyzed by this anxiety! In fact, while you may have thought all your life that you're not good at math, or that your brain isn't wired to understand it, the truth is that you may have been conditioned to think this way. From your earliest school days, the way you were taught affected the way you viewed different subjects. And the way math has been taught has changed.

Several decades ago, there was a shift in American math classrooms. The focus changed from traditional problem-solving to a conceptual view of topics, de-emphasizing the importance of learning the basics and building on them. The solid foundation necessary for math progression and confidence was undermined. Math became more of a vague concept than a concrete idea. Today, it is common to think of math, not as a straightforward system, but as a mysterious, complicated method that can't be fully understood unless you're a genius.

This is why you may still have nightmares about being called on to answer a difficult problem in front of the class. Math anxiety is a very real, though unnecessary, fear.

Math anxiety may begin with a single class period. Let's say you missed a day in 6th grade math and never quite understood the concept that was taught while you were gone. Since math is cumulative, with each new concept building on past ones, this could very well affect the rest of your math career. Without that one day's knowledge, it will be difficult to understand any other concepts that link to it. Rather than realizing that you're just missing one key piece, you may begin to believe that you're simply not capable of understanding math.

This belief can change the way you approach other classes, career options, and everyday life experiences, if you become anxious at the thought that math might be required. A student who loves science may choose a different path of study upon realizing that multiple math classes will be required for a degree. An aspiring medical student may hesitate at the thought of going through the necessary math classes. For some this anxiety escalates into a more extreme state known as *math phobia*.

Math anxiety is challenging to address because it is rooted deeply and may come from a variety of causes: an embarrassing moment in class, a teacher who did not explain concepts well and contributed to a shaky foundation, or a failed test that contributed to the belief of math failure.

These causes add up over time, encouraged by society's popular view that math is hard and unpleasant. Eventually a person comes to firmly believe that he or she is simply bad at math. This belief makes it difficult to grasp new concepts or even remember old ones. Homework and test

293

grades begin to slip, which only confirms the belief. The poor performance is not due to lack of ability but is caused by math anxiety.

Math anxiety is an emotional issue, not a lack of intelligence. But when it becomes deeply rooted, it can become more than just an emotional problem. Physical symptoms appear. Blood pressure may rise and heartbeat may quicken at the sight of a math problem – or even the thought of math! This fear leads to a mental block. When someone with math anxiety is asked to perform a calculation, even a basic problem can seem overwhelming and impossible. The emotional and physical response to the thought of math prevents the brain from working through it logically.

The more this happens, the more a person's confidence drops, and the more math anxiety is generated. This vicious cycle must be broken!

The first step in breaking the cycle is to go back to very beginning and make sure you really understand the basics of how math works and why it works. It is not enough to memorize rules for multiplication and division. If you don't know WHY these rules work, your foundation will be shaky and you will be at risk of developing a phobia. Understanding mathematical concepts not only promotes confidence and security, but allows you to build on this understanding for new concepts. Additionally, you can solve unfamiliar problems using familiar concepts and processes.

Why is it that students in other countries regularly outperform American students in math? The answer likely boils down to a couple of things: the foundation of mathematical conceptual understanding and societal perception. While students in the US are not expected to *like* or *get* math, in many other nations, students are expected not only to understand math but also to excel at it.

Changing the American view of math that leads to math anxiety is a monumental task. It requires changing the training of teachers nationwide, from kindergarten through high school, so that they learn to teach the *why* behind math and to combat the wrong math views that students may develop. It also involves changing the stigma associated with math, so that it is no longer viewed as unpleasant and incomprehensible. While these are necessary changes, they are challenging and will take time. But in the meantime, math anxiety is not irreversible—it can be faced and defeated, one person at a time.

False Beliefs

One reason math anxiety has taken such hold is that several false beliefs have been created and shared until they became widely accepted. Some of these unhelpful beliefs include the following:

There is only one way to solve a math problem. In the same way that you can choose from different driving routes and still arrive at the same house, you can solve a math problem using different methods and still find the correct answer. A person who understands the reasoning behind math calculations may be able to look at an unfamiliar concept and find the right answer, just by applying logic to the knowledge they already have. This approach may be different than what is taught in the classroom, but it is still valid. Unfortunately, even many teachers view math as a subject where the best course of action is to memorize the rule or process for each problem rather than as a place for students to exercise logic and creativity in finding a solution.

Many people don't have a mind for math. A person who has struggled due to poor teaching or math anxiety may falsely believe that he or she doesn't have the mental capacity to grasp mathematical concepts. Most of the time, this is false. Many people find that when they are relieved of their math anxiety, they have more than enough brainpower to understand math.

Men are naturally better at math than women. Even though research has shown this to be false, many young women still avoid math careers and classes because of their belief that their math abilities are inferior. Many girls have come to believe that math is a male skill and have given up trying to understand or enjoy it.

Counting aids are bad. Something like counting on your fingers or drawing out a problem to visualize it may be frowned on as childish or a crutch, but these devices can help you get a tangible understanding of a problem or a concept.

Sadly, many students buy into these ideologies at an early age. A young girl who enjoys math class may be conditioned to think that she doesn't actually have the brain for it because math is for boys, and may turn her energies to other pursuits, permanently closing the door on a wide range of opportunities. A child who finds the right answer but doesn't follow the teacher's method may believe that he is doing it wrong and isn't good at math. A student who never had a problem with math before may have a poor teacher and become confused, yet believe that the problem is because she doesn't have a mathematical mind.

Students who have bought into these erroneous beliefs quickly begin to add their own anxieties, adapting them to their own personal situations:

I'll never use this in real life. A huge number of people wrongly believe that math is irrelevant outside the classroom. By adopting this mindset, they are handicapping themselves for a life in a mathematical world, as well as limiting their career choices. When they are inevitably faced with real-world math, they are conditioning themselves to respond with anxiety.

I'm not quick enough. While timed tests and quizzes, or even simply comparing yourself with other students in the class, can lead to this belief, speed is not an indicator of skill level. A person can work very slowly yet understand at a deep level.

If I can understand it, it's too easy. People with a low view of their own abilities tend to think that if they are able to grasp a concept, it must be simple. They cannot accept the idea that they are capable of understanding math. This belief will make it harder to learn, no matter how intelligent they are.

I just can't learn this. An overwhelming number of people think this, from young children to adults, and much of the time it is simply not true. But this mindset can turn into a self-fulfilling prophecy that keeps you from exercising and growing your math ability.

The good news is, each of these myths can be debunked. For most people, they are based on emotion and psychology, NOT on actual ability! It will take time, effort, and the desire to change, but change is possible. Even if you have spent years thinking that you don't have the capability to understand math, it is not too late to uncover your true ability and find relief from the anxiety that surrounds math.

Math Strategies

It is important to have a plan of attack to combat math anxiety. There are many useful strategies for pinpointing the fears or myths and eradicating them:

Go back to the basics. For most people, math anxiety stems from a poor foundation. You may think that you have a complete understanding of addition and subtraction, or even decimals and percentages, but make absolutely sure. Learning math is different from learning other subjects. For example, when you learn history, you study various time periods and places and events. It may be important to memorize dates or find out about the lives of famous people. When you move from US history to world history, there will be some overlap, but a large amount of the information will be new. Mathematical concepts, on the other hand, are very closely linked and highly dependent on each other. It's like climbing a ladder – if a rung is missing from your understanding, it may be difficult or impossible for you to climb any higher, no matter how hard you try. So go back and make sure your math foundation is strong. This may mean taking a remedial math course, going to a tutor to work through the shaky concepts, or just going through your old homework to make sure you really understand it.

Speak the language. Math has a large vocabulary of terms and phrases unique to working problems. Sometimes these are completely new terms, and sometimes they are common words, but are used differently in a math setting. If you can't speak the language, it will be very difficult to get a thorough understanding of the concepts. It's common for students to think that they don't understand math when they simply don't understand the vocabulary. The good news is that this is fairly easy to fix. Brushing up on any terms you aren't quite sure of can help bring the rest of the concepts into focus.

Check your anxiety level. When you think about math, do you feel nervous or uncomfortable? Do you struggle with feelings of inadequacy, even on concepts that you know you've already learned? It's important to understand your specific math anxieties, and what triggers them. When you catch yourself falling back on a false belief, mentally replace it with the truth. Don't let yourself believe that you can't learn, or that struggling with a concept means you'll never understand it. Instead, remind yourself of how much you've already learned and dwell on that past success. Visualize grasping the new concept, linking it to your old knowledge, and moving on to the next challenge. Also, learn how to manage anxiety when it arises. There are many techniques for coping with the irrational fears that rise to the surface when you enter the math classroom. This may include controlled breathing, replacing negative thoughts with positive ones, or visualizing success. Anxiety interferes with your ability to concentrate and absorb information, which in turn contributes to greater anxiety. If you can learn how to regain control of your thinking, you will be better able to pay attention, make progress, and succeed!

Don't go it alone. Like any deeply ingrained belief, math anxiety is not easy to eradicate. And there is no need for you to wrestle through it on your own. It will take time, and many people find that speaking with a counselor or psychiatrist helps. They can help you develop strategies for responding to anxiety and overcoming old ideas. Additionally, it can be very helpful to take a short course or seek out a math tutor to help you find and fix the missing rungs on your ladder and make sure that you're ready to progress to the next level. You can also find a number of math aids online: courses that will teach you mental devices for figuring out problems, how to get the most out of your math classes, etc.

Check your math attitude. No matter how much you want to learn and overcome your anxiety, you'll have trouble if you still have a negative attitude toward math. If you think it's too hard, or just have general feelings of dread about math, it will be hard to learn and to break through the anxiety. Work on cultivating a positive math attitude. Remind yourself that math is not just a hurdle to be cleared, but a valuable asset. When you view math with a positive attitude, you'll be much more likely to understand and even enjoy it. This is something you must do for yourself. You may find it helpful to visit with a counselor. Your tutor, friends, and family may cheer you on in your endeavors. But your greatest asset is yourself. You are inside your own mind – tell yourself what you need to hear. Relive past victories. Remind yourself that you are capable of understanding math. Root out any false beliefs that linger and replace them with positive truths. Even if it doesn't feel true at first, it will begin to affect your thinking and pave the way for a positive, anxiety-free mindset.

Aside from these general strategies, there are a number of specific practical things you can do to begin your journey toward overcoming math anxiety. Something as simple as learning a new note-taking strategy can change the way you approach math and give you more confidence and understanding. New study techniques can also make a huge difference.

Math anxiety leads to bad habits. If it causes you to be afraid of answering a question in class, you may gravitate toward the back row. You may be embarrassed to ask for help. And you may procrastinate on assignments, which leads to rushing through them at the last moment when it's too late to get a better understanding. It's important to identify your negative behaviors and replace them with positive ones:

Prepare ahead of time. Read the lesson before you go to class. Being exposed to the topics that will be covered in class ahead of time, even if you don't understand them perfectly, is extremely helpful in increasing what you retain from the lecture. Do your homework and, if you're still shaky, go over some extra problems. The key to a solid understanding of math is practice.

Sit front and center. When you can easily see and hear, you'll understand more, and you'll avoid the distractions of other students if no one is in front of you. Plus, you're more likely to be sitting with students who are positive and engaged, rather than others with math anxiety. Let their positive math attitude rub off on you.

Ask questions in class and out. If you don't understand something, just ask. If you need a more in-depth explanation, the teacher may need to work with you outside of class, but often it's a simple concept you don't quite understand, and a single question may clear it up. If you wait, you may not be able to follow the rest of the day's lesson. For extra help, most professors have office hours outside of class when you can go over concepts one-on-one to clear up any uncertainties. Additionally, there may be a *math lab* or study session you can attend for homework help. Take advantage of this.

Review. Even if you feel that you've fully mastered a concept, review it periodically to reinforce it. Going over an old lesson has several benefits: solidifying your understanding, giving you a confidence boost, and even giving some new insights into material that you're currently learning! Don't let yourself get rusty. That can lead to problems with learning later concepts.

Teaching Tips

While the math student's mindset is the most crucial to overcoming math anxiety, it is also important for others to adjust their math attitudes. Teachers and parents have an enormous influence on how students relate to math. They can either contribute to math confidence or math anxiety.

As a parent or teacher, it is very important to convey a positive math attitude. Retelling horror stories of your own bad experience with math will contribute to a new generation of math anxiety. Even if you don't share your experiences, others will be able to sense your fears and may begin to believe them.

Even a careless comment can have a big impact, so watch for phrases like *He's not good at math* or *I never liked math*. You are a crucial role model, and your children or students will unconsciously adopt your mindset. Give them a positive example to follow. Rather than teaching them to fear the math world before they even know it, teach them about all its potential and excitement.

Work to present math as an integral, beautiful, and understandable part of life. Encourage creativity in solving problems. Watch for false beliefs and dispel them. Cross the lines between subjects: integrate history, English, and music with math. Show students how math is used every day, and how the entire world is based on mathematical principles, from the pull of gravity to the shape of seashells. Instead of letting students see math as a necessary evil, direct them to view it as an imaginative, beautiful art form – an art form that they are capable of mastering and using.

Don't give too narrow a view of math. It is more than just numbers. Yes, working problems and learning formulas is a large part of classroom math. But don't let the teaching stop there. Teach students about the everyday implications of math. Show them how nature works according to the laws of mathematics, and take them outside to make discoveries of their own. Expose them to math-related careers by inviting visiting speakers, asking students to do research and presentations, and learning students' interests and aptitudes on a personal level.

Demonstrate the importance of math. Many people see math as nothing more than a required stepping stone to their degree, a nuisance with no real usefulness. Teach students that algebra is used every day in managing their bank accounts, in following recipes, and in scheduling the day's events. Show them how learning to do geometric proofs helps them to develop logical thinking, an invaluable life skill. Let them see that math surrounds them and is integrally linked to their daily lives: that weather predictions are based on math, that math was used to design cars and other machines, etc. Most of all, give them the tools to use math to enrich their lives.

Make math as tangible as possible. Use visual aids and objects that can be touched. It is much easier to grasp a concept when you can hold it in your hands and manipulate it, rather than just listening to the lecture. Encourage math outside of the classroom. The real world is full of measuring, counting, and calculating, so let students participate in this. Keep your eyes open for numbers and patterns to discuss. Talk about how scores are calculated in sports games and how far apart plants are placed in a garden row for maximum growth. Build the mindset that math is a normal and interesting part of daily life.

Finally, find math resources that help to build a positive math attitude. There are a number of books that show math as fascinating and exciting while teaching important concepts, for example: *The Math Curse; A Wrinkle in Time; The Phantom Tollbooth;* and *Fractals, Googols and Other Mathematical Tales.* You can also find a number of online resources: math puzzles and games, videos that show math in nature, and communities of math enthusiasts. On a local level, students can compete in a variety of math competitions with other schools or join a math club.

The student who experiences math as exciting and interesting is unlikely to suffer from math anxiety. Going through life without this handicap is an immense advantage and opens many doors that others have closed through their fear.

Self-Check

Whether you suffer from math anxiety or not, chances are that you have been exposed to some of the false beliefs mentioned above. Now is the time to check yourself for any errors you may have accepted. Do you think you're not wired for math? Or that you don't need to understand it since you're not planning on a math career? Do you think math is just too difficult for the average person?

Find the errors you've taken to heart and replace them with positive thinking. Are you capable of learning math? Yes! Can you control your anxiety? Yes! These errors will resurface from time to time, so be watchful. Don't let others with math anxiety influence you or sway your confidence. If you're having trouble with a concept, find help. Don't let it discourage you!

Create a plan of attack for defeating math anxiety and sharpening your skills. Do some research and decide if it would help you to take a class, get a tutor, or find some online resources to fine-tune your knowledge. Make the effort to get good nutrition, hydration, and sleep so that you are operating at full capacity. Remind yourself daily that you are skilled and that anxiety does not control you. Your mind is capable of so much more than you know. Give it the tools it needs to grow and thrive.

Thank You

We at Mometrix would like to extend our heartfelt thanks to you, our friend and patron, for allowing us to play a part in your journey. It is a privilege to serve people from all walks of life who are unified in their commitment to building the best future they can for themselves.

The preparation you devote to these important testing milestones may be the most valuable educational opportunity you have for making a real difference in your life. We encourage you to put your heart into it—that feeling of succeeding, overcoming, and yes, conquering will be well worth the hours you've invested.

We want to hear your story, your struggles and your successes, and if you see any opportunities for us to improve our materials so we can help others even more effectively in the future, please share that with us as well. **The team at Mometrix would be absolutely thrilled to hear from you!** So please, send us an email (support@mometrix.com) and let's stay in touch.

> **If you'd like some additional help, check out these other resources we offer for your exam:**
> **http://mometrixflashcards.com/MoGEA**

Additional Bonus Material

Due to our efforts to try to keep this book to a manageable length, we've created a link that will give you access to all of your additional bonus material.

Please visit https://www.mometrix.com/bonus948/mogea to access the information.

301

Made in the USA
Monee, IL
02 October 2020